WORSHIP
AND CHURCH

2019

To: Peter

    With fond memories, and with gratitude for your sending me your *Ordo* year after year!

    Time for you to slow down and read books like this one.

Fondly,
Jerry

WORSHIP AND CHURCH

An Ecclesial Liturgy

ESSAYS IN HONOR OF GERARD AUSTIN, OP

EDITED BY
SALLIE LATKOVICH, CSJ,
AND PETER C. PHAN

Paulist Press
New York / Mahwah, NJ

The Scripture quotations contained herein are from the New Revised Standard Version: Catholic Edition, Copyright © 1989 and 1993, by the Division of Christian Education of the National Council of the Churches of Christ in the United States of America. Used by permission. All rights reserved.

Cover image by Chaiwat Graphic / Shutterstock.com
Cover design by Lynn Else
Book design by Sharyn Banks

Library of Congress Cataloging-in-Publication Data

Names: Austin, Gerard, honouree. | Latkovich, Sallie, editor.
Title: Worship and church : an ecclesial liturgy - essays in honor of Gerard Austin, OP / edited by Sallie Latkovich, CSJ, and Peter C. Phan.
Description: New York : Paulist Press, 2019.
Identifiers: LCCN 2018050173 (print) | LCCN 2019014426 (ebook) | ISBN 9781587688164 (e-book) | ISBN 9780809154241 (pbk. : alk. paper)
Subjects: LCSH: Catholic Church—Liturgy—History. | Liturgics—History.
Classification: LCC BX1970 (ebook) | LCC BX1970 .W67 2019 (print) | DDC 264/.02—dc23
LC record available at https://lccn.loc.gov/2018050173

ISBN 978-0-8091-5424-1 (paperback)
ISBN 978-1-58768-816-4 (e-book)

Published by Paulist Press
997 Macarthur Boulevard
Mahwah, New Jersey 07430
www.paulistpress.com

Printed and bound in the
United States of America

CONTENTS

—❦—

v

Contents

INTRODUCTION

Our friend and colleague Jerry Austin is not only an excellent scholar, professor, preacher, and presider but also a man who *lives* liturgy. He often says that the most important day of his life was his baptismal day. He is a man who is committed to community life as a Dominican and in the many communities to which he belongs, and who celebrates life with others in his welcoming hospitality, always as a congenial host.

There is no doubt of Jerry's serious scholarship, his personal study and writing. He was an engaging professor, a model and mentor to many. He often came to class bearing books to recommend to students to enhance their learning. Jerry's teaching and speaking were captivating. In addition, his advisement of students was always pastoral and with fine direction.

Jerry's family community remains important to him and he to them. He remains connected to and interested in the lives of his nieces and nephews, who fondly call him "Uncle Neil." That family community carries over to Jerry's Dominican community. He loves community life and prayer. Beyond these, Jerry's community of friends is wide. All the authors in this collection are counted among them.

Jerry's colleagues at Catholic University speak of the hospitality he provided in his office, where he welcomed colleagues for meetings, both formal and spontaneous. At the Blessed Edmund Rice School, Jerry loved to invite colleagues and other guests for home-cooked meals. He was a superb host from wine and appetizers to dessert.

Thus, the essays contained in this collection reflect Jerry Austin, whose life is liturgy itself. It is intended as a textbook for upper-level undergraduate and graduate students who are studying liturgy. It is also hoped that those who are the primary providers of liturgy—

priests, parish liturgists, catechists—will find this text a useful tool to update themselves in both the history and practice of liturgy in our church.

It is my pleasure to thank Peter Phan, my coeditor. Peter's experience in projects like this has been an enormous help in bringing it to completion. It was my delight to be in communication with contributors to this volume, whose relationship with Jerry allowed them to say yes to writing, even amid very busy schedules. Donna Crilly at Paulist Press has been very kind in her editorial help to produce this volume. Heartfelt thanks to Paulist Press for accepting this book for publication.

We celebrate you, dear Jerry, with this Festschrift.

It is fitting to conclude this introduction with the words of the 2017 Berakah Award presented to Fr. Charles Gerard Austin, OP:

Formed in deep Dominican sources of thought
and practice.
Seasoned by fifty-six years of teaching and ministry.
Marked by untiring passion for ecumenical dialogue.
Animated by the joy of life-giving friendships.
Your teaching and writing have steadfastly
called us all to a profound baptismal spirituality—
to a vison of
True baptismal priesthood in the Body of Christ.
From Providence to l'Institut Catholique
to the Catholic University of America continuing in
innumerable conferences and global itinerary.
Your life and teaching radiate a clear resilient light.
For all these gifts you give and share so generously
This Academy gives thanks and praise to God.

Sallie Latkovich, CSJ
Catholic Theological Union

Part I

FOUNDATIONS

LITURGY AND THE BIBLE

—〽—

Barbara E. Reid, OP

It is a distinct honor to contribute to this volume honoring our beloved brother and colleague. I knew Jerry by reputation from his years of teaching at Aquinas College in Grand Rapids, Michigan, in the early 1960s, but my first personal encounters with him were when I was studying Scripture at The Catholic University of America in the 1980s. He was well known not only for his brilliant teaching but especially for his kindness and concern for struggling graduate students. He was particularly attentive to us young Dominicans. How we relished dinner invitations with him, where laughter abounded amid serious theological discussions! Jerry's continued support and friendship is truly a lifelong gift. In this essay, I offer reflections on how the renewed emphasis on Scripture since Vatican II, particularly in the liturgy, has been a blessing, while some unfulfilled hopes remain for how to bring the Word alive more fully in the lives of the faithful.

SCRIPTURES IN THE LITURGY IN A VATICAN II CHURCH

It is now fifty-five years since the Second Vatican Council impelled us toward a renewal of the liturgy and a revival of the use of the Scriptures, especially within the liturgy. Jerry Austin was a budding young scholar in those heady days and became a significant figure in bringing the renewal to life. The Constitution on the Sacred Liturgy, *Sacrosanctum Concilium*, promulgated by Pope Paul VI on December 4, 1963, was the first Council document to be promulgated. One of its emphases is the importance of the Scriptures within the liturgy:

> Sacred scripture is of the greatest importance in the celebration of the liturgy. For it is from scripture that lessons are read and explained in the homily, and psalms are sung; the prayers, collects, and liturgical songs are scriptural in their inspiration and their force, and it is from the scriptures that actions and signs derive their meaning. Thus to achieve the restoration, progress, and adaptation of the sacred liturgy, it is essential to promote that warm and living love for scripture to which the venerable tradition of both eastern and western rites gives testimony. (no. 24)[1]

It also urges, "In sacred celebrations there is to be more reading from holy scripture, and it is to be more varied and suitable," and the sermon "should draw its content mainly from scriptural and liturgical sources, and its character should be that of a proclamation of God's wonderful works in the history of salvation, the mystery of Christ, ever made present and active within us, especially in the celebration of the liturgy" (no. 35).

In speaking about the sacred mystery of the Eucharist, the document advises, "The treasures of the bible are to be opened up more lavishly, so that richer fare may be provided for the faithful at the table of God's word. In this way a more representative portion of the holy scriptures will be read to the people in the course of a prescribed number of years" (no. 51). *Dei Verbum* likewise highlights how "in the liturgy, the faithful receive the bread of life from the table both of God's word and of Christ's body" (no. 21).[2] Now Pope Francis continues to highlight the importance of liturgical proclamation of the Word of God, especially in the eucharistic assembly, as "a dialogue between God and his people, a dialogue in which the great deeds of salvation are proclaimed and the demands of the covenant are continually restated" (*Evangelii Gaudium* 137).[3] Pope Francis also stresses how what is heard in that dialogue at Mass "passes into daily life."[4]

BIBLICAL ACCOUNTS OF THE READING OF SCRIPTURE IN WORSHIP

That the Scriptures take a central place in our liturgical life is not a new invention. The reading and study of Scripture became central to the worship of our Jewish ancestors in faith once there was no temple. In ancient Israel, worship centered on sacrificial offerings of various kinds.[5] A connection between the Word of God and sacrificial ritual can be seen, however, in the sealing of the covenant in Exodus 24: "Moses came and told the people all the words of the LORD and all the ordinances; and all the people answered with one voice, and said, 'All the words that the LORD has spoken we will do.' And Moses wrote down all the words of the LORD. He rose early in the morning, and built an altar at the foot of the mountain, and set up twelve pillars, corresponding to the twelve tribes of Israel. He sent young men of the people of Israel, who offered burnt offerings and sacrificed oxen as offerings of well-being to the LORD" (vv. 3–5). Moses then read the book of the covenant in the hearing of the people, who responded, "All that the LORD has spoken we will do, and we will be obedient" (Exod 24:7). He took the blood from the sacrifices and dashed half of it on the altar and the other half on the people, saying, "See the blood of the covenant that the LORD has made with you in accordance with all these words" (Exod 24:8).[6] Christians will hear echoes of Jesus's words to his disciples at his last supper with them (see Mark 14:24; Matt 26:28; Luke 22:20).

The Old Testament names various places where altars were erected and sacrifices were made: Bochim (Judg 2:1–5), Ophrah (Judg 6:24), Shiloh (1 Sam 1:3), Beth Shemesh (1 Sam 6:14–15), Mizpah (1 Sam 7:5), and Gilgal (1 Sam 10:8). Archaeologists have also uncovered near Dothan a large open-air shrine dating to the twelfth century BCE and another at Mount Ebal that was used from 1225 to 1100 BCE. A household shrine with two horned stone altars and cultic vessels dating to the time of Solomon was discovered at Megiddo. Another was found not far away in Taanach, also from the time of Solomon.

With the establishment of the monarchy came attempts to centralize all worship in Jerusalem.[7] King David brought the ark of the covenant to Jerusalem (2 Sam 6), and there his son Solomon built his temple (1 Kgs 6). In the ancient Near East, a temple was considered a god's earthly dwelling, into which only the king and priests were allowed to enter. Temples were generally constructed with three parts: a vestibule, a central court, and the holy of holies (see the description of Solomon's temple in 1 Kgs 6–7 and of the restored temple in Ezek 40–43). It was in the courtyards outside the temple that worshipers gathered as the priests offered the sacrifices on their behalf (see Luke 1:10, where the whole assembly of the people is outside while Zechariah is making the incense offering in the sanctuary).

Sacrificial worship continued in the first temple in Jerusalem until it was destroyed by the Babylonians in 587 BCE. With support from the Persian government, the returned exiles rebuilt the temple in 515 BCE. In Roman times, Herod the Great renovated and expanded the temple. Many scenes in the Gospels are set in or refer to this temple, which stood in the time of Jesus and was in use until it was razed in the sack of Jerusalem in 70 CE.

Once there was no temple, worship shifted from a sacrifice-based cult to one centered on prayer and the reading and study of Scripture. Another important development was the rise of the synagogue, where liturgy could be enacted in every village of the land, no longer centralized in Jerusalem. The origins of the synagogue are much debated. Rabbinic tradition traces the beginnings of the synagogue to the Mosaic period, while literary theories locate its origins anywhere from the late seventh century BCE to the first century CE. Synagogues are never mentioned in the Hebrew Scriptures. In the Septuagint, *synagōgē* refers not to a building but to a liturgical or secular assembly of people. The New Testament and Josephus have ample references to synagogues, but it is not certain that these indicate single-purpose buildings for worship. More likely, worshipers met for communal prayer and reading and study of the Scriptures in buildings that were used for multiple purposes. Archaeological evidence suggests that it was not until the third century CE that there were distinct synagogue buildings.[8]

As the synagogue developed, it had a threefold function: a house of assembly (*Beth-ha-Kenneset*), a house of prayer (*Beth-ha-Tefilah*), and a house of study (*Beth-ha-Midrash*). Just as there had been morning, afternoon, and evening sacrifices in the temple, so there were morning, afternoon, and evening prayers in the synagogues. The central prayers in Jewish liturgy today are the *Shema* (Deut 6:4–9) and the *Shemonei Esrei* (Eighteen Benedictions), developed in the fifth century BCE. Because the latter prayer is recited standing, it is also called the *Amidah* ("standing"). The other key part of the liturgy is the reading of Torah (Pentateuch) and the Prophets.

There are several references in the Gospels to Jesus teaching and healing in synagogues. One scene in the Gospel of Luke gives us a glimpse of the synagogue liturgy and the reading of Scripture therein. Jesus goes to his hometown synagogue in Nazareth

> on the sabbath day, as was his custom. He stood up to read, and the scroll of the prophet Isaiah was given to him. He unrolled the scroll and found the place where it was written:
>
> "The Spirit of the Lord is upon me,
>   because he has anointed me
>   to bring good news to the poor.
> He has sent me to proclaim release to the captives
>   and recovery of sight to the blind,
>   to let the oppressed go free,
> to proclaim the year of the Lord's favor." (Luke 4:16–19)

Jesus then begins to interpret the text and points to the ways in which this Scripture is fulfilled by means of his mission, on which he is about to embark (Luke 4:21). Similarly, in the Acts of the Apostles, Paul and his companions, after arriving in Antioch in Pisidia, went to the synagogue on the sabbath. "After the reading of the law and the prophets, the officials of the synagogue sent them a message, saying, 'Brothers, if you have any word of exhortation for the people, give it.' So Paul stood up and with a gesture began to speak" (Acts 13:15–16). In Acts 15, when James makes his decision at the council in Jerusalem that the Gentiles need "abstain only from things polluted by idols and from fornication and from whatever has been strangled and from blood," he explains, "For in every city, for generations past,

Moses has had those who proclaim him, for he has been read aloud every sabbath in the synagogues" (vv. 20–21).

The reading and breaking open of the Scriptures, central to the synagogue worship, set the basic pattern for what would become the Liturgy of the Word in Christian eucharistic worship.[9] Moreover, a portion of the wording in the Liturgy of the Eucharist is drawn directly from the gospel accounts of Jesus's last supper. There could be no Christian liturgy without the Scriptures.

SCRIPTURES IN THE LITURGY: HOPES FOR THE FUTURE

The renewed emphasis on Scripture in the liturgy in the decades following Vatican II has brought rich blessings. There are yet a number of unfulfilled hopes for the future concerning the construction of the *Lectionary*, the translation of the Scriptures, and preaching from the Scriptures.

The Bible Recontextualized

When the Scriptures are proclaimed in the liturgical assembly, they are being recontextualized in a way that creates a new meaning. The ways in which selections from the Old Testament and the New Testament are combined with prayers from the liturgical season influence the way the biblical texts are understood.[10] While this recontextualization creates a rich banquet to feed our spirits, there are some cautions to keep in mind. One way in which the meaning of texts is altered in a liturgical context is the manner in which Old Testament selections are paired with New Testament passages in a typological way. For example, the account of the near sacrifice of Isaac (Gen 22:1–18) is the second reading assigned for the Easter Vigil. In this liturgical context, a link is forged between Abraham's willingness to sacrifice his beloved son Isaac and God's willingness to "give up" Jesus. Some Christians also see a parallel between the Johannine Jesus who carries his own cross (John 19:17, heard on Good Friday) and

Isaac, upon whom Abraham lays the wood for the burnt offering (Gen 22:6).

Two difficulties result. First, the passage from Genesis has its own meaning in its original biblical context that is overshadowed when it is read as pointing toward Jesus. Second, the impact of including the story of the near sacrifice of Isaac in the Easter Vigil liturgy can lead to an interpretation of the death of Jesus that can have very deleterious effects. Abraham's willingness to give up his beloved son is usually lauded as the proof of his extraordinary faith. Likewise, Jesus "became obedient to the point of death—even death on a cross" (Phil 2:8). But the parallel is not exact; Genesis 22 says nothing about whether Isaac was accepting of the sacrifice his father was planning.[11] Moreover, this line of interpretation creates chilling images of God. In Genesis, God seems a cruel trickster who tests a faithful father until the "test" is called off. And when God is thought of as the Father who sends Jesus to die for us (a formulation nowhere found in the Scriptures), it is, as Rita Nakashima Brock has observed, tantamount to divine child abuse that gives approbation to humans to do likewise.[12] In her book *Abraham on Trial*, Carol Delaney wonders why Abraham never bargained for his son's life, as he did for the people of Sodom and Gomorrah (Gen 18:22–33). And why, she queries, "is the willingness to sacrifice one's child *the* quintessential model of faith, why not the passionate protection of the child?[13] Would not the story of the woman who was willing to relinquish her son to another woman who claimed him as her own, rather than let the child be cut in two (1 Kgs 3:16–28), be a better foundational story?" The rabbis asked similar questions. Some proffered that God did not test Abraham at all. Rather, Abraham misunderstood God. In *Genesis Rabbah*, a midrash written sometime between 300 and 500 CE, God says to Abraham, "What, do you think I meant for you to slay him? No! I said only to take him up. You have taken him up. Now take him down" (*Gen. Rab.* 56:8).[14]

One hope for the future is that interest in studying the Bible may continue to grow, both in parish settings and in formal academic venues. It is in such settings that people can learn the meaning of biblical texts in their original historical, literary, and cultural contexts—a kind of exploration that is not possible to do in the homily at liturgy.

The *Lectionary*

One of the guiding principles for the general arrangement of the *Lectionary for Mass*, taken from *Sacrosanctum Concilium*, is that there should be "more reading from holy scripture, and it is to be more varied and suitable" (no. 35). Furthermore, "the treasures of the bible are to be opened up more lavishly, so that richer fare may be provided for the faithful at the table of God's word. In this way a more representative portion of the holy scripture will be read to the people in the course of a prescribed number of years" (no. 51). Indeed, the three-year cycle of Scripture readings has largely succeeded in these aims. However, there is also a good deal of selectivity in the choice of readings. One glaring omission is that texts featuring important female characters in the biblical narrative are absent or marginal apart from those in which they are giving birth to sons. As Ruth Fox notes, "Women's books, women's experiences and women's accomplishments have been largely overlooked in the assigned scripture readings that are being proclaimed in our churches on Sundays and weekdays."[15]

One example is on Monday of the Fifteenth Week in Ordinary Time, Year I (*Lectionary* no. 389), where the first reading is from Exodus 1:8–14, 22. After hearing of the forced labor of the Hebrews as they increased in number in Egypt (Exod 1:8–14), the story of Shiphrah and Puah, the Hebrew midwives who defied Pharaoh's orders to kill the Hebrew babies (Exod 1:15–21), is totally passed over and the reading concludes with verse 22, Pharaoh's second plan—to throw into the river all the Hebrew baby boys. A story of women who are devoted to bringing forth life and who together use their intelligence and wit to devise a way to withstand a murderous ruler is never heard in our liturgies. The same kind of excision happens with Huldah, the seventh-century prophet who was a contemporary of Jeremiah and an adviser to King Josiah. On Wednesday of the Twelfth Week in Ordinary Time, Year II (*Lectionary* no. 373), the lectionary passage (2 Kgs 22:8–13; 23:1–3) tells of the finding of the scroll in the temple and the reading of it to all the inhabitants of Jerusalem, but it skips over the part that recounts how the royal delegation of priests took the scroll to Huldah to verify, after which they reported her words to the king (2 Kgs 22:14–20). Other powerful women from the Old Testament who are absent or only minimally present in the *Lectionary* include Deborah, Ruth, Esther, and Judith.

Similarly, there are many New Testament women who are passed over or excised from lectionary readings. On Saturday of the Thirty-First Week in Ordinary Time, Year I, the reading from Romans 16 begins with verse 3, omitting Paul's recommendation of Phoebe, deacon (*diakonos*, translated by NAB as "minister") of the church of Cenchrae, and his note that "she has been a benefactor to many and to me as well." Also missing from the lectionary selection (Rom 16:3–9, 16, 22–27) is Paul's greeting to his female coworkers Tryphaena and Tryphosa and "beloved Persis, who has worked hard in the Lord" (v. 12), as well as Julia and Nereus's sister (v. 15). One other important thing to note in this reading is the translation of verse 7, where Paul greets "Andronicus and Junias, my kinsmen and fellow prisoners; they are outstanding apostles, and they were in Christ even before I was." The translation that renders Andronicus's companion a male is erroneous.[16] The worshiping community is left with a skewed image of Paul and his companions in spreading the gospel when we do not hear about Phoebe's ministry and leadership as a deacon, or the female apostle Junia, or Paul's esteemed female coworkers.

Another lamentable choice is the relegation to Easter Tuesday of the account of the risen Christ's appearance to Mary Magdalene at the empty tomb and her faithful fulfillment of his commission to her (John 20:11–18). Every Easter Sunday we hear the first part of the account, with Mary Magdalene discovering that the tomb is empty and Peter and the Beloved Disciple racing there and finding the wrappings (John 20:1–9). But only the few who attend weekday Mass will hear of the powerful revelation to Mary as she turns from seeking and weeping to knowing him alive in a new way and announcing the good news to the others.

These are only a few of the many examples of the omission of women from the *Lectionary*. In addition, many of the texts about women that do appear in the *Lectionary* are edited in ways that perpetuate gender stereotypes. One example is the reading from Proverbs 31 on the Thirty-Third Sunday in Ordinary Time, Year A (*Lectionary* no. 158). As Ruth Fox describes,

> The lectionary omits verses 14–18 and 21–29, which praise the woman's initiative, business acumen, dignity and wisdom: "Like merchant ships she secures her provisions from afar....She picks out a field to purchase; out of her earnings she plants a vineyard. She is girt about with strength....She makes garments and sells them....She is clothed with strength and dignity." The lectionary does, however, include the passages that praise the woman for serving her husband and being his "unfailing prize." The gospel for this same day is Matthew 25:14–30, which is about the three servants who are given silver pieces. Only with the reading of the complete passage of the industrious woman will listeners be able to find a connection to the industrious male servant of the gospel.[17]

Among the suggestions Fox offers for remedying such omissions are these: the homilist could tell the whole story, calling attention to the excised verses; in addition, there could be an article in the bulletin citing the whole passage and providing commentary. Another approach is to use biblical passages about women that are omitted from the *Lectionary* on other occasions in parish life: "on evenings of formation or reflection, or for the commissioning of ministers, for example. For catechists, Anna the prophet, Priscilla and Acquila, Lydia, Lois and Eunice; for musicians, Miriam or Judith leading the singing with tambourines; for lectors, Huldah, the prophet; for ministers of hospitality, the women who welcome prophets in 1 Kings 17 or 2 Kings 4; for ministers of communion, Martha's confession in John 11."[18]

Again, study of the Scriptures can help bring to consciousness the fuller biblical story. Christians whose sole experience of the Scriptures is from what they hear at liturgy are only exposed to portions of the rich treasures of the Bible. Reading and studying a Gospel as a continuous narrative, for example, instead of hearing only disconnected snippets of it each week, helps believers understand the Scriptures more fully and move more deeply into embracing the spiritual riches they offer.

Translation of the Scriptures for Liturgical Use

The English translation of the Bible that has been adopted in the revised *Lectionary* for use in the United States is the *New American Bible*, first published in 1970, and then with the revised New Testament in 1986. This translation is based on the original Hebrew and Greek text, a great advantage over previous Catholic translations that were based on the Vulgate. Aiming to render accurately the nuance and form of the original Hebrew and Greek, it also "recasts the language to make it compatible with the rules and style of modern English and in harmony with traditional Catholic interpretations of Scripture."[19]

In 2001, when the Congregation for Divine Worship and the Discipline of the Sacraments issued *Liturgiam Authenticam*,[20] some of the gains that were made with the new translations from Greek and Hebrew were lost. Among the general principles on the translation of liturgical texts into vernacular languages was the following: "the new translations must be made directly from the original texts, namely the Latin, as regards the texts of ecclesiastical composition, or the Hebrew, Aramaic, or Greek, as the case may be, as regards the texts of Sacred Scripture. Furthermore, in the preparation of these translations for liturgical use, the *Nova Vulgata Editio*, promulgated by the Apostolic See, is normally to be consulted as an auxiliary tool, in a manner described elsewhere in this Instruction, to maintain the tradition of interpretation that is proper to the Latin Liturgy" (no. 24).

"CUP" TO "CHALICE"

As a result, some of the changes in language in the new Roman Missal (implemented November 27, 2011) came from wooden and literal translations, using archaic words and sometimes unintelligible phrases. One jarring change was when the word *chalice* was substituted for *cup* in the words of institution. In all the Gospel accounts of the Last Supper, the word in Greek is *potērion*, the term for an ordinary drinking cup. The Latin word *calix*, "chalice" (*kylix* in Greek), denotes a large ceremonial vessel. There is more at stake in this inaccurate rendering than simply the kind of vessel *chalice* implies. Jesus's drinking of the cup is part of the Passover ritual. As John R. Donahue points out, "To call this cup a 'chalice' disguises the relation of the Christian Eucharist to an *anamnesis* (enacted memorial) of the Paschal Meal celebrated by the Jewish Jesus as he approached his suffering and death. The events surrounding the Passion of Jesus have caused great difficulties and sorrow in Jewish-Christian relations. The suppression of the memory of the Jewishness of Jesus in the Christian Eucharist is another example of 'de-Judaizing' Jesus, and will erect another barrier to appreciation of our Jewish heritage, to mutual understanding, and to a proper liturgical catechesis."[21]

Another unfortunate consequence is that the image of Jesus using a "chalice" distances him from his disciples and us, as he uses not a common drinking cup but a vessel more proper to kings and priests. No longer does the text convey a message that the divine may be found in *lo cotidiano*, the ordinary stuff of everyday life. Not only that, important resonances with meanings of "cup" in other parts of Scripture[22] are lost. In Psalm 23:5, "my cup [*kôsî*] overflows" evokes God's largess in caring for and providing for the ones s/he shepherds. Likewise, when Psalm 16:5 speaks of God as "my chosen portion and my cup," it connotes the abundance of life. Psalm 116:13 speaks of "the cup of salvation," an offering made in thanksgiving for all the good God has bestowed. Jeremiah 16:7 refers to the "cup of consolation" offered to mourners. There are also several references to *cup* where it has the sense of an ominous destiny, as in the "cup of wrath" (Isa 51:17; Jer 25:15) or "the cup of staggering" (Isa 51:22). The connotation of ominous destiny is what is evident in Jesus's plea in Gethsemane to the Father to let the cup pass him by (see Mark 14:36; Matt 2:39; Luke 22:42; cf. John 18:11). This is also the sense of *cup* in Mark 10:38–39 where Jesus responds to James and John's request to sit at his right and left: "Are you able to drink the cup that I drink, or be baptized with the baptism that I am baptized with?" These rich theological overtones are lost when *cup* becomes *chalice*.

FROM "ALL" TO "MANY"

Another difficult change in the words of institution is the rendering "the blood of the new and eternal covenant, which will be poured out for you and *for many* for the forgiveness of sin." These words are taken from Matthew 26:28, where the Greek *peri pollōn* is ordinarily translated "for many." This reflects a Semitic expression where *many* is the opposite of *one*, thus the equivalent of "all." In English, "for many" implies that not all are included, which is not the meaning in the original. The translation "for all" in the Roman Missal issued by Pope Paul VI in 1969 captures well this important theological nuance.

BACKTRACKING ON INCLUSIVE LANGUAGE

The New American Bible, the approved translation for liturgical use in the United States, takes a compromise stance when it comes to inclusive language. "Where the original biblical language clearly intends a generic reference to human beings, the translation is careful to use inclusive language."[23] Where the original text uses a gender-specific reference, however, such as references to God with male pronouns, no attempt to use inclusive language is made.

Accordingly, when the NAB translation of Matthew 6:7–15 was read on Tuesday of the First Week of Lent (no. 225), we heard, "If you forgive others [*tois anthrōpois*] their transgressions, your heavenly Father will forgive you. But if you do not forgive others [*tois anthrōpois*], neither will your Father forgive your transgressions" (Matt 6:14–15, NAB). The Greek masculine plural *tois anthrōpois* is rightly translated inclusively here. The Sermon on the Mount, of which this is part, is addressed to Jesus's disciples (Matt 5:1), which clearly includes a wide circle of women and men. Certainly, these verses that come at the conclusion of the Our Father are meant for all current followers of Jesus, not only males. In the wake of *Liturgiam Authenticam*, however, the translation now being used is this: "If you forgive men their transgressions, your heavenly Father will forgive you. But if you do not forgive men, neither will your Father forgive your transgressions." The slight gains toward inclusivity, where it was clearly intended in the biblical text, have been erased by such unfortunate choices.

Breaking Open the Word

In addition to offering a fuller fare of biblical readings in the liturgy since Vatican II, there has also been a renewed emphasis on preaching from the Scriptures. *Dei Verbum* asserts, "All the preaching of the Church must be nourished and regulated by Sacred Scripture" (no. 21), and among the ministries of the Word, "the liturgical homily must hold the foremost place" (no. 24). In 1982, the U.S. bishops issued *Fulfilled in Your Hearing: The Homily in the Sunday Assembly*, which directs that the homily "flow from the Scriptures which are read at that liturgical celebration, or, more broadly, from the Scriptures which undergird its prayers and actions."[24] The most recent document by the U.S. Conference of Catholic Bishops, *Preaching the Mystery of Faith: The Sunday Homily*,[25] issued in 2013, reaffirms that the lectionary readings are the basis for the homily (p. 18) and that "the goal of the homily is to lead the hearer to the deep inner connection between God's word and the actual circumstances of one's everyday life" (p. 29). Similarly, Pope Benedict XVI wrote, "The homily is a means of bringing the scriptural message to life in a way that helps the faithful to realize that God's word is present and at work in their everyday lives" (*Verbum Domini* 59).[26]

In the fall of 1995, my colleague Leslie Hoppe, OFM, professor of Old Testament at Catholic Theological Union, and I undertook a study of the ways in which Roman Catholic preachers were basing (or not!) their homilies on the Scriptures in their Sunday preaching. We evaluated one hundred homilies of priests who had benefited from excellent theological education in Scripture and homiletic preparation at seminaries and schools of theology that had embraced the vision of Vatican II. What we found was that although the participants had a very high appreciation for the importance of preaching, study, preparation, and crafting homilies that flowed from the Scriptures, the actual preaching most often did not reflect this in practice. Only one-fourth of the homilies exhibited the kind of understanding of the text that would come from exegetical study. Many used a word or phrase from the text as a jumping-off point to take the homily in a direction that had little to do with the Scriptures. Many resorted to moralistic exhortations that were not always true to the original direction of the text. We concluded that there was not enough attention in theologates to helping students learn how to move from biblical exegesis to liturgical proclamation that flows from the Scriptures. After hosting a conference with two dozen biblical scholars and homiliticians, we crafted recommendations about the initial formation of preachers, their ongoing education, and greater collaboration among biblical professors and teachers of preaching. While it has now been twenty years since our study was published,[27] my experience of listening to homilies in the Sunday assembly continues to be mostly disappointing. It is a rare treat when one hears a homilist who is truly skilled in understanding the Scriptures and connecting their meaning to the lives of the congregation. Much work remains to be done to achieve the goal more widely that the liturgical homily flow from the Scriptures and illumine their meaning in everyday life.

The Preacher of the Word

A final hope for the future is that the circle of those who are authorized to break open the Word at liturgy may be expanded to include qualified women and men who are not ordained. Many who are not ordained have the requisite skill to interpret the Scriptures and have the gift of inspired preaching. When the aim of the homily is to help the gathered assembly relate the Scriptures to their daily lives, how much better could that be accomplished when the preacher's station in life and experiences and language closely match those of the hearers? The Congregation for Divine Worship recognized this in their *Directory of Masses for Children*, issued in 1973. They allow the following: "With the consent of the pastor or rector of the church, nothing forbids one of the adults who is participating in a Mass with children from speaking to the children after the gospel reading, especially if the priest finds it difficult to adapt himself to the mentality of children" (no. 24). We might ask, is it not as important for laywomen and laymen to hear the Word broken open in their own language as it is for children? Might not a laywoman or layman or a brother or sister be more adept at doing so?

In the conclusion of *Preaching the Mystery of Faith*, the U.S. bishops hold up Mary, the mother of Jesus, as a model for preachers: "Mary as Hearer and Bearer of the Word—Mary, the Mother of God and Mother of the Word Incarnate, can serve as an example for those who preach the Sunday homily." They characterize the preacher as a man of holiness, a man of Scripture, a man of tradition, and a man of communion. Might we hope that in the future ecclesiastical authorities may recognize that women preachers also resemble Mary and exhibit these same qualities? And Pope Francis, in his wonderful section on preaching in *Evangelii Gaudium* 135–59, speaks of preaching as "A Mother's Conversation": "The Church is a mother, and...she preaches in the same way that a mother speaks to her child....Just as all of us like to be spoken to in our mother tongue, so too in the faith we like to be spoken to in our 'mother culture,' our native language (cf. *2 Macc* 7:21, 27), and our heart is better disposed to listen" (no. 139). Can we hope that in the not too distant future actual mothers and single and vowed women might also be able to serve as preachers at Eucharist? Women are taking advantage of other venues and noneucharistic liturgies to break open the Word,[28] but what an impoverishment it is for the whole church when the circle of preachers at eucharistic liturgies is restricted to ordained males.

CONCLUSION

There has been a great revival of use of the Scriptures since Vatican II. This has been evident not only in the liturgy but also in the growth of interest in study of the Bible, in both formal programs and informal faith-sharing groups. The inclusion of a wider array of biblical texts in the liturgy and the emphasis on preaching from the Scriptures has been a great gift to the church. And yet there is still more that can be done to bring the Scriptures alive in the liturgical life of the church. Some of the hopes articulated above can be accomplished through creative ways of working within the norms; others would require sustained voicing of concerns to those who have the decision-making power to change the texts and practices. These are not selfish aims but the desire to receive even more abundantly from the gift of the Word we are given, and this in turn impels us to share these riches with others. As Pope Francis has said, "Attentive hearing of the Word, particularly in a liturgical setting, and receiving it with an open heart, moves us toward being missionary disciples, impelled to proclaim the Word with our lives" (*Evangelii Gaudium* 119–21). So may it be.

Notes

1. For the full text, see http://www.vatican.va/archive/hist _councils/ii_vatican_council/documents/vat-ii_const_19631204 _sacrosanctum-concilium_en.html.

2. *Dei Verbum* is the Dogmatic Constitution on Divine Revelation promulgated by Pope Paul VI on November 18, 1965. For the full text, see http://www.vatican.va/archive/hist_councils/ii_vatican_council/ documents/vat-ii_const_19651118_dei-verbum_en.html.

3. For the full text of this apostolic exhortation issued on November 24, 2013, see http://w2.vatican.va/content/francesco/en/apost _exhortations/documents/papa-francesco_esortazione-ap_20131124 _evangelii-gaudium.html.

4. See his weekly audience address on January 31, 2018: http:// www.catholicworldreport.com/2018/01/31/find-good-readers-for -mass-pope-francis-says/.

5. See Hayim Goren Perelmuter, "Sacrifice," in *The Collegeville Pastoral Dictionary of Biblical Theology*, ed. Carroll Stuhlmueller (Collegeville, MN: Liturgical Press, 1996), 856–59.

6. Biblical quotations are from the New Revised Standard Version (NRSV) unless otherwise noted.

7. See Leslie J. Hoppe, "Temple," in *The Collegeville Pastoral Dictionary of Biblical Theology*, 977–80.

8. See Leslie J. Hoppe, "Synagogue," in *The Collegeville Pastoral Dictionary of Biblical Theology*, 969–71, and Haym Goren Perelmuter, "Synagogue: Later Developments," in *The Collegeville Pastoral Dictionary of Biblical Theology*, 971–72.

9. Jerome Kodell, "Worship," in *The Collegeville Pastoral Dictionary of Biblical Theology*, 1105–7.

10. See the commentaries by Dianne Bergant with Richard Frago-meni (*Preaching the New Lectionary*, 3 vols. [Collegeville, MN: Liturgical Press, 1998, 1999, 2000]) that use a method of interpretation with a lectionary hermeneutic.

11. In the Jerusalem Targum on Genesis 22, there is willingness on the part of Isaac, who says to his father, "My father, bind my hands rightly, lest in the hour of my affliction I tremble and confuse thee, and thy offering be found profane, and I be cast into the pit of destruction in the world to come."

12. Rita Nakashima Brock, *Journeys by Heart: A Christology of Erotic Power* (New York: Crossroad, 1988). Similarly, Joanne Carlson Brown and Rebecca Parker, "For God So Loved the World?" in *Christianity, Patriarchy, and Abuse: A Feminist Critique*, ed. Joanne Carlson Brown and Carole R. Bohn (New York: Pilgrim, 1989), 1–30.

13. Carol Delaney, *Abraham on Trial: The Social Legacy of Biblical Myth* (Princeton, NJ: Princeton University Press, 1998), 5.

14. See further in chap. 2 of my book *Taking Up the Cross: New Testament Interpretations through Latina and Feminist Eyes* (Minneapolis: Fortress Press, 2007).

15. Ruth Fox, "Women in the Bible and Lectionary," reprinted from *Liturgy 90* (May/June 1996) at https://www.futurechurch.org/women -in-church-leadership/women-and-word/women-in-bible-and -lectionary.

16. The name in the Greek text is *Iounian*, in the accusative case, which can be either masculine or feminine. The evidence is overwhelmingly in favor of the name being feminine, Junia, which is well attested. To date, the masculine name Junias has not been found in any Latin or Greek inscriptions or in any ancient literature. Early commentators on Romans, such as John Chrysostom, Origen of Alexandria, and Jerome, all took Junia to be a woman. See further Bernadette Brooten, "'Junia...Outstanding among the Apostles' (Rom 16:7)," in *Women Priests: A Catholic Commentary on the Vatican Declaration*, ed. Leonard Swidler and Arlene Swidler (New York: Paulist Press, 1977), 141–44.

17. Fox, "Women in the Bible and Lectionary."

18. Fox, "Women in the Bible and Lectionary."

19. Donald Senior, "General Introduction," in *The Catholic Study Bible* (Oxford: Oxford University Press, 1990), RG6.

20. For the full text, see http://www.vatican.va/roman_curia/congregations/ccdds/documents/rc_con_ccdds_doc_20010507_liturgiam-authenticam_en.html.

21. John R. Donahue, "Cup or Chalice? The Large Implications of a Small Change," *Commonweal* (May 21, 2012). Available online at https://www.commonwealmagazine.org/cup-or-chalice.

22. See Harry Hagan, "Cup," in *The Collegeville Pastoral Dictionary of Biblical Theology*, 192–93.

23. Senior, "General Introduction," RG6.

24. The Bishops' Committee on Priestly Life and Ministry, *Fulfilled in Your Hearing: The Homily in the Sunday Assembly* (Washington, DC: United States Catholic Conference, 1982), 17. Available at http://www.usccb.org/_cs_upload/8090_1.pdf. The General Instruction of the Roman Missal also allows that the homily be based on a liturgical text: "It should be an exposition of some aspect of the readings from Sacred Scripture or of another text from the Ordinary or from the Proper of the Mass of the day and should take into account both the mystery being celebrated and the particular needs of the listeners" (no. 65).

25. Available at http://usccb.org/search.cfm?site=newusccb&proxystylesheet=newusccb_frontend&q=preaching&lang=eng.

26. Post-synodal apostolic exhortation of the Holy Father Benedict XVI to the Bishops, Clergy, Consecrated Persons and the Lay Faithful on The Word of God in the Life and Mission of the Church, issued September 30, 2010. Available at http://w2.vatican.va/content/benedict-xvi/en/apost_exhortations/documents/hf_ben-xvi_exh_20100930_verbum-domini.html.

27. Leslie J. Hoppe and Barbara E. Reid, *Preaching from the Scriptures: New Directions for Preparing Preachers* (printed by Assumption BVM Province Franciscans, 1998). Available upon request from breid@ctu.edu.

28. E.g., www.catholicwomenpreach.org; http://www.preacherexchange.com/dominican_preaching.htm.

2

PRINCIPLES AND PRACTICES OF EARLY CHRISTIAN LITURGIES

—⁂—

Anne McGowan

Those exploring the contours of early Christian liturgy for the first time will quickly find themselves immersed in the familiar and the foreign. The basic patterns for many liturgical practices were established by the late fourth or early fifth century in forms that remain recognizable today. Sources from this period, for example, recount threefold rites of initiation featuring water baptism, sealing with the Holy Spirit, and sharing in holy communion. Late ancient manuscripts preserve early evidence for the essential subunits of the eucharistic prayer that have been variously combined by Eastern and Western Christian traditions ever since. Meanwhile, emergent theological reflection links the eucharistic elements with Christ's Body and Blood and identifies the Eucharist as the church's sacrifice. The core seasons and feasts of the liturgical year have assumed their places on the church's annual calendar, and a regular regimen of daily prayer is proposed for all Christians (although probably only maintained in its entirety by the most devout). A further reason for the familiarity is that recent Western liturgical reforms have selectively appropriated aspects of the theology and practice of the early church[1]— such as calls for frequent communion, the restoration of the catechumenate for adults, the hope of situating sacramental manifestations of God's forgiveness in a broader social and ecclesial context, and the renewal of Holy Week and the Triduum as the annual celebration par excellence of Christ's dying and rising—and of the Christian's passage from death to life in Christ that begins in baptism and culminates at the eternal heavenly banquet.

The literary and material evidence of Christian liturgy between the close of the New Testament era, when the connection to living apostles began to fade, and the beginning of the medieval period also feature practices and theological interpretations that might be perceived as rather jarring or even odd today—like Christians experiencing the "second birth" of baptism in fonts whose shape resembled the birth canal by which they emerged from the watery womb of their first human birth.[2] While it is not surprising that early Christians prayed to God when life circumstances called for healing, it may seem unusual to find blessing prayers that suggest consecrated oil for the sick was not only outwardly applied but also inwardly ingested, and to learn that the minister of anointing was not invariably a bishop or priest but that oil blessed by the bishop could be taken home and administered to oneself or others as needed, just as the eucharistic bread shared in the gathered assembly on Sundays might be saved for self-communion during the week.[3] Furthermore, some early eucharistic communities were content to celebrate the Eucharist with bread and *water* (to avoid associations between wine, pagan sacrifices, and libations offered to the gods).[4] Dining with the dead was common, as early Christians paralleled the Greco-Roman practice of *refrigerium* ("refreshment"), memorializing the dead by celebrating the Eucharist in cemeteries; such gatherings on the anniversaries of martyrs' deaths contributed to the development of the liturgical year and impacted the liturgical landscape as shrines and eventually churches were built on or around the earthly remains of some of early Christianity's most significant saints. In some places, widows were *ordained*, serving the local church through their prayer, through their ministry to other women, and by "persevering at the altar night and day"; although urged to remain silent in church, they were seated in a place of honor near the bishop during liturgies (see *Testamentum Domini* 1.19, 2.8, 1.54).[5]

23

A THEOLOGICAL APPROACH THROUGH PRINCIPLES AND PRACTICES

In the midst of evidence affirming the familiar and also reminding us that liturgy in the first five centuries puts us in a different world than the one we know now, some principles underlying early liturgical practices begin to emerge. These "principles" amount to characteristic features or trends that will serve as guideposts in this brief and highly selective survey. This essay will focus on three such principles, explored primarily through consideration of the central Christian practices of baptism and Eucharist, with some attention to other rites. The first principle is a trend toward increased organization that parallels the growth of the church more generally. During this time period, tremendous initial diversity in liturgical practice and accompanying theological interpretation settles into increasing standardization on both fronts, especially after the revolutionary changes precipitated by the imperial acceptance of Christianity beginning with Emperor Constantine in the early fourth century and the consequent shift of Christianity from a way of life for a highly committed and converted chosen few to the religion of the masses subscribed to along a continuum running from extreme devotion through genuine faith to nominal adherence. The second principle involves the interconnection between the theology conveyed through liturgical rites and theological reflection on liturgical rites, with the practical result that the church's liturgical life did inform the church's theology—at the same time as theological developments left their mark on the evolution of liturgical rites. (In other words, the adage *lex orandi, lex credendi*[6] works both ways.) The third principle is implicit in the other two: early Christian liturgy developed in close conversation with culture.[7] As the distinctive practices of the Christian cult developed in dialogue with regional cultures, the beginnings of Christian theological reflection on worship and sacraments often proceeded by spiritualizing widely held concepts in light of their new context when undertaken by people who were new creations in Christ. Over time, the early church was increasingly principled in its practices while also seeking to instill its theological principles through liturgical practices that inscribed the bodies of individual Christians and incorporated them into the church as Christ's Body.

Before launching into this discussion, a note on sources for liturgical theology in the early church is in order since theological reflection in this era so often transpired in and around, from and for the celebration of the liturgy in particular communities. Many eminent theologians were also bishops and pastors who articulated a theology of liturgical celebration in the context of Christians' practical and pastoral engagement of the rites as mediating God's love, grace, and mercy, on the one hand, and the human response of thanksgiving and worship, on the other. As an activity of God unfolding through the mediation of Christ under the auspices of the Holy Spirit, an expression of human faith, and a witness to the church incarnating its mission in the world, the history of *how* rites were celebrated by people in the first few postapostolic centuries is therefore a worthwhile topic of theological interest; furthermore, this paradigm invites theologians of any age to ponder how "all true Christian theology must be liturgical theology—that is, doxological, involved with God's unending saving activity and men's and women's prayerful response to it throughout the ages."[8]

The most prevalent witnesses to the worship of this period are textual ones since manuscripts (and copies of them) and inscriptions have survived the centuries in the greatest abundance.[9] In general, the written documentary evidence for early Christian worship becomes more abundant as the centuries progress. The early Christian Scriptures—both the canonical ones eventually enshrined in the New Testament and apocryphal texts—are shaped by the memories of what Jesus and his first followers did but are also likely informed, especially where descriptions of worship practices are involved, by what Christian communities were doing in their worship at the time they were written. From the second to fifth century, some of the most detailed information about Christian worship is preserved in a genre of so-called church orders, many of which are composite documents claiming the authority of the apostles but reflecting accumulated layers of traditions. Since these documents circulated widely in various versions, they illuminate the evolution of many liturgical rites and forms of prayer (among other matters that would be of

interest to those concerned with the good governance of local ecclesial communities) while quite possibly presenting liturgies that no
church anywhere ever *actually* celebrated as written.[10] This category
includes the *Didache* (late first/early second century), the *Apostolic
Tradition* (various layers dating from the second to the fourth century), the *Didascalia Apostolorum* (late third/early fourth century),
the *Apostolic Constitutions* (late fourth century), and the *Testamentum
Domini* (fifth century).

Records of the content of preaching and teaching that touched
on the church's liturgical life to a greater or lesser degree are another
fruitful source for gathering information about the rites of the early
church and their theological interpretation. Catecheses addressed to
those in the final stages of baptismal preparation and/or lectures to
the newly initiated during the Easter octave (which more fully
unfolded the meaning of baptism, chrismation, and Eucharist) sur-
vive from several renowned bishops from the late fourth and early
fifth centuries—like Ambrose of Milan, Cyril of Jerusalem, John
Chrysostom, Theodore of Mopsuestia, and Augustine of Hippo.
Preaching associated with various feasts helps map the development
and interpretation of the liturgical year in various centers of the
ancient world and reveals how early Christians saw themselves as participating sacramentally in the mysteries of Christ's life re-presented
with particular intensity at Easter, Ascension, Pentecost, Christmas,
and Epiphany. Homilies also help to trace the nascent development
of lectionary systems and provide a glimpse of an emerging "ministry of the Word" in the early churches. In biblical commentaries,
bishops in their role as preachers and exegetes frequently address
scriptural texts associated with Christian rites (such as John 3, Rom
6, and 1 Cor 11) and sometimes explore concepts pertinent to early
Christian liturgical theology, such as "mystery," "sacrament," and
the unfolding of salvation history through the Jewish and Christian
Scriptures and the ongoing life of Christian communities.

There are also apologies defending the Christian faith (including its worship practices) against critics, the most important liturgical source being Justin [the] Martyr's *First Apology* from the

mid-second century, which will be discussed further later. Some early Christians wrote theological treatises on topics such as baptism, the Eucharist, and Christian prayer.[11] Poetry and hymns give insight into the theology that was sung in the midst of early Christian worshipers.[12] Letters provide further information; for example, a letter of Pope Innocent I responding to questions from Bishop Decentius of Gubbio in 416 provides some of the earliest evidence for what became the Roman practice of confirmation. The decrees of councils and synods sometimes record decisions on liturgical matters—such as the conclusion of the Council of Nicaea in 325 to henceforth celebrate Easter on the Sunday after the first full moon on or after the spring equinox—in distinction to the practice of some Christian communities, dubbed the Quartodecimans ("Fourteeners"), of scheduling their annual celebration to coincide with the Jewish feast of Passover on the fourteenth day of the Jewish month of Nisan. Prohibitions are illuminating as well, since there is little need to forbid people from doing things that have never happened.[13]

Fewer objects produced and used by early Christians have survived. For the most part, materials used in worship during this period would have been indistinguishable from those intended for ordinary daily use, although wealthy patrons might donate apparel or implements to enhance the beauty and dignity of the sacred rites. Some of the earliest extant materials are associated with death: the art on catacombs and burial chambers suggest how early Christians viewed their "end" in Christ and hope in the resurrection while witnessing to some aspects of Christian funeral and burial practices. As mentioned earlier, baptismal fonts attest to how Christians perceived the formal ritualized culmination of the beginning of their new life in Christ. By the fourth century, architectural sites built or adapted for Christian worship and their adornment become a more prominent source for exploring how early Christians worshiped and how they understood what they were doing when they did. Music and movement are ephemeral aspects of early Christian worship that have not been abundantly preserved in the historical record, but considerable commentary *about* these topics has survived.[14]

PRINCIPLE ONE: FROM DIVERSITY TO STANDARDIZATION

The earliest layers of liturgical development reflect tremendous diversity, coalescing into a more recognizable unity over time. Some local practices were displaced by the growing influence of more dominant liturgical centers and/or official efforts to promote alternative practices; others were more deliberately discarded as greater theological precision rendered some formerly acceptable ideas and rites no longer tenable on the other side of disputes over orthodoxy. The trend toward standardization and cross-fertilization peaked in the second half of the fourth century as more open exchange of Christian people and ideas between places contributed to the circulation of ritual components across great distances and as the decisions of ecumenical councils were implemented broadly. The short-lived synthesis achieved during this period has been viewed by many as a "golden age" when the liturgy flourished; however, some fourth-century liturgical developments more likely represent the response of a church facing a "crisis" of rapid expansion.[15] The move from diversity toward uniformity is particularly evident in early Christian practices of initiation and Eucharist.

Tertullian asserted that "Christians are made, not born" (*Apol.* 18.4), which means that new Christians must be "made" in every age if the church is to remain as a witness to the way of Christ in the world until he comes again. The basic underlying pattern of Christian initiation has remained relatively stable through the centuries; its order features at least a minimal amount of prebaptismal catechesis (at least for those old enough to benefit from it), baptism in water (perhaps with some accompanying prebaptismal and/or postbaptismal rites that heighten and reinforce the theological significance of what is happening to the baptized), sharing in the Eucharist at some point after baptism, and living thereafter a Christian life (sometimes aided by further teaching and/or intensive guidance on the part of the community). Beyond this common foundation, the trend from initial diversity to later standardization in theology and practice is illustrated well in the process of "making" new Christians.

The earliest witness to baptism outside the New Testament is from the *Didache*:

> Concerning baptism, baptize thus: having first recounted all these things [i.e., catechesis on the "way of life" and the "way of darkness"], baptize in the name of the Father and of the Son and of the Holy Spirit in living water; if you do not have living water, baptize in other water; if you cannot in cold, then in warm; if you do not have either, pour water three times on the head in the name of Father, Son, and Holy Spirit. Before the baptism let the baptizer and the one to be baptized and any others who can fast; you shall instruct the one to be baptized to fast one or two [days] before. (*Didache* 7)[16]

In terms of ritual practice, the basic pattern presented above is the only information to be gleaned; another part of the text indicates that the Eucharist is to be reserved to the baptized (see chapter 9), but it is unclear whether the Eucharist typically followed immediately after baptism. Beyond a broadly trinitarian context (which might reflect later emendation of the text at a time when trinitarian theology was more developed than ca. 100) and the preference for "living" water, there is no indication of the theology of the rite.

The following chart gives a representative sample of the initiatory process as depicted in rites from the Christian East and West in texts likely from the second and third centuries (although some layers of the church order *Apostolic Tradition*, which exhibits the most detail, may postdate the third century). The length of the stated preparation process varies significantly (although *Apostolic Tradition*'s "three years" may reflect an ideal rather than a regularly experienced reality). Notice also that the Eastern rites presented here are devoid of postbaptismal rites beyond sharing in the Eucharist whereas the Western rites have minimal prebaptismal components, especially compared to the highly significant ritual and theological role prebaptismal anointing(s) plays in Syria.

Figure 1: A Comparative Overview of Pre-Nicene Initiatory Rites[17]

	EAST		WEST		
	Syrian Documents (*Didascalia, Acts of Thomas*)	Egypt (Clement of Alexandria, Origen)	Justin Martyr (from Syro-Palestine, wrote in Rome)	*Apostolic Tradition* (Rome? Egypt? Elsewhere in the Christian East?)	North Africa (Tertullian and Cyprian)
Prepara-tion	Catechesis (three weeks?)	Preparatory catechesis	Instruction in "the truth"; fasting and prayer	Three-year catechumenate Election to baptism Immediate preparation with fasting, prayer, and daily exorcism	Catechesis (unspecified length); with vigils, fasting, and prayer
Prebap-tismal Rites	Anointing(s) associated with the gift of the Holy Spirit	Anointing associated with the Holy Spirit?		Blessing of water and oils Renunciation of Satan Anointing/ Exorcism	Sanctification of the waters Renunciation of Satan
Baptism Proper	Baptism with trinitarian formula (i.e., invocation of the "divine names"); themes of new birth, adoption	Themes of regeneration and new birth; associated with crossing the Jordan; baptismal formula or question-response	Baptized are regenerated and illuminated/ enlightened, with possible interroga-tions	Baptism connected to threefold interrogation and profession of faith	Baptism connected to threefold interrogation and profession of faith

Figure 1 *continued*

Postbap-tismal Rites			Led to assembly for common prayers and kiss	Anointing by presbyter Handlaying prayer for "grace" by bishop Anointing by bishop with consignation (+)	Anointing Sign of the cross (Tertullian) Handlaying with prayer related to the Holy Spirit Consignation (Cyprian)
Eucharist	Eucharist as culmination	Unclear if Eucharist followed immediately	Eucharist as culmination	Included "milk and honey"	Included "milk and honey"

At least three different ritual patterns and dominant models of theological interpretation are represented here:

1. Anointing(s), baptism, Eucharist [Syria and Egypt]

   The central paradigm is Christ's baptism by John in the Jordan River; Christian initiation is the means by which humans are reborn, through the Holy Spirit (see John 3), into a new life as followers of Jesus, the Anointed Messiah. In Syria, anointing of the head and/or head and body prior to baptism is the high point of the rite, with water baptism playing a secondary supporting role. Epiphany, as an opportunity to celebrate the manifestations of Christ to the world, including his baptism, would be an ideal time for Christians to celebrate baptism according to this model—although the sources above express no preference regarding the timing of baptism.

2. Baptism, anointing, handlaying, Eucharist [North Africa]

3. Baptism, anointing, handlaying, second postbaptismal anointing, Eucharist [Rome]

With the latter two paradigms, after some prebaptismal rites associated with purification and/or exorcism (to expunge evil spirits), the candidates' old selves are put to death in a watery "tomb" so that they might rise to new life in Christ and receive the *Holy* Spirit. Easter's emphasis on Christ's death and resurrection aligns well with this theology of initiation.

In the fourth and fifth centuries, the process of preparation for baptism becomes a more standardized catechumenate (which proved especially useful to manage the large number of converts seeking to join the church). After the Council of Nicaea, the final, more intensive period of baptismal preparation typically aligned with the season of Lent. The initiatory rites themselves became more elaborate in terms of pre- and postbaptismal ceremonies; their sensory and dramatic appeal (e.g., turning to the West and spitting to renounce Satan, clothing in a white garment after baptism) were calculated in part to facilitate genuine conversion in the candidates if this had not already transpired. The theological focus of the prebaptismal rites becomes invariably preparatory or exorcistic; ritualization of the reception of the Holy Spirit has shifted to a location during or more usually *after* the water bath. The candidates are invited to affirm their faith according to formulas whose content reflected the theological debates of the fourth and fifth centuries. The first reception of the Eucharist that now clearly forms the conclusion of the immediate process of initiation everywhere is treated with special dignity. Mystagogical lectures provided the newly baptized with opportunities to reflect further on what they had experienced and deepen their appropriation of its theological significance.

The development of the Eucharist follows a similar trajectory to the one just observed with initiation. In the mid-second century, Justin Martyr, a native of Syro-Palestine residing in Rome, describes the Sunday gatherings of the Christian community to which he belongs. The gathering occurs on the day called after the sun and features readings from the "apostles" and "prophets" as long as time permits, followed by the presider's address to the assembly urging those gathered to put the teachings they have just heard about into practice in their lives. Prayers are made, then bread and wine are brought forth with the presider giving thanks over them "to the best of his ability" (and presumably extemporaneously); the people affirm the blessing by responding, "Amen." The "eucharistized" bread is distributed to those gathered and taken to those absent, and other items that have been collected are distributed to those who need them.[18] As with baptism, it seems that there is a foundational pattern for the way a community gathers to celebrate the Eucharist that is quite ancient and persists in its major outlines until today. However, alongside the seemingly "familiar" elements there is a considerable lack of detail. This "Sunday" gathering might occur as early as Saturday evening (if Justin's community follows the Semitic pattern for marking the beginning of a new day at sunset) or as late as Sunday evening. Reference to a mixed cup of wine and water may reflect the consolidation of "bread and wine" and "bread and water" groups of Christians in this community's history. In the following several centuries, eucharistic rites become more elaborate, expanded especially around the gathering rites, the preparation of the elements to be blessed, and the rite for receiving communion.

Surviving examples of eucharistic prayer *texts* from the first few centuries are rare, as extemporaneous prayer was the normal expectation. Eucharistic prayers tend to feature two central components: *anamnesis* (thankful remembrance of what God has done in the past that grounds the gathered community's activity in the present) and *epiclesis* (petition or invocation that invites God's further blessings in the present and future). Some of the earliest extant eucharistic prayer texts feature aspects of *anamnesis* and *epiclesis* with little other content at all, as in this example of the blessing of the bread from the *Didache*:

> We give thanks to you, our Father, for the life and knowledge which you have made known to us through your child Jesus; glory to you for evermore. As this broken bread was scattered over the mountains and when brought together became one, so let your Church be brought together from the ends of the earth into your kingdom; for

yours are the glory and the power through Jesus Christ for evermore.[19]

By the fourth and fifth centuries, many other elements are added and certain prayer components, like the Sanctus (Holy, Holy, Holy) and the institution narrative (featuring some reference to Jesus's words, "This is my body" and "This is my blood" in relation to the bread and cup) become nearly universal. By the late fourth century, a time that witnessed debates about the equal divinity of the Holy Spirit, many eucharistic prayers reframe the epicletic component of the prayer as a more explicit invocation for the Holy Spirit to be sent upon the eucharistic gifts of bread and wine, on the people gathered, or on both gifts and people—so that the Holy Spirit might begin to bring about the fruits of communion in those who will soon consume them. The following chart provides a visual representation of this expansion of components:

Figure 2: Development of the Eucharistic Prayer

Early Core (late first/ early second century)	Developed Form (by late fourth century)		
	West Syrian	East Syrian	Alexandrian
Anamnesis (remembrance)	Preface (Praise of Father for creation)	Preface	Preface
	Sanctus	Sanctus	Thanksgiving/Offering
	Post-Sanctus (thanksgiving for redemption)	Post-Sanctus (thanksgiving addressed to Christ)	Intercessions
	Institution narrative	Institution narrative	Sanctus
	Anamnesis	Anamnesis	Epiclesis I
	Offering ("sacrifice of praise")	Intercessions	Institution Narrative

34

Figure 2 *continued*

Epiclesis (petition)	Epiclesis (petition for sending the Holy Spirit and the fruits of communion)	Epiclesis	Anamnesis/Offering
	Intercessions	Doxology	**Epiclesis II**
	Doxology		Doxology

There are more examples of eucharistic prayer texts from the third and especially the fourth centuries, which make it easier to trace the development of early eucharistic praying and its standardization in the sense that while the *content* of these particular subunits might vary from prayer to prayer and their exact arrangement within the prayer differed between regional liturgical "families," most of the components listed above came to be included in most newly composed prayers or inserted in older ones that remained in active use. (There are some exceptions, however, to this general trend: The East Syrian anaphora of Addai and Mari has no institution narrative, and what became the standard form of the Roman Canon has no epiclesis of the Holy Spirit.) The second column in the chart above represents the West Syrian or Antiochene pattern of eucharistic praying, which has been influential in recent Western liturgical revisions.

A wide variety of images and metaphors expresses early eucharistic theology: the Eucharist is holy food, healing "medicine" of immortality, awe-inspiring mystery, and sacred coal. Some further metaphors emerge not so much in eucharistic prayer texts themselves but in discussions of the Eucharist in homilies and other sources, such as reflection on God's gift of food and drink in analogous terms of a mother's self-offering to her child as breast milk.[20] Two theological strands with enduring significance emerged rather early as well—the issue of Christ's true *presence* in the Eucharist and the connection between Eucharist and sacrifice. In terms of presence, the theological focus was on what the blessed bread and wine ultimately become for those who *receive* it in communion rather than the technical details of any transformation that might be operative within the bread and wine, which will become acute concerns of later ages in the West. In the orbit of the early church, affirming that Christ was really present in the Eucharist was helpful in arguing that Christ's earthly, incarnated presence was real in general (in contrast to the views of some early Christian groups with Gnostic or Docetist leanings). Regarding sacrifice, the earliest Christians viewed their cultic practices in contrast to what they understood of Jewish temple sacrifices and the pagan sacrifices of surrounding cultures and in view of Christ's offering of the ultimate sacrifice to reconcile God and humanity. When the Eucharist is presented in early Christian reflections and prayers, it is typically as a sacrifice *of praise*. Toward the end of the period under consideration here, the developing understanding of the Eucharist as a memorial or re-presentation (but *not* repetition) of Christ's once-for-all sacrifice on the cross gained a foothold. As eucharistic prayers begin to combine remembrance of Christ's institution of the Eucharist with the *anamnesis* of his sacrificial death and resurrection, the eucharistic action itself is open to interpretation as a memorial sacrifice since the sacrifice of Christ is remembered and celebrated at every eucharistic gathering.[21] Unfortunately, the combined result of dramatic additions to the eucharistic rite that heightened its solemnity and historicized allegorical interpretations connecting various aspects of the eucharistic rite to the passion, death, and resurrection of Christ—along with bishops' admonitions to receive the Eucharist in a worthy manner—was that those who deemed themselves *unworthy* assumed the role of noncommunicating spectators rather than sacrificial "consumers" whose communion reinforced the call to *become* a living sacrifice through their lives.

PRINCIPLE TWO: A RECIPROCAL *LEX ORANDI, LEX CREDENDI*

Building on the discussion above, a few examples will suffice here to illustrate how practice and doctrine in the early church often grew out of acute pastoral concerns, on the one hand, with the theological ramifications articulated concurrent with or subsequent to the liturgical expression of the church's pastoral response. On the other hand, there are also instances where developments in doctrine clearly influenced the church's way of praying.[22]

The typical candidate for Christian initiation in the early church was a person mature enough to actively participate in the preparation process and profess his or her faith in the immediate context of baptism. At a relatively early stage, however, some children were included in the process, seemingly indicated by directives such as this one from *Apostolic Tradition* 21.16: "Baptize first the children, and if they can speak for themselves let them do so. Otherwise, let their parents or other relatives speak for them." The practice of baptizing children, however, spawned a theological question: If baptism forgives sins, what sort of sins could infants and very young children have committed? The reflections of Western theologians on this point, especially Cyprian of Carthage and Augustine of Hippo, contributed to a developing theology of what would become known in the West as "original sin"; what was forgiven through baptism in the case of the youngest members of the church was not sins they personally had committed but a state of sin they had received as a quasi-inheritance simply from being born into the human race. This theology would in turn affect practice: Christian parents were encouraged to present their children for initiation at a young age; after a few centuries, the time between a Christian's first biological birth and second spiritual birth in baptism tended to shorten such that, by the early Middle Ages, the newest Christians were most often infants rather than adults.

Baptism could be administered by people who were not models of holiness and even by Christians who were in schism, leading to theological reflections on the baptismal status of Christians who had gone through the outward rite of baptism in cases where the minister's claims to holiness left something to be desired. Could sinful ministers serve as effective conduits for God's grace? Against the Donatists, who claimed that those who had renounced their faith in the time of persecution could not mediate the church's faith to others through baptism, Augustine argued that the true minister of baptism (and, by extension, other sacraments) is *Christ*, not any human person. He developed a sacramental equation of sorts: if a word is added to an element, the result is a *sacramentum*; therefore, any baptism using a trinitarian formula and water made a person a member of the church, regardless of who pronounced the words and poured the water. Those baptized by schismatics might need to be *reconciled* to enter communion with the mainstream church, but they did not need to be baptized. Thus the early church's sacramental theology was developed not in the abstract but as a pastoral response to emerging pastoral concerns.

For those who found themselves excommunicated from the church due to serious sins like murder, adultery, and apostasy that threatened the integrity of the church as the ecclesial Body of Christ, a rigorous system of penance was developed to publicly reconcile those who had so publicly sinned. Theologians like Tertullian and Jerome viewed this ecclesially mediated opportunity as a "second plank after shipwreck" that God extended to sinners (Jerome, *Ep.* 130; cf. Tertullian *De penitentia*). Once again practice shaped theology, which in turn, informed practice: by the fourth century, many would-be Christians, including Emperor Constantine, enrolled in the catechumenate but postponed the completion of their initiation process for many years, preferring to take advantage of the rights this connection to the church afforded—yet without the responsibility of committing to the highest standards of Christian ethical behavior or the risk of falling into serious sin after baptism (which would require the recourse of public penance).

The Eucharist provides several examples of cases where developing church doctrine came to shape liturgical practice. Concerns over theological orthodoxy in general put an end to the practice of extemporaneous eucharistic praying, with the expectation that bishops and presbyters would pray using fixed texts that would not intentionally or inadvertently perpetuate questionable theological concepts. Debates about the Holy Spirit's full divinity in the latter half of the fourth century likely contributed to the incorporation of more explicit invocations for the presence and activity of the Holy Spirit in eucharistic prayers during this period and more careful phrasing of trinitarian formulas.

PRINCIPLE THREE: LITURGY AS DIALOGUE BETWEEN CULT AND CULTURE

Although Christians certainly did give distinctive theological interpretations to their practices in light of their growing understanding of the fullness of God's revelation in Christ, many new Christian rituals like baptism and Eucharist developed in ongoing conversation with elements and themes that were already prevalent in the surrounding cultures within which diverse expressions of Christianity took root. Rites of water purification abounded in first-century Palestine, and Christian explanations of baptism for the sake of spiritual cleansing and forgiveness of sins resonated broadly with understandings that non-Christians might have shared; however, unlike other outwardly similar practices, Christian baptism was a definitive, *one-time* event that initiated a new relationship with the God of Jesus Christ. Roman bathing facilities also influenced the architectural surround of Christian baptism. The oldest surviving baptismal "font" is essentially the bathtub in a private home converted for use in Christian worship in the 240s located at the site of Dura-Europos in Syria. As worship transitioned to larger quarters, baptisteries containing pools or fountains were built adjacent to the new basilicas. Roman bathing customs also influenced baptismal practice insofar as men and women were baptized separately (since people stripped naked before entering the water) and anointed with oil before and/or after the bath; in Christianity, the anointing(s) assumed messianic and/or pneumatic connotations. Handlaying as part of prebaptismal exorcistic rites that loosened the bonds of slavery to sin and the devil or postbaptismal rites that further cemented a Christian's new allegiance to Christ had parallels in Rome and North Africa to manumission rites in which a handlaying ritual freed slaves and established new client-patron relationships.[23] Feeding the newly baptized a mixed cup of milk and honey at their first reception of the Eucharist transformed biblical symbols into "a gustatory icon of the promised land"[24] but also conveyed luxury and abundance to people steeped in Greco-Roman culture. Some communities in northern Italy, North Africa, Spain, and Gaul incorporated footwashing, a practical ritual of hospitality, into their initiation rites; Ambrose of Milan calls footwashing a sacrament (in an era predating definitive decrees about the precise number of sacraments) and cites its necessity based on Jesus's command in John's Gospel: "Unless I wash you, you have no share with me" (John 13:8; Ambrose, *On the Sacraments* 3.5).

Even though Christianity was a countercultural cult insofar as it lacked temples, ritual sacrifices, and traditional priests, its central meal, the Eucharist, arose against the backdrop of a banquet culture that would have made the Christian meal recognizable in its broad outlines across the Mediterranean world as a characteristic feature of social groups bonded by a common religion, profession, or other shared interest (ranging from philosophy to provision of a dignified burial). The "supper" (*deipnon*) was followed by a *symposion*, or drinking party featuring entertainment and conversation; the menu and structure of the meal varied according to the social status of participants and the occasion. Tertullian describes a gathering in his community in North Africa ca. 200 that is typical of this basic pattern, if somewhat subdued:

> We do not recline until we have first tasted of prayer to God; as much is eaten as to satisfy the hungry; only as much is drunk as is proper to the chaste. They are satisfied as those who remember that they have to praise God even in the night; they talk as those who know that the Lord is listening. After water for washing the hands, and lights, each is invited to sing publicly to God as able from holy scripture or from their own ability; thus how each has drunk is put to the test. Similarly, prayer closes the feast. (Tertullian, *Apol.* 39.17–18)[25]

What would have been most unusual is that Christians celebrated their bond with God and among themselves "not by pouring libations for the emperors but by remembering a crucified victim of their rule."[26] Over time, and as Christian communities grew larger and celebrations moved from private homes to larger public spaces dedicated to Christian worship, their eucharistic gatherings were reduced from a full meal featuring bread and wine (or water)—but which might have included a variety of other foods as well—to appetizer-sized portions of blessed bread and wine typically shared at a morning meeting rather than an evening feast.

Social and cultural ties bonding the living with the dead also influenced the shape of early Christian worship. In the first few centuries, much activity of great importance to ordinary Christians transpired neither in house churches nor in other spaces built for Christian worship but outside the city walls in its cemeteries where Christians would gather on a small scale to commune with their beloved dead and on a much larger scale to celebrate the "birthdays" of the martyrs into eternal life on the anniversaries of their death. Some ancient tombs contained holes or pipes that permitted visitors to pour a libation of wine inside and thus to commune with the deceased.[27] The Greco-Roman custom of *refrigerium*, or "refreshment," of the dead in their graves evolved into a Christian celebration of the Communion of Saints by celebrating the Eucharist at the *martyria*—shrines erected at martyr's tombs or built to house relics transferred from elsewhere.[28] Otherwise, the "customs on display were taken over for the saints from the traditional family rites: staying up late, often all night, and eating, drinking, and dancing in a celebratory fashion, exactly as non-Christians had always done in honor of their own dead and as they continued to do in the same cemeteries, or next door."[29] On the one hand, bishops encouraged veneration of local saints and new saints introduced to regional consciousness and the annual liturgical calendar through the movement of relics. On the other, they critiqued popular practices that transgressed elite sensibilities about proper Christian decorum.[30] "Official" and "popular" expressions of liturgical piety often overlapped but sometimes conflicted.

The practices and principles of early Christian liturgies provide valuable perspective for understanding the structure and theology of contemporary liturgical rites and potential insights for shaping creative pastoral responses to situations that might arise in the future. Liturgy is an important component of the church's living tradition through which God is still coming to meet us in Christ and through the Holy Spirit—a tradition that remains vital in the present by maintaining an informed connection with its past that often warrants celebration, sometimes inspires reassessment, and always promotes conversion and sanctification. As Robert Taft has noted, "Historical scholarship cannot tell the church what it must do. It can only help the church to see what it could do if those in the pastoral ministry deemed it feasible."[31] For example, might it be possible to restore full initiation, including communion, for all, infants and adults alike?

Could the early church's ways of emphasizing the unity of the local church around the bishop's Eucharist be adapted if regular celebration of the Eucharist in all a diocese's churches becomes impossible? How could liturgies continue to proclaim and celebrate the good news of salvation in Christ to all people through bold yet faithful liturgical inculturation representing innovative *and* organic development of the Christian tradition? The intervening centuries contributed their own principles and practices, making it unwise to adopt or adapt aspects of the early church's liturgical celebration and theological interpretation either uncritically or without consideration of contemporary pastoral needs. Yet the legacy of early Christian liturgy might also inspire us to more fruitfully respond to the intersection of God's activity and human hopes in our own time as the embodied experience of the church at worship continues to shape the worship of the church.

Further Reading

Bradshaw, Paul F. *Early Christian Worship: A Basic Introduction to Ideas and Practice.* 2nd ed. Collegeville, MN: Liturgical Press, 2010.

Bradshaw, Paul F., and Maxwell E. Johnson. *The Origins of Feasts, Fasts and Seasons in Early Christianity.* London: SPCK/Collegeville, MN: Liturgical Press, 2011.

Ferguson, Everett. *Baptism in the Early Church: History, Theology, and Liturgy in the First Five Centuries.* Grand Rapids, MI: Eerdmans Publishing Company, 2013.

Gerhards, Albert, and Benedikt Kranemann. *Introduction to the Study of Liturgy.* Translated by Linda M. Maloney. Collegeville, MN: Liturgical Press, 2017.

Jensen, Robin M. *Baptismal Imagery in Early Christianity: Ritual, Visual, and Theological Dimensions.* Grand Rapids, MI: Baker Academic, 2012.

Johnson, Lawrence J. *Worship in the Early Church: An Anthology of Historical Sources.* 4 vols. Collegeville, MN: Liturgical Press, 2009.

Johnson, Maxwell E. *Praying and Believing in Early Christianity: The Interplay between Christian Worship and Doctrine.* Collegeville, MN: Liturgical Press, 2013.

McGowan, Andrew B. *Ancient Christian Worship: Early Church Practices in Social, Historical, and Theological Perspective.* Grand Rapids, MI: Baker Academic, 2014.

Phillips, L. Edward. "Prayer in the First Four Centuries A.D." In *A History of Prayer: The First to the Fifteenth Century*, edited by Roy Hammerling, 29–58. Leiden: Brill, 2008.

Notes

1. On this phenomenon see, e.g., Paul F. Bradshaw, "The Homogenization of Christian Liturgy—Ancient and Modern," *Studia Liturgica* 26, no. 1 (1996): 1–15; and Frederick R. McManus, "Back to the Future: The Early Christian Roots of Liturgical Renewal," *Worship* 72, no. 5 (1998): 386–403.

2. On architectural evidence for maternal imagery in baptismal fonts, see Robin M. Jensen, *Baptismal Imagery in Early Christianity: Ritual, Visual, and Theological Dimensions* (Grand Rapids, MI: Baker Academic, 2012), 162–65.

3. For examples and discussion, see Charles W. Gusmer, *And You Visited Me: Sacramental Ministry to the Sick and the Dying*, rev. ed., Studies in the Reformed Rites of the Catholic Church(New York: Pueblo Publishing Company, 1989), 6:11–21. On communion practices, see Robert F. Taft, "The Frequency of the Celebration of the Eucharist throughout History," in *Between Memory and Hope: Readings on the Liturgical Year*, ed. Maxwell E. Johnson (Collegeville, MN: Liturgical Press, 2000), 77–96.

4. See Andrew B. McGowan, *Ascetic Eucharists: Food and Drink in Early Christian Meals* (Oxford: Clarendon Press, 1999).

5. On this broad understanding of *ordinatio* as "a religious and liturgical act which was a consecration, a blessing or a sacrament," see the *Catechism of the Catholic Church* 1538.

6. A condensed formulation of this concept was captured by Prosper of Aquitaine in the fifth century, although its actual application is older still. In the context of making an anti-Pelagian argument, Prosper observed that the Church in its solemn intercessions makes supplication for all sorts of people, in essence asking God to give the grace of faith to all according to their need. Therefore, he concluded, *ut legem credendi lex statuat supplicandi* (that the law or "rule" of [intercessory] praying

[might it establish] the law of believing)—in this case believing in the absolute priority of God's grace over human initiative. For a more extensive discussion of *lex orandi, lex credendi* and its reciprocal manifestations in the early Church, see Maxwell E. Johnson, *Praying and Believing in Early Christianity: The Interplay between Christian Worship and Doctrine* (Collegeville, MN: Liturgical Press, 2013).

7. For a more sustained treatment of the interaction between liturgy and culture, see Martin D. Stringer, *A Sociological History of Christian Worship* (Cambridge: Cambridge University Press, 2005); Frank Senn, *The People's Work: A Social History of the Liturgy* (Minneapolis: Fortress Press, 2006); and Mark R. Francis, *Local Worship, Global Church: Popular Religion and the Liturgy* (Collegeville, MN: Liturgical Press, 2014).

8. Robert F. Taft, "Liturgy as Theology," in *Beyond East and West: Problems in Liturgical Understanding* (Rome: Edizioni Orientalia Christiana, 1997), 234–35; quote from 235.

9. The overview in this section is based on the more extensive one in Basil Studer, "Liturgy and the Fathers," in *Handbook for Liturgical Studies*, vol. 1, ed. Anscar J. Chupungco (Collegeville, MN: Liturgical Press, 1997), esp. 54–60. While it was common until recently to speak of the "Fathers" or "Patristics" in reference to this time period, the terminology has been shifting more recently; see Elizabeth A. Clark, "From Patristics to Early Christian Studies," in *The Oxford Handbook of Early Christian Studies*, ed. Susan Ashbrook Harvey and David G. Hunter (Oxford: Oxford University Press, 2008), 7–41.

10. The eucharistic prayer proposed for a bishop's ordination liturgy in *Apostolic Tradition* 4 has since inspired Eucharistic Prayer II in the current Roman Rite and several other eucharistic prayers widely used by churches in North America.

11. On baptism, see Tertullian, *De baptismo*; Cyprian, *Epist.* 69–75; Augustine, *Opere antidonatiste*. On the Eucharist, see Cyprian, *Epist.* 63. On prayer, see Tertullian, *De oratione*; Origen, *De oratione*; and Cyprian, *De oratione*.

12. What we think of as congregational hymn singing would have been relatively rare during this period. Scriptural texts might have been "chanted" or cantillated, and psalms were "read" by an appointed singer with the assembly contributing a prescribed response. See Edward Foley, *Foundations of Christian Music: The Music of Pre-Constantinian Christianity* (Collegeville, MN: Liturgical Press, 1996) and John Arthur Smith,

Music in Ancient Judaism and Early Christianity (Farnham, UK: Ashgate, 2011). Hymns would have been sung more often by soloists or choirs to praise God and enlighten the congregation, whether gathered in place or in a procession from one place to another.

13. On a related note, John Chrysostom felt the need to admonish his congregation when he was a presbyter in Antioch toward the end of the fourth century: "You must stop going to the synagogue, you must not think that the synagogue is a holier place than our churches are," suggesting that at least some among his flock *were* observing Jewish feasts as well as Christian ones and that the close connection between Judaism and Christianity that existed at Christianity's origins endured for several centuries in some places. See Homily 47, *Against the Jews* and, for context, Robert L. Wilken, *John Chrysostom and the Jews: Rhetoric and Reality in the Late 4th Century* (Berkeley: University of California Press, 1983).

14. The nontextual aspects of early Christian worship are explored well in Andrew B. McGowan, *Ancient Christian Worship: Early Church Practices in Social, Historical, and Theological Perspective* (Grand Rapids, MI: Baker Academic, 2014); and Edward Foley, *From Age to Age: How Christians Have Celebrated the Eucharist,* rev. and exp. ed. (Collegeville, MN: Liturgical Press, 2009). See, e.g., McGowan's chapter on "Music: Song and Dance" and Foley's treatment of architecture, music, books, and vessels applicable to each historical period.

15. Paul F. Bradshaw, *The Search for the Origins of Christian Worship: Sources and Methods for the Study of Early Liturgy,* 2nd ed. (Oxford: Oxford University Press, 2002), 213. The entire volume offers a representative survey of the liturgical trend toward greater standardization.

16. ET from Kurt Niederwimmer, *The Didache* (Minneapolis: Fortress Press, 1998).

17. Adapted from Maxwell E. Johnson, *The Rites of Christian Initiation: Their Evolution and Interpretation* (Collegeville, MN: Liturgical Press, 2007), 111; see 63ff. for discussion of the interpretive challenges posed by the Egyptian sources in particular.

18. Justin Martyr, 1 *Apol.* 67; ET in R. C. D. Jasper and G. J. Cuming, *Prayers of the Eucharist: Early and Reformed,* 3rd ed., rev. and enlarged (Collegeville, MN: Liturgical Press, 1990), 29–30.

19. *Didache* 9, ET from Jasper and Cuming, *Prayers of the Eucharist,* 23.

20. See Teresa Berger, *Gender Differences and the Making of Liturgical History: Lifting a Veil on Liturgy's Past* (Burlington, VT: Ashgate, 2011), 72–86.

21. For more on this theological development, see Paul F. Bradshaw, *Early Christian Worship: A Basic Introduction to Ideas and Practice*, 2nd ed. (Collegeville, MN: Liturgical Press, 2010), esp. 62–69 and Bradshaw, *Eucharistic Origins* (London: SPCK, 2004).

22. For further examples and discussion, see Johnson, *Praying and Believing*.

23. See Senn, *The People's Work*, 32–34; Bryan D. Spinks, *Early and Medieval Rituals and Theologies of Baptism: From the New Testament to the Council of Trent* (Burlington, VT: Ashgate, 2006), 35–36.

24. Aidan Kavanagh, "A Rite of Passage," *Liturgy* 70, no. 8 (1977); and McGowan, *Ancient Christian Worship*, 160–63.

25. ET from McGowan, *Ancient Christian Worship*, 22.

26. McGowan, *Ancient Christian Worship*, 22.

27. For discussion and examples, see Ramsay MacMullen, *The Second Church: Popular Christianity A.D. 200–400* (Atlanta: Society of Biblical Literature, 2009), 24–26, 77.

28. For considerations of how *martyria* situated within church complexes might accommodate vigils, popular devotions, and the eucharistic liturgy, see Lizette Larson-Miller, "The Altar and the Martyr: Theological Comparisons in Liturgical Texts and Contexts," in *Worship Traditions in Armenia and the Neighboring Christian East*, ed. Roberta R. Ervine (Crestwood, NY: St. Vladimir's Seminary Press/St. Nersess Armenian Seminary, 2006), 237–60.

29. MacMullen, *The Second Church*, 107.

30. See, e.g., MacMullen, *The Second Church*, 91–94.

31. Robert F. Taft, "Response to the Berakah Award: Anamnesis," *Worship* 59, no. 4 (1985): 311.

3

WESTERN LITURGY IN THE MIDDLE AGES

—ɯ—

Tom Elich

Several narratives are possible when looking at liturgy in the Middle Ages. One may focus on the hard evidence of the liturgical texts, but the mechanisms of an oral culture also remained operative at least until the twelfth century. On the one hand, one may focus on the gradual ascendancy of the Roman liturgy and see a growing unity developing throughout the West; but, on the other hand, in a manuscript culture there is always local variation, and it is only the printing press in the fifteenth century that allowed liturgical uniformity. One may focus, as many writers do, on the clericalization of the liturgy and the progressive exclusion of the laity from the liturgical action, but there is also a dimension to be recognized that speaks of lay involvement in the liturgy. The plural term *Middle Ages* reminds us that there are many stories to be told.

This chapter does not attempt to tell them all. There were different centers in the West that maintained their own liturgical traditions into the medieval period: Milan, Spain, and Gaul, for example. Celtic elements brought to the continent by missionary monks are found as far south as St. Gall in Switzerland and Bobbio in Italy. The story told in this chapter figures most prominently the mutual influence of Roman and Gallican traditions. Monasteries and the Liturgy of the Hours they celebrated, important though those stories are, receive only passing mention.

LITURGICAL BOOKS

The first centuries of what we call the Middle Ages see the development of a library of liturgical books. Their changing form tells us a lot about the evolution of the liturgy itself. At first, a few collects or a formulary for a particular Mass were set down in writing on a page or leaflet (*libellus*). A collection of these booklets from the fifth and sixth centuries is preserved in a seventh-century manuscript at Verona; sometimes called the Sacramentary of Verona, it groups multiple formularies for certain feasts under the months of the year. Much of the liturgy, however, was improvised or known by heart.

Since each book was copied and often illustrated by hand, books were rare and precious. An earlier book might be copied later and edited to omit elements that were not required or to add pieces that seemed to be lacking. Older books were used alongside newer ones. Each manuscript was unique.

Sacramentary. This is a book for the presider, containing his texts for Mass and other rituals. Roman sacramentaries can be classified into two types: one called the Gelasian is a presbyteral book; the other called the Gregorian is a papal book (though it also exists in an adapted form for presbyteral use). Sacramentaries of the Gelasian type are divided into three sections: first the Christmas–Easter cycles, then the cycle of saints' days, and finally the Masses for ordinary days together with the Canon of the Mass and Masses for various occasions; each Mass formulary opens with two collects. The second type, the Gregorian, combines the seasons and saints into a single part, and each Mass formulary has just one collect before the Prayer over the Gifts.

Neither of these types exists in its pure form. The Gelasian, for example, is found in an eighth-century manuscript in the Vatican Library (Vat. Reg. 316). Its title announces it as a sacramentary of the Roman church, but already it includes Frankish sections (for ordinations and the consecration of virgins, the dedication of a church, the blessing of water and funerals). Then there is a group of manuscripts called the Frankish Gelasian of the eighth century. They combine the Gelasian content, the structure of the presbyteral form of the Gregorian, and further Frankish material. These versions came about because pilgrims visiting Rome apparently brought back books for use north of the Alps. Monks took part in this informal exchange, and the important work of compiling and copying these sacramentaries took place in Frankish monasteries.

Ordines. An ordo is a description of how a liturgical rite takes place. Ordines contain the "stage directions" or the rubrics alongside the texts of prayers, readings, and chants that are generally indicated just by their first words (*incipit*). Compiled in Gaul in the eighth and ninth centuries, these books contain collections of *Ordines Romani* and hybrid Frankish ordines, covering the Mass, Christian initiation, and innumerable other rites, destined for either parish, cathedral, or monastic settings. The famous *Ordo Romanus I*, for example, describes a papal Mass in Rome at the end of the seventh century; *Ordo Romanus XI* gives a description of baptism in Rome that may be read as a companion to the Gelasian sacramentary.

Lectionaries. Throughout the Middle Ages, patterns developed for reading from Scripture. The Roman Rite had two readings (epistle and gospel), and when the Roman liturgy made its way north, it supplanted the Gallican tradition of three readings. Because the Gospels were carried by the deacon and venerated with special solemnity in the liturgy, the Book of Gospels or the evangeliary was frequently the most beautifully bound and illuminated.

Several systems of identifying the liturgical readings from Scripture coexisted:

- *Marginal notes*: a copy of the Bible (or New Testament) was marked with crosses or other reference signs in the margins. This worked well when the readings listed were relatively few and before the early thirteenth-century division of the biblical text into chapter and verse.

- The *capitularia*: lists that gave the beginning and ending of each reading (the *incipit* and *explicit*) for each liturgical day. Sometimes separate lists were developed for gospel and non-gospel readings, and sometimes the capitularia was added to a biblical text with marginal notes. This system of identifying readings would have been easier for people living in a largely oral culture where much of the New Testament would have been known by heart.

- The *Lectionary, evangeliary,* or *epistolary*: arranged like the capitularia, these books gave the full text of the reading. This was an expensive option but became more common toward the end of the Middle Ages—and correspondingly the system of marginal notation became less common.

Chant Books. Among the Roman books that found their way over the Alps was the antiphonary. These books contained the texts to be sung but not the music. The melodies and modalities of the chant were memorized and transmitted orally.

The first musical notation appears in the second half of the ninth century in the form of neumes. These were graphic signs written over the text, and they functioned as an aide-memoire for the cantor. At first, only some pieces were notated and often the neumes were later additions to the written text. Guido of Arezzo in the eleventh century placed marks on horizontal lines, thus establishing accurate intervals. He demonstrated his method for the pope at the time who was astonished and impressed that the schola could sing a chant that they had never heard! Proportional notation introduced in the early thirteenth century meant that at last one could truly "read the music."

Charlemagne. Pope Leo III crowned Charlemagne emperor of the Holy Roman Empire on Christmas Day in 800. Like his father, Pepin (crowned king of the Franks in 751), he promoted political and ecclesiastical unity across his territory, which extended from Rome to the North Sea. The Roman liturgy was an important tool in his work of unification. A single people, he argued, should celebrate a single liturgy. So books and ministers were brought from Rome in an attempt to supplant the Gallican traditions of the Frankish Church.

This was easier said than done. Manuscripts were rare even in Rome. Pepin worked with the Frankish Gelasian, but Charlemagne wanted to go further. The most famous story concerns Charlemagne's request of Pope Hadrian I for an authentic and pure Roman sacramentary to serve as a model. The pope sent him a lavish manuscript in 785, but it was a Gregorian sacramentary (for use in papal liturgy).

As such it was too limited for the needs of the church in Gaul. So Charlemagne commissioned a supplement to fill in the gaps. Probably the work of Benedict of Aniane, it drew on Gallican sources. Therefore, despite Charlemagne's best efforts, the Roman liturgy again absorbed Gallican material.

Unifying the liturgical chant was even more difficult because, without notation, the entire repertoire of music was still learnt by heart and taught orally. So Roman cantors were brought to the north to teach the chant and the techniques, or Frankish cantors would be sent to spend time in Rome. As he travelled, Charlemagne noticed on several occasions differences between the Roman chant and the Gallican. Where, he asked, is the water purer, at the source or in the current? We, he added, who have been drinking polluted water from the stream must return to the source. He sent clerics to Rome. How these differences were interpreted depended on one's point of view: on the one hand, John the Deacon from Rome blamed the barbaric throats and grinding voices of the northern cantors that, he said, prevented them from following the delicate inflections of the Roman cantillation; on the other hand, Notker of St. Gall accused the Roman cantors of jealousy and subterfuge, saying that they taught different things in different parts of Gaul so that the Roman superiority would never be threatened. These stories illustrate the impossibility of maintaining a uniform chant in an oral culture.

Moreover, we see the same diversity in the chant texts themselves. Even after Charlemagne's work, ninth-century Amalarius of Metz (an important center for music) found that antiphonaries differed. He was sent to the pope to borrow an authorized Roman copy, but the pope did not have one to lend—they had been sent to the monastery of Corbie for copying. So Amalarius went to Corbie and compared Rome and Metz. He discovered differences in both the texts and their ordering. "I was astonished," he wrote, "to see how much mother and daughter differed from each other." His solution was to compose a new antiphonary drawn from both traditions!

Otto I. Upon Charlemagne's death in 814, the empire was divided between his two sons. Much later, in 962, Otto I, king of Germany, was crowned Holy Roman Emperor in Rome. He and his successors used the bishops (and the pope) to maintain control of the empire. They celebrated the Gallicanized Roman liturgy and brought the hybrid liturgical books from the north back to Rome. With several German popes in the eleventh century, the Franco-Germanic liturgy was established even in the Lateran Basilica. After a difficult century, the papacy reasserted itself with the election of Gregory VII in 1073. His focus was on the reform of the clergy and the centralization of liturgical administration, but he also thought to revise the liturgy itself to retrieve the more sober Roman tradition. Papal power grew to its high point in the thirteenth century.

One of the key books that had been brought to Rome in the tenth century was an influential compilation of a dramatic new kind, the *Romano-Germanic Pontifical*. This offered the bishop the convenience of having everything (apart from the Mass and Office) in a single volume: rubrics, prayers, blessings, readings, and even homilies and liturgical commentaries. This book would be revised and simplified for the Roman curia in the twelfth and thirteenth centuries. It reached its medieval high point in the Pontifical of William Durand, bishop of Mende, at the end of the thirteenth century. William organized the material as a book for use in the liturgy, omitting extraneous material and anything that did not pertain to the bishop. Meanwhile, the presbyteral material for the sacraments developed into a book called the *Ritual*.

Missal and Breviary. Likewise, liturgical books for the Mass were evolving. By the eleventh century, the sacramentary was often combined with the epistolary, evangeliary, and antiphonary to form a plenary *Missal*. Sometimes the parts were juxtaposed, sometimes interwoven. During the twelfth century, the Missal became far more common than the sacramentary. What happened here for the Mass occurred soon after for the Liturgy of the Hours as the various Office books evolved into the *Breviary*.

The Missal and Breviary were adopted by the papal household, whose legates were often on the move because it was not possible to celebrate in community with a full complement of ministers. In the thirteenth century, these portable books were taken up by the mendicant orders (particularly the Franciscans) whose missionary activity supported the diffusion of the Roman liturgy throughout Europe.

The form of the missal and breviary represents a significant change of mind-set with respect to the ecclesial nature of the liturgy. As the various books were combined into one, so the roles of those who used them (the subdeacon, deacon, and cantor/choir) are subsumed by the priest. Even when these ministers performed their roles, the priest simultaneously needed to vocalize the texts himself.

Going hand in hand with the spread of the Missal were new ways of celebrating the Mass: the priest would say Mass privately, facing east away from the people in the nave; the number of Masses was multiplied, especially in monasteries; and the priest prayed large parts of the Mass silently, adding private prayers of his own.

THE MASS

Architecture for Celebrating Mass. In the early Christian basilica, the cathedra was placed in the apse and the altar was placed forward in the nave. The priest would stand on whichever side allowed him to face east, symbolic of the dawn of the resurrection. With no seating in the nave, the people were able to move freely around the altar. In this case, whether the apse was at the east end or the west end of the church made little difference. In the time of Charlemagne, the apse tended to be placed on the eastern side, meaning that the priest and many of the people all faced east. But the Franks had also received the Roman practice of placing the altar above a crypt that contained the tomb of a martyr. This tended to raise the altar and separate it from the nave.

In ninth-century Gaul, Latin was not generally understood by the people and the priest began to pray the eucharistic prayer in silence. This added a "mystical distance" to the liturgy that was also expressed by progressively moving the altar back into the apse; lines of demarcation appeared between nave and sanctuary. The altar was eventually placed against the back wall and decorated with an altarpiece to articulate a theology of the Eucharist. The chancel was expanded to make provision for the choir of monks and/or clergy, and the demarcation became a rood screen (so called because it was topped by a crucifix). In monastic churches, the choir stalls for the

Liturgy of the Hours sometimes extended into the nave, creating an enclosed space facing the high altar.

As the priest prayed silently in Latin, there was a growing sense that the priest offered the Mass for others. At first, all those present were presumed to make the offering. In the Roman Canon, the priest said *omnium circumstantium...qui tibi offerent* ("all those present... who offer to you"). Under Charlemagne, it is augmented to emphasize the particular role of the priest: *omnium circumstantium...pro quibus tibi offerimus, vel qui tibi offerent* ("those present...for whom we offer you, or who offer to you"). Further, in this context it was natural that the priest developed a repertoire of private prayers. In the eleventh century, many prayers of unworthiness (*apologiae*) were included among the Mass prayers.

Throughout the Middle Ages, the cult of relics grew in importance and with it the practice of pilgrimage. Important relics were enshrined in additional altars that were located in the ambulatory, a passageway for pilgrims encircling the chancel and choir.

Death and judgement were an ever-present reality for medieval believers: they might have entered the church under a dramatic Last Judgement scene sculpted over the main west door or perhaps they viewed the Mass under the rood crucifix and against a painted Doom on the chancel arch. The Mass offered a way to escape the clutches of the devil, who could be seen dragging the condemned into a horrible hell-mouth. Thus, it became important for the priest to offer Mass for the dead, and this too led to the multiplication of Masses and side altars. And it was only after the eighth century that the *Memento* for the dead was introduced into the Roman Canon—it was not in the Sacramentary that Pope Hadrian sent to Charlemagne!

To respond to the growing need, many of the monks in large monasteries were ordained and altars were built to accommodate the larger number of private Masses. For example, Abbot Suger (1081–1151) of the royal abbey of St. Denis, who rebuilt his monastery church in the brilliant new Gothic style, incorporated twenty altars in his plan (eleven in the choir and nine in the crypt).

All these developments are generally adduced as evidence for the clericalization of the liturgy during the Middle Ages and the consequent exclusion of the people. No doubt, this is true to a large extent, but it is not the whole story.

In many ways, the multiplication of Masses and the proliferation of side altars made the Mass more accessible to laypeople. Ironically, even blocking off the high altar by the clergy choir was countered by the erection of a nave altar in the midst of the people. Chantry chapels were erected at the head of the side aisles or in the transepts of parish churches. These were generally the work of laypeople and were under lay control. Sometimes a confraternity or guild would sponsor such an altar, furnishing it and providing the lights, as well as employing the priest to offer daily Mass there. In the later Middle Ages, a bequest might be left for the establishment of a chantry where Mass would be offered in perpetuity for the soul and family of the deceased. A Mass stipend gave a person a stake in the priest's offering and might even determine the Mass texts the priest would use, whether a votive Mass, for example, or a Mass for the dead.

While the Sunday parish Mass might have been experienced from a distance and seen through the rood screen, the most common experience of Mass for devout laypeople—just at arm's length— would have been the weekday Mass in a chantry chapel or at a side altar. This allowed people a close involvement in the action of the Mass. Contemporary illustrations of the Mass, whether carved on the side of seven-sacrament fonts in East Anglia or in paintings and illuminations of the Mass of St Gregory, show laypeople beside the altar or looking over the railings at the elevation of the host. Often, they are shown holding the torches or ringing the bell at the elevation. Many hold up their hands in a gesture of prayer. People were quite free to move about the church space. Churches may have had some stone benches along the walls where people could sit, but rows of wooden pews only appear toward the end of the Middle Ages. The pew-filled nave keeping people in their place was a postmedieval phenomenon.

What, then, was it like for people at a medieval Mass? Two examples open up the experience for us: receiving communion and liturgical catechesis.

Receiving Communion. Communion practice was shaped by the developing theology of the real presence of Christ in the Eucharist.

The ninth century juxtaposed the ultra-realist position of Paschasius Radbertus with the sacramental position of Ratramnus. In the eleventh century, Berengarius of Tours was forced to adopt an intensely realist position. The debate was eventually resolved in favor of a sacramentalist view with the doctrine of transubstantiation. This was defined by the Fourth Lateran Council in 1215 and articulated by the scholastics through the Aristotelian metaphysics of substance and accidents. Nevertheless, divergent understandings continued to coexist. Popular stories of seeing the child in the host, the host turning to flesh, or images of the Mass of St. Gregory expressed the reality of Christ in the Eucharist in quite a literal way. The fourteenth-century *Ave Verum Corpus*, sung at the elevation of the host, captures the eucharistic devotion of the time: *Hail, true Body, born of the Virgin Mary, having truly suffered, sacrificed on the cross for humankind, from whose pierced side water and blood flowed.*

This awesome reality led people to fear receiving communion unworthily. Councils recommended receiving communion three or four times a year, and the Fourth Lateran demanded at least an annual Easter communion. (There were always exceptions, such as the fifteenth-century mystic Margery Kempe who confessed to her spiritual director and received communion weekly.) The people's communion, not mentioned in the Order of Mass, sometimes became a supplementary rite rather like the communion of the sick.

Unleavened bread left fewer crumbs and was easier to reserve in the tabernacle; it became the norm in the eleventh century. Communion was received on the tongue (as it was given to the sick) and, to make it easier to administer, the communicant knelt. With the awareness that the living Christ was received under either species and recognizing the danger of spillage, communion from the cup was gradually withdrawn in the twelfth and thirteenth centuries. Thomas Aquinas (1225–74) gives witness to this changing practice (*Summa* III.80.12).

The focus of people's attention became the elevation of the host. In the West Midlands around 1400, John Myrc wrote his *Instructions for Parish Priests* in English in rhyming couplets. He encouraged priests to teach people, young and old, to kneel when they hear the bell ring at the consecration, to hold up both their hands, and to say these words softly to greet the Lord at the elevation (lines 290–93):

> Jesus Lord, welcome thou be
> in form of bread as I thee see.
> Jesus! For thy holy name,
> shield me today from sin and shame.

There are many examples of these "salutations of Christ" written in the vernacular so that laypeople could memorize them and pray them at the elevation. They derive from the priest's own communion prayers where he addressed Christ in the consecrated elements. The Sarum Missal from England, for example, has the priest say, "Hail forever, most holy flesh of Christ, before all else and above all else, the highest sweetness."

So the elevation became a key moment for lay participation in the Eucharist. Officially sanctioned for the first time at the Synod of Paris early in the thirteenth century, the elevation spread quickly. At the end of the Middle Ages, Thomas Cranmer, with rhetorical humor, would lament that people ran to the altar and from altar to altar *peeping*, *tooting*, and *gazing* at the host held up by the priest.

As the host was raised on high so that it could receive the gaze of the faithful, people were encouraged to bow or kneel with devotion and reverence. This practice is best regarded as a form of receiving holy communion (rather than a pious devotion that takes the place of receiving communion).

In a medieval understanding, seeing took place when the rays sent out by an object were received by the eye. Sight involved a quasi-physical contact between the person and the perceived object, in this case between the believer and the host. In the scholastic theology of transubstantiation, what is perceptible remains unchanged (the "accidents"), but the reality (the "substance") changes: it is no longer bread but Christ. At Mass, we make physical contact with the accidents (the sacrament) but the reality we encounter is Christ. So whether we access the sacrament by tasting or seeing is less important than the fact that, through the senses, we enter into communion with the Body of Christ.

People were taught that a glimpse of the host, like receiving communion itself, was rewarded with the promises of extraordinary blessings from Christ: one would not go hungry, idle words would be pardoned, one would be kept safe, and if death should come, it would count as viaticum. Given the fear of eating the bread unworthily and thereby eating judgement against themselves (1 Cor 11:27–30), it is not surprising that people were encouraged to make daily physical contact with the host through their eyes rather than their mouths.

This led people to focus on a spiritual communion, particularly their vicarious participation in the priest's communion. For example, the early fourteenth-century poet and priest from Kent, William of Shoreham, writes of the mystical Body in his poem on the seven sacraments: Christ is the head, the priest is the mouth, the people are the limbs; God's flesh is taken as the mouth takes food, and the food is transmitted to the limbs. Thus, people's sacramental encounter, even when they do not actually receive holy communion, is placed into an ecclesial context.

The practice of visual eucharistic participation in the Mass provides a helpful perspective for understanding the development of Corpus Christi and the display of the consecrated host in the monstrance. The moment of the elevation of the host was extended to make the encounter with Christ available for people at other times and places. The feast was introduced in Liège in 1246 and spread throughout Europe in the fourteenth century. Corpus Christi guilds were founded to honor Christ in the blessed sacrament; they organized processions with banners, garlands, and lights that became major civic events. Progressively in paintings and manuscripts, instead of illustrating the Eucharist with the elevation at Mass, images of the Corpus Christi procession or just the monstrance itself appeared instead. (The monstrance developed from reliquaries in the fifteenth century.)

Liturgical Catechesis: Two Approaches. Two quotations describing the reading of the gospel at Mass illustrate two very different approaches to helping people in the Middle Ages understand and participate in the liturgy. They are roughly contemporary.

4.23.1 …The priest rises and, moving to the left part of the altar, he proclaims the Gospel, signifying that Christ did not come to call the just but rather the sinners, according to what he himself said in the Gospel: *it is not the healthy who need a physician, but those who are sick* (Lk 5:31); for the right side signifies the just, while the left signifies the sinners, on account of which the Lord, on Judgement Day, will place the sheep on his right and the goats on the left…

4.24.6 [The deacon] takes the Gospel book, as some claim, from the right side of the altar because the Church of the Jews, from which our Church originated, was in ancient times, on the right side; he places it in his left hand while placing his right hand on top of it, according to the text: *His left hand is under my head and his right hand embraces me* (Song 2:6, 8:3). And this is done for three reasons.

First because the Evangelist teaches that celestial things, which are understood by the right side, are placed above earthly things, which are understood by the left.

Second the Gospel book is borne on the left arm to note that the preaching of Christ will pass from the Gentiles to the Jewish people: *In his days, Judah shall be saved* (Jer 23:6).

Third, because the Gospel must be preached in this earthly life, which is signified by the left hand.

4.24.23 Fittingly, the Gospel is heard standing, not sitting, just as Pope Athanasius decreed, to note the readiness of going into battle in the service of faith in Christ; thus *Let him who has no sword sell his tunic and buy one* (Lk 22:36). And since his teaching raises our minds to the love of celestial things, to designate the same sort of readiness, while the Gospel is being read, some take off their cloaks; this is also done to note that all earthly things must be renounced to follow Christ, according to the text of the Gospel: *Behold we have left everything and we have followed you* (Mt 19:27).

• William Durand, *Rationale Divinorum Officiorum, Book IV: On the Mass and Each Action Pertaining to It*, translated from Latin by Timothy M. Thibodeau, Corpus Christianorum in Translation (Turnhout: Brepols, 2013).

151–96. If they sing the Mass or say it, always repeat your *Pater Noster*, until the deacon or priest reads the gospel. Stand up then and pay close attention. For then the priest carries his book north to the other corner of the altar and, making a cross upon the text with his thumb, he goes one better and afterwards makes another upon his face, for he has great need of grace: for then an earthly man shall utter the words of Jesus Christ, the Son of God from heaven. Both the readers and the hearers have great need, I think, of teachers—how they should read and should hear the words of God, so pleasing and dear.

People ought to have great dread, whether they hear it or else read it, and also to love that sweetness which soothes our woes with these words. But since our subject is of hearing, of that now shall be our learning. Clerics hear in one way but another way of learning is right for lay people.

At the beginning take care to make a large cross on yourself. Stand and say in this manner as you see it written here:

In the name of the Father and Son and the Holy Spirit, a faithful God of power and might; may God's word be welcome to me; and glory and praise be to you, Lord.

While [the gospel] is read, do not speak, but think about him who bought you so dearly, saying in your mind thus, as you find it written here:

My Jesus, grant me your grace and the strength and time for amendment, to keep your word and do your will, to choose the good and leave the bad; and that it may be so, Good Jesus, grant it to me. Amen.

Repeat this often in your thought: until the gospel is ended, do not forget it. Besides, when it is ended, make a cross somewhere and then kiss it.

• *The Lay Folks Mass Book or the Manner of Hearing Mass with Rubrics and Devotions for the People*, Early English Text Society (London: Trübner & Co., 1879). Adapted from the translation of the Middle English by R. N. Swanson, *Catholic England: Faith, Religion and Observance before the Reformation*, Manchester Medieval Sources (Manchester: University Press, 2013).

Bishop William Durand of Mende (c. 1230–96) wrote in Latin for a literate and educated clergy. These quotations from his commentary on the gospel reading are fragments of a much longer exposition that offers explanations of how the deacon takes the book from the altar, his blessing by the bishop, his movement to the ambo, the incense and candles, the form of the ambo, the signing with the cross, the kissing of the book, and so forth. The *Rationale* is an encyclopedic compilation of allegorical liturgical commentary, drawn from Patristic exegesis and earlier medieval sources such as Amalarius, ninth-century bishop of Metz. In eight books, it covers the symbolism of the church building, clerical orders, vestments, the Mass, the Office, the temporal and sanctoral cycles, and computing the calendar. Immensely popular, it may be regarded as the zenith of medieval liturgical understanding.

The allegorical commentary starts from the texts and gestures of the liturgy and then proceeds to reveal the hidden mysteries contained within each liturgical detail. Durand himself introduces the nature and scope of his project:

Whatever belongs to the liturgical offices, objects and furnishings of the Church is full of signs of the divine and the sacred mysteries, and each of them overflows with a celestial sweetness when it is encountered by a diligent observer....Here the celestial model that was shown to Moses on the mountaintop will be revealed to me [c.f. Ex 20], so that I can unveil and explain clearly and openly each object or ornament that belongs to the ecclesiastical services, what each of these signifies or represents figuratively, and set forth their rationale, according to what has been revealed. (Prologue 1, trans. Thibodeau)

The Lay Folks Mass Book demonstrates that, for laypeople, there was a different way of appreciating the liturgy. It too takes the action of the liturgy as its point of departure. But this book was written in the vernacular for a lay audience—originally in French in the mid-twelfth century and then translated into Middle English around 1300. Before this time, English was largely the spoken language of the illiterate;

after this time, there was increasingly a literature in English used by laypeople for devotion and recreation, for business and administration. Notwithstanding the official Latin liturgy and its arcane explanations for the clergy, the *Mass Book* shows that laypeople were by no means excluded from understanding and participating in the liturgy. As presented here, their prayer and devotion is not just an overlay of private popular piety but a real engagement with the structure and actions of the liturgical celebration itself. Laypeople are encouraged to notice what is happening at the Mass; they are led to understand the meaning of the various parts of the Mass and then to pray in harmony with the liturgical action.

While obviously such a book is addressed to a literate public, all laypeople could access its content if they heard it read aloud, if they progressively memorized the vernacular prayers, and if they learned to watch the priest and imitate the postures and gestures of other laypeople. The presumption of the book is that it would not be read at Mass but that the postures, gestures, and prayers would be memorized for use in the church at Mass. "I have told you how you should spend your time at the Mass; now I will end. It is good to look at the rubrics from time to time but to know the prayers without the book" (622–26).

THE SACRAMENTS

There are seven sacraments of the new Law, namely baptism, confirmation, eucharist, penance, extreme unction, orders and matrimony, which...both contain grace and bestow it on those who worthily receive them....By baptism we are reborn spiritually; by confirmation we grow in grace and are strengthened in faith. Once reborn and strengthened, we are nourished by the food of the divine eucharist. But if through sin we incur an illness of the soul, we are cured spiritually by penance; spiritually also and bodily as suits the soul, by extreme unction. By orders the Church is governed and spiritually multiplied; by matrimony it grows bodily.

Identifying and settling on the seven sacraments occurs late in the Middle Ages. Students of liturgical history should take care not to impose this sevenfold sacramental system anachronistically on earlier evidence. The definitive list was first given by Peter Lombard (1100–1160) in the mid-twelfth century and was then taken up and developed by Scholastics such as Thomas Aquinas (1225–74). The text given above is the first official church listing and comes with a commentary by the Council of Florence in its Decree for the Armenians in 1439. Identifying the seven sacraments became a staple of liturgical catechesis at the end of the Middle Ages.

Baptism and Confirmation. In light of the theology of the necessity of baptism for salvation, the high level of infant mortality in the Middle Ages encouraged the practice of baptizing infants as soon as possible (*quam primum*). Laypeople could be the ministers of the sacrament when necessary, and memorizing the baptismal formula in Latin or the vernacular was a basic part of catechesis for laypeople. John Myrc's *Instructions for Parish Priests* gives the following fearsome advice for midwives:

> She is to have clean water at the ready for baptism. And though the child be but half-born, head and neck and no more, bid her nevertheless christen it and cast on water; and if she can only see the head, ensure she baptises it without hesitation. And then if the woman dies, teach the midwife that she hasten to open her with a knife in order to save the child's life and move quickly that it be christened for that is a deed of charity. (lines 88–102)

Baptism celebrated quickly within days of birth meant that the mother would rarely be at the baptism, for she would not yet be "churched" (purified) after the birth. It was the godparents who presented the child and lifted him/her out of the font after immersion, who taught the child the basic prayers and ensured he/she was confirmed in the first years of life. Gradually—earlier in Europe and later in England—immersion in water was replaced by pouring water on the child's head.

Until the Carolingian reform, Christian initiation in Gaul included no specific episcopal postbaptismal rite of the imposition of hands or the anointing with chrism. An episcopal rite was adopted from the Roman Rite (with an emphasis on the anointing over the handlaying) and it took on its own identity in Christian initiation. In many places, this rite of the Holy Spirit, which came to be called *confirmation*, was delayed until the bishop could be present. At the end of the Middle Ages, iconography in Europe shows young children walking to the bishop to be confirmed. William Durand nominated youths of twelve or fifteen years of age and his Pontifical describes a formal liturgical setting: "Those to be confirmed are kneeling down with their hands joined before their hearts." The Sarum Rite in England, however, said that baptized children should be brought to the bishop whenever he came within seven miles. Confirmation could be administered very simply as a blessing in the open air and legislation specified that this should not be delayed beyond three or five years. Indeed, confirmation iconography in pre-Reformation England consistently shows the confirmation of babes-in-arms and sometimes the bishop dressed in his street clothes.

Eucharist and Penance. As communion from the cup was withdrawn from laypeople during the thirteenth century, one of the common ways for the newly baptized infant to receive communion also disappeared. The Fourth Lateran Council (1215) decreed that receiving communion was not obligatory for those before the age of discretion and these guidelines became the norm. From this age, all were required to confess and receive communion at least once a year at Easter. Consequently, the parish church was busy with these sacraments at Eastertime.

The first centuries of the Middle Ages had seen the development of a more personal form of penance, centered on confession. It had grown from the monastic practices of Celtic missionaries. For Thomas Aquinas, the confession of sins expressing contrition was the *matter* of the sacrament and the absolution pronounced by the priest was its *form*; doing penance followed (*Summa* III.90.1–2). People went to the place where their parish priest was seated with his hood drawn over his head. They knelt beside him or before him to whisper their confession. It took place in the open in a busy church, and the fact of who did or did not make their annual confession was a matter of public knowledge. This set up the parish for Easter communion. John

Myrc summarized, "They shall all come to church and be shriven, one and all, and receive communion quietly all together on Easter Day; on that day by custom, you shall receive communion, one and all" (*Instructions*, lines 238–43).

Extreme Unction. The Carolingian reform reserved to the clergy the use of the oil blessed by the bishop for the sick. The text of a rite is found beside the prayers for the commendation of the dying and the forgiveness of sins, and this shaped the understanding of the rite. Anointing different parts of the body was seen to address the sins committed through the five senses. The theologians of the twelfth century began to speak of "extreme unction," and it was interpreted as anointing the dying person for entry into glory. "When that he is so worn-out that he may no longer live, then he shall be anointed, and not before, I warn you," wrote John Myrc in the late fourteenth century (*Instructions*, lines 1701–4). This official Latin rite developed alongside extensive vernacular instructions and interrogations aimed at helping a dying person in the "crafte for to dye well."

Ordination. The sacramentaries and ordines of the early Middle Ages show us a basic Roman model of ordination for bishops, priests, and deacons, focused on the laying on of hands and an ordination prayer. These rites were richly augmented in the following centuries, first in the *Romano-Germanic Pontifical* of the tenth century and later elaborated in the Pontifical of William Durand. The ordination sequence changed, running through the minor orders of porter, lector, exorcist, and acolyte, and leading to subdeacon, deacon, and priest, while the ordination of the bishop was juxtaposed with the crowning of the king. To the sign of peace and the seating of the ordained were added anointing, vesting, presentations, and explanatory texts. The bishop's head was to be anointed with chrism and the Gospels imposed on it; the crozier, ring, and Gospels were handed over as a sign of his authority, and he was invested with miter and gloves. The hands of the newly ordained priest were anointed, and he was clothed in his vestments (fully unfolded at the end) and presented with the chalice, bread, and wine; he received a second imposition of hands for the power to forgive sins, and he promised obedience. The deacon was vested and given the Book of the Gospels. Scholastic interpretation of these ordination rites saw the presentation of the symbols of office as the essential sacramental moment rather than the laying on of hands.

Marriage. Marriage in the Middle Ages was a lay affair. It came into being by the mutual consent of the couple. This could be a promise to marry (*I will take you to be my wife/husband*) followed by cohabitation or an actual exchange of consent at home or in another place (*I now take you to be my wife/husband*). The couple would normally hold hands because their consent brought their union into being. The involvement of the priest was simply to bless the marriage, perhaps blessing the couple at home in bed or in the church during a nuptial Mass. Clandestine marriage, however, created problems because the free consent of the woman and the public status of the couple were uncertain. Consequently, the Fourth Lateran Council asked for the publication of the banns of marriage and the church vigorously promoted the public exchange of consent in front of the priest at the doors of the church. Marriage rituals for giving and receiving consent (which include large amounts of the peoples' vernacular) appear in the eleventh and twelfth centuries. But Thomas Aquinas speaks for the age: the wedding liturgy is not related to the essence of marriage but belongs rather to its solemnization (*Summa Suppl.* 45.5). It was only after the Middle Ages, at the Council of Trent, that the public wedding ritual in church before the priest became constitutive for establishing a valid marriage.

CONCLUSION

The story of Western liturgy in the Middle Ages is often told in terms of disintegration and decline, clericalization and exclusion. This chapter has tried to cover the same territory but with alternative narratives. It is an attempt to understand without judgement and to receive the story on its own terms.

Two typical medieval images serve as our conclusion. We might return to the grand depiction of the last judgement found sculpted on the west portal or painted on the chancel arch. It stirred up a healthy fear of the Lord for people who entered the church to commune with Christ in beholding the elevated host at Mass. The liturgical space offered them this image of hope and inclusion. The chain gang of the damned dragged along by the devil often included a bishop and a king, while those being led by an angel in the opposite direction to their places in the choirs of heaven were mostly ordinary folk like themselves. People's participation in the liturgy put them on the right side of the picture.

We might also note the popular late medieval image of Mary, Mother of Mercy. Like the Last Judgement, it is an ecclesial image of inclusion where people could see themselves. The Virgin Mary holds her arms wide and people crowd under her mantle, the great and the low, the rich and the poor. The image was prolific in central Italy and Spain from the thirteenth century. As an altarpiece, it was in the closest possible relation to the celebration of the Mass. The eye received the image of the host and the Virgin Mary simultaneously. The protection promised by a glimpse of the elevated host was illustrated by the depiction of the maternal care of the Virgin of Mercy.

Further Reading

Bryant, Geoffrey, and Vivien Hunter. *"How Thow Schalt Thy Paresche Preche": John Myrc's Instructions for Parish Priests* (Part 1: Introduction and Text). Barton-on-Humber: Workers' Educational Association, 1999.

Chupungco, Anscar, ed. *Handbook for Liturgical Studies*. 5 vols. Collegeville, MN: Liturgical Press, 1997–2000.

Duffy, Eamon. *The Stripping of the Altars: Traditional Religion in England 1400–1580*. New Haven: Yale University Press, 1992.

Fisher, J. D. C. *Christian Initiation: Baptism in the Medieval West; A Study in the Disintegration of the Primitive Rite of Initiation* (with an Introduction to the North American Edition by Gerard Austin). Chicago: Hillenbrand Books/LTP, 2004.

Foley, Edward. *From Age to Age: How Christians Have Celebrated the Eucharist*. Collegeville, MN: Liturgical Press, 2008.

Jungmann, Josef. *The Mass of the Roman Rite: Its Origins and Development*. 2 vols. New York: Benziger Brothers, 1950.

Kroesen, Justin, and Regnerus Steensma. *The Interior of the Medieval Village Church*. Leuven: Peeters, 2012.

Martimort, A. G., ed. *The Church at Prayer*. 4 vols. Collegeville, MN: Liturgical Press, 1986–88.

Palazzo, Eric. *A History of Liturgical Books from the Beginning to the Thirteenth Century*. Collegeville, MN: Liturgical Press, 1998.

Rubin, Miri. *Corpus Christi: The Eucharist in Late Medieval Culture*. Cambridge: Cambridge University Press, 1991.

4

LITURGY AND THE
REFORMATION

—◦—

Don E. Saliers

One of my most memorable experiences of friendship with Gerard Austin occurred in our mutual engagement in an official ecumenical dialogue on the Eucharist. Following the Second Vatican Council, a series of theological conversations were held between Roman Catholic and various Christian denominations. Fr. Austin and I participated in one of these dialogues for several years (1977–84), exploring liturgical and sacramental issues between Roman Catholic rites and the newly received United Methodist worship reforms. As Kurt Cardinal Koch has observed, "Christian persons and churches certainly come closer to one another in the praise of God in liturgical doxology than in theology alone."[1] This essay emerges from that ecumenical friendship, common prayer, and joint efforts at mutual understanding invited by the process of liturgical reform.

REFORMATION AND
FAITHFUL PARTICIPATION

To speak of Christian liturgy and the Reformation opens a vast historical inquiry. Hundreds of books and essays have described the complexity of the several patterns of reformed liturgy among a proliferating number of sixteenth-century church bodies. It is not possible here to trace the details of all the attempted liturgical reforms. The social/ecclesial forces and doctrinal debates involved are immensely complex. In what follows I wish to focus on two crucial aspects of the legacy of sacramental and liturgical reforms of the sixteenth century: (1) the changing nature of "liturgical participation" and (2) theological foundations of liturgical reform. Or, in slightly different terms, this essay highlights the ways in which all major efforts at liturgical reform—then and now—reconfigure relationships between liturgical/ sacramental participation in Christ and questions of moral and spiritual theology.

Allow me first a lighthearted but serious characterization of the Protestant Reformation. An image from Walt Disney's *Fantasia* comes to mind. It is the "Sorcerer's Apprentice" sequence and the music of Dukas. Mickey Mouse is given the task of cleansing a palace room with brooms and water. He dons a magician's hat and, waving a magical wand, conjures the brooms and water buckets to split and double to do more work. At first all goes well, but then he discovers that he cannot stop the splitting brooms: first two, then four, then eight, until the room and Mickey are overwhelmed, and the music comes to its thundering climax. What begins as a legitimate task of correction can lead to an uncontrollable multiplication of forces. This image, some would claim, pictures how Christian liturgy in the West and its purported ecclesial unity were irretrievably shattered.

At the same time, embedded in impulse for liturgical and sacramental change among the reformers was a search for true and authentic worship of God "in, with, and through" Jesus Christ. This search was and is, I contend, at the heart of all major liturgical reforms. The achievement of what is held in common among Christian communions by revisions to rites and texts continues to elude us. Perhaps it is because liturgical revision cannot, in itself, guarantee full ecumenical unity. This points to both the necessity and the limitations of all such attempts at liturgical reform.

We often think of the Protestant Reformation as the second great rupture in the Western (European) church, the first being the eleventh-century split between the Catholic and Orthodox churches. Yet any assessment of the rise of Protestant attempts at reform and renewal reveals both continuity and discontinuity with antecedent medieval Catholic traditions. Even more significant, the sixteenth century is part of the long and continual history of liturgical reforms, beginning within the New Testament literature itself, stretching back through the Hebrew prophetic critiques of worship practices. The most central questions generated by the reforms of public worship during the Reformation period concern the how and why of liturgical participation of the faithful. In what sense were the changes wrought by Luther, Calvin, and others radically discontinuous with the inherited faith and practice of the saving mystery of Christ? In what sense must we also discern continuities with various reform movements prior to the sixteenth century? Subsequently, we turn to the efforts and accomplishments of the twentieth-century liturgical reforms generated by the Second Vatican Council in the Constitution on the Sacred Liturgy (*Sacrosanctum Concilium*) and its related documents. The revitalization of Christian liturgy for the faith and life of the Christian churches can be viewed as simultaneously a prophetic/ theological critique and a quest for a faithful ecclesial and spiritual identity in Christ.

In the major liturgical reforms of the sixteenth century carried out by Luther, Calvin, Bucer, Zwingli, and others, we recognize essential proposals. Among these are the restoration of vernacular languages in worship and prayer, a renewed focus on Scripture and biblical preaching, the centrality of congregational singing, a purification of theological distortions, and a restoration of the assembly's public role in the Eucharist and baptismal rites. These are, along with the rallying cry of "priesthood of all believers," hallmarks of the Lutheran and Reformed critique of received liturgical practices of the inherited Western "Catholic" traditions. The critique of existing liturgical practices and the theological foundations supporting them required changes—sometimes radical—in ritual and pastoral practices. This was especially the case with respect to the abuse of indulgences and the quantification of sacramental grace. At stake in all these changes, ideally, was the goal of faithful participation in liturgies more transparent to freedom and grace in Christ.

It would be a mistake to think that those liturgical and sacramental reforms suddenly appeared with the nailing of ninety-five theses on the Wittenberg church door by the Augustinian monk Martin Luther. The reforming impulse was already present earlier in fourteenth- and fifteenth-century figures such as John Wyclif in England

and especially Jan Hus in the Bohemian lands. Critique of ritual practices has a long history well before Luther's revolt. It would be equally misleading to think of "The Reformation" as a coherent, unified, singular movement. The contexts and differences, for example, between Luther's reforms in Germany, Calvin's in Geneva, and Zwingli's in Zurich show remarkably different impulses and consequences. All were, in some sense, attempts to purify and activate the faith life of the churches, often based on an appeal to the early church and—as with the Anabaptist developments—the appeal to a pure New Testament church. The Protestant critique wished to renew a true and vital catholicity, but inevitably became embedded in particular cultural, social, and political contexts. Thus, specific liturgical and sacramental reforms led to great tensions and strife among the several Protestant reformers and their emerging churches.[2] The social history of Protestant/Catholic hostility, not to mention bloodshed, over liturgical practices and fundamental theologies of church and sacraments continues well beyond the sixteenth-century rupture. That history is filled with ironies when considered from a more recent ecumenical engagement with the problem of misunderstandings in doctrine and practice.

There is no doubt that the major reformers desired a renewal of sacramental life and hence of the true Christian identity of church communities. But as Lutheran church historian Yngve Brilioth has claimed, "At the re-birth of sacramental life at the Reformation, the idea of Communion-fellowship begins by filling the whole service with its inspiration but ends by being refused a place within it."[3] This is a result of multiple factors: the retention of an individualistic late medieval piety, intense emphasis on preaching/hearing the Word, restricting access to the eucharistic table, and the role of political/ civil government. Despite the theological purification of the texts and rites from corrupt or misleading theology (e.g., Luther's fullscale attack on the "corrupt doctrine of sacrifice") there resulted what Frank Senn has called the "dissolution of the social body in Reformation communions."[4]

In assessing the Protestant critique of Catholic theology and practice, we note that even in such heralded reforms as "back to Scripture and biblical preaching," the implementation of reforms themselves failed to restore the unity and identity of the church; the tendency toward sectarianism was ever present. The reformers were steeped in polemic, in the achievement of identity "against" other churches perceived to be in error. Yet, the positive legacy of the Reformation is undeniable. The vigor and force of the reforms unleashed ideas and practices that would reemerge in subsequent centuries in which numerous attempts at reform gave evidence, beginning with the Catholic response sometimes known as the "counter-Reformation." Questions about the liturgical changes in the Reformation period depend on discerning how the theological foundations were subject to social, cultural, and historical forces that shape the specific theological concerns, for good and for ill.

Sixteenth-century liturgical and sacramental debates, however culturally, aesthetically, and politically complex, were about restoration of the worship life of the faithful. Questions of aesthetics and pastoral relevance mattered deeply. Architecture, music, art, rhetoric, and vesture are necessary to actual worship practices. Verbal languages (sermons, prayers, hymns, blessings) employed in whatever native tongue, always depend on the nonverbal elements for depth and point. So, too, gesture, touch, and the ethos of hospitality and care are intrinsic to qualities of liturgical participation. Aesthetic and pastoral details become theologically significant when they are embodied features of the divine/human "transaction" of living liturgy, as Aidan Kavanagh reminded us.[5] The Protestant Reformation was thus involved in negotiating the cultural and political idioms of cities in which the reforms were being carried out.

Theological foundations for reform emerge when the church confronts basic contradictions and misunderstandings that have developed over time in actual practice. In the judgement of Protestant reformers, developments over time had obscured Scripture and the inner relationship of Word and Sacrament. The faithful were perceived to be held captive to church law and to a whole system of sacramental legislation and control. Luther and others were convinced that the whole range of Scripture in proclamation and song was not nourishing the faith of ordinary believers. Consequently, the whole range of prayer and song needed to be returned to the worshiping assembly in order to purify and restore true sacramental participation.

72

In the case of Luther, hymns were composed to carry the biblical and theological themes of grace and freedom. With Calvin, a renewal of biblical psalms was central. In both cases the emphasis was on hearing and responding to the Word of God as a corrective to non-biblical and perceived idolatrous doctrines. At the same time, both Lutheran and Calvinist reformers wished to restore the Eucharist itself to the faithful, in contrast to its clericalization. The matters of both frequency and adequate catechetical preparation were central to the reform's task. The number of new Lutheran and Reformed catechisms testify to the effort to teach theology and faith to the laity, thus enhancing understanding of the spirituality of liturgical participation.

In this way the reformers were, in one sense, reclaiming the idea of prophetic self-critique for the church. Despite the incessant anti-Catholic and intra-Protestant polemics, the notion that "reform" is co-natural to Christian worship of God was clear. Could it be shown that Jesus Christ stands in the living tradition of the prophets precisely in his priesthood (which now refers to both pastors and people)? The aim was to reassert the baptized assembly gathered to hear the biblical Word proclaimed, to share in the Eucharist, and to embody the mercy of God in everyday life. Viewed from this perspective, the liturgical concerns of the sixteenth-century reformers were not a "rupture" within the church but a call for authentic Christian faith and life.

SEMPER REFORMANDA FROM THE BEGINNING

Already with the New Testament witness there are signs of prophetic critique and nascent theological/liturgical reform. St. Paul brought Christ-initiated concerns to the church at Corinth, particularly to their practices surrounding eucharistic participation. In chapter 11 of his First Letter to the Corinthians, we find a vigorous ethical critique. When some in the community arrive early and consume all the food, this is regarded as more than a breach of etiquette. This Paul sees as a theological misunderstanding that needs correction.

Perhaps we could say that Paul's basic intention is "formative" rather than officially "reformative." It was ritual criticism from a moral/ethical discernment of what is essential to eucharistic worship.

There is evidence of what recent reforms have called "inculturation" as well. The great prayer in the opening chapter of Ephesians can be seen as a major form of negotiation between biblical and Greek patterns. Based on antecedent Jewish *berakoth*, the author gives a new form "in the name of Jesus Christ." This is not a rejection of the earlier theological pattern found in the *berakoth*. It is an adaptation and reorientation.

The prophetic critique and reformist impulse arises from the communal remembering (*anamenesis*) of what Jesus said and did. The narrative of his person and work, read and proclaimed in the assembly—with distinctive accents in the four gospel books—already shows both ritual and ethical criticism of worship patterns. "The sabbath was made for humankind, and not humankind for the sabbath" (Mark 2:27). "Stop making my Father's house a marketplace" (John 2:16). "Whenever you pray, do not be like the hypocrites" (Matt 6:5). Teachings such as these are embedded in the significance of who Jesus is and what he does—now remembered and practiced precisely because of his suffering, death, resurrection, and Spirit-giving. The prophetic critique and reformist impulse are therefore part and parcel of the gospel proclamation.

Not all historical development is intentional ecclesial reform. Liturgical reform requires a critical assessment of tradition that aims at correcting recognized flaws in the concrete celebration of the liturgy and its textual foundations. As Martin Klöckner observes, a liturgical reform has accountable stakeholders (councils, synods, ecclesial/political leaders) but especially "a broad ecclesial anchoring among the people of God."[6] In this sense the Reformation itself is a complex period of liturgical reform. Yet it must be seen as part of a longer history of such attempts, ranging from early councils, monastic reforms, and culminating in the reforms of Vatican II. This twentieth-century reform, I contend, is best read as an official wholescale rereading of the Reformation impulse toward *semper reformanda*.

There can be no true liturgical reform without critically reassessing what it means to be the Body of Christ in its fullness. Thus, reform of Christian worship and its liturgical expression entails a theological appreciation and critique of the church and its various ministries, as recent discussions by scholars such as Massimo Faggioli[7] and John Baldovin[8] have made clear. To be a faithful community of the "dangerous memory of Jesus Christ" is to be a community intercession. For it is Christ's continuing liturgy to intercede for all humanity and the created order. This implies a theology of the multiple presences of Christ in sacramental action, proclamation, prayer, and song and in the very assembly itself. All of these themes were present in the Constitution on the Sacred Liturgy. This is why that reform has had such a profound effect on the churches of the Reformation as well.

We cannot disconnect the actual life of the church in the world and the eschatological promises of God. Two difficulties keep reappearing in history: either the church is too closely identified with the rule and reign of God, or the claims of the kingdom and the church are disconnected. The first can result in claiming too much continuity and institutional hubris; the second can result in unchecked cultural captivity, and even in false apocalypticism—as in extreme sectarianism. I contend that the impulse for reform of liturgy and church springs to life precisely when ecclesiology becomes fossilized and ceases to stand under the eschatological vision of God for church and world. Here we must stand between the "already" and the "not yet" of the kingdom of God in humility and hope. This links the *best* impulses of the Reformation with the promises of liturgical reforms emerging from Vatican II.

Despite the risk of historical-critical issues, I think it appropriate to invoke the fourfold characterization of the early Christian community from the second chapter of Acts (2:42–47) as a touchstone to the questions we have been exploring. There we read that this community, idealized though it may be, continued in the apostolic teaching, the *koinonia* of mutual care, the prayers of the faithful for the world, and the shared meals in the name of Christ—the "breaking of the bread." These four elements of "being church" seem necessary to think *with* (as well as *about*) in light of both the Reformation and the Second Vatican Council's reforms. These do not provide a doctrinal set of truths for renewal, and each element is "open-textured." Rather, they point to and await communal action among the baptized into the death and resurrection of Christ. They contain the crucial interrelationship of verbal and nonverbal signs that are "performative," not discursively doctrinal. In this sense they are guiding images awaiting reception in emerging social/historical contexts. They are also interrelated practices in the ongoing liturgy of Jesus Christ. When conflict and controversy demand doctrinal definition, these must be coupled with articulated "marks of the church." When we distort or ignore the full witness of the apostolic teachings, the criterion of faithfulness to the gospel is diminished or held captive. When the church becomes factionalized (as overheard in Paul's admonitions to the churches in Corinth or Galatia) or split into rival camps, self-critical intention in the worship of God is called for. When prayers no longer draw from the rich traditions of Scripture and the faithful witnesses imbued with prophetic discernment, something crucial is lost. Reform is called for. When meals together and the service of the poor are subordinated to law or reduced to mere cultural fellowship, reform is called for. The socially embodied saving efficacy of Christ is at stake.

None of this would make sense, of course, if doing these things took place in forgetfulness of the divine economy of salvation in creation and history. For Christian churches' liturgical life this means "in the name of Jesus Christ by the power of the Holy Spirit." A robust trinitarian conception of God is entailed. This still leaves room for human ambiguity, as the history of various reform movements in Christianity testifies. This again points to the ongoing character of self-critical element of *semper reformanda*. Humility is required, along with a sense of the limitations of specifically liturgical reforms in any age.

In confessing baptismal faith expressed in the creeds, we proclaim "one, holy, catholic, and apostolic" church. Luther, Calvin, Melanchton in the sixteenth century, when asked what characterizes a human assembly as the church of the crucified and resurrected Christ, cited a list of signs or notae. This was a flexible list of the "marks" of the church-in-life. When some of the churches of the Reformation coined the watchword "always in the process of reforming," they aimed at the always present range of misunderstandings and flaws born of the cultural, political, and ideological forces that are always influencing Christian liturgy. Later, more formal "marks" emerged from the Nicene Creed, particularly among Anglicans in controversy with Roman Catholic theological ecclesiology. These marks were not possessions of the churches so much as received gifts and graces, including participation in the suffering of humanity. Such reforming passions can, and did, easily generate other misunderstandings when translated into doctrinal warfare about liturgical participation. The advantage of reminding reforms of Acts 2 is that these are practices to be *lived into over time* rather than dogmatic truths to be defended. So, a key question for the implementation of liturgical and sacramental reforms is this: How shall we interpret and liturgically enact these "marks?"

The question of faithful, authentic liturgical life is integral to questions about the faithfulness of the visible form of the church in the world. Just as the Nicene-Constantinopolitan Creed names the church "one, holy, catholic, and apostolic" as conditions, so the appearance of unity, holiness, catholicity, and apostolicity are not mere human achievements but gifts of the Holy Spirit made visible, audible, and palpable from the whole life and presence of Jesus Christ. In this sense the "marks" are never possessions but only continually received and made real in specific historical and cultural contexts. As Jürgen Moltmann has insisted, "The four characteristics of the church are...to be seen as messianic predicates of the church in the perspective of the coming kingdom."[9]

The marks of the church are statements of faith and hope; thus, they become intentions of action when seen liturgically. Because Christ is one, and in Christ the community is one, the desire for spiritual unity in worship and life follows. Because Christ is the Holy One incarnate, the community that prays in his name must always seek holiness. Because only by the gift of the Spirit can the church claim holiness, we must pray and work for a "new creation." If the kingdom of God for which we yearn and pray, and of which we have a "foretaste" in the Eucharist, embraces the whole inhabited world, we are to be catholic in sensibility and compassionately prophetic in life. Because the church is born of apostolic witness, life, and proclamation, the liturgical community is to be a liberating force in the face of oppression and from all lamentable cultural captivities.

The social and theological foundations of liturgical reform, therefore, appeal to the recovery of signs and wonders. Luther and the classical reformers also articulated the "marks" to include singing and praying in the vernacular and qualities of the church born into suffering and persecution. *Sacrosanctum Concilium* sought to recover this amplitude within the Roman Catholic context. Every Christian liturgical assembly is called to show forth this amplitude in Christ's ongoing liturgy. Where the gospel is rightly preached with integrity and the sacraments are congruent with the new covenant in Christ made continually real by the Holy Spirit, there is the true church.

All of this is why liturgical life itself must not subvert what the church is yet called to be. Word and Sacrament cannot be truly grounded in Christ without the loving community (*koinonia*) of love and justice. Any liturgical reform of rites and texts worth its salt must face the present ecclesial fractures and the sufferings of all humanity. Our mutual situation is our "divided, fought over, unjust, inhuman world."[10] We ask again and continually with St. Paul: "Has Christ been divided?" (1 Cor 1:13a). Is not the Christ of our Eucharists also the brother of all who are suffering within and outside the church? Can we recognize the gifts of God in one another's faithfulness to Word, Sacrament, song, and prayer even though our "rites" differ? We cannot deny differences in church structure and authority. But in a world of hostility and forgetfulness of God, how shall we receive, celebrate, and live the "dangerous memory of Jesus Christ"?[11] In what ways can the church be sanctified in the Spirit in our world stunned and ravaged by war and human degradation if our liturgies cannot lament or continually intercede? The liturgy alone cannot answer these questions. True liturgical reform is also renewal of faith, of Scripture, of Christian formation in baptism and Eucharist, and in social/ethical engagement. The spirituality of being the Body of Christ alive in and for the world must permeate our moral theology and practice with the desire for God in all things.

THE FUTURE OF THE RENEWAL
OF LITURGICAL LIFE

The claims and proposals for liturgical reform, in any age, but especially in light of the Reformation and Vatican II, stand in tension with actual practice. To lavish the Scriptures as the Word of God, to engage in "full, active, and conscious participation," to reconnect sacramental life with the *missio dei* in ever-changing circumstances: these constitute the agenda of a true *semper reformanda*. This means that Christian communities recognize the gifts and faithfulness of sister churches. To receive and live the radical claims of baptism and Eucharist as the theological heart of the church—these are the high stakes. All flow from God's purposes for the whole creation. Liturgy thus demands personal, social, and cosmic engagement and a continuing vulnerable petition for wisdom, love, and courage.

Here the churches, ecumenically considered, must face genuine differences. Those traditions whose rites are dependent on authorized fixed texts and patterns and that canonically regulate relationships between the fixed and variable aspects of liturgy face the hermeneutical changes born of new social, political, and cultural realities. By contrast, churches that cherish freedom from textual regulation face the problem of cultural captivity or, in the worst cases, the tyranny of novelty and of the present zeitgiest. The world of liturgical traditioning requires supple relationships between form and freedom, stability and improvisation grounded in the ongoing liturgy of Jesus Christ. One thinks of the strong initial resistances and criticism in Anglican traditions of the Prayerbook of 1979 because of the loss of a certain elegant rhetorical style and "too many variables." Yet in the forty years since, we note the renewing force of baptismal prominence and the revisited eucharistic participation.

I am also painfully aware of the continuing emotionally charged debates within many "middle Protestant" communities. "Cultural relevance," "spontaneity," and the reduction of liturgy to a tool of evangelization. A liturgical ("anti-liturgical"?) pragmatism is uncritically practiced in the name of communicating the gospel in a post-Christian world. Here, appeals to broader more complex theological reflection meet with resistance and impatience. True liturgical reform and renewal will bring impatience with the effort to instantiate such textual and ritual reforms. But the aim is renewal of the whole church and the life of faith in the whole inhabited world.

The present travail of the churches worshiping toward unity in Christ brings a much richer hermeneutic than may have existed in previous historical periods. Appreciation and critique are thus bound together. It is senseless now simply to pronounce *anathema sit* or to foster worship practices that cannot bear the seeds of self-reflective critique. This is a search for mature participation in the work of God (as the old phrase has it, "partakers of the divine nature"). Scripture, spiritual discernment, and the existential struggle to live as we pray have emerged despite the limitations of the liturgical reforms of both the sixteenth and twentieth to twenty-first centuries. This can never be a matter of theological abstraction. Doctrinal and dogmatic formulations are crucial, but not without grounding and life-giving practices. Here the liturgical/sacramental turn of *Sacrosanctum Concilium* places a demanding invitation on all subsequent ecclesiologies. This is not an ecclesiology of the textbooks or canons so much as an ecclesiology of a living church. As Alexander Schmemann and others have put it: this is reform and renewal in Christ for the "life of the world."

We cannot retreat from the challenges and limitations of the reforms from the Protestant Reformation's central concerns and from the surprise of fifty years ago in Rome. It envisions a future of fully embracing what true reform asks: our humanity at full stretch before God in the world we now face. So abide these four: the fullness of Jesus Christ, crucified and risen in glory; the continuing work of the Holy Spirit in church and all creation; the messianic promises of God; and fidelity to being and becoming the one, holy, catholic, and apostolic community of memory, hope, and ever-renewed witness.[12]

Notes

1. Kurt Cardinal Koch, "Liturgical Reform and the Unity of the Christian Churches," *Studia Liturgica* 44, nos. 1–2 (2014): 55.

2. See the discussion of intra-Protestant liturgical conflicts in John Bossy, *Christianity in the West 1400–1700* (Oxford: Oxford University

Press, 1985); and essays in Geoffrey Wainwright and Karen B. Westerfield Tucker, eds., *The Oxford History of Christian Worship* (New York: Oxford University Press, 2005).

3. Yngve Brilioth, *Eucharistic Faith and Practice: Evangelical and Catholic*, trans. A. G. Hebert (London: SPCK, 1965), 134.

4. See the extensive discussion of this in Frank C. Senn, *The People's Work: A Social History of the Liturgy* (Minneapolis: Augsburg Fortress, 2006), 183–98.

5. Aidan Kavanagh, *On Liturgical Theology* (Collegeville, MN: Liturgical Press, 1985).

6. Martin Klöckner, "Liturgical Renewal through History," *Studia Liturgica* 44, nos. 1–2 (2014): esp. 16–17.

7. Massimo Faggioli, *True Reform: Liturgy and Ecclesiology in* Sacrosanctum Concilium (Collegeville, MN: Liturgical Press, 2012).

8. John F. Baldovin, *Reforming the Liturgy: A Response to the Critics* (Collegeville, MN: Liturgical Press, 2008).

9. Jürgen Moltmann, *The Church in the Power of the Spirit: A Contribution to Messianic Ecclesiology*, trans. Margaret Kohl (San Francisco: HarperSanFrancisco, 1991), 339.

10. Moltmann, *The Church in the Power of the Spirit*, 341.

11. The phrase is Johannes Metz's. See Karl Rahner and Johannes Metz, *The Courage to Pray* (New York: Crossroad, 1980).

12. Sections 2 and 3 of this paper are substantially based on a revision of a previous essay of mine, "Theological Foundations of Liturgical Reform," given at the 2013 Societas Liturgica Congress of 2013 in Würzberg, Germany. See *Studia Liturgica* 44, nos. 1–2 (2014): 109–17.

LITURGY AND THE COUNCIL OF TRENT

—⁓—

John W. O'Malley, SJ

The Council of Trent met in three distinct periods between 1545 and 1563. Pope Paul III (r. 1534–49) convoked it to respond to the severe controversies that broke out in Europe in reaction to Martin Luther's doctrine of justification by faith alone and his call for the reform of the church. Within a few weeks after the council opened, the prelates determined that its agenda would be, accordingly, two-fold: response to the doctrinal issues raised by Luther and response to the long-standing problem of reform that Luther's call for it had only exacerbated.

The council thus had a very specific plan of action. Unlike the Second Vatican Council (1962–65), it did not undertake a general review of church teaching and practice. It, for instance, said not a word about the great missionary enterprises of the time, which were one of the most distinctive characteristics of Catholicism in the period and of such great consequence for its future.

Although, once again unlike Vatican II, the Council of Trent issued no decree on the liturgy as such, it made several specific decisions that were of particular importance for certain aspects of the liturgy. It generally took these decisions in reaction to Luther's teaching on the sacraments, as expressed especially in his treatise "On the Babylonian Captivity of the Church" (1520).

While Catholics had many problems with Luther's teaching, three were crucial. First, he insisted that there were only two sacraments, baptism and the Eucharist, rather than the seven traditional since the thirteenth century. He allowed for penance but denied that it had any sacramental character that Catholics could recognize. Second, he seemed to deny any intrinsic efficacy to the sacraments, as if they were merely incitements to greater faith. He thus seemed, finally, to minimize the role sacraments play in justification and in the pursuit of holiness. The council set out to respond. As a result, the bulk of the council's doctrinal decrees are on the sacraments, and, hence, on the liturgy.

Since Luther accepted baptism, the council simply repeated the standard teaching on it. Like Catholics, Luther believed in infant baptism, but since other reformers, known as Anabaptists, rejected it, the council reaffirmed it. Between the Lutherans and the Catholics, therefore, the administration and understanding of baptism was virtually identical. For the sacrament of confirmation, the council did little more than assert that it was truly a sacrament instituted by Christ. The same is true for the anointing of the sick, known at the time as extreme unction.

Matters are much more complicated regarding the remaining four sacraments, and for none more so than for the Eucharist. As with its other doctrinal decisions, Luther's teaching and practice were the springboard for the council's teaching. To understand the council's approach, however, two further considerations must be kept in mind. First, during the Middle Ages and even into the twentieth century, the faithful received holy communion most often as a distinctive rite, outside the ritual of the Mass. In other words, although the priest consecrated the wine and hosts during Mass, the Mass and the reception of the Eucharist were two distinct, though closely related, realities.

Also during the Middle Ages, adoration of the eucharistic host had developed apart from any relationship to the Mass. In 1264, Pope Urban IV instituted the Feast of Corpus Christi to commemorate Christ's gift of the Eucharist to the church. As a special mode of celebrating the feast, elaborate Corpus Christi processions developed during which the host was carried through the city streets to be adored. The service known as Benediction of the Blessed Sacrament that concluded the processions and developed in tandem with them became a ritual in its own right. Many places came to celebrate Benediction of the Sacrament every Sunday afternoon or evening.

Second, the council saw itself as fundamentally a legislative or law-making assembly. Many of its doctrinal decrees contained instructional preambles known as chapters that were followed by short ordinances (laws) known as canons, which were the touchstone for interpreting the teaching of the council. Each canon dealt with a specific aspect of the problem under consideration. Use of canons allowed the council to break a problem down into discrete units and thus make dealing with it more manageable.

This process, however, precluded synthesis. It precluded the construction of a document that would reconcile the disparate elements into a coherent totality. It produced, instead, a collection of laws, each of which prescribed or proscribed a certain behavior. The canons ended with an anathema, that is, with excommunication of anybody who acted contrary to the canon.

THE EUCHARIST

These two considerations are especially important regarding the council's treatment of the Eucharist, which resulted, for instance, in its issuing a decree on the Mass and another on the sacrament, almost as if the Mass and the sacrament were not intrinsically related. Regarding the Eucharist as sacrament, the council reaffirmed the real presence of Christ under the form of bread and wine, a doctrine held by Luther but denied by Ulrich Zwingli (1484–1531) and other reformers. Against Luther, the council affirmed that the change of the bread and wine into the Body and Blood of Christ is "properly and appropriately" (*convenienter et proprie*) called *transubstantiation*, a term Luther rejected.

The council had to address, however, the related issue of worship of the eucharistic host, a practice denounced by Luther and others as an abuse and a misunderstanding of the sacrament, in which Christ was efficaciously present only during the rite of the Eucharist and while being consumed during it. The council in its thirteenth session, October 11, 1551, issued a long justification for the Feast of Corpus Christi and the processions as fitting ways to increase devotion and gratitude to God for the marvelous benefit of Christ's eucharistic presence.[1]

The fourth canon of the decree, the core of the council's teaching on the matter, stated,

> If anyone says that after the consecration is completed, the body and blood of Our Lord Jesus Christ are not in this admirable sacrament but only while being taken and not before or after, and that in the hosts or consecrated particles that remain after communion, the true body of the Lord does not remain, let him be anathema.[2]

The council also had to address another related issue. Luther insisted that Scripture required that the faithful receive communion under the form of wine as well as bread and that the church acted illegitimately in withholding from the laity the eucharistic cup. Even as late as the twelfth century, the practice of receiving under both forms had continued in some areas. From that point forward, the practice became even less common and finally disappeared. By the sixteenth century, the single form had become universal but also a subject of contention since early in the previous century by "the Bohemians," that is, the followers of Jacob of Mies and Jan Hus, who agitated for both forms. The Council of Constance (1414–18) reacted by pronouncing that both the Body and the Blood of Christ were present in each of the forms; in receiving under the form of bread, a person received both the Body and the Blood. Thus, the church did not act illegitimately in withholding the cup.

Luther's advocacy of both forms thrust the issue into a new prominence. Catholic theologians held different positions on the issue, but a considerable number were ready to change the discipline. Lateran Council V, which concluded in 1517, just before the outbreak of the Reformation, hoped to effect a reconciliation with the "Bohemians," and it granted its legate to them permission to authorize communion under both forms. Unfortunately, the council was unable to effect a reconciliation.

In 1530, well before the council met, Cardinal Cajetan (Tommaso De Vio, 1469–1534), the most widely respected theologian of the era, drew up a memo for Pope Clement VII (1523–34) in which he suggested allowing the laity to partake of the eucharistic cup.

During the debate in 1551 on the Eucharist, Cardinal Cristoforo Madruzzo of Trent passionately advocated it, as did others. Since at that time the council hoped that a delegation of Lutherans would shortly arrive at the council, it decided to postpone a decision until then. The Lutherans did finally arrive, but for procedural and ideological reasons, negotiations broke down even before they began.

The issue would not go away. During the third and final period of the council, the ambassadors of the Holy Roman Emperor and the duke of Bavaria continued to advocate for it as a simple, urgent, and permissible gesture of reconciliation. But opinion in the council itself was so divided that the council resolved not to decide and to remit the matter to the pope to decide once the council concluded.

During the council, Pope Pius IV (r. 1559–65) had indicated his willingness to grant the cup for certain areas of Europe, and after the council, on April 16, 1564, he did so for the territories of the emperor and the duke of Bavaria. By this time, however, the cup had become such a powerful sign of differentiation between Catholics and Lutherans that soon after it went into effect, even those who advocated it began to regret the decision. Bit by bit the practice began to fade until it finally died out completely by the early seventeenth century. There the matter rested until Vatican II.

In chapter 8 of the decree, the council commended frequent reception of the Eucharist, which will be for those who do so "the life of the soul and the health of their mind."[3] The council thereby took a stand on an issue that divided Catholics of the era. By the late Middle Ages, most Catholics received the Eucharist once or at most twice a year. Even nuns received the Eucharist only a few times a year. In the fifteenth century in the Low Countries, a small movement began advocating reception more often, which meant several times a year or even once a month.

By the time the council opened, some priests and theologians promoted the reception on Sundays and feast days, and a few even supported daily reception. The newly founded Society of Jesus soon took the lead in this regard and had some success, but resistance persisted and the provision of the council had limited success.

Not until Pope Pius X (r. 1903–14) took matters in his own hands and issued the call for monthly, weekly, and even daily communion did most Catholics begin to receive more than at Christmas and Easter. By making frequent reception the norm for Catholic piety, the pope definitively settled the longstanding debate. By the middle of the twentieth century, weekly or daily reception was common among Catholics and no longer considered strange or suspect.

THE MASS

Not until September 1562—eleven years after its decree on the Eucharist—did the council issue its decree "Concerning the Sacrifice of the Mass."[4] The very title of the decree indicates the focus with which the council approached the subject. Luther had denied the sacrificial character of the Mass because he saw it as a "work," as an act performed by human beings to win God's favor. But, according to Luther, God's favor—that is, God's grace—was God's to give or not to give. His denial of the sacrificial character of the Mass was simply an application of his doctrine of justification by faith alone.

Sacrifice is fundamentally the offering to the Deity of a gift, especially a living creature. It has been a widespread practice in religions around the world, and the Old Testament provides many examples of it among the chosen people. Christ's institution of the Eucharist took place in the sacrificial context of Passover and on the eve of his offering himself on the cross. By the Middle Ages, the teaching that the Mass was a sacrifice was virtually universal.

Trent relies on this tradition and, in the first chapter of the decree, provides a succinct statement of it that neatly summarizes the consensus of the times. The problem with this focus on the sacrificial character of Mass is that it precludes any consideration of the Mass as the Lord's Supper. Thus, as we have already seen, the Eucharist and the Mass appear to be two distinct realities. The fathers at Trent surely did not intend this result, but the procedures they adopted almost inevitably led to it.

The other chapters of the decree deal with matters that more directly affected the liturgical character of the Mass. The second chapter, for instance, vindicated the practice of offering Masses for the dead, and the third the practice of offering Masses in honor of the saints. From a twenty-first-century perspective, chapter 8, concerning Mass in the vernacular, is particularly interesting. Few enactments of the council have been so consistently misunderstood and misinterpreted.

The chapter states, "Though the mass contains much instruction for the faithful, the fathers have not deemed it advisable that it be everywhere [*passim*] celebrated in the vernacular tongue." Canon 9 repeats the idea in negative form, "If anyone says that the mass shall be celebrated only in the vernacular...let him be anathema."

With these few words the council in essence deemed simply that Latin was legitimate. It went no further, and, despite what is often attributed to the council, it certainly did not condemn celebrating the Mass in the vernacular or even suggest such celebration was unfitting. One of the ironies of the council is that it approved this provision without controversy, whereas it agonized again and again over what today seems far less radical, the eucharistic cup.

One of the few prelates to comment on the vernacular while the decree was under consideration was the bishop of Krk, the large Adriatic island under Venetian possession. He informed the council that "in the church of the Holy Sepulcher in Jerusalem, masses are celebrated in every language under heaven." Long before the council ended, however, Latin had become such a badge of identity for Catholics that it prevailed unquestioned and unassailable. It became a nonnegotiable issue, allegedly written in stone by the Council of Trent.

Even H. J. Schroeder, OP, the sensitive and astute translator of the documents of the council, could not rid himself of the persuasion that Trent had forbidden the vernacular. He introduced chapter 8 with the heading "The mass may not be celebrated in the vernacular," even though his own translation of the text contradicts the heading.[5]

Chapter 5, which receives little attention in commentaries on the council is nonetheless particularly important for the ethos of Catholic liturgy. It states,

Since human nature is such that it cannot easily raise itself up to the meditation of divine realities without external aids, holy mother church has for that reason duly established certain rites, such as that some parts of the mass be said in quiet tones and others in louder, and it has provided ceremonies such as mystical blessings, candles, incense, vestments, and many other things of this kind, whereby both the majesty of so great a sacrifice might be enhanced and the minds of the faithful are aroused by the visible signs of religious devotion to contemplation of the high mystery hidden in it.

This passage was in effect a manifesto against the radical spiritualization of religion that prevailed in some Protestant writings and religious services. The chapter assumed in human nature a close relationship between the corporeal and the spiritual, between body and soul, and was thus able to justify material enhancements of divine worship. The result was a striking difference between Catholic and most Protestant services.

One of the very last decrees of the council validated and promoted the use of images of Christ and the saints in churches, shrines, and private homes.[6] That decree along with chapter 5 of the decree on the sacrifice of the Mass resulted in church interiors that were immediately recognizable as Catholic and altogether different from Protestant houses of worship.

Although such provisions might seem to be of secondary importance regarding the development of liturgy, they in fact go to the heart of it. The Mass is properly and traditionally a "sacred *action*," and whatever furthers the effectiveness of the action is central to it. "The non-verbal elements [are] possibly the most important part of liturgy."[7]

To the doctrinal decree on the sacrifice of the Mass, the council added a quasi-appendix titled "Decree Concerning Things to Be Observed and Avoided in the Celebration of Mass." Embedded in it was a sentence exhorting the bishops to banish from their churches all such music that whether by organ or by singing a base and suggestive [*lascivum et impurum*] element is introduced and likewise all worldly conduct, vain and profane conversation, wandering about, noise and clamor, so that the house of God may be called and be seen as a house of prayer.[8]

In the original version of this decree, the drafting commission had specifically asked that polyphonic music be forbidden because "it appealed more to the ear than to the soul and served the baseness of morals more than religion." The revised version omitted mention of polyphony but expanded on the quality of music that was appropriate and conducive to devotion and of sufficient simplicity to allow the words of the sacred text to be heard and understood.

The final version was, as we have seen, more general than the earlier ones and abandoned any mention of polyphony and any words suggesting it. The change may have been due solely to the general effort to simplify and shorten the decree. But after the council ended, the story sprang up that Palestrina's masterpieces, especially his "Mass of Pope Marcellus," were sung at Trent and that the effect on the prelates there led to the final wording and thus saved polyphony for the church.

There is no foundation for the story in the official council sources, but the prelates almost certainly heard the sacred polyphony of the Flemish composer Jacob van Kerle as the musical setting for a series of prayers for the success of the council. Even if the prelates did not hear Palestrina's music at Trent, some most certainly were familiar with it and would have been loath to condemn it.

After the council, polyphony began to enjoy a privileged place in Catholic worship and in doing so somewhat sidelined plainchant. In St. Peter's basilica in Rome, it has never lost its appeal. In any case, music became the one art cultivated by both Catholics and Protestants, even though the styles they cultivated were sometimes considerably diverse.

Only in general terms did the decree mention problems of which many of the prelates were painfully aware. Priests, for instance, omitted prayers central to the rite, such as the Our Father, or they introduced prayers that were unauthorized, unfitting, or even superstitious. More general were the textual discrepancies in the many editions of the sacred books, the result of scribal or typographical errors and of local interpolations that sometimes distorted the meaning of the original text.

Although at this point the council did not deal directly with the problem of the liturgical texts, in one of its final decrees it mandated that the pope see to a revision of the texts of the Mass and the Breviary. The purpose was simply to eliminate the discrepancies and abuses that had crept into them and thus provide a standardized text. The council made no further changes in those texts. There was, therefore, no "Tridentine liturgy" beyond the assumption that the traditional Roman Rite would be standard, though not universal, in the Western church.

PREACHING

Luther insisted on the primacy of preaching the Word of God and often receives credit for a revival of preaching in the era. That revival had in fact been under way since the thirteenth century and experienced a further revitalization in the decades preceding Luther. Preaching was, consequently, a concern of the Council of Trent, which insisted on it as one of the most important obligations of bishops and pastors of parishes.

During the Middle Ages and well beyond, most preaching occurred outside the celebration of Mass, usually as a separate occasion during the afternoons of Sundays and feast days. In some places, however, it retained its traditional place during Mass after the reading or singing of the gospel. The dozen or so annual liturgies in the Sistine Chapel during the Renaissance are the most notable instances of this phenomenon. There the new application of classical rhetoric resulted in preachments that resembled the ideal proposed for them in the Constitution on the Sacred Liturgy of Vatican II.[9]

Nonetheless, theologians did not see the intrinsic relationship between the Liturgy of the Word with the Liturgy of the Eucharist. For them, the Mass was one thing and preaching another. The silence about preaching in the decree on the Mass during the Council of Trent unmistakably validated this viewpoint. In the Catholic Church during the Middle Ages and into the present era, theology of the sacraments flourished, while theology of the Word languished.

PENANCE

Late medieval handbooks on penance consistently describe the confessor's role as threefold. He was doctor to help remedy the soul's ills, he was father to comfort the repentant sinner, and he was judge to assess the gravity of the offenses and assign a fitting penalty for them. As canon law became an ever more dominant ecclesiastical discipline, the third of the confessor's roles assumed greater emphasis. Confession thus came to be described as a tribunal, a court of law. As the confessor acted as judge in the tribunal, the penitent became the accused—the self-accused.

The system required that penitents confess their serious sins, indicate the number of times they committed them, and express sufficient sorrow for them. It seems that in practice many confessors acted more as doctors and fathers than as judges and were not too exigent regarding the specificity of sins confessed. Nonetheless, for some confessors and some penitents, the tribunal model weighed heavily on their consciences.

Luther was among them. His inability to find peace of soul in the sacrament was the catalyst for his key insight into justification by faith alone. We are accepted by God as justified, he maintained, not by our striving—certainly not by our striving to confess to a priest each and every misdeed and to summon up from within ourselves sufficient sorrow for them. On the contrary, we must trust in God's promise of forgiveness and grace. Luther's reflections on the sacrament thus cut to the very heart of his message.

He maintained that the gospel prescribed confession of sins but not, as the Catholic Church understood and practiced it. In Scripture, for instance, there was no warrant for the enumeration of sins as the church required. Moreover, the Catholic form of absolution indicated that the priest absolved penitents from their sins. Luther objected that forgiveness of sin rested exclusively with God. After absolution, the priest imposed "works" as penances, as if these were availing unto salvation. In the ritual of the sacrament, faith, as Luther understood it, played no role. The ritual was a striking instance of papal tyranny oppressing Christian consciences and holding them captive.

The council had to answer this broadside attack on the sacrament. It did so in its usual way by breaking the problem down into specific issues. Despite the advantages of such a procedure for facilitating discussion, it prevented the council from seeing it was dealing with the larger reality of Luther's understanding of justification and that it needed to make decisions in accord with that reality.

The council took up the matter during its second period, 1551. For the council, the outstanding question was whether Christ had commanded secret (private) confession of sins. Protestants maintained, correctly, that there was no evidence for it until the Middle Ages. Some theologians at the council agreed with them, or at least that Christ did not demand secret confession.

The decree is long, with nine chapters and fifteen canons.[10] It summarized teaching on the sacrament that developed in the West beginning in the twelfth century when the practice of private confession was becoming widespread outside monasteries. No doctrinal decree of the council had previously betrayed such a strong imprint of medieval Scholastic theology and canon law.

The canons as usual identified the essential points of the decree. Canon 6 condemned anyone who asserted that "confessing secretly to a priest alone, which the Catholic church has always observed from the beginning and still observes, is at variance with the institution and command of Christ, and is a human institution." The wording avoided saying that Christ commanded secret confessions, which took account of the reservations on this point of some bishops and theologians, but it continued the error of asserting that the church had required it "from the beginning."

Canon 9 asserted that the absolution of the priest was a judicial act and thus indicated that sinners present themselves at a tribunal. The council certainly did not intend to minimize the medicinal and consolatory aspects of the sacrament. Chapter 3, in fact, notes that those who properly receive the sacrament are "filled with peace and serenity of conscience and with an exceedingly great consolation of spirit." Nonetheless, the consistent emphasis on obligation and the detailing of the conditions required for a valid confession are the outstanding characteristics of the document. The council not only did not deal with the pastoral problem of the anxiety confession could induce, sometimes in acute forms as with persons as different as Luther and Ignatius of Loyola, but unwittingly contributed to it by its emphasis.

The Council of Trent never mentioned the enclosed piece of ecclesiastical furniture known as the confessional because it scarcely existed at the time. A few decades after the council ended, however, the confessional entered widespread use, largely due to the influence of Carlo Borromeo (1538–84), the saintly archbishop of Milan. It soon became almost ubiquitous. Its prominence in Catholic churches symbolized the greater role the sacrament began to play in Catholic life and worship and came further to differentiate Catholic houses of worship from Protestant.

ORDERS

After a crisis that lasted for a full ten months between September 1562 and July 1563, the council was finally able to address the sacrament of orders, which had been the principal cause of the long stalemate. The crisis was not due to disagreement about Protestant teaching but about two problems within Catholicism itself. First, by what warrant did bishops possess their authority, as a direct result of their consecration (today, ordination) or by concession of the Holy See? Second, by how strict an obligation were bishops bound to reside in their dioceses and tend their flocks? The decree on the sacrament, ratified on July 15, 1563, ended the crisis, but only a skilled eye can detect how it did so. Important and interesting though the solution is, it does not directly concern liturgy.

The decree is relatively short, four chapters and eight canons.[11] Its teaching is, once again, very much the product of medieval Scholasticism and related to the decree on the sacrificial character of the Mass: if the Mass is a sacrifice, it must have a priest to offer it. The decree thus emphasized the sacramental powers ordination confers, especially concerning the Eucharist and penance, and thereby unwittingly minimized its prophetic (proclamation or preaching) dimension. It insisted, rather, that orders is a sacrament instituted by Christ, that orders such as subdeacon and deacon lead to priesthood, that ordination imprints a special character on the soul, and that bishops are true and legitimate successors of the apostles by divine decree.

Ministers in the Lutheran and other Protestant churches married, which raised the issue for priests in the Catholic Church. In Cajetan's remarkable memorandum for Pope Clement VII mentioned earlier, he allowed marriage for priests in Germany. At the council, the ambassadors of the emperor and duke of Bavaria repeatedly pressed for it.

On June 27, 1562, Sigismund Baumgartner, the ambassador of Duke Albrecht V of Bavaria made a passionate plea for married clergy in German-speaking lands, where priests openly kept concubines and where the laity accepted it almost as a matter of course. It was imperative, Baumgartner insisted, that priests be allowed to marry. He said that devout and faithful Catholics had concluded that "a chaste marriage is better than a tainted celibacy" (*castum matrimonium contaminato celibatui preferendum*). The situation would deteriorate further unless, in accordance with the custom of the early church, educated and respected married men be admitted to orders.

The council addressed the issue not in the decree on orders but in the decree on matrimony. Even during the long discussion on matrimony, the celibacy of the clergy received remarkably little attention. The theologians at the council virtually unanimously agreed on the spiritual superiority of celibacy over matrimony, which was not surprising since most of them came from religious orders where chastity was an essential component of identity. They held diverse opinions, however, on whether celibacy was a church law or intrinsic to the sacrament. They accordingly held diverse views on whether the pope could dispense from celibacy a priest already ordained and on whether it was advisable to ordain men already married for troubled areas of the church. For the most part, however, their opinions were conservative.

Although the chapters of the decree on matrimony did not mention the issue, two canons obliquely dealt with it. Canon 10 condemned the view that marriage was more blessed than virginity or celibacy. Canon 9 condemned the view that clerics in holy orders or religious with a solemn vow of chastity could legitimately contract marriage. These minimal statements sidestepped the deeper and more pressing question of whether celibacy was required for ordination to the priesthood and whether the pope could or should allow married clergy at least for German-speaking lands.

The council said no more on the matter, which meant that the problem, like the eucharistic cup, ended up in the lap of Pope Pius IV after the council. The emperor and the duke continued their pressure on him. Pius, undecided how to proceed, created a commission of cardinals in early 1565 to deliberate on the matter and come up with a recommendation, but he died some months later. His successor, Pius V (r. 1566–72), made known immediately after his election that he was utterly opposed to any concession. With that the issue died.

MATRIMONY

The doctrinal decree on matrimony, published on November 11, 1563, just three weeks before the council ended, is brief, consisting in an introduction and twelve canons. It is, once again, a concise and unsurprising summary of medieval theology and canon law concerning the sacrament. Extremely important for the development of liturgy is the reform decree regarding the discipline of the sacrament that accompanied the doctrinal decree.[12]

Of the issues facing the council, matrimony seemed to promise a relatively easy resolution. The members of the council were agreed on two essential points challenged by Luther: matrimony was a sacrament instituted by Christ, and the church had the right to impose conditions for a valid celebration of it. Nonetheless, clandestine marriages emerged as a problem that incited passionate arguments and dashed the hopes for moving ahead with dispatch.

Everyone agreed that the exchange of vows between the man and woman was the essence of the sacrament. What was to be said, however, when they exchanged vows without a witness present? The practice led to many widely recognized problems, caused especially when one of the parties, usually the man, later denied that vows had been exchanged and went on to contract another marriage. The man often left babies as well as his first wife behind.

The council felt constrained to deal with such a pressing problem, but how was it to do so? Could the church legitimately declare a consented-to union invalid? Did the church, in other words, have the authority to impose a condition on the validity of marriage that intruded on the partners' exchange of vows, the constitutive element of the sacrament? After heated discussion, the council was finally able to pass its landmark decree, *Tametsi* ("Even though"), which required a priest witness for validity and prescribed that the ceremony take place "in open church."

Among Christians the rituals regarding marriage had gradually evolved through the centuries from family observances conducted in the home. Bit by bit priests began to play a part, at the invitation of the parents or the spouses, to bless the ring or the marriage chamber or the marriage bed. The church itself became ever more interested in having a priest present to ensure that the consent was free and that the spouses were not blood relatives. By the twelfth century, at least part of the celebration was in some localities celebrated in the parish church. Even at the time of the council, however, practices differed widely across Europe.

No provision of the entire council affected the Catholic laity more directly than *Tametsi*. No provision more radically affected how a sacrament was to be celebrated. It was implemented only gradually and with a great deal of local variation over a long period of time, but it definitively moved the sacrament onto church premises and laid the groundwork for the marriage liturgies in place today. Noteworthy about *Tametsi* in that regard is its statement, "The holy synod earnestly desires that, if any provinces have praiseworthy customs and ceremonies in this matter over and above those mentioned here, they should by all means retain them."

AFTER THE COUNCIL

In the decades immediately following the council, prescriptions concerning the liturgy proliferated and gradually became known as

Tridentine, even though the council sometimes had not even indirectly influenced them. In 1570, for instance, Carlo Borromeo published for his archdiocese an "instruction" on church buildings and furnishings, *Insructiones Fabricae et Supellectilis Ecclesiasticae*. Other bishops took up the instruction and implemented its provisions, so that they soon became standard in churches around the world. Filled with minute specifications, it prescribed, for instance, that the tabernacle containing the reserved Sacrament be placed in the center of the altar and, as mentioned, confessionals be installed for the liturgy of penance. It prescribed that, if possible, the façade of the church face east and, hardly influential at all, that the priest celebrate Mass facing the congregation—*versa ad populum facie.*

Although the council mandated revision only of the missal and breviary, between 1567 and 1614 revisions of other liturgical texts also took place. The able Cardinal Gugliermo Sirleto (1514–85) acted as the principal editor for the missal. He had also been responsible to some extent for the revision of the breviary (1567). Both bulls of promulgation mentioned consultation of manuscripts in the Vatican library as part of the editorial process. The bulls prescribed the use of the Roman Rite unless another was at least two hundred years old. In 1583, the Holy See published a new Martyrology; in 1596, it published a revised Pontifical; in 1600, the *Ceremoniale Episcoporum*, a companion to the Pontifical; and, finally, in 1614, the Ritual.

Of capital importance for liturgy after the Council of Trent was the establishment of the Congregation of Rites by Pope Sixtus V in 1588. For the first time in history, the Holy See through the Congregation explicitly reserved to itself decisions regarding liturgy. Whenever disputes arose about a liturgical practice, the local authorities sent a query (*dubum*) to the Congregation. By the end of the nineteenth century, the Congregation had issued over 8,500 decrees in answer to the queries. It continued to do so at a similar or even accelerated pace until Vatican II.

All these developments contributed to a degree of liturgical conformity in the Latin church that was unknown before. Even so, local liturgical traditions continued to flourish in some areas, most notably in France, into the nineteenth century. The ultramontane movement of that century swept away many such traditions and gave impetus to further uniformity. Not until the Constitution on the Sacred Liturgy of Vatican II did this trend suffer a setback.

Bibliography

D'Avray, David. "Marriage Ceremonies and the Church in Italy after 1215." In *Marriages in Italy, 1300–1650*, edited by Trevor Dean and K. J. P. Lowe, 107–15. Cambridge: Cambridge University Press, 1998.

Ditchfield, Simon. "Tridentine Worship and the Cult of Saints." In *The Cambridge History of Christianity*, edited by R. Po-Chia Hsia, 2:201–24, 640–43. Cambridge: Cambridge University Press, 2007.

McLaughlin, R. Emmet. "Truth, Tradition and History: The Historiography of High/Late Medieval and Early Modern Penance." In *A New History of Penance*, edited by Abigail Frey, 17–71. Leiden: E. J. Brill, 2008.

O'Malley, John W. *Praise and Blame in Renaissance Rome: Rhetoric, Doctrine, and Reform in the Sacred Orators of the Papal Court, c. 1450–1521*. Durham, NC: Duke University Press, 1979.

———. *Trent: What Happened at the Council?* Cambridge, MA: Harvard University Press, 2013.

Power, David N. *The Sacrifice We Offer: The Tridentine Dogma and Its Reinterpretation*. New York: Crossroad. 1987.

Rasmussen, Niels Krogh. "Liturgy and Liturgical Arts." In *Catholicism in Early Modern History*, edited by John W. O'Malley, 273–97. St. Louis, MO: Center for Reformation Research, 1988.

Rubin, Miri. *Corpus Christi: The Eucharist in Late Medieval Culture*. Cambridge: Cambridge University Press, 1991.

Schroeder, H. J., ed. *The Canons and Decrees of the Council of Trent* (1941). Reprint ed. Charlotte, NC: Tan Books, 1978.

Notes

1. See H. J. Schroeder, ed., *The Canons and Decrees of the Council of Trent* (Charlotte, NC: Tan Books, 1978), 76.

2. Schroeder, *The Canons and Decrees of the Council of Trent*, 79.

3. See Schroeder, *The Canons and Decrees of the Council of Trent*, 78.

4. For the decree, see Schroeder, *The Canons and Decrees of the Council of Trent*, 146–52.

5. See Schroeder, *The Canons and Decrees of the Council of Trent*, 150.

6. See Schroeder, *The Canons and Decrees of the Council of Trent*, 218–20.

7. Niels Krogh Rasmussen, "Liturgy and Liturgical Arts," in *Catholicism in Early Modern History: A Guide to Research*, ed. John W. O'Malley (St. Louis, MO: Center for Reformation Research, 1988), 273–97, at 285.

8. Schroeder, *The Canons and Decrees of the Council of Trent*, 153.

9. See John W. O'Malley, *Praise and Blame in Renaissance Rome: Doctrine, Rhetoric, and Reform in the Sacred Orators of the Papal Court, c. 1450–1521* (Durham, NC: Duke University Press, 1979), esp. 7–35, 123–64.

10. See Schroeder, *The Canons and Decrees of the Council of Trent*, 88–99, 102–5.

11. See Schroeder, *The Canons and Decrees of the Council of Trent*, 162–66.

12. See Schroeder, *The Canons and Decrees of the Council of Trent*, 168–84 and 185–92.

6

THE RECEPTION OF
THE LITURGICAL REFORM
OF THE SECOND
VATICAN COUNCIL*

—m—

Gerard Austin

We all know well that the first document considered at Vatican II
was the document on the liturgy. It was a wonderful way to begin
the Council. It seems that there were some seventy prepared sche-
mata (on all the various theological issues) ready in advance, but only
seven had been submitted to the Council members and produced
in printed form. Now of those seven, four had been worked out by
Cardinal Ottaviani's theological commission, and it was judged by
many that to start with one of those would have triggered a real
theological conflict. That left the other three, and providentially two
of those were not completely worked out. That left the schema that
was ready, and that was the one on the liturgy, and that certainly was
a "natural" way to begin. It was a good decision, as so many of the
bishops around the world had written in advance that the Council
should begin with the question of liturgical reform. Starting off with
the very source of the church's life, the liturgy, caused things to start
off with a very positive attitude. It inspired optimism and provided
the Council fathers with a chance to get at the very core of what it
means to be church, *ecclesia orans.*

---

* This chapter originally appeared in *Liturgical Ministry* 17 (Spring 2008): 49–57, and
is reprinted by permission of the author.

Those days marking the opening of the Council were exciting times. Those of us who had been reading journals like *Worship* (and its predecessor, *Orate Fratres*) could scarcely contain our excitement, and we tried to learn as much as possible about what was going on in Rome during those opening months of the Council. On December 4, 1963, the first of the documents, the Constitution on the Sacred Liturgy (*Sacrosanctum Concilium*), was signed. A few months later, my Dominican Provincial wrote me a letter. He had read paragraph 15 of the document, which says, "Professors who are appointed to teach liturgy in seminaries, religious houses of studies, and theological faculties, must be properly trained for their work in institutes which specialize in this subject."[1] I obediently asked where such institutes were located and found out that there was one in Paris and that a well-known Dominican named Pierre-Marie Gy directed it. He told me that he wanted me to go study with that famous Dominican. I obeyed, and my life has never been the same!

Now, over forty years after those exciting times, I would like to do two things: (1) to look at a few of the key, successfully received achievements of the liturgical reform of the Second Vatican Council (I shall pick out three) and (2) to point out a few areas where the reception of the reform seems to be meeting at the moment with mixed or even conflicting interpretations (and again, I shall pick out three).

WELL-RECEIVED LITURGICAL REFORMS OF THE SECOND VATICAN COUNCIL

In approaching this topic, I want to stress right from the start an important point: we cannot talk about the liturgical reform of the Council and limit ourselves only to *Sacrosanctum Concilium*. The obvious reason for this is that the liturgical constitution was the first of the Council documents. The gathered bishops had to learn to work together. They grew in the ability to do that as time progressed.[2] They made mistakes, and they made up for them in later conciliar decrees. Perhaps the best example of this is seen from their treatment of chapter 2 of *Sacrosanctum Concilium*, "The Most Sacred Mystery of the Eucharist." This key chapter never mentions the Holy Spirit! Due to the critical reaction of the Orthodox Christians (and Eastern Catholics), we find subsequent Vatican II documents often bringing in the role of the Holy Spirit whenever the Eucharist is mentioned. A good example would be paragraph 5 of the Decree on the Ministry and Life of Priests (*Presbyterorum Ordinis*): "For in the most blessed Eucharist is contained the whole spiritual good of the Church, namely Christ himself our Pasch and living bread which gives life to men through his flesh—that flesh which is given life and gives life through the Holy Spirit." There is nothing like that in chapter 2 of *Sacrosanctum Concilium*! So, looking at the whole of the Vatican II liturgical reform (including the postconciliar liturgical reforms that flowed from the Council), I would like to pick out three areas for further comment that have been very well received.[3]

An Ecclesiology Based on Baptism

Through our baptism, we are members of the church, the Body of Christ. *Sacrosanctum Concilium* stresses in paragraph 26 that "liturgical services pertain to the whole Body of the Church." Godfrey Diekmann, OSB, himself a *peritus* at Vatican II, writes of the overall thrust of the Constitution on the Sacred Liturgy:

> First and perhaps most importantly, is the priority given to the entire people of God as actively and responsively con- stituting the church, before consideration of the diverse ministries, inclusive of the *diakonia* based on holy orders.... Secondly and correlative to this basic concept of the church, is the constitution's underscoring of the dignity and role of the laity, based on their sacramental deputation to cult through baptism and confirmation.[4]

In view of such a theology, every baptized Christian is seen as an active, co-responsible member of the Body of Christ having a distinct contribution to make in the liturgy. Indeed, the Constitution goes so far as to state that "in the restoration and promotion of the sacred liturgy this full and active participation by all the people is the aim to be considered before all else" (no. 14). This approach is a return to the baptismal theology of the early church, where the *alter Christus* was seen to be the baptized woman or man rather than the ordained person. It is a reversal of a medieval theology that so stressed the prominence of the ministerial priesthood that it almost forced into oblivion the importance of the priesthood of all the baptized.[5]

I once picked the brain of the great church historian John Tracy Ellis by asking him how he thought our post–Vatican II period would go down in history. After a moment of reflective silence, he replied that he thought it would be known as "an era of baptismal consciousness." There is no question that an attention to the riches of baptism (so well elaborated upon by the early church) has returned. Catechists realize that they cannot begin to teach the meaning of the Eucharist until they teach the meaning of what it means to be baptized. As an ordained Catholic priest, I finally realize that the most important day of my life was not the day of my ordination but the day of my baptism! Perhaps the root theological basis of this was expressed by St. Augustine. Pope John Paul II, in his apostolic exhortation on the Laity, *Christifideles Laici*, writes, "All the baptized are invited to hear once again the words of St. Augustine: 'Let us rejoice and give thanks: We have not only become Christians, but Christ himself....Stand in awe and rejoice: We have become Christ.'"[6]

Proper Subject of the Liturgical Action

The second key successful reception of the liturgical reforms of Vatican II that I want to mention is really a corollary of the first one. It is a eucharistic participation based on viewing the gathered assembly as the "proper subject of the liturgical action."

Edward Schillebeeckx writes of the effects of the Constitution on the Sacred Liturgy as follows:

> The fundamental gain of this constitution is that it broke the clergy's monopoly on the liturgy. Whereas it was formerly the priest's affair, with the faithful no more than his clientele, the council regards not only the priest but the entire Christian community, God's people, as the subject of

the liturgical celebration, in which each in his proper place is given his own particular, hierarchically ordered function—a theological view with all kinds of practical repercussions.[7]

This reflects a theology that sees not just the ordained minister but the entire assembly as the proper subject of liturgical actions.

This reflects, according to Yves Congar, OP, a theology that is clearly part of the ancient tradition of the church, a church that is by its very nature priestly. He writes,

> It is not simply a question of a relationship between two terms, the faithful and hierarchical priests: there is a third term, Christ, which encircles the two others, associating them to himself organically. The whole body is priestly, but it is so in virtue of being the body of the first and sovereign priest, Jesus Christ, who acts in the celebrations of his spouse as the first and sovereign celebrant. It is he first and foremost who offers and the Church offers only because she is his body and follows him faithfully in everything. Jesus offers himself and he offers us; his members, the faithful, offer him in their turn and offer themselves with him.[8]

This type of thinking was retrieved when *Sacrosanctum Concilium* stated that "they [the faithful] should give thanks to God. Offering the immaculate victim, not only through the hands of the priest but also together with him, they should learn to offer themselves" (no. 48). This brings us to the very heart of what participation in the Eucharist is all about. The faithful are called to take part in the action of the liturgy, which is the action of both Christ and his church. This important teaching of *Sacrosanctum Concilium* will be reinforced later during the Council in the Dogmatic Constitution on the Church (*Lumen Gentium*):

> In the celebration of the Eucharist these [works, prayers, and apostolic undertakings, family and married life, daily work, relaxation of mind and body] may most fittingly be offered to the Father along with the body of the Lord. And

so, worshipping everywhere by their holy actions, the laity consecrate the world itself to God. (no. 34)

Priests are those who offer sacrifices, and the faithful are priests through their baptism. In the action of the Eucharist they are called to join in with Christ the High Priest and offer the sacrifice of their very lives! This teaching of Vatican II has been truly received. Millions of catechized Catholics now understand the beautiful words of St. Augustine: "If then you are the body of Christ and his members, it is your sacrament that reposes on the altar of the Lord."[9]

Vernacular in the Liturgy

My third and last item to be underscored in the liturgical reform of Vatican II as a well-received achievement is the use of the vernacular in the liturgy. The use (or non-use) of the vernacular in the liturgy was the subject that took up by far the most discussion time during the first session of the Council. The discussions did not lack color. It was not uncommon that glowing panegyrics in favor of Latin were themselves delivered in labored pidgin Latin, while the most forceful advocates of the vernacular expressed themselves eloquently in classical Latin!

When I was a seminarian in the 1950s, Latin was the order of the day. I had studied Latin for a few years in high school, but in college as a sophomore, before leaving for the Dominican novitiate, I took sixteen credit hours of Latin in the course of two semesters alone! Once I embarked on priesthood studies after the novitiate (three years of philosophy and four years of theology), all the major courses were taught in Latin. Our textbooks were written in Latin. We even took our exams, both oral and written, in Latin. Our prayer life was also expressed totally in Latin: the daily Mass and the Liturgy of the Hours. All this time I somehow felt that the Latinity was holding us back. It held us back in our studies; it held us back even more in our prayer life. As well as I knew Latin (and in those days I knew it quite well), it was not "my language," not my normal tongue. For me, it was never a vehicle for intimacy with God.

Sacrosanctum Concilium broke with the immediate past in that, although the use of Latin was preserved in the liturgy, the door was left open to an extended use of the vernacular. Shortly after the Council, the use of the vernacular spread like a brush fire, the chief proponents often being the very bishops who spoke against the vernacular at the Council. It seems that the popular fruits of the vernacular on the part of their people won them over. Progressively, they allowed more and more vernacular to be used.

I personally profited a great deal from the experience of English at Mass. It was a tremendous help to my eucharistic spirituality, and I heard the same thing from the vast majority of the people to whom I ministered. I must confess that I have been a bit amazed in recent years when some people long for the liturgy to be in Latin again. Their knowledge of Latin is quite minimal in comparison to my own. Their most frequent argument is that it helps them find the transcendent in liturgy. For me, the sense of the sacred and the mystery in our liturgy does not result from using a language that is "other." The transcendence of the mystery for me lies precisely in the divine encountering the human, the divine assuming the human. And for me, that is best done in a medium, a language, that is most fully human: my normal mother tongue, English. At any rate, it seems to me from my experience that the overwhelming majority of our faithful cherish the use of the vernacular in the liturgy and that it has fed them spiritually as it has fed me. It seems to me that the vernacular has aided immensely in one of the goals set forth by *Sacrosanctum Concilium*: "But in order that the liturgy may be able to produce its full effects it is necessary that the faithful come to it with proper dispositions, that their minds be attuned to their voices, and that they cooperate with heavenly grace lest they receive it in vain" (no. 11).

NOT-SO-WELL-RECEIVED LITURGICAL REFORMS OF THE SECOND VATICAN COUNCIL

Here, as I said earlier, I would like to point out some areas where the reception of the liturgical reform of Vatican II seems to be presently meeting with mixed or even troubled waters. Again, I have chosen three such areas.

Interrelationship between the Priesthoods

The first is the interrelationship between the baptismal priesthood and the ordained (ministerial) priesthood, especially at the Eucharist. The retrieval of baptismal consciousness and the homogeneous ecclesiology of the documents of Vatican II (e.g., *Lumen Gentium* placing "The People of God" chapter before "The Church Is Hierarchical" chapter because of the ecclesiology begun by *Sacrosanctum Concilium*) certainly served to bring into balance the previous exaggerated role of clerics in the church. As stated, on the one hand, in the years following Vatican II millions of Catholics have become aware that "they are the church" by reason of their baptism. On the other hand, this has resulted in a certain obfuscation of the unique role of the ordained in the church. In recent years this has resulted in a search for identity on the part of many priests. On the pastoral level, it often results in concrete questions such as, "What can I as a priest do that my people cannot do?" (Ironically, the very way the question is posed might be impeding the best answer.)

On a theoretical level, the tension often focuses on the issue of the *in persona Christi* debate. In what way does the priest act at Eucharist in the person of Christ? I'm grateful that there is already a vast array of literature on the topic.[10] The question gathers into itself vital issues such as Christology, ecclesiology, and pneumatology. Different approaches to the question result in different answers, and the different answers seem, at times, to be at odds with each other. Some argue that only the priest acts *in persona Christi* at the Eucharist while others argue that it is not just the ordained but the whole church that acts *in persona Christi*. David Power sums up the situation quite well when he explains,

> Two positions seem to be at odds with one another. One takes the baptismal priesthood as the foundation of ecclesial sacramental celebration and situates the ordained priesthood within this. For the other, the starting point is

the exercise of the ordained priesthood, which is put at the
service of the royal priesthood, invited to take part in what
is effected by the ordained.[11]

It could be argued that the latter position is the one favored by the
magisterium at the moment, but the question is far from being settled
and, happily, theological discussion on the matter continues.

A proper balance is best found by taking into account the intri-
cate interrelationship between the three biblical priesthoods so well
described by Raymond E. Brown: the unique high priesthood of
Jesus Christ, the priesthood of all believers, and the ordained priesthood.[12] Brown predicted that the church will face the problem of
interrelating its three priesthoods for a number of years to come, and
this will entail struggles about the role of the ordained priesthood.
He cautioned, "It is not in terms of power and glory but in terms of
compassion, suffering, and learning obedience that the ordained
priest can imitate Christ the high priest."[13] Again, he states that "privilege and pomp destroy what the ordained priest shares with all believers."[14]

Perhaps a proper balance can be found in looking to the term
synergy, which was a classical term in patristic theology. It connoted a
joint activity or combined energies between the human and the
divine. Such a tradition effected an ecclesiology of communion that
saw church as the communion of God with humanity. Every baptized
member was to enter into the movement of this synergy. An overreli-
ance on the sole role of the ordained goes against the synergy that is
traditionally at work in the Eucharist: a joint activity, or combined
energies, between the Holy Spirit and all the baptized present under
the leadership of the ordained minister.

For me personally, the most helpful source for understanding
the correct interplay between the baptismal priesthood and the ministerial priesthood has been the apostolic exhortation of John Paul
II on the episcopacy. In October 2003, Pope John Paul II released
a lengthy document titled *Pastores Gregis* (Shepherds of the Flock)
that summarized the work of the Synod of Bishops held in 2001 on
the subject of the episcopacy.[15] He wrote, "The interplay between
the common priesthood of the faithful and ministerial priesthood,

present in the Episcopal ministry itself, is manifested in a kind of peri-choresis between the two forms of priesthood" (no. 10). The term *perichoresis* (from the Greek for "around" and "dance") is a marvel-ous word to apply to this context. The theological term was coined to explain how one divine person could be said to be in another divine person, still retaining the notion of one God, expressed, however, in three distinct persons inhering in one another and drawing life from one another. We humans have a hard time seeing distinct things as being equally good. One always has to be "better" than another. John Paul II applies the interplay between the two priesthoods (baptismal and ministerial) on three levels, applying the term *perichoresis* to each:

> ...a *perichoresis* between the common witness to the faith given by the faithful and the bishop's authoritative witness to the faith through his magisterial acts; a *perichoresis* between the lived holiness of the faithful and the means of sanctification that the bishop offers them; and finally a *perichoresis* between the personal responsibility of the bishop for the good of the church entrusted to him and the shared responsibility of all the faithful for that same church. (no. 10)

Certainly such a lofty synergy (or perichoresis) flows from the teach-ings of Vatican II, but it is far from yet being received!

Shift of Emphasis from *res* to *res et sacramentum*

My second area of "troubled waters" concerns the understand-ing of the Eucharist. Using Scholastic terms, we are recently experi-encing a shift of emphasis from the *res* of the Eucharist to the *res et sacramentum*. Ironically, this brings us right back where we were before the Second Vatican Council, when we placed so much empha-sis on the real presence during the post-Tridentine period. I am using here the classical Scholastic terminology that distinguishes the three layers of meaning present in sacraments: *sacramentum, res et sacra-mentum,* and *res*. The *sacramentum* is the outward sign, the exterior rite constituted by the matter and form. By its very nature it is not an end in itself but leads to something further. In baptism this would be the gathered community's using water and the accompanying words and rituals. The *res et sacramentum* is an intermediate reality; it is both something in its own right (as a *res*) and something that points to something further (as a *sacramentum*). In baptism this is the indelible character. The *res* is the final reality signified by the *sacramentum* and the *res et sacramentum*; it is the ultimate purpose of the sacrament. In baptism this is the incorporation into the Body of Christ.

For Roman Catholics, eucharistic faith and practice have been conditioned by history. So much of what we were taught in catechism classes about the Eucharist came down to us from the Council of Trent, which was caught up in an attempt to respond to the reformers. A good example of this is the stress placed on the real presence. Since the eucharistic real presence was being denied (or at least allegedly so) by the reformers, for all practical purposes instruction on the Eucharist for Roman Catholics became instruction on the real presence. We forgot that the real presence was not the end of the line, the *res* of the Eucharist, but was rather the *res et sacramentum*. The final *res* is, in Aquinas's terms, the *unitas corporis mystici*, the unity of the Mystical Body.[16] Even the real presence is ordered to this end.

Immediately before and after the Second Vatican Council there was a shift of emphasis to the traditional *res* of the Eucharist. This is clearly described by Edward Schillebeeckx:

> Holy scripture, the writings of the patristic age, and medieval scholasticism, in contrast to the theology of the post-Tridentine era, always emphasized the *res sacramenti....* Forced by circumstances and already preceded in this by medieval piety, post-Tridentine theology shifted the emphasis. The *res sacramenti* was pushed into the background, while the *res et sacramentum*, that is, the real presence in the sacred host, was emphasized so much that it seemed to be an end in itself and not a *res et sacramentum*, that is, totally oriented toward the *res ultima*: the growth of Christ in the heart of the community. Modern theologians, while accepting the real presence in the eucharist as well as the legitimacy of the adoration of Christ in the

blessed sacrament, want only to replace the emphasis where the New Testament, the fathers, and the great scholastic theologians placed it, that is, on the *res sacramenti*, the end for which Christ instituted it. In my opinion, that is the central point of this whole new theology regarding the eucharist; and to a certain degree it is acknowledged by the Constitution on the Sacred Liturgy. What preoccupies these theologians is the Eucharistic celebration and the active participation of the faithful, culminating in holy communion.[17]

This type of thinking had great influence on the understanding of the Eucharist. More and more, Eucharist was rightfully viewed as a verb (an action of Christ and his church) and not simply as a noun (a sacred thing or person).

My fear is, however, that in recent years, more and more emphasis is being placed, even at Mass itself, on the *res et sacramentum* (the real presence) rather than on the *res* (the building up in unity of the Body of Christ). An understanding of Eucharist is being more and more reduced only to the aspect of real presence. Less and less effort is being made at Mass to avoid distributing previously consecrated hosts. More and more the institution narrative is being robbed of its structural function as part of the recounting of the *mirabilia Dei* and is simply providing an occasion for adoration. The institution narrative at the Mass is becoming a mini-Benediction of the Blessed Sacrament. This misunderstanding brings with it even more related complex misinterpretations. R. Kevin Seasoltz recently wrote,

The exaggerated emphasis on the text of institution as constituting the consecratory moment in the Mass, at least in western theology and practice, resulted in an overshadowing and obscuring of the other essential components of the Eucharistic Prayer, such as thanksgiving, invocation of the Holy Spirit, memorial, and praise. This is certainly a problem that continues down to the present time. Instead of treating the proclamation of the institution narrative as a ritual narrative and an integral part of the Eucharistic Prayer, some presiders tend to transform the text and accompanying gestures into a mime, thus giving the impression that they are literally Christ presiding at the Last Supper. This is surely not the meaning of Vatican II's assertion that the priest acts "*in persona Christi capitis*" (that he functions in the person of Christ as head of the body).[18]

One's Attitude toward the World

My third, and last, item on the agenda of the reception of the liturgical reform of Vatican II that is meeting with troubled waters concerns one's attitude toward the church (and this includes the *ecclesia orans*) and the world. In viewing this area, we must keep in mind what was stated earlier: that one cannot limit Vatican II's teaching on the liturgy only to *Sacrosanctum Concilium* but must include all sixteen documents of the Council and keep in mind the reciprocal relations existing between one document and another. Yves Congar, OP, stresses that

> we can observe the progress made between one document and the other, as to their awareness of the content of the Tradition. The Constitution *Sacrosanctum Concilium* was given its formulation substantially by the pontifical Preparatory Commission. Possibly if it had been composed and discussed after the Dogmatic Constitution *Lumen Gentium*, it might have accentuated even more the points... beyond *Mediator Dei*.[19]

Jean-Pierre Jossua, OP, in his article viewing *Sacrosanctum Concilium* in the entirety of Vatican II, lists six general themes that depend on the reciprocal action from one document to another.[20] He calls his sixth theme "An Indispensable Dialectic: Liturgy and the Church Present to the World."[21]

Let me try to concretize this by speaking from my own personal experience. Many of us have noted in recent years divergence of views that often follow generational lines. Various studies have been done that show that a large number of seminarians and younger priests

113

hold more traditional views and often are less enthusiastic about the reforms of Vatican II than the priests from, say, age forty-five to seventy-five. A few years ago I revisited France and spoke with my own doctoral mentor, Père Pierre-Marie Gy, OP. He said they were experiencing the same thing in France among the French Dominicans. He explained that the now older generation of Dominicans was very much influenced by Père Marie-Dominique Chenu, OP, one of the chief architects of the Pastoral Constitution on the Church in the Modern World (*Gaudium et Spes*), and that these older Dominicans had totally bought the theology of *Gaudium et Spes*. What he meant was that they bought the optimism of that document (an optimism that had begun with the spirit of *Sacrosanctum Concilium*) and its challenge to believers to become involved in efforts to create a more humane society in our world. In a sense they saw the goodness of the world, God's grace at work in the world, which caused a new openness to the world on their part, indeed, a new spirituality that embraced the world. Some of these Dominicans had become very sympathetic to the priest-worker movement that Père Chenu so highly influenced. Those inclined to this side of the coin would cite with enthusiasm *Gaudium et Spes*, which states,

> The world which the Council has in mind is the whole human family seen in the context of everything which envelopes it: it is the world as the theatre of human history, bearing the marks of its travail, its triumphs and failures, the world, which in the Christian vision has been created and is sustained by the love of its maker. (no. 2)

Many of the younger generation, however, would urge a retreat from the world. The older group would feel that such a retreat is not really the Catholic tradition and would be sympathetic to a theologian such as Karl Rahner, who explores the way our worship is related to our experiences of God in daily life. For Rahner, the liturgy of the church is the symbolic expression of the "liturgy of the world," the continual "engracing of the world" with the absolute mystery of God.[22]

The other side would resonate more closely with the writings of Joseph Ratzinger, who, as early as 1965, was critical of Vatican II's

Pastoral Constitution on the Church in the Modern World. He found it insufficiently christocentric, naively optimistic about contemporary culture (and, above all, about the idea of progress), and unclear about the challenge to culture that is the role of the gospel.[23] In Ratzinger's view, this embrace of the world leads to a loss of the sense of the sacred and the loss of the transcendent in liturgical worship.

Probably these two sides, these two "mind sets," reflect the tug-of-war involved in Jossua's "indispensable dialectic" between liturgy and the church's contact with the world. He sees the dialectic in the very documents of Vatican II, stating that *Sacrosanctum Concilium* represents one side of things more traditionally while *Gaudium et Spes* presents the other, with *Lumen Gentium* occupying a middle position between a very intraecclesial and sacramental outlook and a more attentive view of the way to God offered by human life and the secular activities of people in the world.[24]

Perhaps the different poles of the dialectic even reflect different stances on the nature of grace. Some in the church today see sin under every stone picked up, while others, picking up the same stones, see grace. So much of this influences how we view what is "sacred" and what is "profane." Sometimes the different poles of the dialectic are attributed to whether one sees things through the lens of "incarnational theology" or "redemptive theology." Again, some will say the proverbial "optimist twin" views things one way and the "pessimist twin" views things just the opposite.

All of this certainly influences the way one receives the liturgical reforms of Vatican II. Giuseppe Alberigo edited a very helpful work titled *The Reception of Vatican II.*[25] He wrote the first chapter himself and titled it "The Christian Situation after Vatican II." He warns against what he calls "a clear return to attitudes that Vatican II unequivocally disavowed and overcame." He continues,

> A pessimistic vision of history, poisoned by Manichaeism, seems to be spreading abroad. There is a rejection of the Council's call to the churches to become once again pilgrims and missionaries, as though it implied the abandonment of tradition, and finally, a revival of the "closed" ecclesiology of the post-tridentine period in which the

Church is a fortified castle, jealous of its purity and bristling with condemnations.[26]

CONCLUDING REMARKS

Today we seem to be at a whole new crossroad when it comes to positions on the reception of the liturgical reform of the Second Vatican Council. One side is urging a reform of the reform (that is, a reform of Vatican II's liturgical reform), and they argue that Benedict XVI was on their side. The other side argues that such a proposal is truly alarming, and that what is needed is a revitalization of the liturgical reform of Vatican II, a new and deeper catechesis.

In my opinion, the dialogue (the dialectic) can be aided by keeping an eye on the history of liturgy. One of Vatican II's most radical reforms was the opening of the door for the switch to the vernacular. This is not the first time the liturgy changed from a standard common language to the vernacular. Latin itself was the vernacular that took over from Greek. The liturgical historian (and my former professor) Cyril Vogel comments that "the Latin liturgy which came into use at Rome in the IV century was not a simple translation of a Greek but a fresh creation."[27] Adaptation, indeed fresh creation, is something that has always gone on in the history of our liturgy, especially, but not exclusively, in the first millennium. This happens especially in the song of our liturgy. Our chant tradition was at origin essentially an oral tradition. The renowned chant historian Helmut Hucke argues that the transition from oral to written transmission entails "redaction" of the tradition and that what we call Gregorian Chant is such a redaction. He writes,

> The standard version of Gregorian chant originated when the *cantus romanus* was introduced into the Frankish Empire by King Pepin and Charlemagne. It is the result of the adaptation of Roman chants by the Franks, a version of Roman chant created by Frankish cantors, a kind of translation of foreign music into their own musical language. It came into being, not because the Franks wanted to have a

116

different chant, but because of the difficulty of carrying an enormous musical repertory over from one culture to a very distant and different one.[28]

It all sounds familiar, doesn't it! The liturgical reform of the Second Vatican Council calls for a certain redaction of the tradition. A redaction, but remember, it is still "of the tradition"! We are taking the traditional melody and putting it in our own musical language, singing it, as it were, in a new key!

Back in 1969, just before the first celebration according to the *novus ordo* of the Mass, Pope Paul VI said, "It is a further step of the living Tradition."[29] Yves Congar in his famous *La Tradition et la vie de l'Église* states,

Tradition is living because it is carried by living minds— minds living in time. These minds meet with problems or acquire resources, in time, which lead them to endow Tradition, or the truth it contains, with the reactions and characteristics of a living thing: adaptation, reaction, growth and fruitfulness.[30]

For Congar, liturgy is a special witness of the living Tradition. He writes,

In his *Institutions liturgiques* Dom Guéranger wrote: "It is in the liturgy that the Spirit who inspired the Scriptures speaks again; the liturgy is Tradition itself at its highest degree of power and solemnity." No finer expression of the truth could be found.[31]

Certainly the Holy Spirit guided the bishops at the Second Vatican Council (as at all church councils) as the liturgical reforms were being sculpted, and the same Holy Spirit is speaking in the *ecclesia orans* as it lives and celebrates the reformed liturgy passed on by an ecumenical council of the church.

Ladislas Orsy, SJ, writes in a recent article,

Every ecumenical council was an "event" which brought a life cycle of the Church to its closure and initiated a new one; each council was an end and a beginning. Beyond its teaching function (the intellectual enlightenment of the Church), councils always (or mostly) left an existential impact on the Church that sometimes "reverberated" for decades or centuries.[32]

The lived Tradition as expressed in the liturgical reforms of the Second Vatican Council is currently making an existential impact on the church. May it inaugurate a new life cycle of the church, a new beginning where our liturgy is truly a foretaste of heaven, a sign of that kingdom that will know no end, a sign of that kingdom where there will be no Jew or Greek, no slave or freeperson, no male or female, but all will be one, in Christ Jesus!

Notes

1. All translations from the Vatican II documents in this article are from *Vatican Council II: The Conciliar and Post Conciliar Documents*, ed. Austin Flannery, OP, new rev. ed. (Northport, NY: Costello Publishing Company, 1996).

2. A very helpful article for me has been that by Jean-Pierre Jossua, OP, "La Constitution 'Sacrosanctum concilium' dans l'Ensemble de l'Oeuvre Conciliaire," in *La Liturgie Aprés Vatican II*, ed. J. P. Jossua and Y. Congar (Paris: Les Editions du Cerf, 1967), 127–56.

3. An excellent book that I found extremely helpful in viewing the Constitution on the Sacred Liturgy: Rita Ferrone, *Liturgy:* Sacrosanctum Concilium (New York: Paulist Press, 2007).

4. Godfrey Diekmann, "The Constitution on the Sacred Liturgy in Retrospect," *Worship* 40 (1966): 411.

5. In my opinion, the best book on the priesthood of all the baptized is Paul J. Philibert, *The Priesthood of the Faithful: Key to a Living Church* (Collegeville, MN: Liturgical Press, 2005).

6. Pope John Paul II, *Christifideles Laici*, December 30, 1988, no. 17 in *Origins* 18 (February 9, 1989), 569. St. Augustine ref.: *In Ioanne. Evang. Tract.* 21.8: *CCL* 36:216.

7. Edward Schillebeeckx, *Vatican II: The Real Achievement* (London: Sheed and Ward, 1967), 27–28.

8. Yves Congar, "L'Écclesia ou communauté Chrétienne, sujet integral de l'action liturgique," in Jossua and Congar, *La Liturgie Après Vatican II*, 255 (translation my own).

9. St. Augustine, Sermon 272; Latin text: *PL* 36:1246–48; English trans.: Thomas Halton, *The Mass: Ancient Liturgies and Patristic Texts*, ed. André Harnman (New York: Alba House, 1967), 207.

10. As a roadmap to guide one in this important area, I suggest my own article: Gerard Austin, "*In Persona Christi* at the Eucharist," in *Eucharist: Toward the Third Millennium* (Chicago: Liturgy Training Publications, 1997), 81–86.

11. David N. Power, "Roman Catholic Theologies of Eucharistic Communion: A Contribution to Ecumenical Conversation," *Theological Studies* 57 (1996): 607–8.

12. Raymond E. Brown, "An Example: Rethinking the Priesthood Biblically for All," in *The Critical Meaning of the Bible* (New York: Paulist Press, 1981), 96–106.

13. Brown, *The Critical Meaning of the Bible*, 104.

14. Brown, *The Critical Meaning of the Bible*, 105.

15. John Paul II, *Pastores Gregis*, October 16, 2003, in *Origins* 33 (November 6, 2003): 353–92.

16. *Summa Theologiae* III, q. 73, a. 3. I refer the reader to my article: Gerard Austin, "Adoration or Exposition?" *Liturgical Ministry* 13 (2004): 75–80.

17. Edward Schillebeeckx, "Transubstantiation, Transfinalization, Transignification," in *Living Bread, Saving Cup*, ed. R. Kevin Seasoltz (Collegeville, MN: Liturgical Press, 1987), 186–87.

18. R. Kevin Seasoltz, "Eucharistic Devotions and Reservation: Some Reflections," *Worship* 81 (2007): 432.

19. Congar, *La Liturgie Après Vatican II*, 268 (my own translation). Note: Paul J. Philibert, OP, published an English translation of this key article of Congar as "The *Ecclesia* or Christian Community as a Whole Celebrates the Liturgy" in *At the Heart of Christian Worship: Liturgical Essays of Yves Congar* (Collegeville, MN: Liturgical Press, 2010).

20. See n. 2 above.

21. Jossua, "La Constitution 'Sacrosanctum concilium' dans l'Ensemble de l'Oeuvre Conciliaire," 149–56.

22. A good introduction to the understanding of Rahner in this regard is Michael Skelley, *The Liturgy of the World: Karl Rahner's Theology of Worship* (Collegeville, MN: Liturgical Press, 1991).

23. Daniel Donovan, *What Are They Saying about the Ministerial Priesthood?* (New York: Paulist Press, 1992), 68.

24. Jossua, "La Constitution 'Sacrosanctum concilium' dans l'Ensemble de l'Oeuvre Conciliaire," 149.

25. Giuseppe Alberigo, Jean-Pierre Jossua, and Joseph A. Komonchak, eds., *The Reception of Vatican II* (Washington, DC: The Catholic University of America Press, 1987).

26. Giuseppe Alberigo, "The Christian Situation after Vatican II," in *The Reception of Vatican II*, 21–22.

27. Cyril Vogel, *Medieval Liturgy: An Introduction to the Sources*, rev. ed. (Washington, DC: Pastoral Press, 1986), 296.

28. Helmut Hucke, "Toward a New Historical View of Gregorian Chant," *Journal of the American Musicological Society* 13 (1980): 442.

29. Paul VI, November 19, 1969, *Acta Apostolicae Sedis* (1969): 778.

30. Yves Congar, *The Meaning of Tradition* (New York: Hawthorn Books Publishers, 1964), 75.

31. Congar, *The Meaning of Tradition*, 125.

32. Ladislas Orsy, "Law for Life: 'Sacrae Disciplinae Leges'; Forty Years after the Council," *The Jurist* 67 (2007): 19–20.

7

LITURGY IN THE POST–VATICAN II ERA

church worship world

—ɯ—

Gerard Moore

As we take up liturgy in the post–Vatican II era, you may well need to put on your 3-D movie glasses and strap yourself in. The canvas will be a wide panorama, but, like a 3-D movie, things will be brought to your immediate attention—jump out at you so to speak. So be prepared to deal with both the broad sweep and the particulars.

Post–Vatican II liturgy is enacted within a renewed engagement between the church and the world. The initial generation of worshipers who took up the challenge that the church invited them into were steeped in three conciliar documents. Their liturgical practice was guided by the Constitution on the Sacred Liturgy (1963). However, the emerging sense of church, and the vital role of all believers in being responsible for the life of the church, was carried in the Dogmatic Constitution on the Church (1964). Ringing in the ears of the church at prayer was the extraordinary opening paragraph of the Church in the Modern World (1956), which declared that the joys, hopes, sorrows of all people, particularly the poor and afflicted, are the joys and hopes, sorrows and anxieties of the disciples of Christ.

There is one more essential prelude to our excursion. Liturgy is based in texts. The post–Vatican II era can commence only once two momentous steps have been achieved. The first was the revision of all the rites and prayers of the Catholic Church. This massive task covered liturgies so central as baptism, Eucharist, and the Liturgy of the Hours, as well as rites that are less frequently used but part of the fabric of the church, such as the Ceremonial of Bishops through to the Rite of Exorcism. All of these rituals were revised, using the best scholars (liturgical, theological, biblical, and pastoral) and building on at least a century of rigorous study of ancient manuscripts. It was a vast enterprise, done with surprising speed and pastoral acumen, and widely supported by the bishops across the world.[1] Begun in the mid-1960s, the bulk of the work was completed between the mid-1960s and 1970s, though still there are rites that are undergoing modification. What is not so clear to us at this distance is that the revisions were carried out in Latin. The standard ritual books were in Latin and remain in Latin to this day.

Today, however, we encounter the rites and texts of the liturgy in our own language, presumably English for readers of this chapter, though perhaps also Spanish. Consequently, the second step on which the post–Vatican II liturgy is based is that of translation. While this remains an ongoing work, across the period from the mid-1970s to the mid-1980s armies of scholars—liturgical, biblical, theological, pastoral, and linguistic—were marshalled from countries of the major language groups to translate the Latin texts into viable vernacular prayers and liturgical rites. Particular attention was given to the English versions, as these were frequently used as a base for the translations into those languages that had few experts in Latin. I am thinking in particular here of the many languages of the South Pacific region, where there were few native speakers who were Latinists, but the people were not to be denied the right to worship in the vernacular.

It is with the promulgation and publication of vernacular texts that the post–Vatican II era of worship begins.

TRANSFORMED WORSHIP

The worship of the church, based in reformed rituals enacted in the language of the people, was the most visible and profound manifestation of the reforms of the Second Vatican Council. What emerged was a church transformed and now open to the wider culture. Our worship today is characterized by a number of features virtually unimaginable to our predecessors in faith who lived in the year 1963!

Accessible Worship

Though not in any strict order, perhaps the first feature to be named is that the liturgy is accessible to worshipers. The rites of the Catholic Church have returned to their original genius as rites in which the faithful participated from within their own language.[2] We are now able to hear the Word of God, respond to the prayers, rejoice in the chants and hymns, and pray in communion with the priest and ministers in the language of our hearts. We are able to comprehend the invitation to receive holy communion and accept the gift in our mother tongue. We are able to be swept up in the thanksgiving of the Preface, enlightened by the Easter Vigil Exultet, rejoice with the angels in the Gloria, and renew our baptismal vows from within the grace of our own lives.[3] The sick are anointed with oil accompanied by the language through which they have lived their lives. The bride and groom are married into the grammar of their lives together. We are able to bury our dead in the linguistic environment in which they lived out their Christian faith, while grieving their loss directly from our tears. We confess our faith, and confess our sins, in the language of our commitments and our failures, aware that God hears all we say and even what we cannot say (see Rom 8:26–27).

The accessibility re/introduced by the vernacular offers us a further entry point to mystery.[4] The Catholic liturgy, particularly the sacraments, are occasions of encounter between the faithful and the triune God. The renewals of Vatican II envisioned a shift in our conscious sense of ritual, situating our engagement with the revelation of God in the hearing of the Scriptures, in participation in the rites that embody the sacraments, and in the sense of Christ present in a community gathered in his name.

Biblical Worship

The biblical text has taken center place in the contemporary vernacular liturgy. We hear the readings in our language, in translations familiar to us. The Scriptures enter our ears and touch our understanding: their mystery is in the way the words, stories, sayings, songs, and teachings enflame our hearts. To hear the Word of God in our own language is to be with the disciples on the way to Emmaus (Luke 24:32), or to be at the Pentecost preaching of Peter (Acts 2). However, the Scriptures are not only present in the Liturgy of the Word. The vernacular rendition of the rites enables us to hear the biblical resonances at play in the prayers, verses, antiphons, responses, and songs across the liturgy.[5] The closer we examine the text, and the more we pray them alert to their biblical imagery and wordplay, then the stronger we are touched by the biblical beat of our rites. It is important to recognize the momentous nature of this newfound "hearing." Jesus is the Word of God revealed in our midst (John 1:1), a word alive and active that cuts like a two-edged sword between marrow and bone (Heb 4:12), a word that has to be tasted for its sweetness (Ezek 3:3). In terms of ritual books, the renewal of the *Lectionary* with a three-year set of Sunday readings and a broad new range of readings for daily Mass and feasts is unsurpassed as a return of the Scriptures to the people. In the same spirit, the rites of penance are infused with a vast range of options for the biblical readings.[6] In effect, the reimmersion of the faithful in the Scriptures proclaimed at worship has reengaged the Catholic community with the Scriptures as the entry point for encounter with the mystery of the triune God.

Aware of Genre and Ritual Forms

Attention to the biblical nature of the liturgy is in parallel with attention to the nature and genre of the prayers and rites themselves. The renewed liturgy has brought into focus the difference between each of the individual rites that comprise our worship and the effects these variations have on us. The participation that is possible in vernacular liturgy allows us to be shaped by the genre of each ritual form. While the words of prayers have an effect on our thinking, the structure and form of each prayer work to engage our bodies and hearts as well. The Collect is a prayer that invites the faithful to stand as a single body, to pray in a collective silence the petitions of our hearts, and to respond to the presidential prayer with a single gathered Amen. The

Gloria is a song, meant to be sung. The General Intercessions are petitions, given voice by the deacon or lay leader and reflective of the priesthood of the people. Holy communion is in bread and wine and as such is meant to be eaten and drunk. The Sign of the Cross is a shared rite, in which all who are in attendance write on their bodies the crucifixion of the Lord. With the vernacular we are able to unlock the gates to the rites and genres and see a liturgical service somewhat as a garden. To know a garden we have to go into it and allow ourselves—body, senses, spirit, mind—to be touched by the different plants, colors, scents, sounds, and textures. It is now so with the liturgy. Active participation in the multiplicity of genres and forms within the liturgy allows us more opportunities to be engaged by the presence of Christ and the promptings of the Spirit that are made manifest precisely through the liturgy.[7]

This newfound attention to genre has unleashed great creativity and also an appropriate critical sense of what makes up good worship. In terms of creativity, there is no need to go further than the staggering range of new songs, chants, and musical pieces that are available for worshipers of every age and culture. There seems to be no halt to the flow of new music. However, attention to genre also allows for a critical appraisal of forms new and old, allowing the creativity of composers and musicians to serve the liturgical texts.[8]

A Restored Sense of Symbol

Behind genre, form, and structure in worship lies the power of symbol. The nature of symbol is such that its meaning is never clear and forthright, but rather it continues to unfold, even unravel, as we are more and more immersed within it. Nevertheless, symbol is not well served by obfuscation. The mystery in a symbol is not discovered because we have to cut through any of its obscure elements. Rather, there is a sense in which symbols require a certain clarity of form, so that we at least know what we are invited into. The renewed liturgy has allowed us to worship with a deeper appreciation of the symbols that underpin our divine service. We have already noted above that the Sunday Eucharist is replete with the symbol of the Word speaking to us. As well, it is utterly apparent that the central mystery of the

Word enacted in the Eucharist is participation in the blessed bread and consecrated cup through the reception of holy communion. Here we can see that the vernacular liturgy allows the foundational mystery to be manifest, allowing the participants to be more closely attuned to the mystery revealed precisely in and through the various rituals. Consequently, through the vernacular we have a heightened consciousness of the use of water in baptism, of the communal nature of the rites of penance, of the need for healing through anointing, and of the self-giving of the couple in the marriage rite. By this closer alignment of symbol and rite we are more closely bound into the liturgy, more engaged with the celebration, and more open to being transformed ourselves into Christ.

This closer alignment to symbol extends beyond the rites and texts of worship and is expressed in the developments in architecture, art, decoration, music, and movement that invite our communal and corporeal selves into a renewed liturgical world.

Transformative Worship

The renewed liturgy provides fertile grounds for transformation. As we have already seen, worship in light of language, genre, and symbol provides opportunities for grace to work within us and engage us as individuals towards a deeper life in faith.

Without impinging on what will follow in the chapters on justice and ecology, the accessibility of the rites leaves open possibilities of gospel-based challenges to worshipers. Can we continue to ignore the hungry and poor now that we have a restored and heightened awareness that participation in the Eucharist impels us to eat and drink? And we who are so graciously fed by Christ himself, and of himself, are impelled to share the bounty of God's creation with all. The Eucharist teaches unambiguously that we should allow no one to go hungry. If we are required to baptize in water, are we not required to preserve our rivers, wells, skies, and oceans so that we can be cleansed of sin, washed anew, cleaned, and refreshed.[9] Baptism teaches unambiguously that the things of the earth are for the celebration of creation, not to become part of the despoiling of nature and as a consequence the desecration of our sacraments. The forgiveness we receive so readily in the sacrament of penance, particularly with its communal dimensions, challenges us to forgive, to hold life sacred, to be a beacon of hope for prisoners and the condemned. The communal nature of all our worship, and the importance the liturgical reforms have placed on the dignity of the assembly, remind the faithful that in worship all are welcome, and there should be no divisions in the Christian community as all are understood to be fully loved by God. It should come as no surprise, then, that Catholics ought be trenchant in their opposition to the divisions that bedevil our society—whether discrimination on grounds of race, gender, wealth, age, sexuality—because these run counter to the divine values embodied in the Christian community at worship.

Human Experience as Underpinning Worship

As the first wave of translated texts were set in place as the staple form of Catholic worship, a new question slowly emerged. The faithful asked how and whether these texts spoke to their lives. We take up the more challenging aspects of this question later, but some immediate points can be made as we discuss the transformative dimensions of vernacular worship.

In general, our current texts come from three sources. The experts who compiled the rituals were steeped in the ancient and traditional prayers and rites of the church. As the rites were reformed, so prayers and rituals were refreshed in light of their original texts and intentions. However, it soon became apparent that new prayers and forms would be required, so again the experts used their knowledge of the ancient liturgical books to source prayers, or to fuse two ancient prayers to form a new contemporary version. Last, new prayers were composed, often inspired by passages in the documents of the Second Vatican Council and papal texts.

The rites of the Roman church have always added new prayers as required, but usually as a trickle for the admission of a newly canonized saint or the adoption of a new feast. With the reformed liturgy, there was a need to create prayers that were in line with the experiences of humanity in the late twentieth century. You will recall our earlier reference to the Church in the Modern World, where the baptized aligned themselves and their petitions with the hopes, fears, anxieties, and joys of human beings everywhere. The renewed rites were revised within this wider embrace of all God's creation and the plight of all God's people. The vernacular liturgy was now showing that it sought to be relevant to the needs of the faithful and the situation of the world in all its complexity: worship sought to embrace the experience of the faithful, individual, communal, and global.

As the same time, the scholars were disseminating more widely the fruits of the century of research that had uncovered the actual origins of a good number of prayers that are in use today. Many ancient prayers were composed in light of the events of the time, whether various invasions of Rome by enemies of the state and the church, the papal intervention to stop the celebration of the papal festival of Lupercalia, or dissention within a local monastery. Closer examination of the manuscript tradition revealed that later changes to prayers by copyists and liturgical leaders across the Middle Ages gave glimpses of how prayers were adapted to meet the immediate needs of the communities that were praying them. What has become clearer is that within the liturgical tradition there is an expectation that the rites and prayers of the liturgy are related to the experiences and immediate historical situation of the community, and that this expectation is reflected within the range of the liturgical tradition.

Worship Expressed in and through Culture

This discussion around experience paves the way for a reflection on our contemporary recognition of the impact of culture on worship. Culture is to the human community as water is to fish and oxygen to animals and plants. It is the reference point for all human activities and understanding and as such is pivotal to the enactment of worship.

The scholarship behind the liturgical renewal revealed that our prayers and liturgies reflected the cultural values of the Roman Christian community, a period that we can see as coming to a close around the beginning of the ninth century. Western worship was developed in light of the religious sensibilities of the peoples of the city of Rome and the values of that city as interpreted across the

Roman Western Empire. The liturgy reflected their understanding of the Scriptures and was brought to life in the particular Roman preferences for Latin wordplay, grammatical forms, prayer genres, choice of vocabulary, forms of chant, and liturgical gestures. Two examples from the Collect prayers and the Roman Canon will suffice. The Collect prayers that are a staple in the Mass emerged at the time that Roman Christians changed their customary practice of using Greek in worship and created a liturgy wholly in Latin. The then newly created Latin prayers reflected the Roman preference for short, tightly woven, well-constructed prayers, with musical and rhetorical flourishes within the text. Another ancient Latin composition, the Roman Canon, is used still in the Mass today. It contains examples of a favored Roman literary convention of a repetitive building of synonyms to create a rhetorical effect of momentum and significance: *...and bless these gifts, these offerings, these holy and unblemished sacrifices, and....Be pleased, O god, we pray, to bless, acknowledge, and approve this offering in every respect, make it spiritual and acceptable.*

By the nineteenth century, these styles of prayer and rhetorical forms were categorized as elements of the "genius" of the Roman Rite, a rite seen to be characterized by the qualities of simplicity, practicality, sobriety, gravity, dignity, an absence of poetry, and clarity. It was deemed a rite without sentiment and sensuality, but rather with sense and soberness.[10] Our post–Vatican II liturgy is conscious of its roots in a particular cultural world and its recognizable "genius." Our worship lies clearly within an established tradition of Rome-inspired worship.

Post–Vatican II Liturgy
Is Worship in Translation

Contemporary liturgical theology is deeply conscious that our liturgy is celebrated in and through translation. There are ongoing consternations around this, which will be taken up below, however, there is more to being "in translation." First up, a rather broad statement: we are not so much "lost" in translation but rather "found" in translation. We continually underestimate the extent to which we are engaged with translations and choices around translations. Every psalm, lectionary reading, and Scripture verse is a translation from Greek and Hebrew. Further, the history of the reception of the Bible in the Western churches is one of translation, ranging across the first Latin Scriptures to the later Vulgate, then through to vernacular editions, and onto the various Bible translation societies, their development of Bibles in indigenous languages and now their revision. Our love of the Scriptures, our prayer through them, and our song inspired by them is in and through translated texts. The Word is found in translation.

The same can be said for our hymn, prayer, and theological traditions. A broad liturgical music repertoire that includes Luther, Aquinas, and Joseph Gelineau is one steeped in translation. A prayer book that places before us the prayers and meditations of Augustine, Ambrose, Teresa of Avila, Ignatius of Loyola, and Thérèse of Lisieux has invited us into their spiritual environments precisely through translated texts. Our own theological training in figures such as Hildegard, Calvin, Congar, and Lucien Deiss is through the work of linguistic intermediaries.

In effect, the Western Christian tradition has been lived through translation. It is clear that this applies to the larger Christian world itself, as I hear in my own workplace the Scriptures read in Korean and Wesley's hymns sung in Tongan. None of this implies that there is no room for the vernacular, nor does it deny that these texts were originally vernacular texts. Rather, it reveals that we read, sing, pray, and reflect quite normally and intuitively in translation.

Informed by Scholarship

There is an ongoing impact of liturgical scholarship on worship and devotion. The reform of the ritual books and rites themselves was undertaken with a view to incorporating the best scholarship, particularly around the original structure and meaning of rites.[11] Yet this scholarship has not stopped, and ongoing research continues to influence the way we participate in the rituals. One example of the impact of research concerns the eucharistic prayers in the Mass. For virtually fifteen hundred years, the Roman Rite had only one eucharistic prayer, known as the Roman Canon. Yet scholarship has opened up the vast range of eucharistic prayers in use across the liturgical tradition, particularly that of the Eastern churches, a finding that has allowed the post–Vatican II liturgy to have an enlarged number of eucharistic prayers without compromising the liturgical tradition. Furthermore, the theological controversies and pastoral responses during the period that stretched from the year 500 to the present had led the faithful and the clergy to concentrate most closely on the transformation of the bread and wine into the Body and Blood of Christ,[12] with a consequent emphasis on adoration of the consecrated host. Again, without compromising the theology of the real presence of Christ in the Eucharist, liturgical scholarship has opened up for worshipers the grounds of this prayer tradition in thanksgiving, and shown more clearly the necessary link between thanksgiving over bread and cup and the reception of holy communion in the Body and Blood of Christ.

This ongoing dialogue between scholarship and rite promises a more profound connection between the faithful, their lives, and the foundational symbols underneath the liturgy. At the same time, it causes a degree of discomfort when long-held pieties are challenged or seen to be destabilized. This is particularly the case with Catholic devotional practices concerning the Mass. As discussed in earlier chapters, many of these emerged because the faithful were disconnected from the actual rites of the liturgy and so found consolation and spiritual comfort in parallel devotions. One of the features of our life in the reformed liturgy is an ongoing, if not uneven, development of new forms of devotion that are more closely aligned with our engagement in the rites and symbols of our worship.

A Shared Ecumenical Framework

It is difficult to express the extent of the ecumenical blessings that are now so commonplace within post–Vatican II Catholic worship. It is difficult to imagine our church without them. Now that Catholic worship is celebrated in and through the vernacular, however, we are able to invite all Christians to participate[13] actively and consciously in myriad liturgical services, from attendance at the rite of marriage to participation in services of repentance and reconciliation;

the rites of Christian burial; the Liturgy of the Hours; days of prayer for peace, for women, for national disasters; services of praise; charismatic worship; Taizé chant services; and many others.

Alongside this movement has been the sharing of liturgical resources. Again, it is hard to think back to that time when we were impeded in our choice of music, hymns, chants, antiphons, and songs of praise because of discrimination against other Christian denominations and their traditions of liturgical expression. At another level, the scholarship behind the transformation of Catholic rites has had a profound influence on the development and reimagination of the ritual books of Western Christianity. In sum, the Catholic embrace of the vernacular has opened the church to stronger liturgical and ecclesial ties across the ecumenical spectrum.

AN AUTHORITATIVE
ECCLESIAL LITURGY

I would like to end this section on the nature of transformed Catholic worship following Vatican II with a reflection on the ecclesial nature of our worship. Our worship is the church at its most visible. Taking the Eucharist as the key here, each Sunday service is the authentic manifestation of the presence of the church of Christ in the world. The point is made most clearly in the General Instruction of the Roman Missal, where we read that as an action of Christ and the people of God array hierarchically, it is the center of the whole Christian life for the church.[14]

The authority of post–Vatican II worship stems from a number of sources, all of which reflect the intrinsic nature of the church. We have already seen how the liturgy reflects the pillars of Scripture and Tradition. There is also the authorization of our rites by ecclesial authority. The reform of the rites itself emerged as the first of the steps of renewal initiated by the bishops of the world collected at the Second Vatican Council. And clearly our current rites and texts, and the choices and options available within them, are authorized by the ecclesial leaders, whether the Roman curia, the national conferences of bishops, or local bishops themselves.

132

Yet along with this set of official approvals there is another level of authorization: the ongoing acceptance of the faithful who register their approval through participation. Church communities across the Catholic world embrace the forms of worship; take up roles as ministers, leaders, cantors, and the like; seek to have their lives enriched by the rites; and allow their deaths to be interpreted through the liturgy. In part, the authority of the liturgy stems from its ability to meet the pastoral needs of the baptized, to express their faith, and to allow them to be a visible manifestation of the church of Christ.

SECTION SUMMARY

I have used the bulk of this chapter to recognize key features of the ongoing liturgical reform we are experiencing. Somewhere at the front of this book you will find that all the chapters are dedicated to Gerard Austin, my one-time teacher and ongoing friend and mentor. He is a man of great ecclesial conviction and hope in the Holy Spirit. My slim hope is that the points above, covering accessibility, Scripture, rite and genre, symbol, transformation, human experience, culture, translation, scholarship, ecumenism, and authority, will inform your own worship practice and understanding in this remarkable period in which we are living just as Fr Austin has been doing so effectively and faithfully.

New Horizons and Further Transformations

Our liturgical future has its roots in the present. As a teacher, Jerry Austin never shied away from the challenges contained both in the study of liturgical texts and in their application to the reform of our worship. What follows now is an attempt to name some of these challenges and place them within a coherent framework. In fact, a number of these challenges emerge from the nature of the reform itself and are directed to the development of a more open, robust, and pastoral liturgical future.

The Digital Present

Our worship is only beginning to comprehend and embrace the revolutionary change in the digital landscape and the transformation that is being wrought in human culture and history. As students and even for myself as a researcher, it is impossible to imagine the world without the internet, online access through multiple devices, the vast sets of resources now at hand, and the ubiquity of communication. On a larger scale, we are now in a situation where knowledge is compatible with multiple choices and options, where our bodies and physicality are engaging with the earth and community from within a different paradigm, and where the digital economy is struggling to avoid becoming a new form of colonization and control. With an expanded imagination and set of tools, art, music, movies, novels, theatre, drama, dance are exploring ever new possibilities. In this there is a change in the "centering" of culture: there are few fixed points of reference and more opportunities for alternative voices. Yet even in this there is change, as it becomes clearer that the internet is not an open, unregulated free space, but is also under the control of vested interests and concealed political strategies.

My point is neither to decry this situation nor to overly praise its possibilities. Rather, we are now in the midst of a massive cultural shift through which we are already experiencing life differently, and this trajectory of change and disruption will continue. As with all change, the response inspired by the Vatican Council is not to be in reaction to this, but to recalibrate faith and worship to evangelize successfully and present "new" peoples and cultures with the life of the gospel and the church at worship.

Whose Experience?

This recognition of the changing epoch carries with it a challenge implicit in the characteristics identified earlier. As we discussed language, rite, symbol, culture, and experience, we identified that these emerged from particular languages and historical events and specific groups of people. If our liturgical texts are inspired by human experience, we are now compelled to ask whose experience is behind the texts and whose experiences are not reflected in them. Virtually all the scholars who undertook the task of reform, and similarly the first generations of translators, were from Europe and North America and were men. The ancient texts and virtually all the texts of the Catholic tradition were the creation of men. This does not make them invalid but does forcefully ask where the experiences of women, of Asian, African, and Indigenous Christians, of the poor are in our worship. Are they to continue to be excluded? Are we unable to bring the experiences of gender, race, culture, exclusion, poverty, violence, and abuse to God, experiences that shape the very lives of the faithful? While our liturgical texts and symbols are founded in human experience, they will flounder when closed off from ongoing human experience and consequent reformulations of the meaning of our lives in new contexts.

What is being signaled here is the recognition of a significant change that has already taken place but is not yet recognized or explored. In a sense, comprehending this point does depend on where you are sitting right now! As I write from Australia, with friends from New Zealand also contributing to these essays, I am aware that I live within the indigenous peoples of Australia and the South Pacific, that my cultural origins are from the West, but my northern neighbors are from South East Asia. My fellow Christians, students, friends, colleagues, cricket team parents are from Tonga, Fiji, Japan, Korea, Singapore, South Africa, India, Sri Lanka, and Pakistan. The Catholic faith is no longer held within the bounds of Rome or within the parts of the world collectively known as the West. The vast church we belong to is not accurately characterized as either Roman or Western but is a worldwide communion of cultures and languages and peoples celebrating their belief in Christ, offering the eucharistic thanksgiving in communion with their international sisters and brothers, and representing before God a new and diverse set of joys, hopes, sorrows, needs, and anxieties, now understood from outside the prism of Western culture and politics.

The current reform of the liturgy has allowed us to realize that there is an ongoing dance between Catholic worship, experience, culture, and history. Our challenge is to be open to this ever-new context.

Whose Liturgy, Whose Church?

There remains a continuing tension in the liturgical reform around the nature of priesthood and the place of the ordained within worship. To be clear, the debate is not whether the ordained have a place! Rather, there is the question of the nature of the collaboration between the priest and the faithful in the planning and enactment of our worship. The pendulum shifts from the extreme of the priest having total control over every aspect without recognition of the role and rights of the laity, to the faithful perceiving that the rituals are open to any number of changes.

In a rough parallel, there have been difficulties within the upper levels of the hierarchy of the church itself as to the authority over translation and the role to be played by Vatican curia in contrast to the rights and responsibilities of bishops and conferences of bishops in the confirmation of official translations and ritual books.

The rightful participation of the faithful in the reformed liturgy will continue to challenge the church to reimagine how the structures of hierarchy and authority best serve to manifest the nature of the church and further the presence of Christ in the world.

This point is not made in isolation from the situation in which we live. With immediate access to what is happening across the world through digital media, there is a stronger determination to transform the lives of all human beings across the planet, to take responsibility for the condition of the environment, and to call authority to account in the face of abuse, injustice, and violence. From our baptism we find ourselves committed to bringing about the reign of God on earth. The participation of the faithful in worship and in changing the world offers new possibilities for imagining the role of the priest and the significance of Gospel leadership in the liturgy and in the church.

CONCLUDING REMARKS

I would like to conclude with the most obvious of statements. The Catholic Church would have virtually no presence or credibility in the contemporary world if it had remained huddled in worship behind arcane rituals, muttered in a long dead language, reliant on moments of theatrical ritual splendor from a tiny corner of the ancient city of Rome, and demanding only discipline and obedience of its worshipers.

The accessibility of its rites, their openness to mystery through symbol, their unswerving biblical foundation, and their justice imperatives have signified to humanity that the Christian faith is willing and able to engage with the world as it is and has good news to offer it. The larger liturgical events of Catholic mission and identity, such as papal visits and World Youth Day celebrations are testimony to the integrity and evangelical power of the reformed liturgy. The celebration of the sacraments in the language and culture of the faithful has allowed them to speak directly into lives and begin the process of conversion and transformation.

This has also enabled the liturgy of the post–Vatican II era to contribute to the health of human civilization itself. We have already mentioned how participation in the Eucharist is a reminder of our need to feed the poor and eliminate hunger. Our renewed rites of penance have contributed to the grammar of forgiveness that is now an intrinsic part of truth and reconciliation movements internationally.[15] Our reliance on water for baptism is a reminder of our ecological responsibilities.

All this is not to ignore the failings and missteps that the church has taken. They are only too evident. It is, however, to acknowledge that the influence and contribution of the church to society, civilization, and the health of the planet itself is built in part on the credibility of its renewed worship and the coherence of its mission, liturgical expression, and manifestation of the mystery of Christ in the Spirit.

Further Reading

You might want to consult the following resources to continue your awareness of the intention and direction of post–Vatican II worship, Catholic and ecumenical.

- For a discussion of sacraments from a Catholic perspective see:
  Baldovin, John, and David Farina Turnboom, eds. *Catholic Sacraments: A Rich Source of Blessings*. Mahwah, NJ: Paulist Press, 2015.

Irwin, Kevin. *The Sacraments: Historical Foundations and Liturgical Theology*. New York: Paulist Press, 2016.

• An ecumenical view with strong catholic sensibilities is to be found in:

Larson-Miller, Lizette. *Sacramentality Renewed: Contemporary Conversations in Sacramental Theology*. Collegeville, MN: Liturgical Press, 2016.

• To gain an overview of aspects of the Vatican II reforms, with a Southern Hemisphere perspective, see:

Pilcher, Carmel, David Orr, and Elizabeth Harrington, eds. *Vatican Council II: Reforming Liturgy*. Vatican II Series. Adelaide: ATF Theology, 2013.

Turner, Paul. *Whose Mass Is It? Why People Care So Much about the Catholic Liturgy*. Collegeville, MN: Liturgical Press, 2015.

• For an approach to exploring the texts of Christian worship, there is:

Day, Juliette J. *Reading the Liturgy: An Exploration of Texts in Christian Worship*. London: Bloomsbury: T&T Clark, 2014.

Notes

1. The best guide for this is Annibale Bugnini, *The Reform of the Liturgy 1948–1975*, trans. Matthew O'Connell (Collegeville, MN: Liturgical Press, 1990).

2. I draw the reader's attention to the vast body of philosophical and theological scholarship that sets language as a central attribute of our sense of self, our knowledge, and our place in reality.

3. The astute reader might realize here that I am writing this paper in the week leading up to the great celebrations of Easter.

4. An astute guide to the question of worship and mystery is Nathan D. Mitchell, *Meeting Mystery* (Maryknoll, NY: Orbis Books, 2006).

5. The General Instruction of the Roman Missal (GIRM) makes the claim that all the prayers, orations, and songs of the liturgy draw their inspiration and spirit from the Scriptures. See GIRM 391.

6. There are over a hundred options of biblical texts for use in the revised rite of penance alone.

7. Note here how our worship seeks to be highly attentive to the actual faithful who are in the congregation. The General Instruction of the Roman Missal directs that choices around options in the worship must be made in full consideration of the needs and condition of the members of the congregation, as seen in GIRM (2000), 352. The *Directory of Masses with Children* is based on this premise.

8. You will be aware of the three liturgical judgements found in the document from the U.S. bishops, *Music in Catholic Worship* (1972/1983): the musical, the liturgical, and the pastoral. See no. 25 and what follows.

9. For a range of baptismal images, see the extensive blessing of the water in the rite of baptism.

10. I am summarizing in brief the foundational studies of such figures as Englishman Edmund Bishop (1846–1917) and German scholar Anton Baumstark (1872–1948) and the research that has followed from their work. The influence of their theories reached the Constitution on the Sacred Liturgy, which reads: "The rites should be distinguished by noble simplicity. They should be short, clear, and free from useless repetitions" (no. 35).

11. This can be seen in the Constitution on the Sacred Liturgy 21–25, where "sound tradition" and "legitimate progress" are noted as requiring careful investigation that is theological, historical, and pastoral.

12. The Council of Trent acknowledges that this transformation is most aptly named as *transubstantiation*. See Session 13, Canons on the most holy sacrament of the eucharist, 2.

13. I am excluding participation in the sacraments themselves here. The point is that now freed from the constraint that Catholic worship required to be expressed in Latin, we have found ourselves able to worship openly and wholeheartedly with our sisters and brothers in other denominations and churches. It must be noted that a good number of these interdenominational services are led by church leaders themselves.

14. For the full text, see the General Instruction of the Roman Missal (2000), 16.

15. While this point has not been developed within the paper, it is a reminder of the contribution of Catholic liturgy to human culture. See Gerard Moore, "In Touch out of Touch: The Church and Reconciliation," in *Indigenous Australia and the Unfinished Business of Theology: Cross Cultural Engagement,* ed. Jione Havea (New York: Palgrave Mac-Millan, 2014), 113–28.

Part II

SYSTEMATIC ISSUES

8

LITURGY AND CHURCH

—ഝ—

Paul McPartlan

INTRODUCTION

In 1992, the *Catechism of the Catholic Church* (*CCC*)[1] defined the church as follows: "'The Church' is the People that God gathers in the whole world. She exists in local communities and is made real as a liturgical, above all a Eucharistic, assembly. She draws her life from the word and the Body of Christ and so herself becomes Christ's Body" (*CCC* 752). Such a definition, particularly at the level of formal doctrine, would have been unthinkable prior to the mid-twentieth century. It is a fruit of the biblical, liturgical, and patristic renewal movements of the first half of that century—"the century of the Church"[2]—and especially of the Second Vatican Council (1962–65).

In marked contrast to the institutional and juridical definition of the church as a "perfect society" that had dominated Catholic ecclesiology through most of the second millennium, the Council spoke of the church both liturgically and sacramentally. At the start of its Constitution on the Sacred Liturgy, *Sacrosanctum Concilium* (*SC*; 1963), it said, "It is through the liturgy, especially, that the faithful are enabled to express in their lives and manifest to others the mystery of Christ and the real nature of the true Church" (*SC* 2),[3] and it went on to describe the church's twofold nature, both human and divine, visible and invisible, anticipating the profound analogy between the mystery of the church and that of the incarnate Christ himself proposed in the Dogmatic Constitution on the Church, *Lumen Gentium* (*LG*; 1964; see *LG* 8). This and many other correspondences between the two constitutions show how deeply interwoven they are, to such an extent that *LG* can almost be seen as a subsequent dogmatic commentary on *SC*.

Correspondingly, the Council presented the liturgy ecclesially. It is the prayer of the church, not just of individuals, and most truly it is the prayer of Christ the Lord, "who always associates the Church with himself in this great work in which God is glorified and [human beings] are sanctified" (*SC* 7). The church thus participates in the liturgy of Christ himself, our "great high priest" (Heb 4:14). As the Council says, the liturgy "is rightly seen as an exercise of the priestly office of Jesus Christ," in which "full public worship is performed by the Mystical Body of Jesus Christ, that is, by the Head and his members" (*SC* 7). This Christocentric focus is mirrored in *Lumen Gentium*, which begins, "Lumen gentium cum sit Christus" (*LG* 1). Christ himself is the light of the nations, and the church, mystically constituted as his Body by the Holy Spirit (*LG* 7), is called to transmit that light.

The church thus understood, inwardly united with Christ and outwardly radiating his light, is sacramental. "If Christ is the sacrament of God, the Church is for us the sacrament of Christ," said Henri de Lubac in 1938.[4] The Council repeatedly spoke of the church in these terms, and the idea of the church as sacrament again weaves together *SC* and *LG*: the church is "the sacrament of unity" (*SC* 26, also 5), "the universal sacrament of salvation" (*LG* 48, also 1, 9). The Council's Pastoral Constitution on the Church in the Modern World, *Gaudium et Spes* (*GS*; 1965), can in turn be seen as an extended commentary on the opening paragraph of *LG*, and it too focuses on the idea of the church as sacrament: "Every benefit that the people of God can confer on [humankind] during its earthly pilgrimage is rooted in the Church's being 'the universal sacrament of salvation,' at once manifesting and actualizing the mystery of God's love for [humanity]" (*GS* 45).

Being united in Christ, participating both in his worship of God and in his mission in the world,[5] the church should be understood in an intensely dynamic way. Never more truly itself than when gathered for the liturgy and primarily for the Eucharist—St. Paul indeed speaks of gathering for the Eucharist as gathering "as a church" (1 Cor 11:18)[6]—the Christian community is then sent out at the end of the liturgy: *Ite missa est*, a sending so intrinsic to the very meaning of the assembly that it has given to the Eucharist its normal Catholic name, the Mass. In other words, to say that the church *gathers* for the Eucharist expresses only half of the reality; it is equally true that it is from the Eucharist that the church is regularly *sent out* again on mission. We gather and we go, we gather and we go—the eucharistic heartbeat of the church.[7]

By the gift of the Spirit, the church's life in Christ, as his Body, is one of communion (see 2 Cor 13:13), and in the Eucharist the members of the church "receive communion" afresh. They receive the Body of Christ to become the Body of Christ, hence de Lubac's principle: "the Eucharist makes the Church."[8] The Russian Orthodox Alexander Schmemann movingly says, "The Eucharist is the entrance of the Church into the joy of its Lord. And to enter into that joy, so as to be a witness to it in the world, is indeed the very calling of the Church, its essential *leitourgia*, the sacrament by which it 'becomes what it is.'"[9]

The ultimate source of the communion in which the church participates in Christ and the Spirit is the Trinity itself. After considering the church in relation to the Father, the Son, and the Spirit (*LG* 2–4), respectively, the Council says in summary, "The universal Church is seen to be 'a people brought into unity from the unity of the Father, the Son and the Holy Spirit.'"[10] Gathered in Christ and worshiping the Father "through him and with him and in him, in the unity of the Holy Spirit," the church is renewed in its participation in the very life of God and is sent out to minister communion to a divided world: "In her whole being and in all her members, the Church is sent to announce, bear witness [to], make present, and spread the mystery of the communion of the Holy Trinity" (*CCC* 738). Drawing these threads together, it may be said that "the Church as communion is a sacrament for the salvation of the world."[11]

The twentieth-century biblical, liturgical, and patristic renewal that has fostered a sacramental and eucharistic understanding of the church has had a particular impact on Catholic and Orthodox ecclesiology. While de Lubac was responsible for the famous principle quoted earlier, the phrase "eucharistic ecclesiology" was actually coined by the Russian Orthodox Nicholas Afanasiev, to describe an understanding as follows: "Where there is the eucharistic assembly, there is Christ, and there is the Church of God in Christ."[12] Convergence along these lines has been a major factor in promoting Catholic-Orthodox ecumenical dialogue. The programmatic first agreed statement of the international dialogue said in 1982, "The eucharistic celebration makes present the Trinitarian mystery of the Church,"[13] and the dialogue has worked within the framework of a eucharistic ecclesiology ever since. Invoking key patristic figures from East and West, the North American Orthodox-Catholic dialogue likewise said in 1989,

> When it gathers, under the life-giving impulse of the Holy Spirit, to celebrate in the Eucharist the Son's "obedience unto death" (Phil. 2.8) and to be nourished by participation in his risen life, the Church most fully expresses what, in God's order of salvation, it is: an assembly of faithful human persons who are brought into communion by and with the persons of the Holy Trinity, and who look forward to the fulfillment of that communion in eternal glory. So the clearest human reflection of the Church's divine vocation is the Christian community united to celebrate the Eucharist, gathered by its common faith, in all its variety of persons and functions, around a single table, under a single president [*proestos*], to hear the Gospel proclaimed and to share in the sacramental reality of the Lord's flesh and blood ([St.] Ignatius [of Antioch], Eph 5.2–3; Philad. 4), and so to manifest those gathered there as "partakers of the divine nature" (2 Pet 1:4). "If you are the Body of Christ and his members," proclaims St. Augustine, "your divine mystery is set on the table of the Lord; you receive your own mystery.... Be what you see and receive what you are." (Serm. 272)[14]

THE EUCHARIST MAKES THE CHURCH

The link between the Eucharist and the church is particularly clear in Paul's words to the Corinthians: "The cup of blessing that we bless, is it not a sharing in the blood of Christ? The bread that we break, is it not a sharing in the body of Christ? Because there is one bread, we who are many are one body, for we all partake of the one bread" (1 Cor 10:16–17)—the Eucharist makes the church. The letters of the New Testament were written to local communities and read when they gathered for the liturgy on the Lord's day. That eucharistic setting could be presumed by the writers, and it seems to explain the following passage from the Letter to the Hebrews:

> You have come to Mount Zion and to the city of the living God, the heavenly Jerusalem, and to innumerable angels in festal gathering, and to the assembly [*ekklesia*] of the first-born who are enrolled in heaven, and to God the judge of all, and to the spirits of the righteous made perfect, and to Jesus, the mediator of a new covenant, and to the sprinkled blood that speaks a better word than the blood of Abel. (Heb 12:22–24)

It seems that the earthly liturgy gives a foretaste of the last day itself, judgement day, and of the heavenly liturgy in which the whole church (*ekklesia*) is gathered around the throne of God, where Jesus intercedes for us with his blood shed for the salvation of the world.

The *Catechism* teaches that the church, properly speaking, is that final heavenly community—"the goal of all things" (*CCC* 760), the gathering in God's kingdom of the multitude "from every tribe and language and people and nation" (Rev 5:9)—and the Hebrews passage seems to indicate that that heavenly mystery is revealed to the earthly church in the celebration of the Eucharist. If, as *LG* 8 teaches, the church (as sacrament) is "a complex reality," both human and divine, at once "earthly" and "endowed with heavenly riches," it would appear that the Eucharist, when the earthly encounters the heavenly, is its defining celebration and the occasion when it is most truly itself. *Lumen Gentium* 50 indeed says, "It is especially in the sacred liturgy that our union with the heavenly Church is best realized." As *SC* teaches, the liturgical celebrations of the local church, and especially the Eucharist, when all the people gather around their bishop with his presbyters and ministers at one altar, constitute "the principal manifestation of the Church" (*SC* 41). If the church is "the sacrament of the unity of the human race," "the 'sign and instrument' of the full realization of the unity yet to come" (*CCC* 775), the Eucharist would again seem to be the occasion when that is most truly the case. Again, the Eucharist appears to be the church's defining celebration. It is in and from the Eucharist that the church most truly lives.

In the eucharistic context of the Last Supper in John's Gospel, Jesus tells the apostles that the Spirit whom the Father will send will "remind you of all that I have said to you" (John 14:26) and will "declare to you the things that are to come" (John 16:13). It is therefore by the work of the Spirit that the earthly community in the Eucharist regularly receives a foretaste of the heavenly church and is united with that church (*LG* 50). Notably, also, the Lamb being praised by the multitude in the heavenly liturgy as described in the Book of Revelation bore the marks of having been slain (Rev 5:6; cf. John 20:19–20, 26–28). The heavenly praise is a song of victory (Rev 5:9–12). Calvary is not forgotten in heaven; rather, it appears that heaven will be the everlasting celebration of the victory won on Calvary. The foretaste of heaven thus confronts the faithful with the paschal mystery of the death and resurrection of Christ, and in declaring the things that are to come, the Spirit therefore also reminds the faithful of what Christ said and did for our salvation. In other words, it is possible to see the memorial of Christ's passion, which is essential to the Eucharist (*SC* 47), as contained within the foretaste of the heavenly liturgy celebrated in the Holy City of Jerusalem, which is given to the faithful in the earthly liturgy while still on their pilgrim way (*SC* 8).

Whereas it might be thought that the Mass is an occasion when each of the faithful as an individual encounters Christ and is fed by him in a reenactment of the past event of the Last Supper, it is clear that that picture needs a threefold complement: it is the church that is fed, not just individuals; not only Christ is present, but the Spirit also; and as well as being a memorial of the past, the Eucharist is also a foretaste of the future kingdom. The bond between the Eucharist and the church is thus best understood with the help of a strong pneumatology and eschatology. The latter have traditionally been found more in the Christian East, but ecumenical dialogue has enabled those gifts to be shared. The three complementary perspectives are notably strong in the 1982 Catholic-Orthodox agreed statement[15] and in other ecumenical agreements on the Eucharist.

Thus, the church is fashioned in the Eucharist. The earthly, pilgrim church is strengthened and uplifted as it encounters the heavenly church but is also called to conversion and repentance for its sins.[16] It is shaped and molded for its heavenly destiny: the Eucharist makes the church. "Everything in the Church is organized with a view to the 'new creature' [2 Cor 5:17],"[17] says de Lubac, and that activity culminates in the Eucharist: "we must all be molten in that crucible of unity which is the Eucharist."[18] With the regular celebration of the Eucharist likewise in mind, the Greek Orthodox John Zizioulas memorably says that the church "is what she is by becoming again and again what she will be."[19]

WORD AND SACRAMENT

As has been mentioned, de Lubac coined the principle, "the Eucharist makes the Church."[20] He produced major works not only on ecclesiology but also on spiritual exegesis, and in connection with the writings of Origen, he said the following:

> The life of the Church has its source in Scripture. It has it no less in the Eucharist. Scripture and Eucharist, moreover, appear closely associated in everything, since it is in the midst of the same assembly, in the course of the same liturgy, that the Bread of the Word is broken and the Body of the Lord is distributed....It is not possible for Scripture and the Eucharist not to be made, so to speak, from the same material and not to constitute at bottom the same Mystery, since in both of them it is the same Logos of God who comes to us and lifts us up to him. Just as there is a spiritual sense of Scripture, so there must be a spiritual sense of the Eucharist, and if we get to the bottom, we will find that it is identical in both.[21]

It would seem, therefore, that we must also say that Scripture (or the Word) makes the church. However, lest we think that this has now blurred the focus, and that we need to develop another line of thought alongside the one we have pursued here, let us notice de Lubac's unifying pointer to the single Mystery at work: both in Scripture and in the Eucharist, the same Logos comes to lift us up to himself.[22] Vatican II stressed that the two parts of the Mass, the Liturgy of the Word and the Liturgy of the Eucharist, "form but one single act of worship" (*SC* 56).[23] However, particularly since Word and Sacrament have been tragically polarized in Catholic-Protestant polemic over the years, we must be wary lest we simply juxtapose the two parts. The unity between them must be grasped in depth, as Schmemann indicates:

> Western Christians are so accustomed to distinguish the Word from the sacrament that it may be difficult for them to understand that in the Orthodox perspective the liturgy of the Word is as sacramental as the sacrament is "evangelical." The sacrament is a manifestation of the Word. And unless the false dichotomy between Word and sacrament is overcome, the true meaning of both Word and sacrament, and especially the true meaning of Christian "sacramentalism" cannot be grasped in all their wonderful implications. The proclamation of the Word is a sacramental act par excellence because it is a transforming act. It transforms the human words of the Gospel into the Word of God and the manifestation of the Kingdom. And it transforms the man who hears the Word into a receptacle of the Word and a temple of the Spirit.[24]

St. Paul's teaching is an essential reference point in this regard: "as often as you eat this bread and drink the cup, you proclaim the Lord's death until he comes" (1 Cor 11:26). As it is more satisfactory to see "the whole eucharistic prayer as consecratory" rather than simply isolating the words of consecration,[25] so it may be helpful to see the entirety of the Mass as both Word and Sacrament, rather than demarcating too rigidly the Liturgy of the Word and the Liturgy of the Eucharist. The necessary integration was nicely expressed by Catholics and Orthodox in the 1982 agreed statement:

> The Eucharist is inseparably Sacrament and Word since in it the incarnate Word sanctifies in the Spirit. That is why the entire liturgy and not only the reading of the Holy Scriptures constitutes a proclamation of the Word under the form of doxology and prayer. On the other hand, the word proclaimed is the Word made flesh and become sacramental.[26]

It is also important to recall that the New Testament actually took shape in and around the eucharistic celebration of the early church. As Denis Farkasfalvy says, "All New Testament Scripture has a Eucharistic provenance."[27] Not only does the New Testament tell us *about* the Eucharist; it is itself "the product of the apostolic church's eucharistic practice."[28] The church followed the instruction of the Lord to "Do this in remembrance of me" (1 Cor 11:24–25) from the start, but only gradually determined the canon of New Testament writings through their usage in the liturgy. Zizioulas similarly bids us recognize that "without the Church's liturgical experience we would not have the New Testament, certainly not in its actual content and form."[29] In a sense, therefore, as the Word is sacramentalized in the Eucharist, so the Eucharist is "verbalized" in the New Testament. Not forgetting that the Liturgy of the Word contains also the Old Testament, which is intimately linked to the New,[30] we see again how deeply united with the Liturgy of the Eucharist it is.

LITURGY AND STRUCTURE

If the church is considered in a liturgical and sacramental way rather than primarily juridically, then in accord with its sacramental nature, there are two aspects of the church that need to be considered, namely, the outer and the inner, the church's structure and its life. This section and the following one consider these in turn.

That the liturgy has structural implications for the church, and that the church should indeed be structured on that basis, has been clearly affirmed from both Catholic and Orthodox standpoints in recent times and constitutes one of the most remarkable and consequential points of convergence between Catholics and Orthodox. In an account of "The ecclesiology of the Second Vatican Council," Joseph Ratzinger states, "The Church lives in eucharistic communities. Its worship is its constitution, since of its nature it is itself the service of God and thus of men and women, the service of transforming the world."[31] In his book *The Church of the Holy Spirit*, Afanasiev likewise firmly states, "The structure and order of the Church originate in the eucharistic assembly, the foundation of the Church's entire organization."[32] Stressing the trinitarian source of the church's life, the international Catholic-Orthodox dialogue made a strikingly comprehensive statement in its opening document similarly relating the church's institutions to the Eucharist:

> The church finds its model, its origin and its purpose in the mystery of God, one in three persons. Further still, the eucharist thus understood in the light of the Trinitarian mystery is the criterion for functioning of the life of the church as a whole. The institutional elements should be nothing but a visible reflection of the reality of the mystery.[33]

As is very clear in the opening quotation from the *Catechism* stated earlier, eucharistic ecclesiology highlights the local church. As we have already noted, Vatican II saw the eucharistic celebration of the local church around its bishop as "the principal manifestation of the Church" (*SC* 41), implicitly recognizing that liturgically there is no such thing as a universal celebration of the Eucharist around a universal bishop. The pope is the bishop of Rome (the "Roman Pontiff") and "pastor of the universal church" (*LG*; *Nota Explicativa Praevia* 3; also *LG* 22 and *Nota* 4), but not a universal bishop. This is a point of great historical importance, since, as Yves Congar notes, in the Gregorian Reform of the late eleventh century, popes began to embrace the ideas of the church as "a single diocese" and of the pope as "the universal bishop."[34] It was the development of this pyramidal understanding of the church, and of the pope as having the fullness of power (*plenitudo potestatis*) and a universal jurisdiction, that precipitated the schism of 1054 between West and East. Theologians in the new mendicant orders developed this understanding of the church as a "perfect society," fully equipped to run its own affairs independently of the state or the empire, while the East maintained a "sacral order" according to which "each local church fully realized the mystery of the Church."[35] Given this background, it can clearly be seen why the development of a eucharistic ecclesiology with a renewed emphasis on the local church in recent theology, both Catholic and Orthodox, has led to such a rapprochement between West and East.

Fundamental to that ecclesiology is the idea of the bishop as "high priest," pastor of his local church and presider at its liturgy. Leading the church and presiding at the liturgy were twin responsibilities in the early church.[36] If the Eucharist makes the church, then the pastor of the local church will naturally have particular care for the Eucharist and be its primary presider (see *LG* 26). One of the hallmarks of Scholastic theology was its separation of those responsibilities, in accord with its understanding of the exercise of two powers in the church: power of order and power of jurisdiction. The power of order culminated in the power of the priest to consecrate bread and wine into the Body and Blood of Christ in the Mass; thus, though the phrase was not used at that time, priests had "the fullness of the sacrament of orders." Bishops had the same power of order as priests but additional power of jurisdiction, received from the pope who had the fullness of power, as we have seen. Thus, in short, priests celebrated the Eucharist, while the pope and the bishops governed the church. It was understood that the pope called bishops "*in partem sollicitudinis,*" that is, to share in his solicitude for the church, and this idea was closely associated with the new title for the pope that Innocent III (1198–1216) adopted: "vicar of Christ."[37]

Ratzinger refers to "the separation of the doctrine of the eucharist and ecclesiology, which can be noted from the eleventh and twelfth centuries onwards," as "one of the most unfortunate pages of medieval theology."[38] The separation, compounded by the juridical developments just described, was actually precipitated by the eucharistic controversy provoked by Berengar of Tours (c. 1000–1088), who denied the transformation of bread and wine into the Body and Blood of Christ in the Mass. As a result, that transformation, instead of being understood as enabling those who then received the Eucharist to be transformed themselves into the Body of Christ, itself became the major focus of eucharistic theology in the West, and the second half of the eucharistic mystery, so to speak, whereby the Eucharist was understood as making the church, was neglected and eventually forgotten. As de Lubac regretfully says regarding the Eucharist, "The mystery to be understood" became "the miracle to be believed."[39] A static picture replaced the fathers' dynamic understanding, and uniting the church became a juridical task (of the pope and the bishops) separate from celebrating the Eucharist (a priestly task). Some theologians were troubled by not finding the real presence as clearly expressed as they might wish in patristic teaching. De Lubac urged them to recognize that the real presence was actually implicit in the patristic doctrine that the Eucharist really makes the church! "Eucharistic realism and ecclesial realism…support one another, each is the guarantee of the other."[40] Such people should realize, he said, that "the essential perspective of the [patristic] texts is not that of a presence or of an object, but that of an action and of a sacrifice."[41]

We shall return to that crucial notion of sacrifice in the final section, but first we must note how fully Vatican II repaired the long-standing separation between Eucharist and church. In various phrasings, *LG* teaches at several points that the Eucharist makes the church (see *LG* 3, 7, 11, 26), and it formally declares that episcopal consecration is to be understood as "the fullness of the sacrament of Orders," that fullness which the fathers of the church call "the high priesthood" (*LG* 21). The Scholastic idea of the ordained exercising two powers in the church, a view that left the laity powerless at the bottom of the pyramid, is replaced by the idea of all of the baptized participating in the three offices (*munera*) of Christ, as prophet, priest, and king (*LG* 31), with the ordained receiving further participations in those same three offices in order to fulfill their particular ministries (*LG* 21, 28, 29). It is said that bishops receive all three *munera* in their episcopal ordination (*LG* 21), implicitly amending the view that they receive the juridical power of the kingly office from the pope, though it is stressed that the offices of teaching and ruling "of their very nature" can be *exercised* only in communion with the pope and with the other bishops (*LG* 21).

This sacramental understanding of the bishop leads immediately to the Council's teaching on collegiality, whereby the bishops form a college headed by the pope, and together with him have "supreme and full authority over the universal Church" (*LG* 22). We are thereby led to see collegiality itself as having a sacramental rather than a purely juridical basis: each bishop presides over the Eucharist of his local church, but the fact that there is only one Eucharist by which Christ the Lord feeds his church draws them all together in care for the church as a whole. Likewise, since each bishop "takes the place of Christ himself, teacher, shepherd and priest, and acts in his person [*in eius persona*]" (*LG* 21; amended trans.), and since there is only one Christ, all bishops are profoundly united in Christ, caring as one for his church. Following this logic, the Council states that all bishops are to be understood as "vicars and legates of Christ" and not as "vicars of the Roman Pontiff" (*LG* 27), which was always a danger in the pyramidal view. Consolidating the shift from a pyramidal to a communional view of the church, the Council teaches that the local or particular churches are "constituted after the model of the universal Church" and that it is "in these and formed out of them that the one and unique Catholic Church exists," such that the Mystical Body can be understood as "a corporate body of Churches" (*LG* 23).[42]

The fact that each local church celebrates the one Eucharist of the church means that all the local churches are fundamentally open to one another and to the church universal. Zizioulas emphasizes this essential openness and sees the early development of councils of bishops as an important expression of it.[43] In 1992, the Congregation for the Doctrine of the Faith also emphasized "the necessary openness of every celebrating community, of every particular Church," and it proposed that the Petrine ministry, which Catholics believe to be "a foundation of the unity of the episcopate and of the universal Church," should therefore be understood as bearing "a profound correspondence to the Eucharistic character of the Church."[44] This is an important example of the remarkable development in Catholic theology in recent times toward seeing the universal primacy of the pope not primarily as a juridical office but rather as a ministry symbolizing and serving the eucharistic unity of the church.[45] This development clearly has great ecumenical potential, particularly with regard to Catholic-Orthodox relations.[46]

LITURGY AND LIFE

Having considered how the liturgy, and especially the Eucharist, shapes the structure of the church understood as a sacrament, let us now finally consider how the liturgy, and especially the Eucharist, shapes the actual life of the church. As we have seen, de Lubac emphasizes that the Eucharist is "an action and...a sacrifice."[47] He insists that it is not just a human "gathering": "The memorial of the Passion, the offering to the heavenly Father, the conversion of the heart: these...are the totally interior realities without which we will never have anything but a caricature of the community that we seek."[48] In other words, the inward grace of communion that should accompany the outward sign of communion in the church as sacrament of communion is a gift of God and can only be received from him by repentance and prayer in and through the one sacrifice of Christ.

Vatican II likewise highlights the aspect of sacrifice in its description (*LG* again echoing *SC*) of the dynamic relationship between the liturgy and the church.

> The liturgy is the summit toward which the activity of the Church is directed; it is also the fount from which all her power flows. For the goal of apostolic endeavor is that all who are made [children] of God by faith and baptism should come together to praise God in the midst of his Church, *to take part in the Sacrifice* and to eat the Lord's Supper. (*SC* 10; emphasis added)

> Taking part in the *eucharistic sacrifice*, the source and summit of the Christian life, [the faithful] offer the divine

victim to God and themselves along with it. (*LG* 11; emphasis added)

The "full, conscious, and active participation" (*SC* 14) of all the faithful in the liturgy that the Council urges therefore means participating in the one, unrepeatable sacrifice of Christ and joining the sacrifice of oneself to it, and that by definition is a priestly activity. Elaborating the teaching of *SC*, *LG* says, "By virtue of their royal priesthood, [the faithful] participate in the offering of the Eucharist" (no. 10).

As we saw earlier, the liturgy is "an exercise of the priestly office of Jesus Christ," in which Christ associates the church with himself as his bride and his Body, such that the church through him "offers worship to the eternal Father" (*SC* 7). This is how the injunction given in the First Letter of Peter is fulfilled: "like living stones, let yourselves be built into a spiritual house, to be a holy priesthood, to offer spiritual sacrifices acceptable to God through Jesus Christ" (1 Pet 2:5). Christ unites all the faithful with himself as he offers his own sacrifice, and through him and with him and in him they offer the sacrifice of themselves. St. Augustine gave a matchless description of the dynamism of the eucharistic sacrifice in his *City of God*:

> The whole of that redeemed city, that is, the congregation or communion of saints, is offered as a universal sacrifice to God through the High Priest who, "taking the form of a servant," offered Himself in His passion for us that we might be the body of so glorious a Head....
>
> Such is the sacrifice of Christians: "We, the many, are one body in Christ." This is the Sacrifice, as the faithful understand, which the Church continues to celebrate in the sacrament of the altar, in which it is clear to the Church that she herself is offered in the very offering she makes to God.[49]

Though the time of persecution was over, Augustine taught that the idea of sacrifice was as important as ever. He recalled the teaching of Paul: "I appeal to you therefore, brothers and sisters, by the mercies of God, to present your bodies as a living sacrifice, holy and acceptable to God, which is your spiritual worship" (Rom 12:1). He also said that there is "a true sacrifice in every work which unites us in a holy communion with God." He noted that *sacrificium* (*sacrum + facere*) refers to what is made holy by being offered to God.[50] Our bodies and souls should be dedicated to the service of God.[51] As Christ and the church together form the "*totus Christus, caput et corpus*,"[52] so the church's sacrifice when joined with his becomes the *totum sacrificium*: "it is we ourselves who constitute the whole sacrifice."[53]

So we see the immense significance of the renewal at Vatican II of the idea that all of the baptized participate in the three offices of Christ, as prophet, priest, and king, as noted earlier, and we see also that the priestly office in a sense unites the other two. Just as all of Christ's preaching and service (as prophet and king, respectively) were part of his perpetual self-offering to his Father that culminated on the cross (see Heb 5:7–9), so too all that the faithful say and do is meant to be taken up as spiritual sacrifices in their own self-offering. The Council's description of that offering is comprehensive:

> The laity, dedicated as they are to Christ and anointed by the Holy Spirit, are marvelously called and prepared so that even richer fruits of the Spirit may be produced in them. For all their works, prayers and apostolic undertakings, family and married life, daily work, relaxation of mind and body, if they are accomplished in the Spirit—and indeed [*imo*] the hardships of life if patiently borne—all these become spiritual sacrifices acceptable to God through Jesus Christ (cf. 1 Pet 2:5). In the celebration of the Eucharist these may most fittingly be offered to the Father along with the body of the Lord. (*LG* 34; amended trans.)

The above paragraph concludes with a most remarkable statement: "And so, worshipping everywhere by their holy actions, the laity consecrate the world itself to God" (*LG* 34). Clearly, the consecration of the world, which is the task of the church as the "universal sacrament of salvation" (*LG* 48),[54] depends on the priestly activity of the laity, and that priestly activity depends on constant interaction with the priesthood of Christ and with his one sacrifice. The role of the ministerial priesthood of bishops and presbyters is precisely to make Christ and his priesthood and his sacrifice sacramentally present and accessible so that that vital interaction can occur:[55] "the common priesthood of the faithful and the ministerial or hierarchical priesthood are...ordered one to another; each in its own proper way shares in the one priesthood of Christ" (*LG* 10).

Let us finally recognize the essential link between the priesthood of all the faithful and the universal call to holiness to which *LG* devoted a whole chapter (nos. 39–42). As Jean-Pierre Torrell says, "[The] Christian and ecclesial holiness preached by the Council...has a priestly modality."[56] As the Council drew to a close, Pope Paul VI himself made the connection with great urgency. With reference to the teaching of St. Augustine above, he notes that the Council reiterated the "wondrous doctrine" that "the whole Church plays the role of priest and victim along with Christ, offering the sacrifice of the Mass and itself completely offered in it," and says that he is "filled with an earnest desire to see this teaching explained over and over until it takes deep root in the hearts of the faithful," because "it is a most effective means of fostering devotion to the Eucharist, of extolling the dignity of all the faithful, and of spurring them on to reach the heights of sanctity."[57]

If sanctity is participation in the communion life of God, and if the church is truly to be "*the home and the school of communion*,"[58] we may surely say that the liturgy, and most especially the Eucharist, is our inspiration and our classroom.

Notes

1. *Catechism of the Catholic Church* (Rome: Libreria Editrice Vaticana, 1997).

2. See Henri de Lubac, *The Splendor of the Church*, trans. Michael Mason (San Francisco: Ignatius Press, 1986; French orig. 1953), 27: "It seems as if, as far as the development of doctrine is concerned, the twentieth century is destined to be 'the century of the Church.'"

3. Unless otherwise noted, Vatican II quotations are taken from Austin Flannery, ed., *Vatican Council II: The Conciliar and Post Conciliar Documents* (Dublin: Dominican Publications, 1975).

4. Henri de Lubac, *Catholicism: Christ and the Common Destiny of Man*, trans. Lancelot C. Sheppard and Sr. Elizabeth Englund, OCD (San Francisco: Ignatius Press, 1988), 76.

5. See Pope Benedict XVI, Apostolic Exhortation, *Sacramentum Caritatis* (Rome: Libreria Editrice Vaticana, 2007), 55.

6. See *CCC* 752; also, John Zizioulas, *Being as Communion* (London: Darton, Longman and Todd, 1986), 148.

7. See Paul McPartlan, *Sacrament of Salvation: An Introduction to Eucharistic Ecclesiology* (Edinburgh: T & T Clark, 1995), 61.

8. Henri de Lubac, *Corpus Mysticum: The Eucharist and the Church in the Middle Ages*, trans. Gemma Simmonds with Richard Price (London: SCM, 2006), 88. See also, Paul McPartlan, *The Eucharist Makes the Church: Henri de Lubac and John Zizioulas in Dialogue*, 2nd ed. (Fairfax, VA: Eastern Christian Publications, 2006). Joseph Ratzinger notes, "'Communion ecclesiology' is in its inmost nature a eucharistic ecclesiology"; *Pilgrim Fellowship of Faith: The Church as Communion*, ed. Stephan Otto Horn and Vinzenz Pfnür, trans. Henry Taylor (San Francisco: Ignatius Press, 2005), 131.

9. Alexander Schmemann, *For the Life of the World: Sacraments and Orthodoxy* (Crestwood, NY: St. Vladimir's Seminary Press, 1973), 26. See Pope Francis, Apostolic Exhortation, *Evangelii Gaudium* (Rome: Libreria Editrice Vaticana, 2013), 5.

10. *LG* 4; quoting St. Cyprian, *De Orat. Dom.* 23 (PL 4:556).

11. "The Church in the Word of God celebrates the mysteries of Christ for the salvation of the world," Final *Relatio* of the 1985 Extraordinary Assembly of the Synod of Bishops, II, D, 1, in *L'Osservatore Romano*, weekly edition, December 16, 1985, 6–9, at 9.

12. Nicholas Afanasiev, "Una Sancta," in *Tradition Alive*, ed. Michael Plekon (Lanham, MD: Rowman and Littlefield, 2003), 3–30, at 14, 18. For the influence of Afanasiev on the drafting of *LG*, see Paul McPartlan, "Eucharistic Ecclesiology," *One in Christ* 22 (1986): 314–31, at 325–27.

13. Joint International Commission for Theological Dialogue between the Roman Catholic Church and the Orthodox Church, "The Mystery of the Church and of the Eucharist in the Light of the Mystery of the Holy Trinity" (1982), I, 6, in *The Journey towards Unity: The Orthodox-Catholic Dialogue Statements*, ed. Ronald G. Roberson, Thomas FitzGerald, and Jack Figel, 2 vols. (Fairfax, VA: Eastern Christian Publications, 2016), 2:29–42, at 32.

14. North American Orthodox-Catholic Theological Consultation, "On Conciliarity and Primacy in the Church" (1989), 3, in Roberson, FitzGerald, and Figel, *The Journey towards Unity*, 1:91–95, at 92.

15. See "The Mystery of the Church and of the Eucharist," e.g., I, 4; I, 5; and I, 2, respectively.

16. See McPartlan, *Sacrament of Salvation*, 1–13.

17. "So if anyone is in Christ, there is a new creation: everything old has passed away; see, everything has become new!"

18. De Lubac, *The Splendor of the Church*, 147–48.

19. John Zizioulas, "The Mystery of the Church in Orthodox Tradition," *One in Christ* 24 (1988): 294–303, at 301.

20. In fact, he elaborated a double principle: "the Church makes [*fait*] the Eucharist" and "the Eucharist makes [*fait*] the Church." But it was the latter that he wanted to restore as the proper complement of the former. Church and Eucharist, he said, stand "as cause to each other": "the one Body...builds itself up through this mysterious interaction in and through the conditions of our present existence up to the day of its consummation" (de Lubac, *The Splendor of the Church*, 134, also 152).

21. Henri de Lubac, *History and Spirit: The Understanding of Scripture according to Origen*, trans. Anne Englund Nash and Juvenal Merriell (San Francisco: Ignatius Press, 2007), 407, see also 418. On the links between de Lubac's work on spiritual exegesis, on ecclesiology, and on nature and the supernatural, see Kevin L. Hughes, "The Spiritual Interpretation of Scripture," in *The T & T Clark Companion to Henri de Lubac*, ed. Jordan Hillebert (London: Bloomsbury, 2017), 205–23.

22. We might recall the phrase that Augustine heard in his encounter with the Word of God, words subsequently applied by de Lubac to the Eucharist: "You will not change me into you...[but] you will be changed into me" (Augustine, *Confessions*, 7, 10, 16; see de Lubac, *Corpus Mysticum*, 178; *Catholicism*, 99–100; McPartlan, *The Eucharist Makes the Church*, 67–68).

23. In the Mass, the faithful are nourished both "at the table of God's word" and "at the table of the Lord's Body" (*SC* 48, 51). Later, in its Dogmatic Constitution on Divine Revelation, *Dei Verbum* (*DV*; 1965), the Council notably integrated these ideas: in the sacred liturgy, the church offers "the bread of life" to the faithful "from the one table of the word of God and the Body of Christ" (*DV* 21; amended translation).

24. Schmemann, *For the Life of the World*, 32–33.

25. See John H. McKenna, *The Eucharistic Epiclesis: A Detailed History from the Patristic to the Modern Era* (Chicago/Mundelein: Hillenbrand Books, 2009), 204–6.

26. "The Mystery of the Church," II, 2; in Roberson, FitzGerald, and Figel, *The Journey towards Unity*, 1:36 (translation amended to reflect the capitalization in the French original).

27. Denis Farkasfalvy, *Inspiration and Interpretation: A Theological Introduction to Sacred Scripture* (Washington, DC: The Catholic University of America Press, 2010), 63.

28. Denis Farkasfalvy, "The Eucharistic Provenance of New Testament Texts," in *Rediscovering the Eucharist: Ecumenical Conversations*, ed. Roch Kereszty (Mahwah, NJ: Paulist Press, 2003), 27–51, at 28. See, e.g., the above interpretations of the Letter to the Hebrews and the Book of Revelation.

29. John Zizioulas, "The Existential Significance of Liturgical Time" (unpublished paper), quoted in McPartlan, *The Eucharist Makes the Church*, 133–34.

30. Using a memorable image, Henri de Lubac says that "as the seed gives way to the fruit in which the seed again appears," so "the Old Testament lives on, transfigured, in the New"; *Scripture in the Tradition*, trans. Luke O'Neill, intro. Peter Casarella (New York: Crossroad, 2000), 175; see also *DV* 14–16.

31. Joseph Ratzinger, "The Ecclesiology of the Second Vatican Council," in *Church, Ecumenism and Politics* (Slough: St. Paul Publications, 1988), 3–20, at 8. The similarity between this statement and the opening quotation from the *Catechism* is no coincidence. Cardinal Ratzinger was president of the commission that drafted the *Catechism*.

32. Nicholas Afanasiev, *The Church of the Holy Spirit*, trans. Vitaly Permiakov, ed. and intro. Michael Plekon (Notre Dame, IN: University of Notre Dame Press, 2007), 136.

33. "The Mystery of the Church," II, 1 (see also III, 2); in Roberson, FitzGerald, and Figel, *The Journey towards Unity*, 1:35 (also 39–40). The precise meaning and implications of this principle, especially with regard to universal primacy, are still being worked out; see Paul McPartlan, "Primacy and Eucharist: Recent Catholic Perspectives," in *Primacy in the Church: The Office of Primate and the Authority of Councils*, ed. John Chryssavgis, vol. 1 (Yonkers, NY: St. Vladimir's Seminary Press, 2016), 217–36.

34. Yves Congar, "De la communion des églises a une ecclésiologie de l'église universelle," in *L'Épiscopat et l'Église Universelle*, ed. Y. Congar and B. D. Dupuy (Paris: Cerf, 1964), 227–60, at 238.

35. Yves Congar, *L'ecclésiologie du haut Moyen-Age* (Paris: Cerf, 1968), 388–90.

36. See Hervé-Marie Legrand, "The Presidency of the Eucharist According to the Ancient Tradition," in *Living Bread, Saving Cup: Readings on the Eucharist*, ed. R. Kevin Seasoltz (Collegeville, MN: Liturgical Press, 1987), 196–221.

37. See Paul McPartlan, *A Service of Love: Papal Primacy, the Eucharist and Church Unity*, 2nd ed. (Washington, DC: The Catholic University of America Press, 2016), 31–34.

38. Joseph Ratzinger, "The Pastoral Implications of Episcopal Collegiality," *Concilium* 1, no. 1 (1965): 20–34, at 28.

39. De Lubac, *Corpus Mysticum*, 240.

40. De Lubac, *Corpus Mysticum*, 251, 253. See also, *The Splendor of the Church*, 158n134.

41. De Lubac, *Corpus Mysticum*, 65. Also advocating a dynamic view, Zizioulas says that the Eucharist should be "understood primarily not as a *thing* and an objectified means of grace but as an *act* and a *synaxis* of the local Church, a *'catholic'* act of a *'catholic' Church*" (*Being as Communion*, 145; italics in original).

42. Whether what is meant by the "universal Church" in *LG* 23 is the final eschatological church or simply the current worldwide church is a moot point; see Paul McPartlan, "The Local Church and the Universal Church: Zizioulas and the Ratzinger-Kasper Debate," *International Journal for the Study of the Christian Church* 4 (2004): 21–33; also Walter Kasper, *The Catholic Church: Nature, Reality and Mission* (London: Bloomsbury, 2015), 275.

43. Zizioulas, *Being as Communion*, 156–58.

44. Congregation for the Doctrine of the Faith, *Letter to the Bishops of the Catholic Church on Some Aspects of the Church Understood as Communion (Communionis Notio)* (1992), n. 11. Zizioulas himself acknowledges the possibility of identifying a "Petrine task" within a eucharistic understanding of the church; *Being as Communion*, 203n115; see also Metropolitan John (Zizioulas) of Pergamon, "Primacy in the Church: An Orthodox Approach," in *Petrine Ministry and the Unity of the Church*, ed. James F. Puglisi (Collegeville, MN: Liturgical Press, 1999), 115–25.

45. See also *CCC* 1369.

46. See McPartlan, *A Service of Love.*

47. De Lubac, *Corpus Mysticum,* 65.

48. De Lubac, *Corpus Mysticum,* 261. See likewise, Pope John Paul II, Apostolic Letter, *Novo Millennio Ineunte* (Rome: Libreria Editrice Vaticana, 2001), 43.

49. St. Augustine, *City of God,* 10, 6; in *St. Augustine: The City of God, Books VIII–XVI,* trans. G. Walsh and G. Monaghan. The Fathers of the Church, vol. 14 (Washington, DC: The Catholic University of America Press, 2008), 126–27.

50. See also Pope Benedict XVI, *Sacramentum Caritatis,* 70.

51. *City of God,* 10, 6; in *St. Augustine: The City of God, Books VIII–XVI,* 125–26.

52. See, e.g., Augustine, *Enarr. in Psalmos* 17, 2 (PL 36:148).

53. *City of God,* 10, 6; in *St. Augustine: The City of God, Books VIII–XVI,* 127.

54. See Pope Francis, *Evangelii Gaudium,* 112.

55. See Albert Vanhoye, "Common Priesthood and Ministerial Priesthood: Difference and Relations," *Josephinum Journal of Theology* 23 (2016): 4–16, at 11–12.

56. Jean-Pierre Torrell, *A Priestly People: Baptismal Priesthood and Priestly Ministry* (Mahwah, NJ: Paulist Press, 2013), 183. See also "a holy priesthood" (1 Pet 2:5) and "a living sacrifice, holy and acceptable" (Rom 12:1).

57. Pope Paul VI, Encyclical Letter, *Mysterium Fidei* (Rome: Libreria Editrice Vaticana, 1965), 31.

58. Pope John Paul II, *Novo Millennio Ineunte,* 43 (emphasis in original).

9

BAPTISM

—w—

Helen Bergin

It is a delight to contribute to a Festschrift honoring Dr. Gerard Austin, OP, and his wonderful gifts—especially those linked with theology and liturgy. Equally important is to honor Jerry's engaging friendship, which I and many others have been so blessed to experience.[1] Thank you, Jerry!

This chapter begins with an extensive overview of baptism in the New Testament. Second, it examines the theology of baptism as presented especially in the Rite of Christian Initiation of Adults (RCIA). Third, it raises theological issues pertinent to baptism that may confront contemporary believers. Fourth, it reflects on the relationship between baptism and faith. Fifth, it considers the role of the Holy Spirit in baptism. Sixth, it considers ecumenical dimensions of baptism. The chapter concludes with several short reflections on baptism.

The theme of baptism is of particular significance within several New Testament writings. We begin by considering the Gospels.

BAPTISM IN THE GOSPELS

The Baptism of Jesus

All four Gospels testify to Jesus's baptism in the Jordan River and to the presence of God's Spirit upon him.

The river Jordan was a place of important symbolic significance for the Jewish people. The First Testament Book of Joshua, especially in chapters 3 and 4, describes how the Jewish people, together with the ark of the covenant, crossed over the river Jordan into the land of freedom that God had promised.

Six or seven centuries later, John the Baptist chose this river for a renewal of his people, suffering under centuries of occupation, when they came to him at the Jordan River. There he invited them to a symbolic baptism, a washing and a crossing over into a renewed faith in God's promise for them as the new Israel in their own land. It is within this context that Jesus came to John to be baptized.

The four Gospels each highlight a different aspect of Jesus's identity. By doing so, they alert the reader to Jesus's true identity as will be revealed in the rest of the gospel story. The three Synoptic Gospels each express John's awareness of God's delight in Jesus, who is variously described at his baptism as "Favored," "Beloved," and the One who brings God great joy. In John's Gospel, John the Baptist confesses Jesus both as the Son of God and as the Lamb of God, thus already linking Jesus's baptism with his death.

The above baptism in the Jordan is especially significant since it marks Jesus's transition from his hitherto largely unknown life into his public life and ministry. But the transition from the waters of the Jordan also includes an important phase. Mark, Matthew, and Luke each alert readers to the fact that Jesus's baptism in the Jordan River is followed by a forty-day withdrawal into the wilderness for fasting, solitude, and prayerful reflection. The event of Jesus's baptism thus begins a commitment that ultimately includes a journey to the cross, rejection, death, and—significantly—resurrection. Not only does Jesus as a Jewish male fulfill the baptismal requirements of his contemporaries but he goes beyond the mission of John the Baptist who had been preparing the new Israel among those who had approached him for baptism. Jesus's focus, however, will be preaching and bringing about the impending reign of God—not at the Jordan but to all the Jewish people in their towns and villages throughout the land.

Thus, baptism is central to Jesus's life and mission. At the same time, it occurs with divine acknowledgment that Jesus is deeply loved and is the One in whom God rejoices.

We might also say that, in undergoing baptism, Jesus aligns himself with struggling human beings in every era and place and with the dependence of all people on God's grace. His mission will demonstrate the availability and power of that grace.

Jesus Is Missioned from Baptism

According to John's Gospel (John 3:22), a rite of baptism was part of Jesus's ministry. However, while Jesus's disciples baptized, it is not clear whether Jesus himself baptized. Nonetheless, it is especially at the beginning of Jesus's ministry that one fully recognizes the significance of the Spirit that came upon him at his baptism.

When Jesus in the local synagogue outlines his mission (Luke 4:18), he recognizes the Spirit as calling him to "go out" and gladden the hearts of the poor, heal the sick, unburden the downhearted, and offer God's forgiveness to those who have strayed.

Later, Luke's Gospel reminds readers that baptism has consequences. Not only do people make a commitment to following Jesus as disciples, but after Jesus had taught the disciples to divest themselves of material goods and to prepare for the Son of Humanity's coming, he utters strong words. Jesus says, "I came to bring fire to the earth, and how I wish it were already kindled! I have a baptism with which to be baptized, and what a stress I am under until it is completed!" (Luke 12:49–50). It seems that Jesus is describing his death as a baptism, beyond that of John the Baptist, beyond the baptism of his own ministry.

From a crossing of the Jordan River, Jesus is to cross over into eternal union with God. Jesus reminds his hearers that one consequence of baptism—whether gifted to children, youths, or adults—will involve the inclusion of God at the center of their lives. For many people, fidelity to their baptismal call is often costly.

Baptized into the Name of the Father, into the Name of the Son, into the Name of the Holy Spirit: Jesus's Missionary Invitation in Matthew's Gospel

The disciples inherit Jesus's mission to proclaim the good news of the kingdom of God. But Matthew adds something more specific.

He states, "All authority in heaven and on earth has been given to me. Go therefore and make disciples of all nations, baptizing them in the name of the Father and of the Son and of the Holy Spirit, and teaching them to obey everything that I have commanded you. And remember, I am with you always, to the end of the age" (Matt 28:18–19).

Of particular interest in Jesus's command is the phrase "in the name of." As our common translation stands, Jesus tells his disciples to baptize in the name of someone else—in the name of the Father, and of the Son, and of the Holy Spirit. However, the Greek word underlying this translation is *eis*—which more commonly is translated as *into*. This latter translation suggests that the person being baptized is baptized "into," or grafted "into," the name of God. Some fundamental insights follow from this translation.

First, it means that baptism is a journey rather than a destination. It is the beginning of a journey *into* the mystery of God, into the life and love of each trinitarian person—as well as a journey into the communal divine love of the Trinity. Catherine of Siena's wonderful trinitarian image is pertinent here. She says, "You, eternal Trinity, are a deep sea. The more I enter you, the more I discover, and the more I discover, the more I seek you."[2]

"Journeying into the deep ocean" is a strong image for baptism. Its vastness and depth transcend the beautiful but limited images of sprinkled water that so often accompany the reception of this sacrament. At the same time, this image also reminds us of our personal journeys into the mystery of God who is always "ever greater."

Second, Matthew's command "Go therefore and make disciples…" applies to each divine person. Let us look at each in turn. We are baptized *into* the name of the Father. While Jesus intimately described God as *Abba*, at the same time, Bernadette Farrell's song "God Beyond all Names" reminds human beings of our inadequacy in naming God who is the ultimate and eternal Divine Source.[3]

We are baptized *into* the name of the Son, whose earthly life and mission stand at the heart of the gospel and whose presence with us—always—is its constant foundation. The journey *into* knowing both the earthly Jesus and his risen presence in our lives (as evidenced in all our prayer and worship) is our life's joy and mission.

We are baptized *into* the name of the Spirit, who is our teacher, helper, advocate, and guide into truth (See John 14:26—16:14). North American theologian Eugene F. Rogers states, "The Spirit incorporates human beings into the body of Christ and distributes the life of God not only in the resurrection of Jesus and the celebration of the Eucharist but paradigmatically in baptism."[4]

Third, we too are missioned through our baptism to hand on Jesus's command to those whom we meet, and to following generations, even to the end of time. The word *into* expresses God's desire for an ever-growing communion with every human being, every animal and species—the world itself. This is our baptismal task and mission. The baptized are ultimately invited to build and nourish the Body of Christ.

Consequently, baptized persons are invited to discover God's rich love in their own lives and to offer God's love freely to others. This occasionally daunting mission occurs because at baptism each person, whether an infant, youth, or adult, has been a recipient of Matthew's words at the end of his Gospel, which state, "Go therefore and make disciples of all nations, baptizing them in the name of the Father[5] and of the Son and of the Holy Spirit" (Matt 28:19). Pope Francis reiterates Matthew's invitation when he says, "In virtue of their baptism, all the members of the People of God have become missionary disciples" (*Evangelii Gaudium* 120).[6]

Our focus now moves to select references from the writings of Paul in order to supply a theological context for the baptismal ritual and issues concerning baptism that will follow.

BAPTISM IN SELECTED WRITINGS FROM PAUL

In Paul's letters, the theme of baptism is central. Fundamentally, Paul emphasizes that through baptism each recipient becomes a member of Christ's Body. Thus, the reality of one's "being in Christ" and "belonging to Christ" infuse his baptismal theology.

In Galatians 3:28,[7] Paul reminds the community that they are "all one in Christ Jesus" and that because of their baptism, they are to look beyond differences of race (whether Jews or Greeks), status (whether slaves or free), and gender (whether male or female). It is through each person's believing in and belonging to Jesus that faith in Jesus and love toward others might gradually grow.

However, Paul expands the notion of each disciple belonging individually to Christ Jesus. In 1 Corinthians 12:13,[8] he says, "In the one Spirit we were all baptized into one body—Jews or Greeks, slaves or free—and we were all made to drink of the one Spirit." Paul understands each baptized person as being profoundly linked not only with Jesus and the Spirit but also with all of Jesus's disciples throughout time and space.

The above connectedness is highlighted in 1 Corinthians 12:27, which states, "Now you are the body of Christ and individually members of it." Once one member is linked with Christ in baptism, that one member is linked with all other past, present, and future baptized persons. A further emphasis on the Body of Christ comes late in Romans 12:5[9] when Paul says, "We, who are many, are one body in Christ, and individually we are members one of another." Not only do members share the life of Christ with others but Paul emphasizes that through each one's baptism a sense of responsibility toward another enables one member to bear the burdens of the other and even sometimes identify with the other.

For Paul, the Spirit's inclusive mission might be expressed today in the witness and engagement of baptized human beings from different ethnicities, religious denominations, genders, social classes, and disparate areas of the globe. Paul then lists a variety of Spirit-inspired gifts—including healing, leadership, and the assumption of responsibility—that each contribute to shaping a healthy body. Finally, Paul highlights the gift of love as indispensable to a vibrant body.

Paul does not, however, confine baptism to care for Christ's Body alone. For Paul, from one's baptismal commitment emerges one's spreading of the knowledge and love of Christ through mission. In Romans 6—8, Paul outlines both the framework and goal of baptism. He describes disciples as being "baptized into [Christ's] death" and then he adds "so that, just as Christ was raised by the glory of the Father, so we too might walk in newness of life" (Rom 6:3–4). For Paul, Christian discipleship, which "officially" begins in baptism, is very likely to involve multiple "deaths and resurrections" during life's journey.

The sacrament of baptism offers Christians the joys and challenges of participating in a worldwide communion of Jesus's disciples. Whether gifted to infants, teenagers, or adults, baptism surpasses a celebratory event occurring among friends and relations. Baptism begins a challenging yet enriching faith journey in which Jesus's followers navigate joys, struggles, deaths, and resurrections such as Jesus experienced in fidelity to the Source of life—his *Abba* God.[10]

In the following section, we focus on elements from the Second Vatican Council, or Vatican II, which have contributed to a renewal of the theology and practice of baptism.

BAPTISM AND THE RCIA

The Second Vatican Council (1962–65), overseen by Popes John XXIII and Paul VI, enriched the whole church. From this Council, important liturgical insights emerged.

First, the document on the liturgy, *Sacrosanctum Concilium*,[11] was significant as the first of four major constitutions to emerge from the Council in 1963.

Second, since this document affected both the Sunday and daily worship of Catholics, any liturgical changes were felt by all. This was theology in practice—not only in principle!

Third, in order to introduce practical changes within sacramental celebrations, people needed to understand the reasons behind the changes.

In relation to the sacrament of baptism, however, there were also significant fruits. *Sacrosanctum Concilium* included the introduction of the third-century ritual of the catechumenate with the introduction of a special Rite of Christian Initiation for Adults (RCIA) along with the Rite of Christian Initiation for Children (RCIC). Our focus will be on the former rite.

The baptism of infants continued as previously—although the manner of celebrating baptism would include greater congregational participation.

The significance of liturgical change for Catholics not only high-lighted important theological principles about baptism but also suggested the importance of ritual that attempts to express the meaning behind sacraments and their related words. Australian professor of religious education Richard Rymarz describes the significance of ritual when he says, "Without expressive events, any culture will die. In the absence of ceremony or ritual, important values have no impact."[12] Since Vatican II, the power of ritual in regard to the celebration of the sacraments has been powerfully reclaimed.

We now examine the RCIA, which since 1972 has been transforming the entry into the Catholic Church of many adults.

RECALLING THIRD-CENTURY ORIGINS

The RCIA[13] stems from early church practice, especially from the *Apostolic Tradition* of third-century Hippolytus. In recent years, this rite has enriched many participants—along with their sponsors and the wider community.

Hippolytus was a presbyter/priest in Rome and a theologian who was greatly influenced by St. Irenaeus of Lyons. He contributed the following guidelines for those seeking baptism:

- Once approved for baptism, candidates became catechumens[14] who spent up to three years reflecting on God's Word and doing good works in the community.[15]

- Then, prior to baptism, they were examined on issues such as sobriety and their visiting of the sick.

- On Thursday before Easter, they washed.

- On Good Friday, they fasted.

- At the Easter Vigil, the bishop blessed the catechumens with the oil of exorcism and they renounced Satan.

- Then, the presbyter gave catechumens a threefold immersion in water while the latter pronounced their trinitarian faith in a threefold response—"I believe!"

- Finally, when clothed, the catechumens were anointed with the oil of thanksgiving and were led into the waiting community. The Kiss of Peace concluded the ceremony.

Adapting Hippolytus for Today

Today, the RCIA offers a framework, influenced by Hippolytus's wisdom and practice. Particularly important is that this rite is an experience in which catechumens and the congregation participate together. We note this in the following steps.

In the first stage of the RCIA process, newcomers are welcomed into the Order of Catechumens and are affirmed by sponsors and the parish community. Once the candidates have pondered the Scriptures and been anointed, they are again presented to the community and leave the church prior to the celebration of Eucharist.

Later, still within the period of the catechumenate, catechumens are formally "elected" or enrolled into the local faith community and leave the community before the preparation of Eucharist.

In the second stage of this process, after having listened to the gospel and the homily with their godparents, the catechumens are chosen (or elected) for the next step. Again, they leave the community to reflect on their personal journeys.

Then follows a series of education into the Catholic faith—ideally occurring during the final three weeks of Lent.

On the first Sunday (Third Sunday of Lent), catechumens are presented with the Creed and the people's prayers support them. On the next Sunday (Fourth Sunday of Lent), further prayers are offered for each of the newly elect and a prayer of exorcism is offered. Again, the catechumens leave the community. Finally, on the Fifth Sunday of Lent, after the homily, the catechumens receive the Lord's Prayer and, for a final time, leave the community.

The process then approaches its climax.

At the Easter Vigil, once the congregation has pondered the biblical readings concerning God's liberating power among generations of Israelites, both catechumens and the parish community renounce sin and pray together an ancient creed. Then, the catechumens are invited to baptism in the newly blessed Easter water. If they choose immersion in the baptismal pool, their gesture reminds all present of their own baptisms into the life, death, and resurrection of Jesus Christ.

Final tasks for the newly baptized are an anointing with oil that alerts all present to their dependence on the Holy Spirit; being clothed in white to signify the new life of baptism; and, finally, receiving a lighted candle for guidance on life's journey.

It is at Easter that Christians reconnect with the gift of their baptism. It is also a time when people's joys and pains link with the ultimate human hope—resurrection!

In summary, the celebration of baptism that is the goal of the RCIA or the catechumenate[16] depends to a large extent on the participation, over several months, of candidates listening to, reflecting on, praying with, and responding to the Word of God. At each preparatory stage, regular attention to God's Word shapes the candidate's readiness to receive the sacrament. Moreover, those preparing catechumens for baptism also ponder the same daily or weekly Word of God and all are invited to include the catechumens in prayer.

The importance of at least some parish members becoming familiar with biblical texts appropriate to each sacrament is well captured in the following statement: "Sacred Scripture is of paramount importance in the celebration of the liturgy....It is necessary to promote that warm and living love for Scripture to which the venerable tradition of both Eastern and Western rites give testimony" (*Sacrosanctum Concilium* 24).

ISSUES LINKED WITH BAPTISM

Considering the previous section in which the positive contribution of baptism has been highlighted, it is now pertinent to highlight three contemporary issues in which the gift of baptism might present challenges to the Catholic community.

The first issue concerns reasons for which some parents seek baptism for their children. Many people in countries from "the first world"—including Aotearoa New Zealand, Australia, and North America—live in environments that often experience benefits from relatively healthy economies and high standards of living. Such countries also attempt to support people of diverse ethnicities, religions, genders, cultures, and financial status.

One consequence of such diversity, and thus the first issue regarding baptism in a secular society, is that many citizens cannot avoid daily immersion in liberal and individualistic values. Thus, many baptized people can easily overlook Sunday faith commitments because sports, work requirements, or special events take precedence over religious practices that may formerly have been undertaken on Sundays.[17]

The reality is that baptism, which many people receive in infancy, and confirmation, which consolidates baptism, both signal commitment to the discipleship of Jesus and to the Body of Christ. Yet, while each disciple's attitudes and practices are known only to God, the church when gathered on Sunday often suffers from the absence of many baptized members.

The second issue concerns young people within Catholic high schools requesting to be baptized because school friends are Catholic, and they too wish to participate in the school faith community. It is laudable that teenagers ask questions about the faith of their peers and that they are willing to undergo instruction prior to baptism. But there may be reasons that suggest otherwise.

The first query is whether the influence of encouraging Catholic school friends means that a school-aged youth is ready to take a step into Christian baptism. It is possible that some parents may approve of their child's decision for baptism but might feel unable to support the faith life of their young daughter or son. The concern is whether the youth is sufficiently mature to participate weekly in a parish Eucharist—with or without support from family and friends.

The second query is whether the baptism of young people within a school community is wise. The sight of young people receiving baptism in front of peers is indeed moving for those witnessing the baptism and for the baptized youths themselves. Yet, baptism is fundamentally a commitment to Jesus Christ and to the community of Christians or church in which Jesus is central. Baptism is not commitment to a group of select Christians but commitment to the wider Body of Christ. If the only experience of church that some youth know is that of their school or college, a large part of Christ's Body, namely, the local parish and wider diocese, may be absent—and may always remain so.

The third issue pertains to an understanding of baptism as removing original sin. While today this image may be communicated less often in churches, this traditional belief attempts to explain elements of discord present within history, human communities, and individual persons. Despite the grace of Jesus's life, death, and resurrection greatly outweighing the reality of original sin, nevertheless, as stated in the Council of Trent, "Revelation gives us the certainty of faith that the whole of human history is marked by the original fault freely committed by our first parents."[18] A baptismal focus on fundamentally removing original sin has predominated for many generations of Christians.

Since the Second Vatican Council, the emphasis on baptism as removing original sin has been less emphasized—but not denied. It has been replaced positively by baptism conferring on each candidate God's overwhelming grace and liberation.

Lumen Gentium 7 states,

> Through baptism we are formed in the likeness of Christ: "For in one Spirit we were all baptized into one body" (1 Cor. 12:13). In this sacred rite, a union with Christ's death and resurrection is both symbolized and brought about: "For we were buried with him by means of Baptism into death." And if "we have been united with him in the likeness of his death, we shall be so in the likeness of his resurrection also" (Rom 6:4–5).[19]

In this statement, baptism invites the baptized into the one Body of Jesus Christ. Thus, baptized individuals are challenged to belong to Christ and *also* to one another. In companionship with Jesus, each disciple is challenged to die to sin and be raised to life. Neither invitation is cost free. Yet, the overwhelming realization remains that those who have responded to Jesus's invitation to love others will, in God's goodness, rejoice eternally with Christ.

Later, *Lumen Gentium* 11 states,

Incorporated into the Church through baptism, the faithful are consecrated by the baptismal character to the exercise of the cult of the Christian religion. Reborn as [children] of God, they must confess before [people] the faith they have received from God through the Church.[20]

In this quotation, baptism into Christ's Body invites Christians to worship the God of Jesus Christ and as God's children to live out their faith in Jesus. In short, baptism is not primarily an invitation to a party! It is an invitation to rejoice with family, friends, and parishioners because through their common inclusion within the Body of Christ, there are strong reasons to be grateful.

At this point, it is important to consider the gift of faith that underlies and accompanies baptism.

FAITH AND BAPTISM

First, *faith* might be broadly described as trusting in persons or in another human being. Children, for example, depend on parental figures. When a baby cries or smiles, a parent responds and the child gradually learns to engage with parents and caregivers. In time, a mutual bond of familiarity emerges, and the child's dependence on others beyond the family unit gradually grows. Faith in an "other" deepens.

Second, "Christian faith" offers a further dimension. One does not physically see Jesus or any member of the Trinity when one prays, "I believe in Jesus Christ, the only-begotten Son of God, born of the Father before all ages...." Yet, with appropriate support, one may gradually absorb a sense of "believing in Jesus or in God" as something healthy and helpful. When families are also supported by schools in which Christian faith is important, young people experience an atmosphere in which God-conversations are acceptable. Faith grows within an ambience of family, friends, and the wider community. Yet, faith can be tested in difficult times. In periods of death or betrayal, it may be much later that people can really accept that God is fundamentally good.

Third, when one links faith with baptism, two elements come to the fore—faith in God and faith in the Christian community. The words spoken at baptism: "I baptize you in the name of the Father and of the Son and of the Holy Spirit," draw the one being baptized into the trinitarian life of divine communion as well as into a relationship with each divine person. The baptized person is invited in a unique way to experience God's trinitarian love. While such love belongs to the three Divine Persons who continually offer and receive love, human beings may at various times glimpse something of this profound love. Perhaps it is during moments of quiet or in experiences of human love that a yearning for God's love might break into individual lives.

In addition, humans sometimes find themselves being drawn more deeply to know the mysterious God at the heart of their lives. Sometimes they feel themselves being companioned by Jesus on a path of discipleship. Or, they might recognize the Spirit's presence in the resolution to a problem that has been troubling them. In such times, people may implicitly express belief in the triune God.

However, baptism links Christians not only with the Trinity but also with the church, since it is within the Body of Christ that baptism is lived out. Random recent surveys indicate that many Christians express an empathy toward Jesus Christ but a lesser allegiance to the church. Perhaps the church or the Body of Christ appears messy, lukewarm, and divided. Nonetheless, it continues to be Christ's graced body wending its way through time and space, bearing the good news. At the beginning of each Eucharist, a community is gathered "in the name of the Father and of the Son and of the Holy Spirit." The church always assembles in the name of the mysterious yet incarnate God and not in the name of any specific group, culture, or nation.

It is the responsibility of each parish and diocese to ensure that particular expressions of church—whether shaped by age, ethnicity, location, or history—welcome others and express God's hospitality to all. While some baptized persons express their faith on the fringes of society, others prefer to practice their faith within secure structures. It is the living out of faith in a loving environment that keeps the church relevant and welcoming. Pope Benedict XVI, when speaking about

178

parents bringing children for baptism, expressed the ultimate parental hope. He commented that baptism is not primarily about being socialized into the church or being welcomed into the church. Rather, he says, "The parents...expect that faith, which includes the corporeal nature of the church and the sacraments, will give life to their child—eternal life" (*Spe Salvi* 10).[21] Parents often have wonderful dreams for their children. For many parents the dream may well include their family's eternal happiness with God and with God's renewed creation.

We turn now to the indispensable role of the Holy Spirit within the preparation and living out of the sacrament of baptism.

THE ROLE OF THE HOLY SPIRIT IN BAPTISM

Intermittently, within global and local communities, particular people emerge with insights that suggest that something precious has been silently coming to light. Likewise, it is often with hindsight that human beings appreciate the impact on themselves of particular persons, communities, or events. At such times, Christians might well ponder the ongoing and self-effacing presence of God's Holy Spirit regarding individuals, communities, and events.

Some will recall the philosopher Aristotle, whose impact on the Catholic community was highlighted in Thomas Aquinas's engagement with faith and reason in his *Summa Theologica*. For centuries, Thomas's writing has encouraged people of various religious traditions to engage in thought, debate, and prayer in order to involve themselves in personal journeys toward the divine. Might one not ask whether it could have been the Divine Spirit quietly working in the labor, research, and writing of both Aristotle and Aquinas—and in their readers?

Attention to the Spirit often involves individuals and communities setting out on a journey of faith, the fruits of which often emerge sometime later. Moreover, such journeys are often accompanied by nudges from an ever-present but gently working Holy Spirit. So, let us now ponder briefly the role and timing of God's Spirit in relation to baptism.

We raise three questions: Might it be the Holy Spirit who prompts parents to desire baptism for their child or children? Might it be the Holy Spirit who encourages grandparents to express a desire for the baptism of grandchildren that is eventually "heard" by the children's parents? Might it be the Holy Spirit expressed in a couple's joy at their child's impending baptism that tempts other parents to seek baptism for their child as well?

The sacrament of baptism depends in multiple ways on the contribution of the Divine Spirit engaging with parents, grandparents, and caregivers when the time is right.

A homily or a presentation on baptism may be an opportune time for Christians to recall specific moments, either in the present or the past, that may have revealed the Spirit's activity in their lives. A congregation may recall such moments gratefully—and possibly with amazement. Early in the "General Introduction" to *Christian Initiation*[22] there is a description of baptized persons as "a new creation through water and the Holy Spirit" (no. 2). Baptized persons are graced with life-giving newness.

In the same vein, the recalling of baptism may alert us to the Spirit's role within families, communities, work and leisure relationships, as well as in passing relationships with many others. Could it be that we expect the Spirit to be more present within churches and faith practices than in our daily acquaintances and chance meetings? Yet, is it not the latter that consumes a greater portion of our days? Where might the Spirit be within the latter?

Moreover, might we not reflect on ways through which the Spirit might affect our relationships within our local communities and in relation to social and environmental issues in our neighborhoods?

God's Spirit is indispensable within the journey of faith. Sometimes, the Spirit nudges persons throughout a lengthy period toward an eventually significant decision. At other times, the Spirit unobtrusively opens possibilities—a chance meeting, a newspaper item, a billboard advertisement—that encourage a deepening of faith or of one's baptismal commitment many years earlier.

Our focus will now turn to baptism as the sacrament that is shared with our Christian sisters and brothers. It is baptism that offers deep hope.

ECUMENICAL DIMENSIONS OF BAPTISM

Baptism into the Body of Christ means that all baptized Christians share the dignity of being united in a personal way with Jesus. But baptism is also about being incorporated into an ecumenical body of Christians in space and time who have committed themselves to being God's people through following the way of Jesus Christ.

In the sacrament of baptism, each recipient—whether Methodist, Anglican, Baptist, or so on—is invited to experience the communion of divine love or the Trinity. When one struggles to fathom the nature of God, might it not be the first person of the Trinity (variously named as Father, Mother-Sophia,[23] Creator...) to whom one is drawn in prayer, study, or wonder? If, however, one seeks resolution to a challenge in life, might it not be God's Spirit with whom one engages for wisdom? And, if one is drawn toward God's truth, might it not be Jesus, the Son of God, in whose footsteps one attempts to walk?

At the same time, each baptized woman or man is linked with millions of others also incorporated within the Body of Christ. *Lumen Gentium* affirms that Catholics are joined with all other Christians through baptism. After citing elements common to Christians such as reverence for Scripture, religious zeal, respect for Mary, and union in the Spirit, *Lumen Gentium* says of our sister and brother Christians, "These Christians are indeed in some real way joined to us in the Holy Spirit who acts in them and has caused many to shed their blood" (no. 15). The Spirit also encourages both the desire and action among Christ's disciples for eventual unity "as one flock under one shepherd" (*Lumen Gentium* 15). Each baptized person is thus a prized member of the Christian community within a particular place and time.

Dutch Catholic theologian Anton Houtepen wrote challenging words when he said of baptism, "It is about being given an identity, as people who belong to the free children of God, who want to spend their lives becoming what they are."[24] For Houtepen, such an identity might involve putting to death one's former practices (see Col 3:9–11) or drinking the cup that Jesus would drink (see Mark 10:38). Baptized Christians are invited to express the consequences of baptism according to the pattern of the living, dying, and risen Jesus.

The Second Vatican Council document *Unitatis Redintegratio*[25] emphasized the importance for Catholics of acknowledging and appreciating their familial bond with Christians of other faiths. It said, "All who have been justified by faith in baptism are incorporated into Christ; they therefore have a right to be called Christians, and with good reason are accepted as brothers [and sisters] by the children of the Catholic church" (no. 3).

Significant dialogue between Catholics and other Christians[26] has occurred since the Second Vatican Council, and the baptism of members within each tradition provides a rich and life-giving foundation from which all might keep growing into deeper faith, knowledge, and love.

In fidelity to Jesus's invitation, Christians respond to his words: "Go therefore and make disciples of all nations, baptizing them in the name of the Father and of the Son and of the Holy Spirit" (Matt 28:19). Christians are missioned to invite others into the communion of love or into the Trinity that is God's gift to all who seek the divine. Pope Francis confirms this call when he urges, "In all the baptized, from first to last, the sanctifying power of the Spirit is at work, impelling us to evangelisation" (*Evangelii Gaudium* 119).

Finally, in a world where millions of people commit to faiths other than that of Christianity, it is incumbent upon Christians to respect people from every nation, remembering words from another Council document, *Nostra Aetate*, "The Church always held and continues to hold that Christ out of infinite love freely underwent suffering and death because of the sins of [all] so that all might attain salvation" (no. 4).[27] While Christian baptism enables human beings to receive the privilege of belonging to Christ's Body, those not formally within the Body also share the fruits of Jesus's life, death, and resurrection. The mission of Jesus Christ, the Son of God, was "for all."

BAPTISM AND THE FINAL COMMENDATION

It is salutary that at the end of one's life, when the human body is brought to a chapel or church for farewells, the baptism of the deceased person is highlighted by the church. If there is a vigil for a deceased person, the casket is first sprinkled with holy water while the celebrant says, "In the waters of baptism, N. died with Christ and rose with Him to new life. May she/he now share with Him in eternal glory." If there has been no vigil service, the same words will occur at the Christian funeral.

It is baptism that recalls the journey of faith that for many people will have been part of their journey from beginning to end. It is also baptism that calls to mind the many unexpressed "deaths" a Christian will have undergone during his or her life of faith. Christians have been baptized into the life, death, and resurrection of Jesus Christ. Is that not the supreme privilege?

FINAL THOUGHTS

In light of the preceding biblical, theological, and liturgical reflections on baptism, it seems helpful to cite Ladislas Orsy, SJ, who noted an imbalance within sections of the most recent Code of Canon Law. He said of the latter, "It regularly speaks of 'sacred pastors' but never of the 'sacred laity.' Yet, there would be no sacred orders without sacred baptism!"[28]

It is baptism into the name of the Trinity that gives Christians identity, hope, and equality. Furthermore, baptism invites every Christian, within their particular denomination, to participate with Jesus Christ in his living, dying, and being raised from death—for the good of the world and for the future of God's amazing universe.

Whether baptism be followed by confirmation and Eucharist (as for Orthodox Christians) or whether baptism be followed by Eucharist and then confirmation (as for many Western Christians), ecumenical dialogues will continue to nourish and challenge us all.

We conclude this chapter with four pertinent baptismal reflections that have been offered some years apart.

The first is from Basil of Caesarea who said in the fourth century, "For if to me my baptism was the beginning of life, and that day of regeneration the first of days, it is plain that the utterance uttered in the grace of adoption was the most honorable of all."[29]

The second is from the fifteenth-century Council of Florence, which stated, "Baptism is the gateway to the whole spiritual life."[30]

The third is from the late North American theologian Paul Philibert who said in 2005, "The most fundamental ecclesiological reality is the unity of the baptized in the one Body of Christ."[31]

And, the closing words are from New Zealander S. M. Loreto, OP, whose final diary entry in 2015 was "I am especially grateful for my Baptism, ninety-three years ago and still my greatest gift."[32]

Further Reading

Austin, Gerard. "The Church as Worshipping Community." In *The Gift of the Church: A Textbook in Ecclesiology*, edited by Peter Phan, 177–91. Collegeville, MN: Liturgical Press, 2000.

"Baptism." In *Baptism, Eucharist and Ministry*. Faith and Order Paper No. 111. Geneva: World Council of Churches, 1982.

Best, Thomas F. *Baptism Today: Understanding, Practice, Ecumenical Implications*. Collegeville, MN: Liturgical Press, 2008.

Duffy, Regis A. "Baptism and Confirmation." In *Systematic Theology: Roman Catholic Perspectives*, edited by Francis Schüssler Fiorenza and John P. Galvin, 2:213–30. Minneapolis: Fortress Press, 1991.

International Commission on English in the Liturgy. *The Rites of the Catholic Church*. Vol. 1: Study Edition. New York: Pueblo Publishing Co., 1976.

Jungmann, Josef A. "Baptism and Preparation for Baptism." In *The Early Liturgy to the Time of Gregory the Great*, translated by F. A. Brunner, 74–86. London: Darton, Longman & Todd, 1960.

Philibert, Paul J. *The Priesthood of the Faithful: Key to a Living Church*. Collegeville, MN: Liturgical Press, 2005.

Second Vatican Council. *Lumen Gentium* (Dogmatic Constitution on the Church). London: Geoffrey Chapman, 1964.

———. *Sacrosanctum Concilium* (The Constitution on the Sacred Liturgy). London: Geoffrey Chapman, 1963.

Wood, Susan K. *One Baptism: Ecumenical Dimensions of the Doctrine of Baptism*. Collegeville, MN: Liturgical Press, 2009.

Notes

1. Jerry was a mentor and close friend of all "down under" (New Zealand, Australia, Pacifica) students at Catholic University of America. I am privileged to count myself among them. I was delighted to welcome Jerry on a visit to New Zealand.

2. Catherine of Siena, *The Dialogue*, trans. Suzanne Noffke, OP (New York: Paulist Press, 1980), no. 167, p. 364.

3. This song was released by Bernadette Farrell in Great Britain in 1991.

4. See Eugene F. Rogers, *After the Spirit: A Constructive Pneumatology from Resources outside the Modern West* (Grand Rapids, MI: Wm. B. Eerdmans, 2005), 158.

5. I note the male imagery for the divine within Matthew's proclamation. Essentially, this proclamation invites the baptized to experience something of God's infinite love, which is so rich as to be "three persons" interrelating among one another within the one God. It is difficult, however, for many women to sense that God is "beyond male" when God is mostly described in male images and language. The journey toward inclusivity is yet incomplete.

6. Pope Francis, *Evangelii Gaudium* (Strathfield, Australia: St. Paul's Publications, 2013).

7. The Letter to the Galatians was most likely composed by Paul in the late 40s or early 50s CE.

8. The First Letter to the Corinthians was likely composed between 55 and 56 CE.

9. Paul's Letter to the Romans was likely composed about 57 CE.

10. Elizabeth A. Johnson describes God as "Mother-Sophia" to make inclusive divine names that humans may have overlooked. See *She Who Is: The Mystery of God in Feminist Theological Discourse* (New York: Crossroad, 1993), 170.

11. *Sacrosanctum Concilium* (The Constitution on the Sacred Liturgy), in *The Documents of Vatican II*, ed. Walter M. Abbott (London: Geoffrey Chapman, 1966), 137–78. Hereafter, *SC*.

12. Richard Rymarz, "The Challenges Facing the Church Today," citing Terence Deal and Allan Kennedy, *Corporate Cultures: The Rites and Rituals of Corporate Life* (Reading, MA: Addison-Wesley, 1982), in

Priest, Prophet and Theologian: Essays in Honour of Anthony Kelly, ed. Neil Ormerod and Anthony Kelly (Victoria, Australia: Mosaic Press, 2013), 215.

13. The Rite of Christian Initiation of Children (RCIC) is a similar program for children and youth.

14. A catechumen is one who is receiving faith instruction.

15. "Let catechumens spend three years as hearers of the Word. But if someone is zealous and perseveres well in the work, it is not the time but the character that is decisive." Hippolytus, *The Apostolic Tradition*, no. 17. See http://www.bombaxo.com/patristic-stuff/church-orders/ hippolytus-the-apostolic-tradition/ (accessed December 4, 2018).

16. For further information on the catechumenate, see *SC* 64.

17. This is not to overlook the many people who, unable to participate with the Christian community on Sundays, intentionally choose other days as their sabbath.

18. See Council of Trent, *DS* 1513 in *Catechism of the Catholic Church*, United States Catholic Conference (San Francisco: Ignatius Press, 1994), 98, no. 390.

19. *Lumen Gentium* (Dogmatic Constitution on the Church), in Abbott, *The Documents of Vatican II*, 20.

20. *Lumen Gentium*, in *The Documents of Vatican II*, 28.

21. Benedict XVI, *Spe Salvi* (Vatican City: Libreria Editrice Vaticana, 2007).

22. See *Rites of the Catholic Church* as revised by the Second Vatican Ecumenical Council, vol. 1 (Collegeville, MN: Liturgical Press, 1990), 3.

23. See Johnson, *She Who Is*, 170–87.

24. Anton Houtepen, *People of God: A Plea for the Church* (Maryknoll, NY: Orbis Books, 1984), 91.

25. *Unitatis Redintegratio* (Decree on Ecumenism), in Abbott, *The Documents of Vatican II*, 341–66.

26. E.g., ARCIC III 2017 and Lutheran/Catholic Dialogue in 2017.

27. *Nostra Aetate* (Declaration on the Relationship of the Church to Non-Christian Religions), in Abbott, *The Documents of Vatican II*, 660–68.

28. Ladislas Orsy, *The Church: Learning and Teaching* (Wilmington, DE: Michael Glazier Inc., 1987), 43n23.

29. Basil of Caesarea, *De Spiritu Sancto*, chap. 10, no. 26. See http://www.ccel.org/ccel/schaff/npnf208.vii.xi.html (accessed March 28, 2018).

30. Cited by Gerard Austin, "The Church as Worshipping Community," in *The Gift of the Church: A Textbook on Ecclesiology*, ed. Peter Phan (Collegeville, MN: Liturgical Press, 2000), 177.

31. Paul J. Philibert, *The Priesthood of the Faithful: Key to a Living Church* (Collegeville, MN: Liturgical Press, 2005), 19.

32. Sr. Loreto Meehan, OP, died in February 2016.

10

LITURGY AND SPIRITUALITY BETWEEN CROSS AND RESURRECTION

—⟋⟍—

Michael Downey

What's the point? Why invest time and energy addressing a topic that for so many leads to a dead end? The imposition of the "new" Roman Missal (2010) on English-speaking peoples throughout the world is but one example of how liturgical form can snuff out the work of the Spirit. Gerald O'Collins and John Wilkins have documented the ways in which the agenda of Roman authorities during the pontificates of Karol Wojtyla and of Joseph Ratzinger prevailed in the course of the English translation of the Roman Missal with little or no attention to the work of the Spirit in local churches.[1] Perhaps if the 1998 translation of the Roman Missal, "the Missal that never was," had not been derailed by the misguided principles prescribed by the Vatican's instruction *Liturgiam Authenticam*, there would be occasion to celebrate a living liturgy rather than to lament the emptying of so many churches in the English-speaking world.

Even in moments of impasse such as this there are luminous traces of hope.[2] First, there is the life of C. Gerard Austin, whose prayer, preaching, and doxological living have given witness to countless students, colleagues, and rank-and-file Catholics to what good liturgy can and ought to be. Then, there is this gathering of voices to honor this student and teacher of liturgy whose influence spans more than half a century. Finally, amid the impasse and widespread resistance to Pope Francis's efforts to continue the renewal ushered in by the Second Vatican Council, his *motu proprio Magnum Principium*

offers a glimmer of hope in restoring to local churches a greater measure of authority in determining liturgy's form as a work of the Spirit.

Alongside efforts to straitjacket liturgical form, there is still a
tendency among some to impose rigid practices in the "spiritual life"
in some circles and movements in the church, though these are on the
wane. Indeed, often as a reaction to exaggerated and misguided spiritual practices of bygone eras, understandings of spirituality today
have all too often become slippery and the practices of the spiritual
life soft.

What is called for is what might be referred to as a Christian
"spirituality with spine." In such an approach to spirituality, liturgy
has a formative role. But there is also a recognition that the Spirit
poured out into human hearts, within local communities and in our
world, is vital in shaping the form that liturgy takes, as well as in its
ongoing renewal and reformation.

In most contemporary Christian perspectives, the term *spirituality* does not refer to just one dimension of the Christian life, such as
prayer or the pursuit of virtue, recollection, the interior life, or ascet-
ical practices. Rather, *spirituality* or "the spiritual life" pertains to the
whole of the Christian life, living in and through the Spirit of God,
the Spirit of Christ. Christian spirituality has far-reaching implications
for every dimension of the Christian life: interpersonal relationships,
life in the sociopolitical order, economics, environmental concerns,
and more. Spirituality has as much to do with the proper use and disposition of material goods or the integration and exercise of one's
sexual energy as it has to do with one's "prayer life." Spirituality
entails being conformed to the person of Christ, brought into communion with God, living in right relation with God and others, with
every living creature and all of creation, through the presence and
power of the Spirit.[3]

LITURGICAL SPIRITUALITY?

My concern here is not with liturgical spirituality, and so I
depart from the topic originally assigned to me by the editors of this
volume. My intention is not to demonstrate the necessity or essential

characteristics of a liturgical spirituality that could then be situated in a row alongside Ignatian spirituality, Benedictine spirituality, Franciscan spirituality, Dominican spirituality, or a lay spirituality. Rather, the purpose here is to describe the kind of relationship that exists between Christian spirituality and liturgy. In so doing, I hope that the nature and function of both will be clarified.

A fair measure of thought and writing on liturgical matters has been directed to the question of the formative role of liturgy in Christian spiritual life. Kevin Irwin has offered a carefully defined liturgical spirituality, the essential contours of which are presented in detail.[4] He articulates what he considers to be the constitutive elements of liturgical spirituality. His concern is an important one: Christian prayer and spiritual life suffer when they are not rooted in the liturgical life of the church. What is needed, however, is further reflection on the nature of the relationship between liturgy and spirituality with an eye to spirituality's formative role in the liturgy.

In attempting to understand liturgy and spirituality, the task is not one of culling out of the liturgy specific elements that are thought to have a formative influence on the spiritual life of an individual or a group. For example, one might claim that since the *anaphora* is essentially a prayer of thanksgiving, any authentic liturgical spirituality will be characterized by a spirit of thanks. Or others, in the wake of the Second Vatican Council with the attention given to the importance of the Liturgy of the Word, may maintain that a liturgical spirituality must be marked in a singular way by its focus on the Scriptures. The task is more complex and requires the recognition that the relationship between liturgy and spirituality is reciprocal. Not only does liturgy shape spirituality; spirituality shapes liturgy.

To arrive at a better understanding of this relationship, a glance at two different models may be helpful.

a. Spirituality Derives from Liturgy: Model of Derivation

The first model, which shall be referred to as a model of derivation, is useful in understanding the concerns of those who are primarily interested in the importance of the formative role of liturgy in a person's or group's spiritual life. Looking to this model, the concern is to illustrate the elements of spirituality that flow from the liturgy. Spirituality is shaped by these. In an effort to pin down these elements, there is sometimes an attempt to develop not only the broad contours of liturgical spirituality but also the rather specific elements of a liturgical spirituality or *the* liturgical spirituality. The relationship here is rather one-sided. If there is a conviction that the relationship between liturgy and spirituality is in any sense reciprocal, this is hard to detect, and the concern for the influence of spirituality on liturgy is not apparent.

Indeed, *Sacrosanctum Concilium* supports this model in affirming that liturgy is the "primary and indispensable source from which the faithful are to *derive* the true Christian spirit" (emphasis mine). However, this must be understood in view of the aim "to be considered before all else," which is the "full, conscious, and active participation in liturgical celebration" by "all the faithful" (*SC* 14).

What, precisely, is meant by "full, conscious, and active participation" here? Does it mean staying awake at Mass? Listening attentively to a homily that has no scriptural basis and, like a plane circling an airport in inclement weather, never seems to land? Participation that is full, conscious, and active might be best understood by putting forward a simple question: What do people or peoples bring to the liturgy?

b. Liturgy and Spirituality: Model of Reciprocity and Critical Correlation

In an effort to introduce a more adequate understanding of the relationship between liturgy and spirituality, one that recognizes both the formative role of the liturgy as well as what people bring to the liturgy, a second model is worth considering. This might be referred to as a model of reciprocity and critical correlation. Here the dominant concern is with mutuality of impact. The reciprocal relationship between the two gives rise to a variety of spiritualties and liturgical forms. This view of liturgy and spirituality allows for dynamic interaction, openness to change under the Spirit's lead, and multiplicity of future possibilities. Not only is the Spirit at work in the liturgy; the

Spirit is at work in the persons who are to be invited to full, conscious, and active participation.

THE WAY AND WORK OF THE SPIRIT: SEVEN FOCAL POINTS

In speaking of the Spirit at work in persons, attention is given to seven focal points wherein the Spirit may be seen to be at work. The Spirit works (1) within a culture; (2) in relation to a tradition; (3) in memory of Jesus Christ; (4) in relation to contemporary events, hopes, sufferings, and promises; (5) in efforts to combine elements of action and contemplation; (6) with respect to charism and community; and (7) as expressed and authenticated in praxis. By looking to these, it is possible to envision the broader context of a foundational Christian spirituality within which the nature of the relationship between liturgy and spirituality may be better understood.

Attention to these seven focal areas entails setting aside a notion of liturgy that maintains that it is unaffected by contemporary experience of the Spirit at work, as well as any notion that liturgy *could* remain unaffected. What I have in mind in using the term *liturgical form* is much the same and is characterized by the same flexibility as what Joseph Gelineau describes as an operational model:

> The operational model thus emerges as a form of symbolic behavior which the celebrating group is familiar with, the participants have fully assimilated, and the main actors have adequately mastered. It allows the group to celebrate with peace of mind because the game and the rules are familiar. But it does not paralyse the action. Whatever is done is done, as it were, naturally and instinctively. The liturgy can emerge both as something remembered and as something new. The operational model may be said to be the concrete form that the local way of Christian worship actually takes for a specific human group in a particular area at a given moment.[5]

A variety of liturgical forms emerges precisely in response to the way in which the Spirit is at work within a particular culture, in relation to a specific tradition, in light of different ways of remembering Jesus, and so on. Such liturgical forms are assimilated within various cultures and, given the diversity of cultures, will vary.

To speak of the Spirit in persons, it is necessary to see, in the first place, those persons as located within a culture and in relation to a tradition. Culture is second nature to human beings. Wherever mortals dwell, there is culture. Culture includes the particular customs, rites, myths, narratives, metaphors, and ethos of a people. Culture—the web of meaning, purpose, and value—does not drop from the sky. It cannot be imposed from outside or "from above." The contours of a culture are expressed and impressed through a particular tradition. Traces of the Spirit are to be found in the various cultural patterns and currents of tradition through which persons and groups express their awareness of God's being in the world and humanity's being in God. Thus, the particular culture and tradition of a people, with attention to all those channels that facilitate self-expression, interpersonal communion, and communication, are the very places of the Spirit's operation. We look to the whole network provided by culture and tradition wherein we find the primordial locus of God's self-manifestation that is celebrated in liturgy. It is within the whole gamut of human experience, which is always "situated" within a culture and tradition, that God's Word is first spoken. Whatever is said of liturgy, or said or done liturgically, is to be related to this.

The history of Christianity demonstrates that any number of different spiritualities have emerged in the lives of various people and communities all formed, shaped, or schooled by liturgy. For example, the Holy Founders of Citeaux—Robert, Alberic, and Stephen—and the first followers of Francis and Clare and Dominic were all formed by the same liturgical life of the church. But the spirituality that each group lived was noticeably different from the other, each one with its own distinctive characteristics. Liturgy invites participation of persons who, in memory of Jesus Christ and by the power of his Spirit, respond to the gospel in any number of ways, given the influences of their own historical, cultural context. Such context will determine not only the way in which things are done and said in liturgy but also the response to what is done and said. The variety of traditions and cultures together with the historical particularities of a given person or group all shape the context within which liturgy is celebrated and its meaning communicated and received. When looking to groups like those just mentioned, we find a distinctive liturgical form in each case. What is most striking is that each form emerged from within medieval culture, which was quite remarkably the same throughout Western Europe. Not only is it true, then, that different cultures give rise to different liturgical forms and spiritualities, but a variety of liturgical forms and spiritualities may emerge from within the same culture.

The same may be said of the present day. Recognizing that there are nuances and considerable differences within it, we speak of a North American culture. Yet no one is surprised that the liturgical form operative in a North American Cistercian monastery is considerably different from that of the local parish church. Some may be surprised to hear that a group of aging priests and brothers of a religious congregation celebrates the liturgy at a different time, in a different place, and in a different way than the younger seminarians and brothers in the same house, seeing in this an expression of differences that need to be reconciled. The same may be said of congregations of apostolic women religious. But this is not the only reading of the situation. This may be viewed as a case in point, wherein persons within the very same culture, living under the inspiration of the same founder in the same religious congregation, respond to and shape different liturgical forms, recognizing that they are living different spiritualities.

Another area to be considered in understanding the relationship between spirituality and liturgy is that of contemporary events, hopes, sufferings, and promises. It is a great temptation to think and to write about different topics in spirituality with the aim of retrieving insights from a bygone era, be it that of the New Testament or another, and then applying them to the contemporary situation of a person or group. Far more difficult, yet more to the point, is the task of interpreting and responding to contemporary events—what actually goes on in the world—in remembrance of Jesus Christ by the power of the Spirit.

Response to the divine initiative operative in relation to the contemporary events and hopes of a people will take a variety of forms to meet changing and varied needs and circumstances of the age. Indeed, some responses may find no precedent in the history of Christianity. To the massive crises of our own age, there are simply no easy solutions, and too often the facile application of insights or principles derived from a cursory reading of classical religious texts only aggravates the growing senses of despair. David Power has written of the great hopelessness of our age signaled in the dual holocaust of the bygone century. The first is that of the willed and systematic attempt by the Nazis to annihilate the Jewish people as well as other groups. The second is that of a possible nuclear holocaust still threatening the world today. Considering these events, one a fact, the other a present possibility, how does one profess faith and hope in Jesus Christ?

Lamentably, the tide of humanity's inhumanity to humanity continues unabated into the twenty-first century. It is beyond the scope of this essay to chronicle the horrors that have continued as the end of the second decade of this century draws near. Can liturgy be celebrated as if what actually goes on in the world has no bearing on what is said and done in a people's worship?

What does it mean to profess Christian faith in our terrible and terrifying age? Further, what should be the form of Christian prayer and worship in our age? If there is a reciprocal relationship between liturgy and spirituality, then the Spirit at work in persons in relation to contemporary events, sufferings, and promises will impact the shape the liturgy takes, as persons and communities struggle to articulate prayer and celebrate hope in the face of such tragedies. This requires more than the inclusion of a prayer of petition here and there that God protect us from the threat of nuclear disaster, or that God will show compassion and give hope to those who live in despair. It is rather a question of allowing liturgy and sacrament to enter and so transform the collective human experience of helplessness and hopelessness signaled in the events of our terrifying age, by bringing these experiences to expression and by relating such experience to the memory of Jesus and his abiding presence in the people of God through the Spirit.

195

In words said and things done in memory of Jesus Christ we find another locus of the Spirit's activity. Memory is at the heart of liturgy. The diversity of Christian spiritualities illustrates that Christians have remembered Jesus differently in different times and places. To remember Jesus as triumphant Lord of the universe results in a view of church, ministry, and worship shaped by such remembrance. To remember Jesus as suffering servant results in a different understanding of church, ministry, and worship. Contemporary currents in theology point out the importance of remembering the forgotten, the victims, the oppressed, and those living in solidarity with them, in memory of Jesus Christ. Not only is the role of the liturgy to include in memory the words, actions, and promises of Jesus and his followers throughout the ages of Christian history, but also those who have stood at the edges of history, at the periphery of church and society.[6] Those forgotten through a willed and systematic forgetfulness can be gathered into the memory of Jesus Christ, and with this a certain freedom can be won. Traces of the Spirit are found where persons and groups choose to remember all those who in the course of history have been victimized by systems and by the fears and hatreds inculcated therein: victims of racism, classism, sexism, clericalism, environmental pollution, and the like.

The liturgical forms that result from this kind of remembrance would have little or no room for "high church" motifs. Rather, they would make room for lamentation as well as thanksgiving, and the memory of suffering as well as of hope.

In the efforts to combine elements of action and contemplation, we find another locus of the Spirit's work. The way in which these are blended has formed the core of the rich tradition of Christian spirituality. It is true that both ingredients need to be balanced in any wholesome Christian life, and yet it is also true that one or the other dimension will be accentuated, given the temperament, cultural conditions, and historical circumstances of person and/or group. The way in which these are combined gives rise to different liturgical forms in such a way that we can take notice of the considerable differences between the liturgy of a Poor Clare monastery and that of a Catholic Worker House, or between a l'Arche community and a Newman Center on the campus of a large secular university. Whatever similarities may exist between these groups, the difference in liturgical form in each community results—at least in part—from the way in which their respective members understand the task of integrating work and prayer or combining action and contemplation.

In considering charism and community as the next focus for understanding the Spirit's work, it is useful to point out that liturgy is the activity that fully expresses the faith of a community of believers. This is a community of grace and Spirit whose members, by baptism, have been granted charisms or gifts for the service of the Body of Christ. The gifts differ. The form liturgy takes will vary according to the type and measure of gifts operative within a specific community. Given this diversity of gifts, we might ask if the present state of liturgical affairs is characterized by an openness to diverse charisms, such as prophecy and wisdom. Or is the operative assumption that such charisms are a bit unwieldy and so have no place in the church's liturgy?

Finally, liturgical forms are to be assessed by praxis. That is to say, there is a critical correlation between liturgy and praxis. Here the question is one of the adequacy of the liturgy to the life of a people. David Power has put the question well: "Do common and accepted modes of liturgical expression respond adequately to contemporary ways of perceiving and being, and do they allow for hope in the future when we are threatened with awesome destruction?"[7] Liturgical forms must constantly be assimilated, assessed, critiqued, and reworked in light of their ability to relate to and address the deepest experience of a people wherein the Spirit is at work.

KEEPING MEMORY OF THE KENOTIC CHRIST

Of the seven focal points just discussed, particular attention is here given to the question of the way in which the memory of Christ is kept in liturgy. What is the image of Christ expressed and impressed in liturgy? How might Christ be remembered in a way that responds adequately to contemporary modes of perceiving and being in our terrible and terrifying age?

In the encyclical *Fides et Ratio*, John Paul II calls attention to the importance of the *kenosis*, the self-emptying of God in Christ, for probing the mystery of God (nos. 92–99). He writes, "The very heart of theological inquiry will thus be the contemplation of the mystery of the Triune God" (no. 93). Further, "From this vantage point, the prime commitment of theology is seen to be the understanding of God's *kenosis*, a grand and mysterious truth for the human mind, which finds it inconceivable that suffering and death can express a love which gives itself and seeks nothing in return" (no. 93). In line with Hans Urs van Balthasar, John Paul II suggests that the self-emptying of God in Christ, the divine self-abandon, is the point of entry into the Christian mystery in our own time and place.[8]

While *Fides et Ratio* is of interest principally to theologians and philosophers, *kenosis* may be understood as key to understanding every other Christian mystery, indeed each dimension of Christian faith and practice. This is because in the Christian dispensation, the human relationship with God is made possible by the One who is invisible, intangible, and inaudible, becoming one of us in the person of Jesus Christ so that the love of God beyond all naming can be seen, touched, and heard.

Often thought to be a single event in time and space when the Father's Son and Word comes "down" and is born in Bethlehem, the *kenosis* is better understood as the pattern of Jesus's entire life, ministry, passion, dying, death, and descent. According to some of the fathers of the Syriac churches, such as Isaac, Ephraim, Aphrahat, and Jacob of Sarug, the mystery of the *kenosis* does not begin with the incarnation but rather with Creation and continues not only in a succession of descents in the life of Christ but also in the life of the Christian.

The culmination of this divine self-emptying, this ongoing *kenosis*, is usually thought to be the dying and death of Jesus on the cross. Jesus himself is the very seed about which he had preached to his disciples: "Unless a grain of wheat falls into the earth and dies, it remains just a single grain; but if it dies, it bears much fruit" (John 12:24).

As is to be expected, we usually begin at the beginning—in the incarnation, with the vulnerable flesh of an infant laid low in a manger—as the point of departure for tracing this kenotic pattern.

But what if the kenotic pattern of the life and mission of Jesus were to be charted starting at the end of the continuing *kenosis*, beginning with the culmination and fulfillment of the self-emptying begun in the incarnation?

The creedal affirmation that Christ descended to the dead between cross and resurrection is the optic through which we might better understand the kenotic pattern of Jesus's life mission. What is more, the descent is the interpretive key for understanding the fullness of the paschal mystery in our terribly dark age.[9]

Spiritual chumminess has worn out its welcome in a time when it is altogether clear that we are living between the cross and resurrection. No cross, no resurrection. Christian living is always between memory and hope, between promise and fulfillment. Life in Christ is always *toward* Easter. The mystery of Christ's descent is that "moment" of his Pasch when Christ dwelt among the dead bringing light, life, and love to those who seemed beyond hope, in a world, another world, the netherworld beyond God's reach. Because Christ descended among the dead, we rest assured, rest in peace, in the knowledge that nothing, that no one, is beyond God's reach.

The descent of Christ among the dead is the surest anchor of Christian faith for those living in darkness, faced with personal, communal, and global hellish suffering. Yet the descent finds no liturgical expression except silence and waiting.

If there is a relationship of reciprocity and critical correlation between liturgy and spirituality, what form might liturgy take if the culmination of Christ's *kenosis*—the descent among the dead—were brought to liturgical expression? At a minimum, the Eucharist might itself be understood as continuing *kenosis* summoning those who put their faith in Christ to their own ongoing self-emptying, an ecclesial *kenosis*, so as to be open to the gift of God's love in Christ, which is known in his self-emptying.[10] Perhaps it is only when the church and churches are really empty that we might know in our bones that we are always between cross and resurrection—a Holy Saturday People— and find adequate liturgical forms to express our faith in God incarnate and interred, whose moment of loss, darkness, death, and descent is the very same moment of his luminous exaltation.

CONCLUSION

Rather than providing a blueprint containing specific guidelines for a solid Christian spiritual life, liturgy offers canonical parameters within which particular and quite diverse spiritualities—as expressions of the Spirit at work in persons—may develop. The Spirit at work in persons has given rise to new liturgical forms and expressions to meet the exigencies of diverse and particular persons and communities throughout history. The importance of the formative influence of liturgy on spirituality is taken as a given for both students and teachers of liturgical studies. But the deeper and more challenging concern at moments of liturgical impasse such as we have witnessed in recent decades is how the liturgy might allow for openness to diverse spiritualities and hence spirituality's influence on the multiple forms that liturgy might take.

Suggested Reading

Antonio, David William. *An Inculturation Model of the Catholic Marriage Ritual.* Collegeville, MN: Liturgical Press, 2002.

Chauvet, Louis-Marie. *The Sacraments: The Word of God at the Mercy of the Body.* Collegeville, MN: Liturgical Press, 2001.

Downey, Michael, ed. *The New Dictionary of Catholic Spirituality.* Collegeville, MN: Liturgical Press, 1994. Follow pertinent articles.

Fink, Peter E., ed. *The New Dictionary of Sacramental Worship.* Collegeville, MN: Liturgical Press, 1990. Follow pertinent articles.

Power, David Noel. *Worship: Culture and Theology.* Washington, DC: Pastoral Press, 1990.

Smith, James K. A. *Desiring the Kingdom: Worship, Worldview, and Cultural Formation.* Grand Rapids, MI: Baker Academic, 2009.

Warren, Tish Harrison. *Liturgy of the Ordinary: Sacred Practices in Everyday Life.* Downers Grove, IL: InterVarsity Press, 2016.

Notes

1. Gerald O'Collins with John Wilkins, *Lost in Translation: The English Language and the Catholic Mass* (Collegeville, MN: Liturgical Press, 2017).

2. For the implications of impasse in the Christian spiritual life, see Constance Fitzgerald, "Impasse and Dark Night," in *Living with Apocalypse: Spiritual Resources for Social Compassion* (San Francisco: Harper and Row, 1984), 93–116.

3. Two of the most significant voices in articulating a wider understanding of Christian spirituality are Bernard McGinn and Sandra Schneiders. See Schneiders, "Religion and Spirituality: Strangers, Rivals, or Partners," in *The Santa Clara Lectures* 6, no. 2 (2000).

4. While Irwin's concern for a liturgical spirituality runs through much of his writing, it is given particular attention in his *Liturgy, Prayer, and Spirituality* (New York: Paulist Press, 1984). See also Philip K. Pfatteicher, *Liturgical Spirituality* (Valley Forge, PA: Trinity Press International, 1997).

5. Joseph Gelineau, "Tradition-Invention-Culture," *Concilium* 162 (1983): 15–16.

6. Jorge Mario Bergoglio referred to the existential peripheries in his address to the College of Cardinals before the conclave that elected him to the Chair of Peter on March 13, 2013. His attention to those at the peripheries has been one of the hallmarks of his pontificate. For a fuller understanding of Pope Francis's understanding of peripheries and margins, see Andrea Riccardi, *To the Margins: Pope Francis and the Mission of the Church* (Maryknoll, NY: Orbis Books, 2018).

7. David N. Power, *Unsearchable Riches: The Symbolic Nature of Liturgy* (New York: Pueblo, 1984), 5.

8. See especially Hans Urs Von Balthasar, *Mysterium Paschale: The Mystery of Easter* (San Francisco: Ignatius Press, 2000).

9. I have treated this at greater length elsewhere. See Michael Downey, *The Depth of God's Reach: A Spirituality of Christ's Descent* (Maryknoll, NY: Orbis Books, 2018).

10. For an understanding of the Eucharist vis-à-vis *kenosis*, see Jean Corbon, *Wellspring of Worship* (San Francisco: Ignatius Press, 2005).

11

LITURGY AND ECOLOGY

—꩜—

Kevin Irwin

Gerard Austin, OP, was a mentor and colleague during the two decades when we served together on the liturgical studies faculty at The Catholic University of America. He taught colleagues and students through engaging teaching, insightful research, published articles, and books—as well as by example. Among many things, he was noted for making sure that we reflected an ecumenical orientation in our work as much as possible,[1] that we never forgot the importance of liturgical catechesis from the texts and rites of the liturgy itself, and that we needed careful and precise research into historical and contemporary liturgical sources in order to understand and appreciate the liturgy. These three themes are reflected in what follows. Part 1 concerns recent ecumenical initiatives on ecology and the place of liturgy in these initiatives. Part 2 rehearses how and where creation, the cosmos, and what Pope Francis calls "our common home" with our "fellow creatures" can and should shape how we appreciate the liturgy.[2] Part 3 offers an approach to the study of liturgical sources, by way of the example of water and baptism, that integrates a method that is both comparative and contextual to the point of being "ecological."

RECENT INITIATIVES

In retrospect we can say that 1989 to 1990 was a watershed moment when the Ecumenical Patriarchate of Constantinople, the World Council of Churches (WCC), and the Roman Catholic Church issued statements and either began or continued to address ecology with initiatives that have had long-lasting effects both within commu-nions and ecumenically.[3]

In 1989, Patriarch Dimitrios, with the approval of the Holy Synod consisting of a dozen patriarchs from around the world, issued the first of what have become (almost) annual, brief encyclical letters. The letters contain the seeds of the fundamental theological and spir-itual principles that guide the ecological vision of the Ecumenical Patriarchate. This vision includes the celebration of the liturgy, emphasizing its inherent theological and spiritual meanings. In the 1989 message *The Church Cannot Stand Idle,* Dimitrios declares that the Orthodox churches would from then on celebrate a World Day of Prayer for the Protection of the Environment on September 1, the first day of their liturgical year.[4]

In March 1990, the World Council of Churches sponsored a meeting titled "Justice, Peace and the Integrity of Creation" in Seoul, Korea, whose final document contained the affirmations that "the creation is beloved of God" and "the earth is the Lord's."[5]

On January 1, 1990, Pope John Paul II issued the customary annual Message for the World Day of Peace, titled *Peace with God the Creator, Peace with All of Creation.*[6] The opening paragraph sets up his argument: world peace is threatened by a lack of due respect for nature, by the plundering of natural resources, and by a progressive decline in the quality of life. Faced with the widespread destruction of the environment, people everywhere are coming to understand that we cannot continue to use the goods of the earth as we have in the past.

The intervening years have seen numerous initiatives to deepen church support for caring for the environment. The Ecumenical Patriarchate stands in pride of place for spearheading official teach-ings, research, writings, and seminars that concern relating liturgy with ecology (often under the heading of what *sacramentality* means). The leadership of Patriarch Bartholomew, Dimitrios's successor, has been especially important in these efforts.

The work to relate liturgy with ecology has understandably not been a strong suit for the (international) World Council of Churches given the complexity of their membership, not to say the diversity of their worship traditions.[7] At the same time, books like the collection of essays by ecumenical colleagues in honor of the distinguished Anglican liturgist H. Boone Porter, a truly groundbreaking volume, deserve special and careful attention.[8] One example of a national ecumenical dialogue on ecology that uses the structure of the historic liturgy to frame its arguments about care for creation is the 2011 work of the United States Roman Catholic–United Methodist dialogue.[9]

Taking the lead from John Paul II's Message for the World Day of Peace, many Catholic episcopal conferences, theologians, and liturgists have given more and more attention to relating liturgy to ecology and to the demands the liturgy places on us in terms of correct moral living. The wealth and breadth of this material is indicated in Pope Francis's *Laudato Si'*, which cites twenty documents from episcopal conferences about ecology, including one from the United States Conference of Catholic Bishops (USCCB).[10] Among other initiatives, it is noteworthy that the Environmental Justice Office of the USCCB sponsored four seminars in the 1990s to work through many of the ways that the Catholic theological, spiritual, and liturgical tradition could contribute to environmental theology and ethics.[11] At the very same time, liturgists and church leaders began to devote more attention to liturgy and (social) justice. For example, Benedict XVI's post-synodal exhortation on the Eucharist, *Sacramentum Caritatis* (2007), is framed around three major themes: "A Mystery to Be Believed," "A Mystery to Be Celebrated," and "A Mystery to Be Lived."[12]

In *Laudato Si'*, Pope Francis has laid out an extraordinarily rich, profound, and far-reaching teaching on ecology from the depths of the Catholic theological, moral, spiritual, and liturgical tradition that is aimed toward inviting dialogue "with all people about our common home."[13] Toward the end of the encyclical, he speaks specifically about a number of interrelated issues that include the sacraments, the Eucharist, the Sabbath rest, and concern for others, ending with the insightful summary, "and so the day of rest, centered on the Eucharist, sheds its light on the whole week, and motivates us to greater concern for nature and the poor" (*Laudato Si'* 233–37).[14]

ECOLOGICAL PRESUPPOSITIONS OF AND IN THE LITURGY

Liturgy is ecological in that the celebration of the liturgy almost always presumes on, raises up, reflects, and respects all creatures and the cosmos itself. (Two sacraments that do not presume this reality are penance and marriage in that they are based on biblical proclamation and verbal exchange.[15]) Among many possible examples are the following.

Times for Celebration

The determination of times for celebration of the daily Liturgy of the Hours, the seasons of the church year, and some feast days derive from the rhythm of the cosmos.[16] Dawn for morning prayer and dusk for evening prayer is underscored in the General Instruction on the Liturgy of the Hours, which states that morning prayer is "celebrated...as the light of a new day is dawning" (no. 38). It is appropriate that Zechariah's canticle is always used at this hour:

> The dawn from on high shall break upon us,
> to shine on those who dwell in darkness and the shadow
> of death.
> > (Luke 1:78–79; Morning Prayer)

It is not a coincidence that this same text is used as the communion antiphon for the Solemnity of the Birth of John the Baptist since the date of this feast, June 24, was deliberately chosen in accord with the length of the sun's rays as experienced in the northern hemisphere. Just as the daylight begins to diminish after June 21 (often called "the longest day of the year") the church commemorates the birth of the Baptist, whose saying "[Jesus] must increase, but I must decrease" (see John 3:30) determined the date for this commemoration. The sign of diminishing daylight in the cosmos has determined the feast of the one whose self-effacement ("decrease") led to people's putting their faith in Christ ("the dawn from on high"). That this feast has a rich tradition of liturgical importance is attested to by the fact that the

205

only other births commemorated in the calendar are those of Jesus and the Blessed Virgin Mary. Its significance is further emphasized by the number of Mass formulas honoring the Baptist in the (very early) Verona collection of euchology.[17]

With regard to evening prayer, the General Instruction on the Liturgy of the Hours states that when evening approaches and the day is already far spent, evening prayer is celebrated when "we join the Churches of the East in calling upon the 'joy-giving light of holy glory'...[and we sing in praise] now that we have come to the setting of the sun and seen the evening star" (no. 39). The Jewish tradition of the *lucernarium*, the lighting of the lamps in the temple at evening prayer, is also part of the liturgical ritual traditionally attached to this hour.[18]

The phases of the moon and its location determine the date for our celebration of Easter. The interplay of light and darkness is also reflected in the theory of the origins of Christmas that adapts the pagan light festival of the *Dies Natalis Solis Invicti*.[19] The diminishing intensity of the sun in the northern hemisphere is reflected in subtle ways in the lectionary and euchology of Advent and Christmas, which texts become the more compelling when this natural phenomenon is experienced. Liturgists from the southern hemisphere have appropriately critiqued this facile presumption that the cosmic phenomena of light/darkness in the northern hemisphere at this time of year is an essential part of these celebrations. While these arguments should not be jettisoned in any way, the fact that the debate is over cosmic phenomena underscores our point about the cosmic nature of the dating of both Christmas and Easter. At the same time, in praying the liturgy for Advent-Christmas-Epiphany and Lent-Easter-Pentecost, one should be very careful not to presume that the light/darkness phenomenon in the cosmos is universal. In addition, the cosmic experience of diminished light at Easter in the southern hemisphere could well provide the basis for emphasizing the eschatology of all liturgical feasts and seasons. This is to suggest that cosmic phenomena help us to appreciate that the liturgy is not only a commemoration of historical events of our redemption but an experience of their hoped-for fulfillment in the kingdom of heaven. References in the liturgy's assigned Scripture readings and prayers through Advent-Christmas-Epiphany need not mean that there is increased light in the cosmos, but that these references point to sacred realities that are also transtemporal and metahistorical. It also relays many meanings inherent in the cosmos as this affects how the liturgy is experienced.

Motivation for Celebration

Praise to God the Creator is constitutive of the theology of the Liturgy of the Hours.[20] For example, a hymn of praise for the days of creation has been assigned to ferial evening prayer for each day (except Evening Prayer I for Sunday) in the former and present Roman liturgy.[21] These texts, probably from the same author (some would say Gregory the Great), devote four stanzas to the work of each day of creation. Sunday's vesper hymn, *Lucis creator optime*, reflects the light and darkness motif of evening prayer. It begins with the following verses:

> O blest Creator of the light,
> Who mak'st the day with radiance bright,
> And o'er the forming world didst call
> The light from chaos first of all;
> Whose wisdom joined in meet array
> The more and eve, and named them Day:
> Night comes with all its darkling fears;
> Regard thy people's prayers and tears.[22]

The rest of the evening prayer hymns reflecting praise for the days of creation are *Immense coeli conditor*, "O great Creator of the sky" (Monday); *Telluris alme conditor*, "Earth's mighty maker, whose command / Raised from the sea the solid land" (Tuesday); *Caeli Deus sanctissime*, "O God whose hand hath spread the sky, / And all its shining hosts on high" (Wednesday); *Magnae Deus potentiae*, "O Sovereign Lord of nature's might, / Who bad'st the water's birth divide; / Part in the heavens to take their flight, / And part in ocean's deep to hide" (Thursday); and *Hominis supernae conditor*, "Maker of man, who from Thy throne, / Dost order all things, God alone" (Friday).[23] The hymn for first vespers of Sunday, *Iam sol recedit igneus*, by a different author (perhaps St. Ambrose), moves from the days of creation to praising the Trinity in the morning and evening.[24]

At Sunday morning prayer, the use of the canticle from Daniel 3 (vv. 57–88 on Sunday of weeks I and III; vv. 52–57 on Sunday of weeks II and IV) is significant in this connection. The opening verse— "Bless the Lord, all you works of the Lord praise and exalt him above all forever" (see Dan 3:57)—is followed by a series of acclamations citing various facets of creation and redemption as motives for praising God. These include verses about praise for creation and praise for redemption, with praise for redemption ending the canticle. These same motives for praising God are found in much of the Psalter. In the present arrangement of the Hours, "praise psalms" are used as the third psalm at morning prayer, and many of the psalms contain explicit praise of God for creation (e.g., Pss 19, 65, 147, 148, 150).[25]

That the Liturgy of the Hours classically begins with Psalm 94, paralleling the combined themes of praising God for creation and redemption, is an additional illustration of acclaiming the God of creation.[26] Two phrases from the *Te Deum*, used at the end of the office of readings on most Sundays and solemnities, capture and summarize this theology:

All creation worships you…
Holy, holy, holy, Lord, God of power and might,
heaven and earth are full of your glory.

Fittingly, the last two lines are repeated in the preface acclamation (*Sanctus*) in the eucharistic prayers. These prayers praise God for the *mirabilia Dei*, especially in creation and redemption.[27] They are derived from the "blessing" (*berakah*) and "thanksgiving" (*todah*) traditions of Jewish prayer.[28] This acclamation combines praise for creation with praise for redemption, and it specifies the obedient life, death, and resurrection of Jesus. This combination of themes is part of the "classical" shape of eucharistic anaphoras, even though this motif is all too briefly expressed.[29]

The theology operative in the fourth eucharistic prayer in the present Roman Missal concerns praising God who has made all things and who is the source of all life.[30] It brings out the universal need for the paschal mystery and the universal effects that flow from it. The preface to this prayer refers to the entire creation and to the Father as the ultimate source of creation and the one who is manifested in creation. Human beings fulfill the purpose of creation in giving voice to creation's praise of God by joining in the praise that is voiced in liturgy, in particular the Eucharist.[31] This prayer is a worldview in a capsule form.

In the liturgy, the value of creation, as reflecting the power of God and as the arena in which divine salvation overturns universal estrangement from God, is exemplified by the selection of the first Creation account, Genesis 1:1—2:2, as the first reading at the Easter Vigil.[32] The recounting of this text, which is allied with other such texts called "cosmogonic myths," praises God the Creator, Redeemer, and Sustainer of all life.[33] It has special poignancy because it accompanies the annual re-creation of the earth in the Spring. Its repetition reflects the belief that the act of creation is not simply what happened once in history but something eternally accomplished by God's creative word.[34] In fact, one could argue that this text really recounts what God intended in creation, not what really resulted, and that its annual proclamation at Easter facilitates an interpretation that creation happens among us through Christ even as we yearn for the "new heavens and a new earth" (Rev 21:1).

At the very beginning of the (preface to the) Roman Canon, the Roman liturgy has traditionally used the title *Domine, sancte Pater, omnipotens et aeternae Deus*, containing the three dominant names for God found in most contemporary prayers.[35] Fittingly, the last phrase of the preface contains the phrase (from Isa 6:3) and leads to naming God in the following way: *Sanctus, sanctus, sanctus Dominus Deus sabaoth. Pleni sunt caeli et terra gloria tua.*

The mediating function of creation is exemplified in a specifically christological sense in the liturgical use of such Scripture texts as the Johannine Prologue (John 1:1–14, used in the West on Christmas day) and the christological hymn in the letter to the Colossians (Col 1:15–20, specifically 15–18, used as one of the New Testament hymns at evening prayer). According to the Johannine Prologue, God's creative idea is the Logos, the second divine person. The "high" Christology of the preexistent Logos in the Prologue combined with the introductory words of the Prologue, "in the beginning" (recalling the first words of Genesis proclaimed at the Easter vigil), underscore how Christ was present and active at the creation of the world. John 1:3 summarizes this idea: "All things came into being through him, and without him not one thing came into being." The re-creation of the world was accomplished through the same Christ, cited at the Prologue's end as "the Word [who] became flesh and lived among us, and we have seen his glory, the glory as of a father's only son, full of grace and truth" (John 1:14).

Similarly, the Colossians hymn (Col 1:12–20) emphasizes Christ's preexistence. The purpose of all creation consists in our union with Christ and through him with the Father, the origin and fulfillment of all creation, including humanity. Of particular note is Colossians 1:16: "In him all things in heaven and on earth were created, things visible and invisible...all things have been created through him and for him." Thus, we can assert that the stated motivation for liturgical praise is creation and redemption and that the dynamic of Christian liturgy is to offer back creation to the Creator through Christ, the cocreator.[36]

This emphasis on the christological axis of liturgy, specifically the paschal mystery, has recently been appropriately supplemented by a pneumatologically rich emphasis on liturgy and sacraments as experiences through and in which the church is drawn into the life of the triune God. All liturgy is triune. It is the triune God who makes it occur. Just as Jürgen Moltmann can rightly argue that creation is the result of the power and life of the Spirit, thus ending what perhaps can be regarded as too christological an approach to creation, so we can emphasize that the liturgy is dependent on the dynamism of the Trinity (particularly when understood both immanently and economically).[37]

Explicit faith in the Trinity is also illustrated in the creed:[38]

Credo in unum Deum,
Patrem omnipotentem, factorem caeli et terrae
visibilium omnium et invisibilium
Et in unum Dominum Iesum Christum...
per quem omnia facta sunt....
Et in Spiritum Sanctum, Dominum et vivificantem.

Thus, the act of creation is not limited to the Father; it is equally christological and pneumatological.[39]

AN ECOLOGICAL HERMENEUTIC
OF THE LITURGY

An underlying premise for "liturgical theology" is that the words, gestures, and rites of the liturgy all sustain and convey *theological meanings* and by extension implications for living the Christian life.[40] In addition, it will be argued here that more often than not the liturgy contains and sustains many meanings because the liturgy's "texts and rites" are inherently multivalent, which phrase, *ritus et preces*, is from Vatican II's Constitution on the Sacred Liturgy.[41] While what follows comes from the Roman Catholic liturgy, what is presented is meant to be a contribution to the ongoing ecumenical project of developing a proper method for liturgical studies in general and for liturgical theology very broadly conceived. The instructions from the Liturgy Constitution, article 16, deserve ecumenical attention. The article states that liturgy "is to be taught under its theological, historical, spiritual, pastoral, and juridical aspects," which will be presumed and expanded upon here.

This is intended to be a focused elaboration on my own work on relating "texts and contexts" in delineating a method for liturgical theology.[42] Its intent is to utilize a method that is both comparative and contextual. It is "comparative" in that it compares texts and rites for the blessing of water. This approach to liturgical method is fairly recent and builds on the years of dedicated research that were made possible by the publication of the number and variety of liturgical sources, especially in the past century, that helped to guide and form the liturgical revision of many Christian churches, Roman Catholic included. It is "contextual" in that it raises up theological meanings that occur in rites surrounding water by the very fact that we raise up this primal element to be a part of our worship. The very fact that water is repeatedly raised up and revered in the liturgy shows reverence and respect for this fellow creature on our common home. In addition, the fact that water has been and is misused in our world today and is part of the ecological crisis that we face today needs to be factored into any adequate current liturgical/sacramental theology. The phrasing here is important and deliberate. Verb forms like *we use* and nouns like *object* are deliberately avoided here in favor of the language of *Laudato Si'*. That everything is interconnected and related and that all are "fellow creatures" is crucial to our argument emphasizing relatedness and relationship of all on this good earth. Therefore, we avoid any language that would objectify or reify fellow creatures. The phrase "an ecological hermeneutic" is meant to express the combination of careful textual study with raising up theological meanings from the elements in worship independent of and yet also (obviously) related to the *lex orandi*, and in drawing them together to raise up ways of appreciating what the liturgy means by what it both says and does. This kind of hermeneutic also respects that the very engagement in liturgy and sacraments means that, by their very nature, many meanings can be and are expressed, not all of which can be articulated in texts. Liturgical texts "tether the imagination," but they do not determine how the liturgy is experienced and appreciated.[43]

This exercise is also meant to counter a certain "philosophization" reflected in some contemporary studies about the liturgy. This is to say that our using a phrase such as "the present Roman Rite" invites careful study of where the present "texts and rites" of the liturgy came from, to assess what the present rites say and do, as well as look toward their further revision and inculturation. It is to be admitted that liturgical studies is a relative newcomer to the theological scene. To align the method and results of the study of the liturgy too quickly or too tightly with systematics, for example, is as unwise as it is confounding for appreciating what the liturgy is and does when compared with other branches of theology.[44]

We turn to two examples of the way an "ecological hermeneutic" might function regarding the primal element of water in the former and present Roman liturgy.[45] Among the issues that coalesce here are that all prayers contain a number of images and metaphors, that one prayer can never "say" all that might be said about what is occurring in the liturgy, and that interpreting liturgical texts always requires that the elements raised up in worship, here that of water, are always to be factored into the theological meaning of the rite. Water, as the

212

only primal element, except air, without which we cannot live, always conveys life and baptism as a sacrament of new life.

Prayer to Bless Water—Easter Vigil

One of the most significant adjustments in the reformed Catholic liturgy has been the revision and, in some cases, the adoption of prayers to bless elements raised up for worship. This is decidedly true for the adoption of (major parts of) the *Gelasianum vetus*'s prayer for the descent into the font for baptism, its accompanying litany, and the "blessing of the font" (*Benedictio fontis*). Among the more obvious (and important) adjustments in this rite is the elimination of adding the oil of catechumens and sacred chrism to the water as it was being blessed, as was the practice before the reform.[46] In the previous Roman ritual, the water blessed at Easter was used for the entire next liturgical year, which often meant that the blessed water did not reflect freshness or life-giving properties, having become rancid and sour smelling.

The prayer from the Easter Vigil begins by asserting that God has "prepared water, your creation, to show forth the grace of Baptism" (*et creaturam aquae*, which would have been better translated "creature water").[47] The anamnesis of saving history spans from creation in Genesis 1 to Matthew 28. Among others this includes references to water in saving history: "O God whose Spirit in the first moments of the world's creation hovered over the waters," from Genesis 1 (*Deus, cuius Spiritus super aquas inter ipsa mundi primordia ferebatur*); "God, who by the outpouring of the flood foreshadowed regeneration" (*Deus, qui regenerationis speciem*) "so that from the mystery of the one and the same element of water" (*ut unius eiusdemque elementi mysterio*) "would come an end to vice and a beginning of virtue" (*et finis esset vitiis et origo virtutum*), from Genesis 9; that the crucified "gave forth water from his side along with blood" (*una cum sanguine aquam de latere suo produxit*), from 1 John 5:8, which text gives rise to St. Augustine's profound reflections that the sacraments come forth from the side of Christ; that those who are found worthy "may be found worthy to rise to the new life of newborn children through water and the Holy Spirit" (*in novam infantiam ex aqua*

213

et Spiritu Sancto resurgere mereatur),[48] from Romans 6.[49] Other references to water in this prayer include the petition "May this water receive by the Holy Spirit the grace of your Only Begotten Son" (*Sumat haec aqua Unigeniti tui gratiam de Spiritu Sancto*) for those who are "washed clean through the sacrament of baptism from all the squalor of the life of old" (*sacramemnto baptismalis a cunctis squaloribus vetustatis ablutus*). Another reference to water concerns "the very substance of water" (*aquam natura conciperet*).[50]

In the former prayer used to bless water at the Easter Vigil, the first section speaks generously about what it will effect by using phrases such as "the spirit of adoption to regenerate the new people from the font of baptism" (*recreandos novos populous...fons baptismatis...spiritum adoptionis*).[51] This section does not mention water but rather speaks about the "font," which contains water. The structure of the prayer then imitates the structure of prefaces at Mass (and the *Exsultet*) and acclaims how the Spirit hovered over the waters at Creation (*Deus, cuius Spiritus super aquas*) as well as the flood (*per aquas abulens*), again Genesis 1 and 9. It cites the "nature of water" (*aquarum natura*) as well as "this water of regeneration" (*qui hanc aquam regerationis*). To such positive images are added phrases such as "may all unclean spirits depart" (*omnis spiritus immundus abscedat*) and "may the whole malice of devilish deceit be entirely banished" (*procul tota nequitia diabolicae fraudis absistat*), which phrases are followed by an explicit exorcism of the water. Notably, toward the end of the prayer the singular is used: "I bless you creature water" (*creatura aquae*) and "I bless you also by our Lord Jesus Christ" (*benedico te et per Iesum Christum Filium eius unicum, Dominum nostrum*). The presider says (three times), "May the power of the Holy Spirit descend into the water of this font" (*Descendat in hanc plenitudinem fontis virtus Spiritus Sancti*). He then prays, "Make the whole substance of this water fruitful for rebirth" (*huius aquae substantiam, regnerandi fecundet effectu*). The oil of catechumens is added to the water with the words, "May this font be made fruitful by the oil of salvation" (*et fecundetur fons iste Oleo salutis*), and chrism is added, calling it "the Chrism of holiness [and] the oil of anointing and the Water of Baptism" (*Commixio chrismatis sanctificationis et Olei unctionis, et aquae baptismatis*).[52]

There are clear advantages in the revised prayer, among which are its emphasis on the span of saving history not seen in the former prayer, the use of *we* throughout rather than the singular *I*, and a worldview that emphasizes the positive and life-giving qualities of water as opposed to the former prayer, which exorcizes this primal element.

Some commentators regret that the present prayer for blessing at the Vigil places more (and unprecedented) emphasis on a paschal theology of baptism rather than a theology of "rebirth." But when initiates are immersed in the "creature water," is not the theology of rebirth always operative precisely because of the element water?

Rite for the Blessing and Sprinkling of Water—Sundays

The rite of the blessing and sprinkling of water for use "from time to time" on Sundays as a renewal of baptism, included in the Appendix of the revised Missal, is loosely connected with a similar rite that could take place before one Mass on a Sunday in the previous *Missale Romanum* (i.e., the *Asperges me* and the *Vidi aquam*).[53] References to water abound in the present prayers, but most notable is the invitation. It asks God "to bless this water he has created," which Latin phrase, *ut hanc creaturam aquae benedicere*, explicitly refers to "the creature water" (which would be a better translation both literally and theologically).[54] The first prayer then speaks of water as "the fountain of life and source of purification" (*fontem vitae ac purificationis principium*) through which "souls should be cleansed and receive the gift of eternal life." The priest then asks that God "bless this water by which we seek protection on this your day," then "renew the living spirit within us" and that "by this water we may be defended from all ills of spirit and body" (*omni malo spiritus et corporis*).

A second prayer asks that God "bless this water" (*hanc aquam*) "to implore forgiveness for our sins," "to obtain the protection of your grace," that the "living waters [*aquae vivae*] may always spring up for our salvation," "so may we approach you with a pure heart and avoid all danger to body and soul." A third prayer (for the Easter season) asks God to bless the water (*hanc aquam benedicere tu dignare*) and contains images from saving history (specifically the desert, the Prophets, and Christ in the Jordan). These are accompanied by references to water that God "created...to make the fields fruitful, and to refresh and cleanse our bodies" (*et levamen corporibus donaret et lavem corporibus nostris*). Toward the end, the prayer speaks of baptism as "the bath of regeneration."

While not an exact parallel, the former *Rituale Romanum* contains a prayer for blessing water outside of the Easter Vigil.[55] Its first section is called the "exorcism," containing the then-customary references to what the priest does by stating twice that "I exorcise you" "in the name of Christ" "from every power of the enemy" that this "creature water" (*creatura aquae*) may be a "fountain of water springing up unto life everlasting."[56] The second section is titled "Prayer," naming God as "sanctifier of spiritual waters," who is asked to send "the angel of holiness upon these waters" (*et super has aquas*) so that those who are baptized in it may have "the sins of their past life washed away, their guilt wiped out, that they may be reborn as a pure dwelling place for the Holy Spirit." Then the priest pours both the oil of catechumens and chrism into the water, speaking about their union with "the water of baptism" (*aquae Baptismatis*). The rite concludes with a reference both to the font (the translation says "water" where the Latin reads *fons*) and "those who will be reborn in it."

One distinct advantage of this rite for baptismal renewal on Sundays is that it places a ritual in the Roman Rite that draws out the meaning that every Eucharist is a covenant renewal first forged sacramentally in baptism—"the blood of the new and eternal covenant."

Gerard Austin's legacy is broad, deep, and rich. Might we pray one future gift to the church be the reunion of those who are initiated into "the church" by the rites and prayers that surround new life in water and the Spirit about which he taught so well?

Notes

1. He would always make sure we nuanced our use of the word *church*. See the brief, yet (unfortunately) necessary reminder in Gordon

Lathrop, "The Study of Liturgy: An Ecumenical Rejoinder," *Worship* 92 (January 2018): 46–53.

2. Pope Francis, "Encyclical Letter on Care for Our Common Home, *Laudato Si'*" (May 24, 2015), http://w2.vatican.va/content/francesco/en/encyclicals/documents/papa-francesco_20150524 _enciclica-laudato-si.html. Note especially the subtitle ("On Care for Our Common Home") and no. 92.

3. See my own "Ecology," in *The Oxford Handbook of Ecumenical Studies*, ed. Geoffrey Wainwright and Paul McPartlan (Oxford: Oxford University Press, 2017), http://www.oxfordhandbooks.com/view/10 .1093/oxfordhb/9780199600847.001.0001/oxfordhb-9780199600847 -e-23.

4. Dimitrios, "Patriarchal Encyclical for the Day for the Protection of the Environment, *The Church Cannot Remain Idle*," in *On Earth as in Heaven: Ecological Vision and Initiatives of Ecumenical Patriarch Bartholomew*, ed. John Chryssavgis (New York: Fordham University Press, 2012), 23–25.

5. World Council of Churches, *Now Is the Time, Final Document and Other Texts: World Convocation on Justice, Peace and the Integrity of Creation* (Geneva: WCC Publications, 1990).

6. John Paul II, "Message for the World Day of Peace, *Peace with God the Creator, Peace with All of Creation*" (January 1, 1990), http://w2 .vatican.va/content/john-paul-ii/en/messages/peace/documents/hf_jp -ii_mes_19891208_xxiii-world-day-for-peace.html.

7. Therefore, the WCC's agreed statement on the sacraments from January 1982 is even more remarkable: Faith and Order, *Baptism, Eucharist and Ministry*, Faith and Order Paper 111 (January 15, 1982), https:// www.oikoumene.org/en/resources/documents/commissions/faith-and -order/i-unity-the-church-and-its-mission/baptism-eucharist-and -ministry-faith-and-order-paper-no-111-the-lima-text.

8. Ralph N. McMichael, ed., *Creation and Liturgy: Essays in Honor of H. Boone Porter* (Washington, DC: Pastoral Press, 1993). *Creation and Liturgy* contains essays by very distinguished North American liturgical scholars: Aidan Kavanagh, Thomas J. Talley, Paul F. Bradshaw, Leonel L. Mitchell, Bonnell Spencer, Marion J. Hatchett, Charles P. Price, Byron Stuhlman, Louis Weil, A. MacDonald Allchin, Ralph N. McMichael, Reginald H. Fuller, Nathan Wright, Ormonde Plater, Barbara Carey, Frank C. Senn, John Wilkinson, and Anne Perkins. It is notable that the essays are

divided under the topics "Lex Orandi," "Lex Credendi," and "Lex Vivendi."

9. United States Roman Catholic–United Methodist Dialogue, Agreed Statement, *Heaven and Earth Are Full of Your Glory* (2012), http://www.usccb.org/beliefs-and-teachings/ecumenical-and -interreligious/ecumenical/methodist/upload/Heaven-and-Earth-are -Full-of-Your-Glory-Methodist-Catholic-Dialogue-Agreed-Statement -Round-Seven.pdf. The phrase "the structure of the historic liturgy" means the structures of the liturgy as prescribed and used in mainline "liturgical churches," e.g., the Orthodox, Eastern Christians, Roman Catholics, Anglicans, Episcopalians, Lutherans, Methodists, and others.

10. See my own *A Commentary on* Laudato Si': *Examining the Background, Contributions, Implementation, and Future of Pope Francis's Encyclical* (New York: Paulist Press, 2016), 40–59. The document from the bishops of the United States is United States Conference of Catholic Bishops, *Global Climate Change: A Plea for Dialogue, Prudence and the Common Good* (June 15, 2001), http://www.usccb.org/issues-and -action/human-life-and-dignity/environment/global-climate-change-a -plea-for-dialogue-prudence-and-the-common-good.cfm.

11. See Walt Grazer, "*Laudato Si'*: Continuity, Change and Challenge," in *Creation Is Connected: Voices in Response to Pope Francis's Encyclical on Ecology*, ed. Daniel R. DiLeo (Winona: Anselm Academic, 2018), 32–34. Some of the papers delivered at the USCCB summer seminars are in Walt Grazer and Drew Christiansen, eds., *And God Saw That It Was Good: Catholic Theology and the Environment* (Washington, DC: USCCB, 1996).

12. Benedict XVI, "Post-Synodal Apostolic Exhortation on the Eucharist as the Source and Summit of the Church's Life and Mission, *Sacramentum Caritatis*" (February 22, 2007), http://w2.vatican.va/ content/benedict-xvi/en/apost_exhortations/documents/hf_ben -xvi_exh_20070222_sacramentum-caritatis.html. My own pathways in researching and writing about ecology began at a conference at Georgetown University in 1993 (inspired by John Paul II's 1990 Message for the World Day of Peace), published as Edmund Pellegrino and Kevin W. Irwin, eds., *Preserving the Creation: Environmental Theology and Ethics* (Washington, DC: Georgetown University Press, 1994).

13. Francis, *Laudato Si'*. Notably, *dialogue* is addressed in the text nearly two dozen times (nos. 3, 14, 15, 47, 60, 62, 63, 64, 81, 119, 121,

143, 146, 163, 164 [twice], 176, 189, 199, 201). Several initial reactions indicate the importance this encyclical will likely continue to have. For example, see the collection Vincent Miller, ed., *The Theological and Ecological Vision of* Laudato Si': *Everything Is Connected* (London/Oxford: Bloomsbury, 2017), which originated from a 2015 symposium at the University of Dayton. Also see the articles devoted to *Laudato Si'* in *Theological Studies* 77, no. 2 (June 2016), whose editorial stated that Francis's encyclical is "the most important encyclical ever written in the history of the Catholic Church" (293). It is more than noteworthy that the Catholic Theological Society of America devoted its 2016 convention to the theme "Ecology: Theological Investigations," https://ejournals.bc.edu/ojs/index.php/ctsa/issue/view/977. Among other (what I judge to be) world class meetings on *Laudato Si'* include the invitation-only symposium "Connecting Ecologies," which gathered experts in a variety of fields (theology, ethics, philosophy, politics, science, etc.) at Campion Hall, Oxford, in December 2017; the papers will be published in *The Heythrop Journal* 59, no. 6 (November 2018): 867–1080.

14. For one example of the way a careful reading of *Laudato Si'* can lead to relating creation to the sacraments and how the celebration of the sacraments leads to important (social) justice implications—such as just wages and working conditions, air pollution, and so on—see the talk by Cardinal Peter Turkson, prefect for the Dicastery of Integral Human Development, at the 2016 Eucharistic Congress in the Philippines, "The Eucharist and the Care for Creation" (January 27, 2016), http://www.iustitiaetpax.va/content/dam/giustiziaepace/presidenteinterventi/2016/2016.01.27%20Turkson-Ledesma_IEC_ENG.pdf.

15. The Rite of Marriage repeatedly refers to "the new creation," yet determining the church's *lex orandi* here requires careful research and interpretation.

16. See Jürgen Moltmann's interesting thesis, "The Sabbath: The Feast of Creation," in *God in Creation: A New Theology of Creation and the Spirit of God* (San Francisco: Harper and Row, 1985), 276–95, and the appendix, "Symbols of the World," 297–328. The important place of the Sabbath in Pope Francis's theology goes back to when he edited the episcopal conference of Latin America's *Aparecida Concluding Document* (2007) through to *Laudato Si'*. See Consejo episcopal Latinoamericano, *Aparecida Concluding Document* (2007), www.celam.org/aparecida/Ingles.pdf; my own, *A Commentary on Laudato Si'*, 37–39.

17. There are five Mass formulas for "VII Kalens Iulias Natale Sancti Iohannis Baptistae" in the Verona Collection. *Sacramentarium Veronense,* ed. Leo Cunibert Mohlberg, *Rerum ecclesiasticarum documenta* 1 (Rome: Herder, 1978), nos. 232–56.

18. Insightful descriptions of the *lucernarium* and its influence on Christian vespers are found in Paul F. Bradshaw, *Daily Prayer in the Early Church* (New York: Oxford University Press, 1982), 22, 51, 57, 75–77, 80, 116, 119, 135; George Guiver, *Company of Voices: Daily Prayer and the People of God* (New York: Pueblo, 1988), 62–66, 202–3; Robert Taft, *The Liturgy of the Hours in East and West* (Collegeville, MN: Liturgical Press, 1986), 26–28, 36–38, 55–56, 211–12, 355–56.

19. See Susan Roll, *Towards the Origins of Christmas, Liturgia Condenda* 5 (Leuven: Peeters, 1995). That there is another theory about the origin of Christmas as intrinsically related to the paschal mystery needs to be recalled.

20. The New Testament also explicitly confirms that creation can serve the mediating function of coming to know God. A classic text used to support the notion that creation can lead to knowledge of God is Romans 1:19–20.

21. Besides these hymns for ferial evening prayer, several other texts, prescribed for use in the former Breviary, are similarly inspired by or refer to creation. Among these texts are the following: *Creator alme siderum,* vespers Sundays and weekdays of Advent; *Audi benigne conditor,* vespers Sundays and weekdays of Lent; *Quem terra, pontus, sidera,* matins of the Blessed Virgin Mary without a proper matins hymn; *Rerum creator optime,* Wednesday matins; *Rerum Deus tenax vigor,* none throughout the year; *Salutis humanae sator,* vespers Ascension to Pentecost; *Aeterne rerum conditor,* Sunday lauds; *Ecce jam noctis,* Sunday lauds; *Splendor paternae gloriae,* Monday lauds; *Primo die, quo Trinitas,* Sunday matins; *O sol salutis, intimis,* Lent lauds; *Rex sempiterne coelitum,* Eastertide matins; *Veni creator Spiritus,* vespers and terce on Pentecost and through octave. For vesper hymns translated into English and set to various metrical settings, see *The Hymnal for the Hours* (Chicago: Gregorian Institute of America, 1989), nos. 148–57; *The Summit Choirbook* (Summit: Dominican Nuns, 1983), nos. 179–86.

22. See Matthew Britt, *The Hymns of the Breviary and Missal* (New York: Benziger Brothers, 1922), 74. Britt's work includes Latin texts and

English translations, notes on authorship and a theological commentary. Translations of these hymns are taken from Britt.

23. See Britt, *The Hymns*, 73–85.

24. See Britt, *The Hymns*, 84.

25. The General Instruction on the Liturgy of the Hours states, "The psalmody of morning prayer consists of one morning psalm, then a canticle from the Old Testament…and finally a second psalm of praise, following the tradition of the Church" (no. 43).

26. For example, Bernhard Anderson states, "Creation is the foundation of the covenant; it provides the setting within which Yahweh's saving work takes place. But it is equally true that creation is embraced within the theological meaning of covenant. Therefore psalmists may regard creation as the first of God's saving deeds (Psalm 74:12–17) and in the recitation of the Heilgeschichte may move without a break from the deeds of creation to historical deeds of liberation (Psalm 136)." Bernhard W. Anderson, *From Creation to New Creation: Old Testament Perspectives* (1994; repr., Eugene, OR: Wipf and Stock, 2005), 26.

27. Bernhard Anderson states, "It seems, then, that Israel's earliest traditions did not refer to Yahweh as creator in a cosmic sense but concentrated, rather, on Yahweh's 'mighty deeds' of liberation, through which the Holy God became known and formed Israel as a people out of the chaos of historical oblivion and oppression." Anderson, *From Creation to New Creation*, 23–24.

28. See Cesare Giraudo, *La struttura letteraria della preghiera eucaristica: Saggio sullagenesi letteraria di una forma; Toda veterotestamentaria Berakah giudaica*, Anafora cristiana (Rome: Biblical Institute Press, 1981); and *Eucaristia per la Chiesa: Prospettive teologiche sulla l'eucaristia a partire della "lex orandi"* (Rome: Gregorian University Press, 1989).

29. The use of *classic* in "classical eucharistic anaphoras" indicates those elements that are most generally found in eucharistic prayers in the tradition. It is not meant to suggest that there is but one model for eucharistic praying. In fact, a review of these prayers discloses much variation within the commonly agreed upon anaphoral structure. See, e.g., the useful overview of the ritual and theological differences in Hans Bernhard Meyer, *Gottesdienst der Kirche: Handbuch der Liturgiewissenschaft*, vol. 4, *Eucharistie: Geschichte, Theologie, Pastoral* (Regensburg: Friedrich Pustet, 1989), esp. chap. 3, "Vom Herrenmahl zur Eucharistiefeier," and chap. 4, "Die Ritusfamilien des Ostens und des Westens." A helpful comparison

summary of the Antiochean and Alexandrian anaphoral structure is on page 133. For a collection of such texts and appropriate comparisons within and among liturgical families, see Anton Hänggi and Irmgard Pahl, *Prex eucharistica: Textus e variis liturgiis antiquioribus selecti* (Fribourg: Editions Universitaires, 1968). Also see Joseph Keenan, "The Importance of the Creation Motif in the Eucharistic Prayer," *Worship* 53, no. 4 (1979): 341–56.

30. Louis Bouyer argues that the sources for this prayer are Eastern and include the *Apostolic Constitutions*, the Liturgy of St. James, and the Liturgy of St. Basil. See Louis Bouyer, *Eucharist: Theology and Spirituality of the Eucharistic Prayer* (Notre Dame: University of Notre Dame Press, 1968), 448.

31. Bernhard Anderson states, "Although all God's creatures are summoned to praise their Creator, human beings are the only earthlings in whom praise can become articulate. They are made for conversation with God, for a dialogue in an I-and-thou relation....Israel's calling is to vocalize the praise that wells up from all peoples and nations." Anderson, *From Creation to New Creation*, 34.

32. Anderson, *From Creation to New Creation*, 44, where he cites Herman Gunkel, "The Influence of Babylonian Mythology upon the Biblical Creation Story," trans. Charles A. Muenchow, in *Creation in the Old Testament*, ed. B. W. Anderson (Philadelphia: Fortress Press, 1984), 25–52; Anderson, *Creation Versus Chaos: The Reinterpretation of Mythical Symbolism in the Bible* (New York: Association Press, 1967), chap. 1.

33. On the term *cosmogonic myths* in the history of religions and why it was repeated annually, most usually in the spring, see Mircea Eliade, *Cosmos and Myth*, trans. Willard Trask (New York: Harper Torchbooks, 1959).

34. Anderson, *From Creation to New Creation*, 29–30 (on John 1:1–18).

35. A comparison of the titles for God in the present Latin *Missale Romanum* reveals that, among the most frequently used terms, *omnipotens* is used 277 times, whereas *creator* is used 5 times. See Thaddaus A. Schnitker and Wolfgang A. Slaby, *Concordantia verbalia Missalis Romani* (Westfalen: Aschendorff Munster, 1983), col. 398–99, 1704–16. In *Reviving Sacred Speech*, Gail Ramshaw states, "Thus at the beginning of the Great Thanksgiving, we pray along with Abraham who obeyed the call (Genesis 12:4), with Moses, who received the Torah (Exodus 19:20), and

with Jesus, who was the Word (John 1:1). As we eat bread and wine, we recall Abraham, who shared his food with three mysterious visitors (Genesis 18:8), Moses, who ate and drank with God on Sinai and did not die (Exodus 24:11), and Jesus, who breaking bread on Sunday evening, showed forth his wounds (Luke 24:31)." Gail Ramshaw, *Reviving Sacred Speech: The Meaning of Liturgical Language; Second Thoughts on Christ in Sacred Speech* (Akron, OH: OSL Publications, 2000), 44.

36. See, among others, Jürgen Moltmann, *The Future of Creation: Collected Essays,* trans. Margaret Kohl (Philadelphia: Fortress Press, 1979), 119–30.

37. See Edward J. Kilmartin, *Christian Liturgy* (Kansas City, MO: Sheed and Ward, 1988), esp. 100–199; Jean Corbon, *The Wellspring of Worship,* trans. Matthew O'Connell (New York: Paulist Press, 1988).

38. See Cinette Ferriere, "A propos de *Dieu-potier* Images de la création et foi chrétienne en Dieu créateur," *Paroisse et Liturgie* 48, no. 6 (1966): 533–48.

39. See Moltmann, *God in Creation,* 9–13; and Lukas Vischer, "Giver of Life—Sustain Your Creation!" *The Ecumenical Review* 42, no. 2 (April 1990): 143–49.

40. This suggests that the theology of what happens in and through the liturgy is the theology *of* liturgy, where theology that is embedded in and drawn from the liturgy is theology *from* the liturgy.

41. "The Church, therefore, earnestly desires that Christ's faithful, when present at this mystery of faith, should not be there as strangers or silent spectators; on the contrary, through a good understanding of the rites and prayers [*per ritus et preces*] they should take part in the sacred action conscious of what they are doing, with devotion and full collaboration." Second Vatican Council, "Constitution on the Sacred Liturgy, *Sacrosanctum Concilium*" (December 4, 1963), http://www.vatican.va/archive/hist_councils/ii_vatican_council/documents/vat-ii_const_19631204_sacrosanctum-concilium_en.html, no. 48.

42. See my own *Context and Text: A Method for Liturgical Theology,* 2nd ed. (Collegeville, MN: Liturgical Press, 2018), 1st ed. subtitled "Method in Liturgical Theology" (Collegeville, MN: Liturgical Press, 1994).

43. See my own *The Sacraments: Historical Foundations and Liturgical Theology* (Mahwah, NJ: Paulist Press, 2016), 211–12.

44. Clearly Benedict XVI wrote extensively on the liturgy with a certain (much debated) set of presuppositions and prejudices. It is more than noteworthy, however, that the collection of his essays on the liturgy (never having written a monograph on the liturgy) contains not one reference to a liturgical source. What abound are references to (mostly German) systematic and biblical theologians. See Joseph Ratzinger, *Gesammelte Schriften: Theologie der Liturgie* (Freiburg/Basel/Wien: Herder, 2008). The more popular iteration of Ratzinger's ideas for the English-speaking world is the translation of the first 194 pages of *Theologie* as *The Spirit of the Liturgy*, trans. John Saward (San Francisco: Ignatius Press, 2000). Here Ratzinger lays out some of his (not illegitimate) critiques of the reformed liturgy but does nothing to suggest how to either invite dialogue about them, especially to determine whether his writing is accurate or not, or to ameliorate them. Nor does he refer to a source from the liturgy itself.

45. Among others, see the masterful study by Nicholas Denysenko, *The Blessing of Waters and Epiphany: The Eastern Liturgical Tradition* (Surrey/Burlington: Ashgate, 2012).

46. A related adjustment is that the prayer for blessing in the rite for infant baptism is presumed to be done each time a baptism occurs (except during the Easter season, when the water blessed at the vigil is to be used).

47. Texts from the revised *Missale Romanum* in any number of editions, including *Missale Romanum*, editio typica tertia (Vaticano: Libreria Editrice Vaticana, 2002).

48. When compared with the regular translation of *mereor* verbs in the revised *Roman Missal* as "may merit," the absence of *merit* in this translation is most notable.

49. See the very important studies by Dominic Serra about the changes made in the reformed liturgy from the original in the *Gelasianum vetus*: "The Blessing of Baptismal Water at the Paschal Vigil in the Gelasianum Vetus: A Study of the Euchological Texts, Ge 444–448," *Ecclesia orans* 6 (1989): 323–44; "The Blessing of Baptismal Water at the Paschal Vigil: Its Post–Vatican II Reform," *Ecclesia orans* 7 (1990): 343–68; "The Blessing of Baptismal Water at the Paschal Vigil: Ancient Texts and Modern Revisions," *Worship* 64 (1990): 142–56.

50. Note that the Latin text *natura* is translated here as "substance."

51. These texts are from the "Tridentine" Missal and are found in any number of sources. Translations are from *St. Andrew Bible Missal* (Bruges: DDB Publishers, 1962).

52. *Liber sacramentiorum romanae aeclesiae ordinis anni circuli: Sacramentarium Gelasianum; Cod. Vat. Reg. lat. 316,* ed. Leo Cunibert Mohlberg (1960; repr., Rome: Casa Herder, 1981), nos. 444–48, pp. 72–73.

53. Among others, see *Roman Missal* (New York: Magnificat, 2011), 1441. On the previous practice, see *Liber Usualis* (New York: Desclee, 1962), 10–13.

54. This phrase, which coincides with the theology of *Laudato Si'*, insists that we are all "fellow creatures." If salt is to be blessed and added to the water, it is notable that the phrase is "to bless this creature salt," *ut hanc creaturam salis.*

55. That there were a number of rituals issued after Trent, with differences among the texts, is worth noting, and comparisons among them have been very fruitful studies. The Latin and English texts used here are from *The Roman Ritual,* ed. Philip T. Weller, complete ed. (Milwaukee: Bruce Publishing, 1964).

56. Weller, *The Roman Ritual,* 137.

12

LITURGY AND THE NEW COSMOLOGY

—⚬—

Catherine Vincie, RSHM

Some may wonder what is the New Cosmology and what could be the relationship between the New Cosmology and Christian worship. Both are interesting and important questions. This essay attempts to unfold what the Old and New Cosmology are, and why exploring contemporary scientific cosmology is an important theological task. We have traditionally learned of God by looking at the "book of scripture" and the "book of nature." I will argue that it is exceedingly important for Christian theology and liturgy to engage the new science because such knowledge will expand our knowledge of God and will engage us in the quest for the truth of how things really are. We have learned an extraordinary amount about the "book of nature" in the last four hundred years, and it is imperative that we not remain with an outdated cosmology for the sake of naming God truthfully and naming our reality truthfully. Our liturgies should also reflect an updated cosmology lest we alienate our people by having liturgical prayer present a cosmology we no longer hold, or lead people to think that clashing worldviews between liturgy and contemporary culture is not a problem. I also have a pastoral concern that unless we put science and religion in dialogue, we will lose the next generations that are looking for where the truth of science and the truth of religion coincide.

COSMOLOGY—OLD AND NEW

Early Christianity, its liturgical practices and theological writings, was, of necessity, shaped within the thought-world of the

Mediterranean basin and the ancient Near East at the time of its origins and early development. This included the biblical world of Israel, the world of Greco-Roman thought, as well as the contributions of other great civilizations of the ancient Near East. Christianity had no other choice than to use the concepts, worldview, and cosmology of the world within which it found itself. It had a context and contributed to that context with its own particularity.

Cosmology itself is the search for the understanding of how the world really is; it is the study of the origin and ordering of the universe. It can also be understood as the lens through which reality is seen. Christian cosmology was based primarily on a biblical cosmology outlined in the early chapters of Genesis, although aspects of it are found throughout the Hebrew Scriptures. Biblical cosmology presents a static world, created out of nothing by the one good God who made all there is in six days. Everything was created as we now know it "in the beginning." The earth was flat with waters below the earth and a dome above the earth from where snow, hail, and rain came with variable regularity. Humanity was made in the image of God and was the pinnacle of creation. Paradise, a time and place of right relationships among all God's creations, was an original gift of the past that humankind lost in an act of disobedience. This so-called original sin set humankind at odds with God and with creation. Soteriology, or the study of salvation, has often been explored in light of this original sin.

In addition to the biblical worldview and cosmology, Christianity was also influenced by Greek astronomy, which was generated during the ancient Greek, Hellenistic, Greco-Roman, and Late Antiquity eras. Of particular importance is the work of the Greek thinker Claudius Ptolemy, a mathematician and astronomer who worked at Alexandria in Roman Egypt in the second century. Ptolemy's works on astronomy include the *Almagest*, which is arguably the most influential book on astronomy of its time. Ptolemy's planetary model was a series of seven concentric circles with Earth at the center and the sun and the other planets revolving around Earth at varying distances. His cosmos, like the biblical cosmos, was also a static cosmos; it was an infinite universe in terms of time and was spatially limited to what could be seen with the naked eye aided by mathematics. All creatures were created in fixed forms at the beginning of time, and celestial bodies were made of different material than Earth and work according to different laws. While much more could be said of the biblical and Greek cosmology, it ruled and influenced Christian thought and practice for some fifteen hundred years. We can call this cosmology the "Old Cosmology."

The Earth-centered universe was challenged on a number of levels by what was to become known as modern scientific thinking that developed since the sixteenth century. In the West, Nicholas Copernicus (d. 1543) decentered Earth and placed the sun at the center of our planetary system. Galileo Galilei (1564–1642), using his newly discovered telescope, affirmed Copernicus's model of the planetary system and provided strong observational evidence of his findings. Johannes Kepler (1571–1630) critiqued the circular model of the planets by proving the elliptical shape of planetary motion and laid the foundation for Newtonian physics of the late seventeenth century.

The eighteenth-century geologist James Hutton, in his text *The Theory of the Earth: An Investigation of the Laws Observable in the Composition, Dissolution, and Restoration of Land upon the Globe* (1788), was the first to develop a theory of deep geologic time. In his work, he argued that Earth was millions of years old and was perpetually being formed. In the mid-nineteenth century, Gregor Mendel explored the inheritance of genetic characteristics across generations. Even more startling to our conception of the universe were the nineteenth-century developments that challenged a static understanding of the cosmos. In his groundbreaking work *The Origin of Species* (1859), Charles Darwin built upon the theories of his predecessors and introduced the idea of evolution, which became the operative principle for the development of all earthly matter/creatures. According to Darwin, environment, genetics, chance, and deep time were responsible for the formation, development, and dissolution of species. Little did he know that his evolutive model would dominate cosmology for the next 150 years.

In contrast to the biblical and early Greek cosmology that ruled for fifteen centuries, the outstanding ideas of this new era were that change rather than stasis characterize Earth and the cosmos. Various plants and animals were not fixed in the beginning of time, but they evolved according to heredity, environment, and chance. Humans too have their own story of development. They developed from primates through their hominid ancestors to modern humans over millions of years. We have also learned that suffering and waste are intrinsic to evolution.

The developments in science in the twentieth and twenty-first centuries constitute what may be called the New Cosmology. Beginning with Albert Einstein, Edwin Hubble, and their colleagues, cosmology developed significantly at the macro and micro levels. Through the work of astronomy, astrophysics, and cosmology, we now understand that the known Universe started with the Big Bang, an explosion of an exceedingly small and dense bit of matter and energy. The best estimate of the age of the universe is 13.82 billion years old; scientists are unable to calculate the size of the universe, but they do know that it is still expanding. As of August 2017, they now estimate that there are over 2 trillion galaxies besides the Milky Way. Because of major advances in various kinds of earth and space telescopes, scientists are daily learning the magnitude of the universe and are being forced to acknowledge that any of their findings must be qualified by the proviso "at this time." With the development of string theory, it is proposed that there may be parallel universes although there is no observable evidence of this possibility at the present. In sum, the learnings of the New Science at the macro level are that the universe is extremely large, old, complex, and fine-tuned. Space, time, and mass are related, the Universe is still expanding, and evolution is one of the laws of the cosmos.

At the micro level, scientists have also made astonishing discoveries through particle physics, quantum mechanics, and evolutionary biology. Scientific instruments of note in this area are the quantum microscope and the particle accelerator. In sum, we have posited that everything is related to everything else at the cellular level. As scientists explore reality at the subatomic level, they have come to some surprising conclusions. Somewhat illogically, they have come to understand that something can be a wave and a particle at the same time. What is known as the uncertainty principle suggests that the more precise the measurement of the position of the particle, the more uncertain its movement. Examples could be multiplied, but these are enough to indicate the huge advances in knowledge on the micro level.

In short, Big Bang cosmology suggests that everything is related to everything else. Further, we have come to know that the universe is still expanding and is in evolution. For all that we have come to understand, we have been chastened by the extent of our unknowing. The universe, for example, is made up of 90 percent dark energy and dark matter, about which we know relatively nothing. In an evolutionary cosmos, the emphasis is not on the past or even on the present ongoing creation, but on the future. We now know that the growth of the universe has been from simplicity to greater complexity, diversity, and consciousness. Perhaps most significant, we now understand that the human is the universe come to consciousness. What the cosmos is moving toward, we cannot imagine, but the story of the cosmos is toward the more and toward the future. Theologian John Haught has argued that the most significant finding of the New Cosmology is its narrative character and that humanity finds its own story within this cosmic narrative. God, too, has a place in this narrative for the believer. Haught says, "The narrative pattern of evolution fits comfortably into a worldview that features as its ground, center, and future a self-giving God who offers the universe—and perhaps a multiverse—an open future in which to become actualized in new, though also dangerous ways."[1]

SCIENCE AND RELIGION

In the early centuries of the church, biblical interpretation followed several convictions: Scripture was thought of as having a "plain sense" and a "figurative sense." Therefore, it is *cryptic*, has a hidden or coded meaning; *relevant*, has importance for the current time; *perfect*, has no internal contradictions and does not conflict with the world outside the text; *divine*, is divine speech either authorized or authored by God. From the early church through the early Medieval period, science of the physical world and that of the Bible were seen as compatible. If there was a conflict, the figurative sense of Scripture won out, thus alleviating the conflict. The church/bishops helped to interpret scriptural texts, preventing to some degree wild interpretations of texts.

In the late Medieval world of Christianity, allegorical readings of Scripture became exaggerated. As a result, the figurative sense of Scripture was contested and the authority of the church to regulate scriptural interpretation was questioned. Among the reformers, only the plain sense or the literal sense of the Scriptures was considered as true. In the larger culture, because of developments in science, the authority of the Bible came into question. During the seventeenth and eighteenth centuries, scientific truth rose to equal footing with truth of Scripture, even surpassing it. If scientific knowledge of the universe conflicted with Scripture, the truth of science won out. Increasingly, science and theology went their separate ways.

In the nineteenth and twentieth centuries, fundamentalist churches held that the literal meaning of the scriptural text takes absolute priority. If science and the Bible conflict, the biblical explanation wins out. In other churches (including the Roman Catholic), both a literal and figurative meaning is considered. With the rise of historical-critical interpretation, it became clear that the Bible is not meant to be a scientific handbook. The implication is that scientific and religious truth can coexist, although it did not immediately follow that science and religion could be in dialogue to mutual benefit. Theologian John Haught, a specialist in the religion/science relationship, has argued that four possible relationships could exist between religion and science: (1) Conflict: pits religion and science against one another; (2) Contrast: religion and science are about two different things; (3) Contact or conversation: interaction of science and religion; (4) Confirmation: religion supports the scientific enterprise. His preferred models are Contact and Confirmation.

THE NEW COSMOLOGY AND THEOLOGY

A predominantly literal reading of Genesis 1—11 with its past-centered and static view of creation held sway for much of the history of Christian theology. This changed when an evolutionary approach that was future oriented and dynamic called for a complete rethinking of Christian theology. Unfortunately, for the late nineteenth century and most of the twentieth century, Catholic theology did not meet this challenge. Evolutionary theory has caused considerable dis-ease within the Catholic intellectual community since Darwin first proposed his theory. In the century following Darwin, the official church was generally against theories of evolution, often because they were identified with scientific materialism[2] and also because science now contradicted a literal reading of Genesis 1—11, which was still in vogue. In the second half of the twentieth century, developments in biblical interpretation released us from a literalist reading of the Genesis narrative, and some opening to evolution became manifest. Documents of the Second Vatican Council (namely, *Gaudium et spes*) began to include evolutionary themes, and in 1979, Pope John Paul II acknowledged that evolution was "more than a hypothesis."[3]

In the first half of the twentieth century, paleontologist and priest Pierre Teilhard de Chardin, SJ, made the first significant attempt to bring the findings of modern science into dialogue with Christian thought. Arguing against atheistic scientists and scientific materialists who claimed that the universe was mindless and purposeless, Teilhard argued that the universe is not random, mindless, or purposeless. It is organic and involves a dynamic unfolding process working to a larger purpose. In his *Hymn of the Universe*, he argues that the universe should be likened not to a bundle of elements artificially bound together, but rather to an organic system animated by a broad movement of development. In his mind, the world is in process and everything appears at its proper time and place as required and determined by the good of the whole. For Teilhard, it is not by looking back into history that we find the meaning and purpose of the universe, but by looking ahead to the God who calls us out of the future. The universe is still coming into being, and we cannot understand the story without looking ahead. This requires cosmic patience and hope for the world's future.

In the last twenty years, many theologians have taken up the task of addressing the relationship of the New Cosmology to various topics in Christian theology. Of particular note are Ian Barbour, John Polkinghorne, Arthur Peacocke, Denis Edwards, John Haught, Ilia

Delio, Elizabeth Johnson, among others. What they are doing is recasting the various themes in systematic theology in light of the findings of the New Cosmology. The following gives a taste of what is being done.

On Creation: John Haught suggests that the current turn to the cosmos arouses sheer wonder and awe in us and invites the Christian community to bring praise and thanks to the creating God of this vast cosmos. The one God created all that is at a given point in time; God is its source, sustaining power, and goal. God creates something other than Godself, gives it autonomy, and calls it into participation in God. God is not the absent clockmaker or manager but the God who allures us into the future from ahead as the strange attractor. The goal of the universe is unity in differentiation—as is the nature of God.

On God: Arthur Peacocke writes that the God of creation must be some kind of "diversity-in-unity," a Being of unfathomable richness, capable of multiple expressions and variegated outreach, supremely and unsurpassably rational, omniscient, omnipotent, personal, and supra-personal. Peacocke suggests that like the great musical improviser Johann Sebastian Bach, God unfolds the potentialities of the universe through law and chance. God takes joy and delight in creation and in its laws. Addressing the great question of suffering throughout creation, Peacocke argues that God suffers in, with, and under the creative processes of the world with their costly unfolding in time. There is suffering within God without loss of God's omnipotence or being.

Ilia Delio argues that God and creation are not to be considered as two orders of being but as interrelated divine and created energies. God is the uncreated, implicate order of being, the endless depth, movement, process, and relatedness of being. God is the inner dynamic of the world. God is source and goal of all. Delio suggests that we must move from the "Godhead" to the "God ahead." God is the ground of creation's becoming. God empowers creation from within to transcend itself and become more than what it was. The God of the New Cosmology is the God of promise, the God of the future.

On Christology: Elizabeth Johnson addresses the question of suffering in the cosmos in relationship to Jesus Christ. She writes that we must look to the revelation of God in Jesus Christ, who enters the fray of suffering and transforms it from within. By taking on flesh, God in Jesus Christ takes on the history of the universe as part of God's own story. Through the cross, Jesus takes suffering and death up into God. In his own body Jesus knows suffering—this knowing is embedded in the very heart of God. By taking on flesh, Jesus gives new value to all bodies, to all materiality.

Ilia Delio asks, Can we understand the person of Jesus as the evolutionary divine emergent in history, not only as the mysterious union of natures, but as the integrated being in whom a new field of activity arises that promotes wholeness and evolution toward God? Further, she asks, Can we see Jesus as the exemplar of relatedness for the fullness of evolutionary life?

This summary of some of the new theology on creation, God, and Jesus Christ indicates what is developing in systematic theology at the moment. The challenge remains: how do we worship in light of this developing theology?

THE NEW COSMOLOGY AND WORSHIP

Although predating the previously mentioned theologians by some sixty years or more, Teilhard also addressed the question of what worship means considering the New Cosmology that was just emerging in his time: "To worship was formerly to prefer God to things, relating them to him and sacrificing them for him. To worship is now becoming to devote oneself body and soul to the creative act, associating oneself with that act in order to fulfill the world by hard work and intellectual exploration."[4] He continues, "It used to appear that there were only two attitudes mathematically possible for [us]: to love heaven or to love earth. With a new view of space [and time], a third road is opening up: to make our way to heaven through earth."[5]

What he is indicating is that previously we had a spirituality (and a liturgical tradition) that preferred heaven over the materiality of Earth and cosmos. Under the influence of Platonic and neo-Platonic thought that valued mind over matter and spirit over flesh, Christianity too often became an otherworldly religion. Today, because of the interrelationality of all reality, we cannot leave the cosmos behind and seek union with God alone or even with the human community. All creation will be redeemed in Christ; a new heaven and a new earth are promised as the future for all reality and will be transformed through resurrection.

Before addressing topics in the liturgy that need our attention, I would like to say a general word about the formative nature of liturgy and its ability to orient and reorient us vis-à-vis God, one another, and creation. First, we must acknowledge that liturgy is only a part of the life of the church, and that the transformation of Christian lives to the demands of the gospel takes place through a variety of means in the lives of believers. However, liturgy is an important one of those means. We must come to understand that the liturgy presents a "world" through all its symbolic languages (sound, sight, smell, art, ritual actions, gestures, prayer texts, hymnody, etc.). That is, through these very material objects and actions, the liturgy provides a vision of Christian life in the world; it provides a privileged moment of revelation of the God who saves through Christ Jesus and the Spirit; it provides a privileged moment of encounter with the living God. This vision of the world is like a text offered for interpretation and appropriation through the multiple sense experiences of our bodies. Worshipers journey bodily from the baptismal pool to the place for the celebration of the Word; they sing hymn tunes and texts that literally vibrate within them—through their bodily reproduction of this music—sounds, images, ideas, feelings, scriptural passages, issues of justice, right relationships, praise, and lament. Worshipers gather in places of assembly that to a greater or lesser degree suggest that they come to God as community, not merely as individuals. Through preaching that breaks open the Word, they are invited to shape their lives according to the Scriptures. They are invited to cross their bodies with the sign of Christ's cross, which speaks a very different message than success, wealth, and wellbeing as our culture defines them. Worshipers engage in all of these symbols and more as a rehearsal of right attitudes that they practice week in and week out until those attitudes become so internalized that in one's whole body/spirit one becomes a believer, a disciple. According to philosopher Paul Ricoeur, we take a risk when we enter the world projected by the liturgy; interpretation and appropriation will change us. If we enter it with openness and grace, it changes us into becoming what we proclaim.

Of course, the liturgy cannot do the job of transformation of believers by itself. It must be accompanied by action for justice in and out of liturgical space. It must dialogue with the positive and negative messages sent by our culture of what is of value or what kinds of lives are worth living. It must be accompanied by personal prayer.

Where does this leave us in relationship of the New Cosmology and worship?

As I indicated earlier, our theology and liturgy have been very anthropocentric, that is, they have attended almost exclusively to the human person and the human community in relationship with God. Creation, if it is included at all, appears only in passing in some biblical readings and psalms, but infrequently in our liturgical prayers. Creation/cosmos is not directly addressed as a "partner in praise,"[6] as the ground or source of human life, or as an object of our concern and need for reconciliation. If we are to reorient ourselves in right relation with Earth and the cosmos, then our liturgies must play a role in that reorientation, since they are constitutive of making Christians. Liturgies can either serve to keep us alienated from or, at best, oblivious to creation, or they can engender new patterns of relationship between ourselves and creation that are life-giving for all concerned.

Interestingly, the Bible is a relatively rich source for understanding creation as a partner in praise with the human community, and so the intentional inclusion of pertinent passages would be helpful. Of course, the cosmos, Earth, and its creatures praise God with the natural voices they have simply by being themselves, but the Scriptures present them as subjects capable of sounding praise. Psalm 148 calls on the sun and moon, shining stars, and waters above the heavens to join in praise of the God who created them. Sea monsters, mountains and hills, wild animals, creeping things, and flying birds are all implored to join in praise of the Creator. First Chronicles 16:31–36 is also rich in accounting for creation's praise: "Let the heavens be glad, and let the earth rejoice....Let the sea roar, and all that fills it; let the field exult, and everything in it. Then shall the trees of the forest sing for joy before the LORD."

Creation raises its voice not only in praise but also in lament and in anguish. "The earth dries up and withers, the world languishes and withers; the heavens languish together with the earth" (Isa 24:4). Isaiah 33:9 likewise speaks of the anguish of the land: "The land mourns and languishes; Lebanon is confounded and withers away; Sharon is like a desert; and Bashan and Carmel shake off their leaves." Jeremiah also speaks of the plight of the created world: "How long will the land mourn, and the grass of every field wither?" (Jer 12:4). The prophet Joel speaks too of the pain of the earth and its creatures: "How the animals groan!...Even the wild animals cry to you because the watercourses are dried up" (Joel 1:18, 20). In the First Testament, these tragedies befell creation because of Israel's infidelity to the covenant, but few if any preachers extend this lesson to our own day or join these prophets in a call to accountability and conversion. Using these texts more intentionally in existing or newly created services that focus on creation, we can join our voices in solidarity with creation in our orientation toward right relationship with God and the cosmos.

In our age, it is often because of human behavior that Earth shrivels and dries up through destruction of habitats and of the ecological balance that Earth has developed over millennia. Human solidarity with Earth and its creatures calls us to accountability for the destruction of Earth's ecosystem not only for the sake of nature—which is a worthy project in and of itself—but because it also prevents it from being a partner with us in praise of God. Could not our liturgies exhibit human solidarity with Earth and its creation in acts of praise and lament as a daily event? As Norman Habel asks, "Can we then worship in ways that enable us to lament with other creatures as well as to celebrate with them, and to express our responsibility toward them? If we will do so, only then will we truly join them in worship with integrity, as the God we know in the Bible intends us to do."[7]

Our worship needs to join with creation's praise and lament not only on distinct days (e.g., Earth Day) but in every liturgy and in all seasons. Only through such a thoroughgoing process will we be able to move from our anthropocentrism to a more integrated appreciation of our relationship with the whole cosmos. Only by attending to the turn to the cosmos in all aspects of our liturgical prayer will the liturgies be able to do their formative work on us and convert us to care for Earth and its creatures outside of liturgical space.

I would like to suggest that there are many areas that need attention regarding worship, but I would like to look at just five areas for our purposes. The first is how we name God. Naming God holds an important place in our liturgical tradition. In our effort for truthfulness in God-talk, we have traditionally named God through analogy, metaphor, negative naming, and an abundance of names to indicate to the Christian community that God cannot be contained by any single name. Now the challenge is even larger. How do we include the relationship of God with all creation, all materiality? How do we name God by conceiving of God as "God ahead," calling us into future fullness from up ahead?

The second area is how we present Jesus Christ and redemption. Do we present him as taking on and redeeming all materiality and drawing all this up into God? How do we present his suffering? Do we continue to talk about the necessary sin of Adam and Jesus as the one "Who for our sake paid Adam's debt to the eternal Father, and, pouring out his own dear Blood, wiped clean the record of our ancient sinfulness" as we do in the Exsultet at the Easter Vigil? Would a revised theology of original sin move us away from the Anselmian satisfaction theory that this Exsultet prayer reflects?

The third area is how to address the perennial experience of suffering, not just human suffering, but the suffering of all creation as it goes through its evolutionary process. Can we acknowledge that suffering is taken up into God without threat to God's omnipotence and perfection?

The fourth area is how we retell the salvation history narrative considering the 13.82 billion years of cosmic existence and the possibility of another 13.82 billion years of existence. We heard earlier that the narrative quality of cosmic history includes the narrative of human life; the cosmic story is our story. How do we reframe our salvation history narrative in light of these new insights? What would our eucharistic prayers look like if we included this larger narrative?

The fifth area is liturgical iconography and design as well as liturgical music. After the Hubble Space Telescope pictures, what must our worship spaces look like or what should they portray in paint and glass? Considering the evolutionary character of species development (including our own), what should be painted on murals or cast in bronze on our doors or baptismal fonts? What must our hymnody sound like and what sung texts should we put into the mouths of our congregations regarding God, Christ, the Holy Spirit, and the cosmos?

Clearly, this agenda will take an enormous effort to embellish our eucharistic prayers and collects, other liturgies, our art, and hymnody to reflect all of these new insights. We must expend this effort, however, lest we alienate the Christian community by having them live in two different worlds—the New Cosmology in their daily lives and the Old Cosmology in their worship.

Bibliography

Delio, Ilia. *Christ in Evolution*. Maryknoll, NY: Orbis Books, 2008.

———. *The Emergent Christ: Exploring the Meaning of Catholic in an Evolutionary Universe*. Maryknoll, NY: Orbis Books, 2011.

———. *The Unbearable Wholeness of Being: God, Evolution, and the Power of Love*. Maryknoll, NY: Orbis Books, 2013.

Edwards, Denis. *The God of Evolution: A Trinitarian Theology*. New York: Paulist Press, 1999.

———. *How God Acts: Creation, Redemption, and Special Divine Action*. New York: Fortress Press, 2010.

———. *Partaking of God: Trinity, Evolution, and Ecology*. Collegeville, MN: Liturgical Press, 2014.

Haught, John. *Christianity and Science: Toward a Theology of Nature*. Maryknoll, NY: Orbis Books, 2007.

———. *Resting on the Future: Catholic Theology in an Unfinished Universe*. New York: Bloomsbury Academic, 2015.

Johnson, Elizabeth A. *Ask the Beasts: Darwin and the God of Love*. New York: Bloomsbury, 2014.

Vincie, Catherine. *Worship and the New Cosmology: Liturgical and Theological Challenges*. Collegeville, MN: Liturgical Press, 2014.

Notes

1. John Haught, *Resting on the Future: Catholic Theology for an Unfinished Universe* (New York: Bloomsbury Academic, 2015), 82.

2. Scientific materialism claims that matter is all there is, and it is its own source of being.

3. Pope John Paul II, "Address to the Pontifical Academy of Sciences," November 10, 1979, in *Origins, CNS Documentary Service* 9, 24 (November 29, 1979), 391.

4. Pierre Teilhard de Chardin, *Christianity and Evolution* (New York: Harcourt, 1971), 92.

5. De Chardin, *Christianity and Evolution*, 93.

6. I am indebted to Norman Habel for this phrase. See "Theology of Liturgy in a New Key: Worshiping with Creation," in *The Season of Creation: A Preaching Commentary*, ed. Norman Habel, David Rhoads, and Paul Santmire (Minneapolis: Fortress Press, 2010), 4.

7. Habel, "Theology of Liturgy in a New Key," 10.

13

POPULAR RELIGION, LITURGY, AND CHRISTIAN SPIRITUALITY
An Asian Perspective

—m—

Peter C. Phan

The purpose of this chapter is to explore the connections among popular religion, Christian liturgy, and Asian Christian spirituality. One of the major issues in Catholic theology concerning popular religion as a collection of pious practices is its relationship to Christian liturgy, the official worship of the church. Furthermore, since popular religion, in addition to the liturgy, is an important source of Christian spirituality, there is the need to inquire into the possible ways of incorporating popular religion into the Christian life. Hence, the opportuneness of an inquiry into the relationships among popular religion, Christian liturgy, and Christian spirituality, which will be carried out here from an Asian perspective.

I begin with a discussion of popular religion and its relationship to liturgy. Next, I reflect on Christian spirituality as the context for understanding the role of popular religion in Asian spirituality. This is followed by an examination of the ways popular religion is practiced in major Asian religious traditions, especially Asian Buddhism, to serve as an example of how a major world religion incorporates popular religion into its cult. Finally, I suggest some ways to incorporate popular religion into Asian Christian spirituality.

POPULAR RELIGION AND LITURGY: A CONTENTIOUS RELATIONSHIP

Of all the Christian churches, perhaps none have a richer history and practice of liturgy and popular religion than the Catholic and Orthodox churches. However, the relation between these two forms of Christian piety has not always been harmonious, and their conflict has been more frequent and pronounced in the Catholic Church than in the Orthodox Church. This contentious relationship is caused in part by the fact that whereas there is a high regard for as well as near consensus in the voluminous theological literature on the nature of the liturgy, little appreciation is shown for popular religion, the meaning, nature, and function of which are vigorously contested.

Indeed, Vatican II made the liturgy its primary concern. And the liturgy is the theme of its very first document, the dogmatic constitution *Sacrosanctum Concilium* (*SC*). The Council defines the liturgy as

> an exercise of the priestly office of Jesus Christ (*veluti Iesu Christi sacerdotalis muneris exercitatio*). In the liturgy the sanctification of women and men is given expression in symbols perceptible by the senses and is carried out in ways appropriate to each of them. In it, complete and definitive public worship (*integer cultus publicus*) is performed by the mystical body of Jesus Christ, that is, by the Head and his members. From this it follows that every liturgical celebration, because it is an action of Christ the priest and of his body which is the church, is a preeminently sacred action (*actio sacra praecellenter*). No other action of the church can equal its efficacy by the same title and to the same degree (*eodem titulo eodemque gradu*). (no. 7)[1]

Because of its very nature as "complete and definitive public worship," the liturgy, especially the Eucharist, is the highest form of worship:

> The liturgy is the summit (*culmen*) toward which the activity of the church is directed; it is also the source (*fons*) from which all its power flows. For the goal of apostolic endeavor

is that all who are made children of God by faith and baptism should come together to praise God in the midst of God's church, to take part in the Sacrifice, and to eat the Lord's Supper. The liturgy, in its turn, moves the faithful filled with "the paschal sacraments" to be "one in holiness"; it prays that "they hold fast in their lives to what they have grasped by their faith." The renewal in the Eucharist of the covenant between them and the Lord draws the faithful and sets them aflame with Christ's compelling love. From the liturgy, therefore, and especially from the Eucharist, grace is poured forth upon us as from a fountain (*ut e fonte*), and our sanctification in Christ and the glorification of God to which all other activities of the church are directed, as toward their end (*uti ad finem*), are achieved with maximum effectiveness (*maxima cum efficacia*). (*SC* 10)[2]

Compared to the liturgy, popular religion is placed at the bottom of the ladder of spiritual activities because their efficacy is said to be not *ex opere operato*, not even *ex opere operantis ecclesiae*. As nonliturgical, nonofficial, popular expressions of religiosity, popular religion received scant attention from Vatican II. Article 13 of *SC* treats it only under the aspect of "popular devotions" (*pia exercitia*) and declares,

> Popular devotions of the Christian people, provided they conform to the laws and norms of the Church, are to be highly recommended, especially where they are ordered by the Apostolic See. Devotions proper to individual churches also have a special dignity if they are undertaken by order of the bishops according to customs or books lawfully approved. But such devotions should be so drawn up that they harmonize with the liturgical seasons, accord with the sacred liturgy, are in some way derived from it, and lead the people to it, since in fact the liturgy by its very nature is far superior to any of them.[3]

In the post–Vatican II era, popular devotions suffered a significant worldwide decline in the Catholic Church. To remedy this eclipse, the Congregation for Divine Worship and the Discipline of the Sacraments issued in 2002 a lengthy document titled *Directory on Popular Piety and the Liturgy: Principles and Guidelines.* Though a significant improvement on Vatican II's treatment of popular devotion, the document suffers from its one-sided emphasis on the superiority of the liturgy and its unsophisticated account of the development of forms of liturgical worship from popular religion.[4]

Due to this paucity of treatments of popular religion, it will be helpful to give it more attention here. A variety of terms has been used to refer to popular religion: *popular religiosity, popular piety, pious exercises, religious devotions,* and *common* or *folk religion.*[5] These terms are, of course, not synonymous; rather, each expresses a particular feature of popular religion. By *popular* is not meant "fashionable" (or, in young Americans' parlance, "cool" and "awesome") but "of the people." What is meant by *people* varies according to historical contexts. With regard to popular religion, in the West it refers first of all to the religious practices of the peasantry and rural populations. Traditional peasant societies subsist on sedentary farming; as such they are marked by three common features: they depend on a particular ecosystem, live in particular social arrangements, and are dependent on the wider economic, political, and social networks for which they produce food.

The peasants' religious practices ("popular religion") provide them with ways to deal with these three aspects of their lives. First, to manage their ecosystem, peasants have rituals to mark the cycles of nature, the seasons of the year, day and night, the lunar and solar calendars, and the life cycles of animals and plants. They establish sacred places and times and worship appropriate divinities to ensure the success of their cultivation and husbandry and protection from natural disasters. Second, popular religion also helps peasants maintain the unity of their households according to the norms of the family code, resolve conflicts within and among the households or adjacent settlements, and mark especially important events such as birth, puberty, marriage, sickness, and death. Third, as peasants are necessarily connected with the wider networks of society to whose nutrition needs they cater, their popular religion is unavoidably mixed with the more structured, official, and public religions that provide it with a common, even universal, frame of reference and in which it is expressed and practiced. Indeed, strictly speaking, there is no popular "religion" in the technical sense of the term but rather popular "religiousness" or "religiosity" since peasants are almost always Jewish, Christian, Muslim, Hindu, Buddhist, Sikh, Daoist, and so forth by religious affiliations. It is within, albeit not always in harmony with, their institutional religions that they practice their popular religion.

Since the European Enlightenment, in addition to the Western peasants' religious practices, popular religion has been associated with people newly discovered outside Europe, in particular in Africa, Asia, and Latin America, who were called "primitives." Like that of Western peasants, the language of these people is primarily nonliterate. It consists of oral literature in the forms of folktale, folk song, and myth, and of artifacts such as rituals, music, dance, art, and architecture, and it is in and through these cultural creations that the meaning of their popular religion is to be discovered.

It has been commonly postulated that popular religion of both European peasants and the "primitives" is "archaic," that is, having forms of spirituality *ab origine* in the sense of both older in time and less developed in structure than the literate religions of the urban populations with their sacred texts, approved rituals, codified beliefs, official hierarchy, teachers and priests, and structural organizations ("the little traditions" of popular religion as opposed to the "great traditions" of world religions). Eventually a dichotomy is drawn between popular religion as the religion of the folk, the laity, the lower strata of society, the subclass or minority groups, the uneducated, and the superstitious, on the one hand, and the religion of the elite, the clergy, the upper class, the majority ethnic groups, the educated, and the orthodox, on the other. As a result, there exists a general bias against if not suspicion of and outright contempt for popular religion, especially the popular devotions or pious practices of religions other than one's own, regarding them, at best, as inferior to the official forms of worship (liturgy) and, at worst, as superstitions to be condemned and rejected.

This is true of the Catholic Church in its teaching on the essential difference between the liturgy and popular piety, the former efficacious *ex opere operato*, that is, by virtue of its inherent divine power, and the latter efficacious only *ex opere operantis*, that is, dependent on the subjective spiritual disposition of the performer of these devotions. Such sharp theological distinction, whatever its objective merit, does not reflect the reality on the ground where popular devotions have made an enormous impact, perhaps even greater than that of the liturgy, on the spiritual life of most Christians, especially those who live in the so-called Third World, to which we now turn.

CHRISTIAN SPIRITUALITY IN ASIA

In its broadest sense, spirituality refers first to the human capacity for self-transcendence, which is actualized in acts of knowledge of and love for realities other than oneself. Second, and more narrowly, spirituality refers to the religious dimension of life by which one is in touch with the more-than-human, transcendent reality, however it is interpreted and named (e.g., Emptiness, the Holy, the Ultimate, the Real, the Absolute, Heaven, or God). Third, and more strictly still, spirituality indicates a particular way of living one's relationship with this transcendent reality by means of specific beliefs, rituals, prayers, moral behaviors, and community participation (e.g., Hindu, Buddhist, Jewish, Christian, Muslim, and so on).[6] Needless to say, Asian spirituality embodies all three connotations. It is (1) human self-transcendence, (2) toward the Ultimate Other, and (3) within a particular religious tradition.

Because spirituality is lived in a specific religious tradition or, as is common in Asia, a mixture of religious traditions, there is, of course, no generic spirituality, untethered from a historical and particular tradition and community. Even when one attempts to construct one's own spirituality and elects to be "spiritual but not religious," to use a common contemporary slogan, one can only do so by drawing on various elements of preexisting spiritual traditions. In other words, an institutional dimension is essential to any spiritual quest.[7] A spirituality that is like a Platonic form, floating above space and time, valid always and everywhere, does not and cannot exist. Here, then, is the first essential feature of spirituality: All spiritualities are necessarily and intrinsically local and localized, not only in the spatial sense, but also in all the ways in which a reality is particularized in terms of time, economics, politics, culture, and religion. In a sense, to speak of spirituality as "local" is a redundancy, in Asia as well as elsewhere.

This is also true of Christian spirituality, which is a particular way of relating to God as Father/Mother, mediated by Jesus of Nazareth in his ministry, death, and resurrection, and made possible by the power of the Holy Spirit, who has been poured out on the community called the church. Spirituality is essentially life in the Spirit. It is not antithetical, however, to the body and matter. According to Paul, "spirit" (*pneuma*) and "spiritual" (*pneumatikos*)—from which "spirituality" is derived—are the opposites of "flesh" (*sarx*), "fleshly" (*sarkikos*), "soul" (*psyche*), and "soul-ly" (*psychikos*), but not of "body" (*soma*), "bodily" (*somatikos*), and "matter" (*hyle*). The Pauline opposition is not between two ontological realities: the incorporeal and the immaterial, on the one hand, and the corporeal and the material, on the other. Such metaphysical dualism did not attach to the use of *spiritualitas* until the twelfth century. Rather, the opposition is between two ways of life, one that is led by and in accord with the Spirit ("spiritual") and therefore leading to life, and the other opposed to the Spirit ("fleshly") and bringing about death. Christian spirituality, then, is essentially *life empowered by the Spirit of Christ*, by which men and women are made sons and daughters of God by adoption, brothers and sisters of Christ into whose image they must be fashioned, and of one another. Such a life is adorned with the Spirit's gift of virtues (1 Cor 13:13; Col 1:9; Rom 8:21; Gal 5:13; 2 Cor 3:17), fruits (Gal 5:23–24), and charisms of different kinds to build up the Christian community (1 Cor 12:4–11, 28–30; Rom 12:6–8; Eph 4:11–13).[8] In short, Christian spirituality as relationship with God is *pneumatological* (empowered by the Spirit), *christological* (mediated through and modeled after Christ), and *ecclesial* (realized in the church). Hence, Asian Christian spirituality realizes these three dimensions necessarily in the context of Asian societies, cultures, and religions.

Consequently, an essential part of the church's mission is to incarnate the Christian faith into the local context. Beside interreligious dialogue and liberation, Asian Christian churches must also take on the task of inculturation, namely, making Christianity not only *in* and *for* Asia but also *of* Asia. In the recent past, this task was not always considered an essential part of Christian mission. Western pieties and devotions were imported from the West into Asia, especially in the Roman Catholic Church. Hymns, prayers, songs, liturgical books, sacramental rituals, sacred vestments, plastic arts and architecture, monastic institutions, canon law, and the various spiritualities of religious orders, both male and female, and so forth are imposed on the local churches. At best, these foreign spiritual elements and traditions were adapted to the local conditions; they are, as it were, fully grown trees transplanted into another soil and climate and thus underwent only superficial changes.

In contrast, inculturation (or contextualization or indigenization) is understood as a creative encounter between a particular, already inculturated form of Christianity (there is no a-cultural, pure form of Christianity!) and a particular local culture from which another form of Christianity, a *tertium quid*, will emerge, one that preserves some continuity with past Christianities elsewhere but is not identical with them. It is like a seed planted in a new soil out of which a different tree, though of the same species, will grow. No one form of Christianity should and may be taken as normative for all others. So it is with Asian spirituality. It is, of course, Christian spirituality, as explicated earlier, but in the Asian "style," transformed by the cultural and religious values of each ethnic group and country in Asia.[9] We may call these cultural and religious values and practices as embodied and lived in a particular country "local spiritualities."

These general principles of inculturation show that Christian spirituality is itself a local spirituality to be localized again and again as it enters new cultures and encounters other local spiritualities. This statement can be succinctly justified on two theological principles. The first is the incarnation. Just as the Word of God was made flesh not in a generic human form—there is no such thing—but in a particular Jew, namely, Jesus of Nazareth, who lived in a specific place and during a particular time, with all the specificities and the limitations this embodiment entails, so the Christian faith and, by implication, the Christian way of life must also be incarnated into a particular place and time.

As illuminating as the incarnation analogy is, however, it is misleading regarding the inculturation of the Christian faith and Christian spirituality. It may wrongly suggest that, like the Logos, Christian faith and Christian spirituality are nonspatial and nontemporal realities descending pure and culture-free from heaven, as it were, into a particular culture. Christian faith and spirituality are nothing of this sort, of course. As historical realities, they were first expressed in biblical cultures—Hebrew and Greek—and then in those of the Roman Empire, both East and West; of the Anglo-Saxon and Teutonic worlds; of Spain, Portugal, Italy, Holland, Britain, France, Germany, Denmark, and the United States, just to mention some of the countries from which missionaries came to evangelize Asia. It is the Christianities and Christian spiritualities (note the plural!) of these countries, very different among themselves, that were imported to Asia, not the allegedly pure and culture-free Gospel. Inculturation, then, is not the encounter between the contextually free, culturally universal, and permanently valid Christian spirituality, on the one hand, and the locally situated, culturally limited, and temporarily valid spiritualities, on the other. Rather, inculturation is an encounter, at times harmonious, at other times contentious, between an essentially local Christian spirituality and other equally local spiritualities. Christian spirituality, no less than the other spiritualities of other religions of Asia, are affected by limitedness, partiality, bias, incompleteness, and errors.

The second theological principle is what Andrew F. Walls calls "the translation principle."[10] By *translation* is meant not only the verbal rendering of a text, for example, the Bible, from its original language into another language, either by formal equivalence (word-for-word translation) or by dynamic or functional equivalence (sense-for-sense translation), but also, and primarily, the whole process of cross-cultural transmission of certain elements of one culture (the original culture) into another culture (the receptor or target culture). Missiologists such as Andrew Walls and Lamin Sanneh, among many others, have pointed out that it is through what Walls terms "the infinite translatability of the Christian faith"[11] that Christianity survived the vicissitudes of history and became a world or global religion.[12]

As applied to Christianity, this cross-cultural process of transmission is, Walls notes, governed by two apparently opposing principles.

First, the "indigenizing principle," by which Christianity becomes part of the local culture and thanks to which the newly Christian converts can feel at home in their new religion, engaging in familiar spiritual practices, though now endowed with new meanings. Second, the "pilgrim principle," by which the local culture and, with it, the new Christian converts are brought out of their particularities and transformed into something new, more universal, and that is the Christian way of life.[13] In sum, Christian spirituality is essentially one local spirituality among many, to be localized again and again with other local spiritualities with which it comes into contact.

POPULAR RELIGION AND THE "GREAT TRADITIONS" IN ASIA

Notwithstanding the common distinction between liturgy and popular religion, it is difficult if not impossible to separate them. All the "great traditions," including Christianity and Asian religions, have combined both forms of spirituality, the "great traditions" or the "elite religion" and the "small traditions" or the "folk religion," to shape their worship and religious practices. All Asian religions, especially Hinduism, Buddhism, Islam, Daoism, and Shinto, have popular or folk religion as one of their major building blocks. Indeed, as with Christianity, these religions cannot be fully appreciated without taking into account the ways in which they encounter popular religion. Thus, for example, Buddhism has had elements of folk religion since its inception that may be termed "folk Buddhism." Folk Buddhism is not a later degeneration of the allegedly ideal and normative Buddhism but is its original and constitutive part made up of beliefs and practices dominated by magical-animistic and shamanistic features. Already in India, Buddhism had incorporated forms of worship of deities of the Hindu pantheon. As it moved out of its native country to East, Southeast, South, and Central Asia, it dramatically increased its folk character by taking on elements of indigenous popular religion, especially the belief in benevolent and malevolent spirits and ways to invoke their aid and placate them by means of magic. Indeed, it is precisely by means of this indigenous popular religion that Buddhism quickly and successfully spread in most Asian countries and in turn became a "popular," that is, well-received and vibrant, national religion.

Recent research in anthropology, cultural histories, and history of religion has shown that in such an encounter with popular religion, the great traditions in Asia generally follow a threefold strategy, namely, appropriation, adaptation, and transformation. By appropriation, they select certain symbols, beliefs, and rituals of the local popular religion and amalgamate them into their doctrinal and ritualistic system without making substantive changes to their meaning. In this way the great traditions remain basically unchanged. By adaptation, the great traditions are inculturated or contextualized into the indigenous cultural expressions; in this process they undergo internal changes to make themselves into truly and distinctively local religions. By transformation, the great traditions are so profoundly changed by local cultures and popular religion that the religious innovations are no longer recognizable as faithful and orthodox transmissions of the ideal and normative forms of these religions.

Again, the history of Buddhism in Asia provides illustrative examples of this threefold strategy. In the appropriation strategy, in Sri Lanka, Buddhism takes over the hierarchy of local guardian spirits of villages and regional gods such as Skanda and Vishnu. In Tibet, the gods and goddesses of everyday life become the protectors of the dharma. In Burma (Myanmar), the *nats* become the *devas*. In Thailand, the *devatas, cao,* and *phi* are absorbed into the Buddhist pantheon. In Japan, Buddhism absorbs the *kami*, who are often regarded as the *bodhisattvas*. The same process of appropriation of the gods/goddesses and spirits of popular religion occurred in China, Korea, and Vietnam. Appropriation is also used to take over various rituals of popular religion, especially in the conduct of funerals and death commemorations. In this strategy, Buddhism remains substantially unaffected since the forms of popular religion it takes over are subordinated to the Buddha and normative Buddhism.

In the adaptation strategy, the Buddha himself is transformed from a teacher of enlightenment into a miracle worker; meditation is the means not only to gaining insight but also to acquiring supernatural powers; the cult of Buddha relics and of the Buddha himself as a quasi-divine being is introduced; there is a proliferation of supernatural Buddhas and *bodhisattvas*, such as the savior Buddha Maitreya, Amitabha Buddha who brings people into the Pure Land, and the much-beloved Buddha of compassion, Guanyin (Kannon in Japanese); and monks are revered not only for their holiness but also for their ability to communicate with the spirit world, to predict the future, and to perform miraculous deeds. In this strategy, though Buddhism has undergone significant internal changes in terms of both doctrine and practice by adapting local popular religion, the new forms of Buddhism remain recognizably Buddhist.

Finally, in the transformation strategy, folk Buddhism has generated popular sectarian movements that move beyond the boundaries of orthodox Buddhism. For example, in Thailand, there have been messianic Buddhist groups, often gathered around a charismatic leader who claimed to be Maitryea Buddha. In China, major folk Buddhist apocalyptic movements include the White Lotus movement, a complex of rebel eschatologies active from the twelfth to the nineteenth century, the Maitreya, the White Cloud, and the Lo. The leaders of these movements were charismatic and lay, their doctrines heterodox, their method syncretistic, and their politics militant. Eventually these movements ceased to be Buddhist in doctrine and practice and became a local folk religion. In Japan, from the eighth century, under the influence of Chinese Buddhism, a folk Buddhism was developed outside the circle of official orthodoxy and hierarchy, especially in the Amida Buddha tradition, with its practice of reciting the *nembutsu* (the invocation of the Amida Buddha's name) as a quasi-magical mantra to achieve salvation in the Pure Land. Folk Buddhism is also present in Japanese new religions arising in the nineteenth and twentieth centuries that made syncretistic use of magical rituals and of which the two best known are Risshō Kōseikai and Sōka Gakkai.[14]

POPULAR RELIGION AND ASIAN CHRISTIAN SPIRITUALITY

In the encounter between Christian spirituality and other local spiritualities, one of the most difficult challenges is posed by the pervasive presence of popular religion in both Christianity and other religions. As Greek and Latin Christianities have in the past consistently adopted, adapted, and transformed the religious practices of surrounding religions and have made use of these materials to form their own official liturgies as well as their popular devotions, so in the same way Christian faith is now challenged to incorporate into its spirituality both the public and official forms of worship and the popular piety of other Asian religions.

Not unlike other Asian religions, Christianity, which has a long history of popular religion of its own, had to face the challenges of Asian popular religion when it first came to the continent and in subsequent centuries, especially since the seventeenth. Again, not unlike other Asian religions, Christianity practiced in various degrees the three-pronged approach of appropriation, adaptation, and transformation. To understand this process, it would be helpful to examine the eight elements of popular religion that bear marked affinities with Christianity and its popular piety.

In general, Christian popular religion has eight distinctive elements.[15] First, its image of God or gods is that of a deity at once gracious and stern and constantly involved in the life of the believers, dispensing reward for good deeds and punishment for bad ones. Second, the deity is approached not directly but through a series of mediators who intercede for the believers (in Christianity: Jesus, Mary, the saints, and local patrons). Third, it is kept vibrant by social activities such as periodic celebrations and feastings, processions, eating, dancing, and singing. Fourth, it comprises a plethora of devotional activities such as prayer, novena, vow-making, pilgrimage, and personal cult to a favorite mediator. Fifth, it has a strong material culture including sacred objects such as statues, images, rosaries, relics, medals, sanctuaries, shrines, holy water, candles, and incense. Sixth, it is sustained by associations, societies, and clubs, each with an appropriate supernatural patron. Seventh, it has a distinctive cosmology, characterized by a view of the world as an interconnected and controlled place in which divine favors can be obtained and earthly life is intimately connected with life after death. Eighth and last, popular religion has an extensive albeit ambiguous relationship to official religion. On the one hand, its flourishing depends on the approval of the custodians of official religion and on its being incorporated into it. On the other hand, its practitioners tend to neglect the teachings and practices of official religion.

Despite these common features, Christianity, like other religions, has had an ambivalent, at times friendly, most often hostile, attitude toward popular religion.[16] On the negative side, it can take an elitist view, according to which popular religion is a corruption of the official and orthodox religion into false beliefs and superstitious practices. Or it can adopt the Marxist view, which considers popular religion as the false consciousness imposed by the ruling class upon the proletariat.

On the other hand, there are five positive assessments of popular religion. First, the baseline approach views popular religion as the first and basic complex of religious elements of a particular location and culture that are later taken up and incorporated into a more universal world religion such Hinduism, Buddhism Judaism, Christianity, and Islam. Second, the romanticist approach views popular religion as the genuine religion of the people that is corrupted and brought under control by the institutional religion and its clergy. Third, the remnant approach sees popular religion as elements of religious beliefs and practices of the primal religion that continue to exist, though under different forms and meanings, as constituents of world religions. Fourth, the subaltern approach views popular religion as the symbolic creation of the oppressed class to resist and subvert the domination of the ruling class and its official religion. Fifth and lastly, the social-psychological approach views popular religion as collective responses to the social and psychological needs of displaced people, for example, rural people moving into the cities, to find security, identity, and community.

It is important to note that all seven approaches to popular religion have both strengths and weaknesses and provide helpful insights into its origin, nature, and functions. Given the complex and multidimensional reality of popular religion within both Christianity and Asian religions, it is obvious that the encounter between Christianity and Asian religions is not between a popular-religion-free Christianity and popular-religion-laden Asian religions. Rather, it is a two-way, interacting, and mutually influencing dialogue between the above-mentioned eight elements of popular religion of Asian religions and some elements of the popular religion of Christianity. It is an extremely complex and challenging encounter, fraught with dangers such as syncretism, especially in the transformation strategy discussed earlier. Without undertaking an encounter with Asian popular religion, however, Christianity cannot be planted in the indigenous soil and become a local spirituality of everydayness.

How can such encounter be fruitfully carried out between Christianity and popular religion in Asia in such a way that a genuinely Christian-Asian spirituality may emerge? In the remaining pages I examine one of the four ways that have been proposed by the Federation of Asian Bishops' Conferences for interreligious dialogue, namely, sharing life, cooperation for the common good, theological exchange, and sharing of spiritual experiences. I focus on the fourth and last mode since spiritual sharing is most relevant to the theme under discussion and since popular religion plays an important role in this type of dialogue among Asian religions.

Whereas sharing life, cooperation for the common good, and theological exchange as modes of interreligious dialogue do not usually meet with serious objection, sharing spiritual experiences, especially with the participation of religious leaders and in formal and public settings, or, to use a neologism, "inter-riting," is highly controversial.[17] For monotheistic religions with well-defined doctrines and sharply drawn boundaries such as Judaism, Christianity, and Islam, it would seem that shared ritual participation, wherein members of different religious traditions pray, worship, and celebrate sacred rituals together, is to be rejected since, so it is argued, it inevitably leads to religious relativism and syncretism.

On the other hand, especially in Asia, religions are not seen as impermeable and mutually exclusive institutions, with officially defined dogmas, clearly marked and hermetically sealed boundaries, and for-members-only rituals. Rather, religions are widely viewed as diverse but complementary ways to the Divine and to achieve full human flourishing, and they may be adopted in various ways, depending on a particular need at a particular stage of one's life. Whichever religion is deemed to best satisfy this need is adopted, without scruples about doctrinal orthodoxy, membership requirements, or ritual purity. For instance, there is in China the *san jiao* (three religions) tradition, in which a Mandarin is a Confucian when performing his government functions, a Daoist when he is at home enjoying harmony with nature, and a Buddhist when he dies and is buried. It is also said, perhaps with a trifle exaggeration but not without a grain of truth, that a Japanese is born a Shinto, marries as a Christian, and dies as a Buddhist. In India, inter-riting is a pervasive fact of life, not only among Hindus but also among Muslims. The same thing may be said of most other Asian countries. Perhaps the most interesting case of inter-riting is a religion founded in Vietnam in the 1940s known as Cao Dai, which originated as an intentional combination of Buddhism, Daoism, Confucianism, and Christianity.

Moreover, this inter-riting is inevitable when Christianity enters into dialogue with local spiritualities and popular religion. Indeed, as I pointed out previously, there is no a-cultural Christianity; it is itself a historical product born out of the encounter between the already inculturated Christian faith and local spiritualities and popular religions. This concomitant process of inculturation ("the indigenizing principle") and transformation ("the pilgrim principle") is ever ongoing. Indeed, it is this form of hybrid Christianity that is lived in the everydayness of life and that is most meaningful to ordinary Christians. It is primarily a "way of life" and not a "view of life."

How can this spiritual sharing be done? I would like to suggest two main ways in which this can be achieved. Ritual sharing, as Marianne Moyaert suggests, can be done on two fronts, namely, as a community response to external events ("outer-facing") and as an act of hospitality to members of religions other than one's own to promote interreligious dialogue ("inner-facing").[18] First, outer-facing inter-riting should be strongly encouraged to create a common religious "We" among diverse religious communities to galvanize concerted efforts to meet serious challenges facing the community, such as natural disasters, acts of war and terrorism, and political and economic emergency situations. Inter-riting on those occasions serves to express sadness and mourning for the dead and solidarity with the survivors, to organize relief efforts, and to solidify religious collaboration. Such ritual participation can and should also be organized for major cultural feasts such as New Year's Day, National Independence Day, the Day for the Dead, World Day of Prayer for Peace, and so on.

Second, while outer-facing ritual sharing is widely practiced today and is no longer controversial, inner-facing inter-riting in order to extend hospitality to members of other religions in interreligious dialogue is highly contested and often meets with vigorous opposition, especially on the part of conservative religious authorities.[19] On the opposition side, the main argument is that to be possible and authentic, ritual sharing presupposes common core beliefs; where such shared faith is absent, inter-riting would lead to religious syncretism or indifferentism. In response, supporters of inter-riting point out that ritual performances do more than express belief; they "engage the entire person (not just the mind); they impact on all the senses (vision, hearing, smell, taste, and touch); they evoke powerful emotions (or soothe emotions that are too overwhelming); they stimulate religious experiences, stir the imagination, and attune the body to the divine."[20] Because of the evocative and transformative effects of rituals on the entire person, especially on the body, rituals can and often do alter the community's beliefs. Thus, we must hold both principles, traditionally expressed in the Latin adages *lex credendi, lex orandi* (what we believe determines how we pray) and *lex orandi, lex credenda* (how we pray determines what we believe).

I mentioned earlier that one of the main objections of opponents of ritual sharing is the danger of syncretism. It must be acknowledged that until recently Christian literature on syncretism has for the most part taken a negative stance toward it. It is feared that in this process Christianity will be diluted and even lose its orthodoxy and identity. It is to be noted in passing that the syncretistic movement is a two-way street: not only Christianity borrowing elements of other religions to form new types of Christianity but also other cultures borrowing elements of Christianity to form new religious movements, such as the aforementioned Cao Dai in Vietnam, the Iglesia Filipina Independiente (the Aglypian Church) in the Philippines, numerous new religious movements in Japan and Korea, hundreds of Marginal Churches in China, and thousands of Independent Churches in Africa and Latin America.

It must be admitted that to date syncretism remains a highly controversial and deeply contested phenomenon, and unfortunately there is still much that requires careful study.[21] It is here that Asian theologians can make a valuable contribution to the conversation about popular religion and Christian spirituality. Their research can focus on three areas: first, where Christianity and Asian religions have come to form a new religion or religious movement, with Asian religions providing the basic framework; second, where Christianity provides the basic framework for the syncretistic movement but is radically reinterpreted and substantially reshaped, often without dialogue with and control by church authorities; and third, where selected elements of Christianity are borrowed and incorporated into another religious system.

Furthermore, in studying syncretism, special attention should be given to the phenomenon called "double religious belonging," which is a common practice in Asia. In carrying out this study, Christian theologians may enlist existing historical and anthropological research on how non-Christian religions in Asia, especially Buddhism, have accomplished this syncretistic movement as they spread out of their countries of origin without losing their fundamental identity and structure.

In our globalized world, popular religion has long ceased to be the religion of the peasantry and the "primitives." Furthermore, historical studies of the Catholic liturgy, especially of the Roman Mass, have proved beyond doubt the church's longstanding practice of appropriation, adaptation, and transformation of many forms of popular religion in the West. Furthermore, it is clear that popular religion continues to be present and vibrant in the everyday life of Catholics. (The same thing can be said of the Anglicans and Orthodox, though there is little if at all use of popular religion among Protestants, Evangelicals, and Pentecostals.) Finally, anthropological and theological research on popular religion has fully rebutted the common earlier thesis that popular religion represents a degradation of a pristine, orthodox religion. Indeed, it has been shown that popular religion is present at the birth of all religions, provides them with spiritual sustenance, and contributes to their expansion. Simply put, without popular religiosity there is no religion, and without religion popular religiosity lacks structure and permanence. Finally, popular religion can affect social change, sometimes with peaceful revolutions, as the recent political history in the Philippines and Tibet has shown. This is all the more reason why Christian spirituality, which is essentially *imitatio Christi* in the service of the reign of God, must enlist the help of popular religion in the service of this reign of justice, peace, forgiveness, and reconciliation, for which Jesus lived and died.

Notes

1. All English translations of Vatican II's documents are taken from *Vatican II: Constitutions, Decrees, Declarations*, ed. Austin Flannery (Collegeville, MN: Liturgical Press, 2014).

2. For a study of Vatican II's teaching on the liturgy as *culmen* and *fons* of all the church's activities, see Peter C. Phan, *Being Religious Interreligiously: Asian Perspectives on Interfaith Dialogue* (Maryknoll, NY: Orbis Books, 2004), 257–78. See also Ricky Manalo, *The Liturgy of Life: The Interrelationship of Sunday Eucharist and Everyday Worship Practices* (Collegeville, MN: Liturgical Press, 2014).

3. This relative neglect of and suspicious attitude toward popular religion by Vatican II was one of the results of the triumph of the Liturgical Movement, spearheaded by Dom Prosper Guéranger, at the Council. The Liturgical Movement saw popular religion as rooted in subjective and emotional piety, thus favoring the Enlightenment's individualist tendencies, which it wanted to combat. This belittling of "subjective" or "personal" piety and consequent rejection of "all other religious exercises not directly connected with the sacred Liturgy and performed outside public worship" were criticized by Pope Pius XII as "false, insidious, and quite pernicious" (*Mediator Dei* 30). Papal condemnations notwithstanding, the Liturgical Movement's negative assessment of popular religion found its way into article 13 of *SC*. See Patrick L. Malloy, "The Re-Emergence of Popular Religion among Non-Hispanic American Catholics," *Worship* 72, no. 1 (1998): 2–4.

4. For a commentary on this Directory, see Peter C. Phan, ed., *Directory on Popular Piety and the Liturgy: Principles and Guidelines; A Commentary* (Collegeville, MN: Liturgical Press, 2005). For an insightful and highly accessible discussion of the relation between liturgy and popular

devotions, see Mark R. Francis, *Local Worship, Global Church: Popular Religion and the Liturgy* (Collegeville, MN: Liturgical Press, 2014).

5. Studies on popular religion are legion. For our purposes I strongly recommend Robert Schreiter's lucid and insightful chap. 6 ("Popular Religion and Official Religion") of his book *Constructing Local Theologies* (Maryknoll, NY: Orbis Books, 1985, 2015), 139–64.

6. For a survey of these different spiritualities, see the series of monographs published by Paulist Press titled Classics of Western Spirituality. Beyond Western spirituality, see the series World Spirituality published by Alban Books, Ltd. and World Spirituality published by Crossroad Publishing Co.

7. For a study of Christian spirituality in a global perspective, see James Wiseman, *Spirituality and Mysticism: A Global View* (Maryknoll, NY: Orbis Books, 2006).

8. For a comprehensive history of Christian spirituality, see the three volumes: Bernard McGinn, John Meyendorff, and Jean Leclerq, eds., *Christian Spirituality: Origins to the Twelfth Century* (New York: Crossroad, 1988); Jill Raitt, ed., *Christian Spirituality: High Middle Ages and Reformation* (New York: Crossroad, 1988); and Louis Dupre and Don E. Saliers, eds., *Christian Spirituality: Post-Reformation and Modern* (New York: Crossroad, 1991).

9. See Peter C. Phan, *In Our Own Tongues: Perspectives from Asia on Mission and Inculturation* (Maryknoll, NY: Orbis Books, 2004); and Peter C. Phan, ed., *The Asian Synod: Texts and Commentaries* (Maryknoll, NY: Orbis Books, 2002).

10. Andrew Walls, *The Missionary Movement in Christian History: Studies in the Transmission of Faith* (Maryknoll, NY: Orbis Books, 1996), 26.

11. Walls, *The Missionary Movement in Christian History*, 22.

12. See also Andrew Walls, *The Cross-Cultural Process in Christian History* (Maryknoll, NY: Orbis Books, 2002); and Lamin Sanneh, *Translating the Message: The Missionary Impact on Culture* (Maryknoll, NY: Orbis Books, 1989).

13. See Walls, *The Missionary Movement in Christian History*, 7–9.

14. For a study of Buddhism in Asia, especially the chapter on folk Buddhism by Donald Swearer, see Joseph M. Kitagawa and Mark D. Cummings, eds., *Buddhism and Asian History* (New York: Macmillan, 1989).

15. See Schreiter, *Constructing Local Theologies*, 146–49.

16. See Schreiter, *Constructing Local Theologies*, 149–59.

17. See Marianne Moyaert and Joris Geldhof, eds., *Ritual Participation and Interreligious Dialogue: Boundaries, Transgressions and Innovations* (London: Bloomsbury, 2015).

18. Moyaert and Geldhof, *Ritual Participation and Interreligious Dialogue*, 1–3.

19. For a helpful discussion of the pro and con reasons regarding inter-riting, see Moyaert and Geldhof, *Ritual Participation and Interreligious Dialogue*, 3–10.

20. Moyaert and Geldhof, *Ritual Participation and Interreligious Dialogue*, 7.

21. For a lucid exposition of syncretism as a theological problem, see Robert Schreiter, *Constructing Local Theologies*, 165–81. Other useful studies on religious syncretism include: Gailyn Van Rheenen, ed., *Contextualization and Syncretism: Navigating Cultural Currents* (Pasadena, CA: William Carey Library, 2006); Eric Maroney, *Religious Syncretism* (London: SCM Press, 2006); Anita Maria Leopold and Jeppe Sinding Jensen, eds., *Syncretism in Religion: A Reader* (New York: Routledge, 2004); Charles Stewart and Rosalind Shaw, eds., *Syncretism/Anti-Syncretism: The Politics of Religious Synthesis* (London and New York: Routledge, 1994); Jerald D. Gort, Hendrik M. Vroom, Rein Ferhout, and Anton Wessels, eds., *Dialogue and Syncretism: An Interdisciplinary Approach* (Grand Rapids: Eerdmans, 1989); and William H. Harrison, *In Praise of Mixed Religion: The Syncretism Solution in a Multifaith World* (Montreal and Kingston: McGill-Queen's University Press, 2014).

14

LITURGICAL PREACHING

—ᴟᴟ—

Patricia A. Parachini

INTRODUCTION

As I look back on my developing interest in liturgy and liturgical preaching, I realize that the early seeds were planted in my undergraduate college years at a small Catholic women's college. I was fortunate to begin college just before Pope John XXIII called for the Second Vatican Council and had a good experience of the Vatican II reforms in liturgical practice right at the beginning. The enthusiasm of our two priest-chaplains for the Word of God and their ability to preach effectively in that context were great gifts to us. In my early years in the convent after college, I continued to experience good celebrations of liturgy. During my second summer of graduate studies at La Salle in 1968, I had the good fortune to take the first and only team-taught course in liturgy facilitated by Gerard Austin, OP, to whom this book is dedicated, and the Rev. Louis Weil. We not only studied in depth the Constitution on the Sacred Liturgy, *Sacrosanctum Concilium* (*SC*), but also explored the works of many of the major liturgical scholars of the day whose historical perspective and theological insight helped us to appropriate a new understanding of the centrality of the celebration of the Eucharist in creating a living church: "The liturgy is the summit toward which the activity of the Church is directed; at the same time it is the fountain from which all her power flows" (no. 10).[1] We learned that all of the baptized in the liturgical assembly "celebrate" the Eucharist, with the priest-presider, who gathers the faithful around the table, to remember and make present again the saving act of Christ Jesus, calling us forth beyond that assembly to proclaim Christ's liberating action to all, in both word and deed. We came to understand in a new way the close relationship of the Liturgy of the Word and the Liturgy of the Eucharist in the celebration of the Eucharist, a concept that was foreign to lifelong Roman Catholics at that time, learning that the entire liturgy nourishes and enlightens our faith. I am deeply grateful for the expertise of these two professors of liturgy who provided a solid foundation for my later studies, and I feel privileged to be counted as friend and colleague of these uniquely gifted men of deep commitment and integrity.

In this essay I plan to explore the topic of liturgical preaching by focusing primarily on contemporary Roman Catholic Church practice in the United States. After examining some major liturgical and pastoral issues related to preaching, I raise a few questions for our reflection as we consider how to move forward.

INTEGRAL RELATIONSHIP OF WORD AND SACRAMENT

Central to every celebration of the Eucharist is the act of remembering: "Do this in remembrance of me" (Luke 22:19). This act of remembering is more than merely recalling what Jesus did at his last meal with his disciples; rather, it is a mandate to live as Jesus did. Celebrating Eucharist—the act of remembering Jesus washing the feet of the disciples and breaking bread with them—has an impact on both the present and the future. Don Saliers helps us to understand the significance of the act of remembering:

> Without living remembrance of the whole biblical story there would be no authentic worship, nor could there be such a thing as becoming a living reminder of Jesus Christ for others. Seeking God and embodying holiness in our whole existence depends, in great measure on receiving and exercising the memories of the Scriptures in and through particular forms of communal traditions. Living our lives open to God requires dwelling in a common history, the narratives, the writings of the prophets, the witness of the

apostles, and the extended memories of the community praying and living in accordance with them through time.[2]

The celebration of the Eucharist is the action of the gathered people who remember our foundational stories as a people; we hear the stories proclaimed and preached about in the present, evoking and nurturing our living faith and making us one in communion with the Body of Christ. Through each celebration of the Eucharist, we are transformed anew to become a eucharistic people who proclaim a word of hope for the world by our very lives.

Pope Francis, in an instruction about the Mass given in Rome in March 2018, expressed it this way: "We become what we receive, both in the Word and in the Sacrament of the altar, to conform us to him...to allow oneself to be changed as we receive. Just as the bread and wine are converted into the Body and Blood of Christ, those who receive them with faith are transformed into a living Eucharist....You become the Body of Christ. This is beautiful, very beautiful....We become what we receive!"[3]

One of the major contributions of Vatican II was to place more emphasis on the Word of God in worship. Woefully neglected for centuries after the Reformation, the Word of God in Roman Catholicism was restored to its proper place in worship and in the education of the faithful after Vatican II. Due to the convergence of the biblical, catechetical, and liturgical movements of the 1940s and 1950s in the universal church, the Vatican II documents, especially the Dogmatic Constitution on Divine Revelation, *Dei Verbum* (*DV*), and the Dogmatic Constitution on the Church, *Lumen Gentium* (*LG*), as well as *SC*, reflected a new understanding of the central role of the Word of God in the church and stressed the need for Roman Catholics to study Scripture and to take it seriously as part of their communal worship experience. The published works of liturgists, theologians, and episcopal conferences during the 1950s and 1960s reflected the growing attention to the significance of the Word as it related to the Sacrament in the celebration of liturgy. For example, the French bishops spoke of the Word of God as food that nourishes us: "Comme l'Eucharistie, la parole est un festin de communauté:

pour nourrir avec profeit nos âmes à la table eucharistique, il est bon que nour commencions par alimenter notre foi à la table de la parole."[4]

Theologians such as Yves Congar and Edward Schillebeeckx describe this intimate connection in similar terms, noting that the Word and Sacrament in the liturgy are not to be isolated from one another or separated. For example, Congar speaks of the proclamation of the saving mystery of Christ through Word and Sacrament as opening up the mystery more fully to the present gathered assembly. Through the proclamation of the Word and preaching, the worshiping community is able to experience the saving event of Christ here and now and will be led to fuller participation in the eucharistic action that both proclaims and effects that salvation.[5]

Promulgated at the end of the second session, in December 1963, The Constitution on the Sacred Liturgy (*SC*) was the strongest impetus to recapture the significance of the Liturgy of the Word in contemporary liturgical practice. In contrast to *Mediator Dei* (*MD*), promulgated in 1947, which only hinted at the significance of the Word at Eucharist, *SC* places strong emphasis on the Word in the celebration of liturgy. In speaking of the manner of Christ's presence(s) in the liturgy, specific note is made of Christ's presence in the Word, among the other ways Christ is present. "He is present in His word, since it is He Himself who speaks when the holy Scriptures are read in the Church" (*SC* 7). This article clearly underlines the twofold proclamation of the mystery of Christ's saving action in both Word and rite, indicating no dichotomy between them. *Sacrosanctum Concilium* affirms the understanding that in the celebration of the liturgy, the Word of God gives meaning to the eucharistic action and the eucharistic action enfleshes the Word; it is a twofold movement of Word and rite influencing each other.

In contemporary liturgical practice, the church embraces the integral relationship of Word and Sacrament. The Liturgy of the Word and the Liturgy of the Eucharist can be compared to movements in a symphony having different emphases yet serving the whole of the celebration of the Eucharist, forming one harmonious piece or "one single act of worship" (*SC* 56). Unfortunately, some practices have been reintroduced in parishes or other worshiping communities that seem to downplay the intimate connect between Word and rite, and in fact interrupt the flow of the liturgy from one movement to the next. For example, reading parish announcements after the homily, instead of at the end of Mass before the dismissal, makes an unnatural break and halts the natural flow between the celebration of Word and sacramental rite.

PRIMACY OF SUNDAY

In my first liturgy course referred to in the introduction, we learned about the significance of Sunday in the early Christian community.[6] It was noted that these early communities of Christians newly separated from the synagogue looked upon each Sunday as the Lord's Day, in some places referring to it as the "eighth day"; from the viewpoint of faith, Sunday transcends the full seven-day week. Sunday was the day on which the newly formed community of followers of Jesus rejoiced in the new covenant and celebrated their new life in the Risen One through the breaking of the bread.

Today, we too give prominence to the Sunday Eucharist to celebrate the Mystery of God's saving action in Christ, inviting us to be transformed anew at every Sunday celebration of the Eucharist—to recommit to living our whole lives in Christ Jesus!

Documents of Vatican II and later documents to the present have provided direction and implementation of practices for the Sunday celebration that enrich the celebration of both the Liturgy of the Word and the Liturgy of the Eucharist; today, we continue to implement many of those practices. For example, the new three-cycle Sunday *Lectionary* was developed with an emphasis on the rhythm of the liturgical year, calling for appropriate readings for each season. Also, additional rites from the early church's practice related to the baptism of adults were introduced into the Sunday liturgy, so that all could witness the initiation of new members into the Catholic community and provide support for them. Some of the documents specifically related to the Liturgy of the Word and preaching reflected different viewpoints about the nature of the homily and addressed what kind of preaching was needed given the growing diversity and multicultural nature of our Sunday celebrations.[7]

Parishes and other worship communities continue to give priority to making the Sunday worship experience fully alive and participatory. Liturgy committees work hard to identify specific needs of the various communities that are likely to attend a specific liturgy each week. All stops are pulled out to prepare for and implement the best practices of liturgy each Sunday, giving careful attention to the diverse needs of the specific communities, including the choice of music or the need for the use of other languages within the liturgy, among other concerns.

The homily gained a new prominence within the Sunday eucharistic celebration after Vatican II, "as part of the liturgical service," given the new understanding of the Liturgy of the Word as integral to the celebration of the Eucharist. The terms *homily* and *sermon* have been used at different times in the church to refer to the preaching done in the context of worship. The term *homily* was used as early as the second century. It was replaced by the term *sermon* at the Council of Trent and has been restored to common use since Vatican II. In *SC* and other documents of Vatican II, although *homily* is used more frequently, when *sermon* is used, it is used as a synonym for *homily*. In the documents of Vatican II, a homily primarily signifies the preaching done in the context of the Sunday and daily Eucharist and is a proclamation of the marvels of God accomplished throughout salvation history and made present to us now:

> Since the sermon is part of the liturgical service, the preferred place for it is to be indicated even in the rubrics, as far as the nature of the rite will allow; and the ministry of preaching is to be fulfilled with exactitude and fidelity. The sermon, moreover, should draw its content mainly from scripture and liturgical sources. Its character should be that of a proclamation of God's wonderful works in the history of salvation, that is, the mystery of Christ which is ever made present and active within us, especially in the celebration of the liturgy....By means of the homily, the mysteries of faith and the guiding principles of the Christian life are expounded from the sacred text during the course of the

liturgical year. The homily, therefore, is to be highly esteemed as part of the liturgy itself. (*SC* 35.2; 52)

In *SC*, and in the instructions about implementing it that followed, preaching a homily at the Sunday liturgy was a mandate, not an optional choice of the presider. The Sunday homily was considered an opportune time for the preacher to form the assembled community of faith in the mystery of Christ for the here and now, with the specific readings assigned, so that they would live their everyday lives as disciples of Jesus. Through the ritual action of the Liturgy of the Word and the proclamation of the specific lectionary readings for that Sunday, along with the preached word, the community of faith is led into the ritual action of the sacramental rite to follow. The hope is that after eating the bread of the Word as well as the sacramental Bread, the gathered community will be nourished for the journey of discipleship beyond the liturgical assembly into the marketplace.

For a fuller understanding of the Liturgy of the Word and for more effective preparation for preaching, it can be helpful to understand the way the Sunday *Lectionary* is set up. It uses a cycle of readings for each year of a three-year period: Year A for the readings from Matthew, Year B for the readings from Mark, and Year C for the readings from Luke. The Gospel according to John is used at specific times of the liturgical year, for example, especially during Lent and the Easter/Pentecost season. The Sunday *Lectionary* was structured so that it would highlight the gospel message. With that in mind, the gospel was chosen first, either for its relationship to the liturgical season or to ensure the use of the most significant passages of that specific evangelist during each year; the first reading, taken from the Old Testament or one of the epistles, was chosen next, usually for its relationship to the gospel; and the second reading, chosen last, is usually drawn from the epistles or the Acts of the Apostles in the New Testament. The psalms used in the Sunday *Lectionary* are chosen as responses to the first reading and in conjunction with the gospel verse before the reading of the gospel. The advantages of the Sunday *Lectionary* are many, that is, providing the congregation with a wide exposure to Scripture and the opportunity to learn more about each of the Gospels; assisting the congregation in celebrating the liturgical year; and helping those present at the Eucharist to learn how important the Word of God is to the celebration of the Eucharist. Some of the limitations of the *Lectionary* include the omission of important books or sections of the books of the Bible that could be helpful to formation in the faith; the limited use of the Old Testament, with passages chosen only in relationship to the gospel, rather than chosen for what they reveal about God and our relationship to God in their own context; shortening certain passages from both Old and New Testaments that sometimes results in changing the meaning or leaving people puzzled and, at times, offended.

As conceived early on in Vatican II, the Sunday homily was considered the moment both to evoke the faith of those present and to enhance that lived faith. In this way of describing the purpose of the homily, the homilist was called to speak the faith of the church to the faith of the gathered assembly so that the living faith of both preacher and listeners could deepen and grow. This approach rested on the assumption that those who came to the Eucharist had, at least, an incipient faith.

In his study of the homily, Edward Foley suggests that we may need to consider another purpose of the homily or expand our understanding of its purpose in the contemporary church. Given the growing number of worshipers today who come to the Sunday liturgy not as insiders but from different standpoints—that is, some who are disaffected Catholics or have no articulated faith, and others who come from another religious tradition—the homily might serve another purpose, that of "recovering something of its missiological and evangelizing trajectory."[8] Taking Foley's suggestion to heart could require a paradigm shift, a rethinking of how to use the *Lectionary* in a different way or how to restructure it differently, giving more careful attention to its present limitations and how it might be improved to speak to a broader congregation. For example, how do we address those passages that have been strongly critiqued by several authors for their anti-Semitic bias, proclaimed and preached on with no explanation as the "Word of God"? Or how do we ensure that we use the Old Testament readings in such a way that we affirm the value of those Scriptures as God's revelation to us? Gerard Sloyan critiques the *Lectionary*'s use of the readings from the Old Testament as often a mere springboard for understanding or finding their meaning in the gospel rather than choosing the readings for what they reveal to us in themselves about God and faith.[9] There is no question that as the purpose of the homily continues to evolve, this will have wide-ranging effects, not only for a revised *Lectionary* but also for preaching and other aspects of our Sunday liturgical celebration.

LITURGICAL PREACHING AND THE HOMILY

Although there are different ways of describing liturgical preaching in documents from Vatican II to the present, I use the term *liturgical preaching* in this essay to mean any preaching that takes place in the context of liturgical worship, that is, the celebration of the Eucharist, either Sunday or daily liturgy; the communal celebration of the Liturgy of the Hours; and the communal celebration of the sacraments. It can also refer to preaching at a service of the Liturgy of the Word designed for specific occasions such as a vigil service for the dead or a funeral service that is not a eucharistic liturgy. Considering the above description of liturgical preaching, this author would describe the "homily"[10] as one kind of liturgical preaching; however, it is not the only kind of preaching that is done in the context of the liturgical assembly.

As we described earlier, the homily was given prominence in the celebration of the Sunday eucharistic celebration after Vatican II. Articles 35, 52, and 56 of *SC* previously cited give us a workable description of what was envisioned for a homily in the context of liturgy at that time. Looking at the variety of perspectives expressed in documents since then, however, it is difficult to articulate clearly what we mean by a homily in the contemporary church despite the number of articles and documents that describe it. There seems to be no clear description or explanation of what a homily is. Various types of documents describe it differently, whether it is a Vatican II document or an article from the 1983 Code of Canon Law or a bishops' document about preaching. Considering the range of documents that speak about a homily, it is difficult to ascertain if a homily refers more to the content of what is preached, to the person who preaches it, or to the placement of the preaching in the context of liturgy. Despite the many attempts at definitions and descriptions given in formal and less formal documents on liturgy, the distinction between a homily and other forms of preaching is not that obvious.[11]

Some of the ambiguity is due to the evolution of its development through the years in terms of how a homily was preached as well as the stated purpose and the content of a homily at a particular time. Although on the surface, trying to determine what a homily is in this period of our church's history can appear to be merely a question of semantics, the responses to questions raised about it have serious implications for the preaching ministry in the church, determining who is permitted to preach and on what occasions someone may or may not preach. Some of these questions are addressed in the last section of this chapter as we envision future directions for the preaching ministry.

One of the most influential documents affecting the growth and development of the liturgical preaching ministry in the United States is *Fulfilled in Your Hearing: The Homily in the Sunday Assembly* (*FITH*), published by the U.S. Bishops' Committee on Priestly Life and Ministry in 1982. This document provided the basis for the formation and training of preachers throughout the United States for well over thirty years. Although the formation and training were designed for the ordained, who are considered the ordinary ministers of preaching a homily at the Sunday Eucharist, it was used extensively around the country for preparing lay preachers as well. Many of these lay preachers had permission from their bishop to preach when they exercised specific roles assigned to them, such as the role of parish life administrator, or when they were permitted to preach on special occasions, for example, a children's homily. To its credit, *FITH* takes seriously the active role of the listeners in the preaching event; it encourages good preparation for preaching through the study of Scripture as well as the study of the specific congregation who will hear the preaching; it emphasizes the homily as part of the liturgy itself, taking the liturgical rites and seasons seriously as part of the preparation; and it asks preachers to seek help with both preparation for and feedback about their preaching. Edward Foley, among others, offers one major critique of this document—it gives too little emphasis to considering the entire liturgy as a resource for preaching the homily, what he refers to in other publications as the "liturgical bible."[12] In contrast to this, *FIYH* emphasizes Scripture alone as the resource for preaching the homily. In addressing the follow-up document to *FIYH*, *Preaching the Mystery of Faith: The Sunday Homily* (*PTMOF*), published by the U.S. Catholic Conference of Bishops in 2012, Foley notes that although it speaks of the homily as integral to the liturgy, it too limits the role of the liturgy as a homiletic resource, emphasizing the *Lectionary* or other biblical texts, and encourages a more didactic approach to preaching the homily. He also notes a shift in the designation of "homily" as applying solely to the Eucharist and not preaching done in the context of other liturgies.[13] An important point to highlight here is that the purpose and content of a homily, as well as the ways of describing what it is, continue to evolve today.

PREACHING AT DAILY LITURGY

Although there is evidence of the early practice of Christians breaking bread daily in the Church of Jerusalem (Acts 2:46), a first-century document, *The Didache* (The Teaching of the Twelve Apostles), chapter 14, speaks of celebrating the breaking of the bread on the Lord's Day. Although they believed that the Lord's Day was the opportune time to celebrate the breaking of the bread, it was also understood by the early Christians that whenever they gathered to break bread, they would partake of the bread as well.

Since Vatican II, the celebration of daily Eucharist as well as on Sunday in local parishes throughout the United States has been the norm. A majority of local Roman Catholic parishes throughout the United States continues to offer at least one eucharistic liturgy daily, or at least several times a week. However, some of the smaller, more rural parish communities may have one Sunday Eucharist every week and perhaps a communion service once a week on a weekday, at which a lay leader or a deacon presides. Daily attendance at Eucharist is dwindling in some areas of the country, whereas, in other places, daily attendance at liturgy is at least stable if not increasing. Whatever the case, it can be said by those presiding and preaching, as well as by those who attend a daily liturgy, it is a very different experience from that of a Sunday liturgy, especially from two vantage points: the community present at worship and the type of preaching needed.

The community attending a daily liturgy in a local parish is usually a consistent group of people who choose to attend regularly. Since they tend to sit in the same places, the presider can generally tell who is missing if someone is not there one day. Although they may not spend a great deal of time conversing with one another before or after the liturgy, they often form a common bond because they notice one another present as frequent flyers, so to speak. Some of the regular attendees usually serve as readers and/or eucharistic ministers and assist the presider to prepare for the liturgy ahead of time. The age of those who attend daily liturgy can vary according to the specific location of the church and the time of the liturgy. An earlier morning liturgy closer to town might attract a few who go to liturgy on their way to work, along with the elders in the community who would not miss, even on a snow day! Noon liturgies often attract a small group of younger workers who go to liturgy on their lunch hour; at times, a few college students, if the parish is located near a college or university in a more populated area, especially in the northeastern part of the United States; and, of course, the elders in retirement who attend regularly.

Daily celebration of the Eucharist seems to have a somewhat different purpose from the Sunday liturgy. The Sunday liturgy is the primary act of a local parish community as a whole, building the community of faith and sending it forth to the service of God's people. A daily liturgy seems more focused on supporting and deepening the spirituality of individuals who attend, not always from the same parish, inviting them to discern the best use of their gifts in their daily lives in the service of God's people. Normally, those who attend daily liturgy are practicing Catholics who see the daily Eucharist as supporting their faith and giving them sustenance to live the Christian life.

Preaching to those who attend daily liturgy calls for a very different approach from the preaching done at Sunday liturgy. First, the *Daily Lectionary* has a different structure, using a two-year cycle of readings. There is one reading instead of two before the gospel, chosen either from the Old Testament or a book of the New Testament. The *Daily Lectionary* includes special feasts and memorials to be celebrated throughout the year, offering the preacher more options to consider in preparing to preach. For example, for a major feast of a saint, like St. Teresa of Avila, the preacher might choose to emphasize something from her life or something from her writings, rather than refer to the specific Scripture reading for that day as an option. A second consideration is related to the use of the continuous readings in the daily lectionary cycle. With a stable community of regular worshipers at daily liturgy, it is more possible for a preacher to use the first reading differently, for example, to build on the continuous readings from one day to the next, for a few days or even longer, to develop a themed message that can nourish the gathered community. Third, the length of the preaching needs to be much shorter given the daily character of the celebration. A daily liturgy designed to nourish the gathered community for each day calls for preaching that would be no more than two or three minutes in contrast to a more developed reflection of ten to twelve minutes for a Sunday liturgy. This shorter reflection serves as a brief spiritual lesson or reminder for the day that the listener can relate to during the activities of the day.

Some possible approaches to daily preaching could include, for example, a brief reflection from the gospel or first reading that can carry one throughout the day; a thought from the life of a specific saint being celebrated, inviting the listener to emulate the saint's example; or an inspiration gleaned from the liturgy by way of an image or story that supports or encourages those present to deepen their outreach to others as a sign of carrying out their faithful commitment to God in Christ. Preaching at a daily liturgy is the ideal moment for nourishing the faithful present for their daily journey of discipleship—the following of Jesus in their lives.

PREACHING IN OTHER LITURGICAL CONTEXTS

Liturgical preaching on special occasions such as a wedding or a funeral has its own flavor, quite different from both a Sunday Eucharist or a daily liturgy. By looking at the occasion itself as well as who is likely be present at these special events, we can draw some general principles for liturgical preaching in these settings.

These two occasions, a wedding and a funeral, have certain things in common. Those who attend a wedding or a funeral are usually people who want to be there. We can assume they come from a variety of backgrounds and cultures and are a mixture of religious affiliations or none at all. The adults present represent a range of people we would find at any special occasion, that is, those who are married or have a partner, single or divorced. Also, those present would include young and old, family, friends, and relative strangers. The wide diversity of people gathered for these special occasions would certainly influence the way a preacher would think about and prepare for preaching at such occasions.

Many preachers consider weddings and funerals as significant "teachable moments" because those who come to these occasions want to be there and are open to what they will hear and experience; however, because of the diversity of their backgrounds, some may know little or nothing about Christianity or Roman Catholicism. Each of these occasions can be an opportune time for sharing with those present the best of Catholic beliefs and emphasizing the values of inclusion and hospitality—not only by the words preached, but by the way the entire liturgy is celebrated. Although many who are present do not share the same beliefs or may not be familiar with our rituals, a liturgy well celebrated and preached can witness to the best of our Catholic beliefs and at the same time can offer a way for those with different beliefs to still feel included and respected and to be lifted up as well. No small challenge for both preacher and presider!

Although most people who attend a wedding approach it as a joyful and celebrative occasion, some preachers find it a difficult occasion at which to preach, especially if they do not known the couple very well, do not have a strong relationship with the family of either party to be married, and may not know many of the people who attend. They also fret over how to avoid the pitfalls of saying something that might offend or to use overly familiar clichés in their preaching. They may wonder what readings best reflect the couple's preferences or beliefs, especially if they are not familiar with the Bible or do not want to be involved in the liturgical preparation for the wedding. Also, because of the very nature of a wedding, some preachers find it difficult to preach because they are keenly aware that the focus of those attending is frequently on everything but the Eucharist or the Word service that provides the liturgical context for the exchange of vows.

James Schmitmeyer offers a perspective about preaching at a wedding that is worth exploring, especially for those who find it challenging. He invites the preacher to view the entire liturgical event at a wedding, including preaching, as a way of inviting those present to enter into the deeper meaning of a wedding, viewing it as a sign of hope in the constancy of God's presence in the future.

> The form of the words known as a vow, words spoken in the face of all the unknown of the future, is the overarching form of the marriage rite. The element of futurity and the trust and hope it engenders is the experience which everyone at the rite of marriage longs to witness….The experience of these words moves one to think and wonder about an unknown future. As a homilist, how does one attempt to match the qualities of hope and trust which characterize the rite….The homilist would do well to direct the thoughts of the listeners to the future and the constancy of God's presence within it.[14]

In continuing to explore how to preach this hope in the future, Schmitmeyer cautions against too easy answers, as if the preacher (or anyone else) can predict the future of the couple. Rather, he encourages the preacher to emphasize the "gaps, the unnoticed places (in a marriage) wherein we come to recognize our yearning for God…our dependence on God. These are the fertile areas for a homilist to explore." And how does he propose the preacher do this? "Like the writing of a poem or the drawing of an image, the words of the liturgy and the words of our preaching provide the form in which our lives take their shape. The homilist endeavors to suggest or sketch the outlines of a picture wherein we can see ourselves as living in God."[15]

As we described earlier, a funeral is another significant teachable moment that the preacher can use positively. In contrast to preaching at a wedding, preachers with whom I have spoken consider preaching at funerals as one of their most preferred occasions at which to preach. Because most adults have had some experience of loss and grief, tapping into that very poignant human experience is more accessible for the preacher.

Reading and reflecting on the General Introduction to the *Order for Christian Funerals*, could be good remote preparation for preaching at any of the funeral rites, whether it is the vigil for the deceased or the funeral Mass or a funeral liturgy outside of a Mass. The General Instruction situates the celebration of the funeral rites in the context of the paschal mystery of Christ and invites the community of faith to pray for the deceased as well as those who are grieving their loss:

> At the death of a Christian, whose life of faith was begun in the waters of baptism and strengthened at the Eucharistic table, the Church intercedes on behalf of the deceased because of its confident belief that death is not the end nor does it break the bonds forged in life. The Church also ministers to the sorrowing and consoles them in the funeral rites with the comforting word of God and the sacrament of the Eucharist.[16]

In addressing the kind of preaching needed for the funeral liturgy, the General Instruction speaks of the "homily always given after the gospel." For the vigil service, it is stated differently, noting that a homily "may also be given." However, for both the funeral liturgy and the Vigil service, "there is never to be a eulogy. Attentive to the grief of those present, the homilist should dwell on God's compassionate love and on the paschal mystery of the Lord, as proclaimed in the Scripture readings." The preacher is to help the members of the family and community experience consolation as well as the strength to face this death and loss of one of their members "with a hope nourished by the saving word of God." It is important to note that the General Instruction summarizes the preaching role of a layperson who presides at a vigil service or funeral liturgy outside of Mass with one sentence: "Laypersons who preside at the funeral rites give an instruction on the readings." Is this a case of the person being permitted to preside but not being permitted to give a "homily"? How would "an instruction on the readings" differ from a homily in this context? Puzzling, to say the least.

As with any other kind of preaching, a preacher getting ready to preach at a funeral rite needs to give attention to the context of the whole event. This would require the preacher or other ministers in the parish, attending to the family of the deceased, visiting them and talking with them before the vigil service or the funeral, to find out more about the deceased. It would be helpful to know the age, gender, and manner of death; significant others and state of life, such as married, single, in a partnership, or divorced. Was the deceased person a practicing Catholic or inactive? Or, in the case of a child's death, adapt the questions to that case. The preacher also needs to reflect on how to balance the Christian understanding of death and resurrection with the need to express compassion to those who are grieving, in this context. The choice of readings for the funeral rite(s) may depend on gleaning the above information as well as the possible involvement of one or two significant family members or friends who want to participate in the planning of the liturgy and give input to the preacher.

Although preaching at a funeral is not a eulogy, knowing something about the deceased person's story and social location to prepare for preaching at the funeral rites is essential. This most teachable moment not only brings comfort to those present but also can be instrumental in bearing fruit in their lives as well.

THE PREACHER'S MANDATE

As we consider the new emphasis on liturgical preaching since Vatican II and survey the vast amount of literature published about preaching and its importance, I would be remiss if I did not address, at least briefly, the "role" of the preacher, or what I refer to in this section as the preacher's mandate. Given the limitations of an essay, however, I try not to address the question of immediate preparation for preaching, one aspect of the preacher's mandate. There are numerous books and articles, some of which are included in the selected bibliography at the end of this essay, that speak about effective ways for a preacher to prepare to preach in a specific context. Generally speaking, a preacher would need to give attention to the liturgical season and the specific liturgical context, the readings for that occasion, the listeners who will be present, and anything pertinent that will have an impact on the preaching event. And this preparation is always done in the context of prayer and one's own study and appropriation of the Word of God.

Robert E. C. Browne, an Anglican clergyman, ordained in the Church of Ireland, addresses with great passion the vocation of the minister of the Word in *The Ministry of the Word*, still relevant today, although first published in the late 1950s.

> Effective ministers of the Word are not verbose, obscure or obscurantist; they do not abuse, they do not patronize and they never embarrass; they do not make false simplifications in the interests of being understood; they speak as plainly as their subject matter allows and as their development permits. They have sufficient mastery of their subject and of themselves to be servants of all who will pay attention to them.[17]

Preachers could benefit from meditating on this statement as a spiritual practice, using it as an assessment of the state of their soul as well as of their preaching. As Browne continues to describe the mandate of the preacher, he highlights the need for preachers to be centered in God and within themselves as they deal with their temptations and their resistance. "Great preaching, like great art, cannot be the work of those who know no chaos within them and it cannot be the work of those who are unable to master the chaos within them....The preacher's sermons are a most important part of his behaviour and are made as the result of an incalculable amount of hidden work." He describes the preacher as artist, poet, and prophet; as prophet the preacher does not foretell things to come but rather "tells his audience, at the risk of their displeasure, the secrets of their own hearts."[18] Browne sees the

preaching task as evoking from the congregation their personal experience of God brought into dialogue with the Word of God that is
proclaimed and preached in the assembly. The preacher's mandate in
this regard is to preach in such a way that the congregation is invited
to hear God's call in the depth of their heart as they actively listen to
what is preached in the midst of the assembly.

In another challenging book, using Acts 3:12–26 in the context
of the whole of chapter 3 to illustrate her point, Mary Catherine
Hilkert describes "preaching as the art of naming grace found in the
depths of human experience." She notes that "only after preaching
through concrete action does Peter deliver his formal sermon....As
preacher, Peter interprets what has been operative in the depths of the
community's human experience; he points to the power and the presence of God. He names grace." The preaching task, then, is to
announce that God has defeated the power of sin and death through
the resurrection; however, the good news also calls the community to
repentance and conversion—a turning toward God and a turning
away from sin. And, "The final word of the preaching event is not a
word of judgment....Rather preaching is an invitation to follow; it is
a word of hope rooted in God's promise. Preachers announce a word
of life that empowers the conversion it demands."[19]

Together, the insights of these two authors creatively highlight
the basic ingredients of a preacher's mandate: the depth of spirituality
needed from the preacher reflected in certain qualities of character
such as humility and respect for others; the need for preparation to
preach, not only growing in an appropriation of Scripture and the
beliefs of Christianity, but also in knowing who the participants are
and approaching them with a deep respect for their experience of
faith. Preachers are invited to live a disciplined life—a life of integrity—
implying that it is not possible to preach effectively what you as
preacher have not struggled with personally in your graced moments
of invitation to turn away from sin and turn toward your God. And
finally, both invite preachers to accept for themselves and preach to
others the good news—a word of hope in God's promise through
Christ Jesus, who through his cross and resurrection gave us the
assurance that sin and death do not have the last word.

MOVING FORWARD

Several other chapters of this book have addressed topics that have and will continue to have an impact on our liturgical practice and preaching for the future, for example, the issue of inculturation and the growing multicultural contexts of our worshiping communities, the call to justice as integral to the preaching of the gospel, the impact of evolution, and the New Cosmology. Although preaching in the digital age is not addressed specifically in one of the chapters of this book, we are already surrounded by the impact of growing social media and its effects on both church and society. For a good treatment of this and related questions and their impact on Catholic preaching, see *Connecting Pulpit and Pew.*[20]

In this concluding section of the essay, I raise a few questions pertinent to the topic of lay preaching in the liturgical context that need to be addressed if lay preachers are to exercise their ministry effectively in the future. This seems to be one of the most difficult issues to address. The publication and implementation of the *Directory for Masses with Children* sanctioned lay preaching in liturgy in 1973, and the practice of preaching by laypersons in liturgy has been a practice in the United States since that time, even if sporadic. See the references below for a more extensive treatment of the topic of lay preaching.[21]

The church is long overdue in accepting lay preaching as a viable ecclesial ministry, especially in the context of liturgy, and in creating a process whereby ordained and lay theologians and pastoral ministers can reflect together on how to enhance the practice of this ministry in today's church and for the future. Numerous articles have addressed the issue of the missing voices of laypersons in the pulpit and what a loss that is to the richness of the preached word in liturgy. Throughout the United States there is a great deal of unnecessary confusion about if and when lay preaching is permitted, and in many places it has fallen into disuse because of a lack of leadership. Although the 1983 Code of Canon Law opened the possibility of laypersons preaching in a church or oratory, it also stated explicitly that a layperson cannot preach a homily, at least at Sunday Eucharist (see canons 766 and 767). In 2002, the U.S. Conference of Catholic

Bishops promulgated norms, brief but still rather ambiguous, for lay preaching that permit laypersons to preach, give spiritual conferences, or give instructions with permission, but it also notes that "the diocesan bishop may never dispense from the norm which reserves the homily to the sacred ministers" (referring to Canon 767, art. 1).[22] In the case of preaching at a vigil service for the deceased, discussed previously, even though a layperson is permitted to preside and preach at the service, that preaching is referred to as "instruction" rather than a homily, again creating confusion about the nature of the preaching a layperson does. Is instruction (what a layperson preaches) about the meaning of death and the resurrection different from preaching (a homily) about the "mysteries of faith"? What is it about a homily that a lay preacher can't preach it? One can only conclude that, by definition, a homily is what an ordained person preaches. From the perspective of those who listen to the preaching at a vigil service, does it really matter? What they want to hear from the church and its ministers at such times is a word of comfort and hope.

Elsewhere I have written about ways to approach a resolution of some of these issues; in this essay, I am only pointing to the impasse and asking us to reflect on what prevents us from moving forward. It seems to me that fostering the flourishing of lay preaching as well as the preaching of the ordained will only result in growth for the preaching ministry—bearing fruit in the lives of those gathered for worship.

As we move forward as a worshiping church and consider the many hungers of God's people that need to be fed in our liturgical assemblies, let us come together to exercise our imaginations and take a leap of faith through the power of the Holy Spirit, so that the living church about which we spoke at the beginning of this essay can continue to be that sign of hope in God's promise.

Selected Bibliography

Bellinger, Karla J. *Connecting Pulpit and Pew: Breaking Open the Conversation about Catholic Preaching.* Collegeville, MN: Liturgical Press, 2014.

Bergant, Diane. *Preaching the New Lectionary* (Years B, C, A). Collegeville, MN: Liturgical Press, 1999, 2000, 2001.

Browne, Robert E. C. *The Ministry of the Word.* Philadelphia: Fortress Press, 1976.

Foley, Edward, ed. *A Handbook for Catholic Preaching.* Collegeville, MN: Liturgical Press, 2016.

Hilkert, Mary Catherine. *Naming Grace: Preaching and the Sacramental Imagination.* New York: Continuum, 1997.

Parachini, Patricia A. *Lay Preaching: State of the Question.* American Essays in Liturgy Series. Series edited by Edward Foley. Collegeville, MN: Liturgical Press, 1999.

Saliers, Don E. *Worship and Spirituality.* 2nd ed. Akron, OH: OSL Publications, 1996.

Skudlarek, William. *The Word in Worship: Preaching in a Liturgical Context.* Nashville: Abingdon, 1981.

Wallace, James A. *Preaching to the Hungers of the Heart: The Homily on the Feasts and within the Rites.* Collegeville, MN: Liturgical Press, 2002.

Waznak, Robert P. *An Introduction to the Homily.* Collegeville, MN: Liturgical Press, 1998.

Notes

1. See *The Documents of Vatican II*, ed. Walter M. Abbott (New York: America Press, 1966), 141.

2. Don Saliers, *Worship and Spirituality*, 2nd ed. (Akron, OH: OLS Publications 1996).

3. Pope Francis, a catechetical instruction given March 21, 2018, in Rome. This talk is part of a series of the pope's catechetical instructions given on Wednesdays.

4. Evêques de France, *Directoire pour la pastorale de la messe* (Paris: Bonne Presse-Fleurus, 1955), art. 1, 69, 71, in *L'Homélie: Selon la Constitution de la Sainte Liturgie*, ed. Elie Fournier (Bruxelles: Editions de Lumen Vitae, 1964), 15. "As the Eucharist, the word of God is a community feast: to nourish ourselves beneficially at the Eucharistic table it is good to begin to nourish our faith at the table of the Word" (translation mine).

5. Yves Congar, "Sacramental Worship and Preaching," in *The Renewal of Preaching: Theory and Practice*, Concilium 33 (New York: Paulist Press, 1968), 51–63.

6. See Josef A. Jungmann, *The Early Liturgy: To the Time of Gregory the Great* (Notre Dame: University of Notre Dame Press, 1959).

7. See Con Foley and Richard N. Fragomeni, "Roman Catholic Teaching on Preaching: A Postconciliar Survey," in *A Handbook for Catholic Preaching*, ed. Edward Foley (Collegeville, MN: Liturgical Press, 2016), 26–37.

8. Edward Foley, "The Homily," in Foley, *A Handbook for Catholic Preaching*, 164.

9. Gerard S. Sloyan, "The Lectionary as a Context for Interpretation," *Interpretation: A Journal of Bible and Theology* 31, no. 2 (1977): 135.

10. See a brief overview of the different approaches to describing what a homily is depending on the emphasis at a particular period of history, in the following works: James A. Wallace, *Preaching to the Hungers of the Heart* (Collegeville, MN: Liturgical Press, 2002), vii–xii; and Robert P. Waznak, *An Introduction to the Homily* (Collegeville, MN: Liturgical Press, 1998), chap. 1, 1–27.

11. Patricia A. Parachini, *Lay Preaching: State of the Question*, American Essays in Liturgy, ed. Edward Foley (Collegeville, MN: Liturgical Press, 1999), 53–54.

12. Edward Foley, *Preaching Basics* (Chicago: Liturgy Training Publications, 1998), 13.

13. Foley, "The Homily," 159–61.

14. James M. Schmitmeyer, *The Words of Worship: Presiding and Preaching at the Rites* (New York: Alba House, 1988), 84–86.

15. Schmitmeyer, *The Words of Worship*, 87.

16. National Conference of Catholic Bishops, *Order of Christian Funerals* (Chicago: Liturgy Training Publications, 1989), art. 4.

17. Robert E. C. Browne, *The Ministry of the Word*, First American Edition (Philadelphia: Fortress Press, 1976), 17.

18. Browne, *The Ministry of the Word*, 17–20.

19. Mary Catherine Hilkert, *Naming Grace: Preaching and the Sacramental Imagination* (New York: Continuum, 1997), 44–45.

20. Karla J. Bellinger, *Connecting Pulpit and Pew* (Collegeville, MN: Liturgical Press, 2014).

21. See the following for more extensive treatment of this issue: Patricia A. Parachini and Patrick Lagges, "Charism and Order," in Foley, *A Handbook for Catholic Preaching*, 264–74; Patricia A. Parachini, "Preaching in Many Voices," *Ministry and Liturgy* 35, no. 6 (August 2008): 4–6; Patricia A. Parachini, *Lay Preaching: State of the Question*, American Essays in Liturgy, series ed. Edward Foley (Collegeville, MN: Liturgical Press, 1999); Mary Catherine Hilkert, "Bearing Wisdom—The Vocation of the Preacher," *Spirituality Today* 44, no. 2 (Summer 1992): 143–60.

22. See *Origins* 31, no. 33 (Jan. 31, 2002).

15

LITURGY AND
PASTORAL MINISTRY

—⁓—

Sallie Latkovich

I had the great good fortune, indeed the grace, to be a colleague of Jerry Austin at the Blessed Edmund Rice School for Pastoral Ministry in the Diocese of Venice in Florida. Our school was in alliance with Barry University of Miami and offered the master's degree in pastoral theology. Our primary outreach was to the faithful men and women of the diocese who were engaged in various pastoral ministries in their parishes and other places in the diocese.

Any reader of these essays knows Jerry Austin to be a man of faith, which found expression and devotion in the liturgy of the church. As Jerry himself took part in the parish life of St. Maximilian Kolbe Parish during his time at the Rice School, he himself discovered the important connection between pastoral ministry and liturgy. In fact, they are not two distinct parts of the church but are intricately connected, with a common root in baptism and bonding through the sacramental life of the church.

ROOTED IN BAPTISM

Jerry and I did several presentations together on the very topic of liturgy and pastoral ministry. He always began by citing a presentation by Godfrey Diekmann, OSB, "Christian, Remember Your Baptism," from April 17, 1997. It was startling to some in our audience when Jerry proclaimed that the most important day of his life was his baptism and not his ordination.

The Body of Christ, into which we are baptized, includes three specific areas of pastoral ministry: that of priest, prophet, and king. I would suggest that it is full, conscious, active participation as members of the Body of Christ that brings us to the eucharistic table and the sacraments. Ministry is a facet of baptized life, not the vocation of the few.

Incorporated into the Church by Baptism, the faithful are appointed by their baptismal character to Christian religious worship; reborn as children of God, they must profess before all people the faith they have received from God through the Church. (*Lumen Gentium* 11)

PASTORAL MINISTRY
(PASTOR AS SHEPHERD OF THE SHEEP)

The very term *pastoral ministry* has become commonplace over the years since Vatican II. The word *pastor* derives from the Latin noun *pastor*, which means "shepherd," and relates to the Latin verb *pascere*, "to lead to pasture, set to grazing, cause to eat." In other words, the pastor is called to care for and to nurture the sheep.

The model of the *good shepherd* is one of the images in John: "I am the good shepherd. I know my own and my own know me" (10:14). Knowing and being known by others is fundamental to liturgy, which is always a communal event. Liturgical rituals are never "anonymous events" where the rubrics are followed with little or no relationship among the participants.

Ministry begins with the Christian community, flows out of the community, and thereby nourishes and expands the community. A variety of specific ministries serves to sustain a community because there are many things to be done in a communal life of Word, Sacrament, and sustenance of faith. It is fitting to explore pastoral ministry in the three areas to which we are called in baptism, as members of the Body of Christ.

Anointing After Baptism

God the Father of Our Lord Jesus Christ has freed you from sin, given you a new birth by water and the Holy

287

Spirit, and welcomed you into his holy people. He now anoints you with the chrism of salvation. As Christ was anointed Priest, Prophet, and King, so may you live always as a member of his body, sharing everlasting life.[1]

Priest

It may be difficult to set aside the notion of ordained priesthood in favor of the larger understanding of the priesthood of the whole Body of Christ.

> How beautiful will be the day when all the baptized understand that their work, their job is priestly work; that, just as I celebrate Mass at this altar, so each carpenter celebrates Mass at the workbench, and each metalworker, each professional, each doctor with a scalpel, the market woman at her stand, is performing a priestly office! How many cab drivers, I know, listen to this message in their cab: you are a priest at the wheel, my friend, if you work with honesty, consecrating that taxi of yours to God, bearing a message of peace and love to the passengers who ride in your car.[2]

> The baptized, by regeneration and the anointing of the Holy Spirit, are consecrated as a spiritual house and a holy priesthood, that through all their Christian activities they may offer spiritual sacrifices and proclaim the marvels of him who has called them out of darkness. (*Lumen Gentium* 9)

Thus, the baptized are called and sent forth as *light* in the world, as servants of the people of God. The primary metaphor of priesthood is the servant. Pope Francis emphasized this in the homily of his inaugural Mass: "A priest's authority must be linked to service, especially to the care and protection of the poorest, weakest, the least important and most easily forgotten." This is the call of the priesthood of the faithful: called by baptism, nourished and sent forth by the Eucharist.

The sacred nature and organic structure of the priestly community is brought into operation through the sacraments....Incorporated into the Church by Baptism, the faithful are appointed by their baptismal character to Christian religious worship; reborn as children of God, they profess before others the faith they have received from God through the Church. By the Sacrament of Confirmation, they are more perfectly bound to the Church and are endowed with the special strength of the Holy Spirit. Hence they are, as true witnesses of Christ more strictly obliged to spread the faith by word and deed. (*Lumen Gentium* 11)

Prophet

Teaching the prophetic literature in my own course on biblical foundations of spirituality, I make the connection with the call of baptism to be prophet. A reflection question I pose to the students is this: Why is the call to be prophet so little heard/understood in our culture? The discussion that follows is animated! We in the First World, North America, are taught to be "law-abiding" citizens and servants of civil law. Thus, to be prophet is countercultural to be sure.

The task of the prophet is described by Walter Brueggemann in his book *The Prophetic Imagination* in this way: "Prophetic ministry is to nurture, nourish and evoke a consciousness and perception alternative to the consciousness and perception of the dominant culture around us." This is accomplished through both prophetic criticism and prophetic energizing. In simple words, the prophet speaks the truth to power, calling for justice.

The Hebrew *sdq* refers to a relationship between two parties and implies behavior which fulfills the claims arising from such an involvement. Thus, [justice] is the fulfillment of the demands of a relationship with God, with a person, [or with the earth] when people fulfill the conditions imposed on them by relationship, they are righteous.[3]

This prophetic description is true of the prophets of the Hebrew Bible and is certainly true of the ministry of Jesus. We who are baptized into Christ are baptized as prophets. It is clearly through the nourishment of the Eucharist and the strength of anointing in confirmation that the prophetic call is clear.

Doing justice, being prophet, is accomplished in three ways: education to justice, direct service to the marginalized or oppressed, and changing unjust systems. These prophetic words, works, and actions are pastoral ministry, as they take Jesus as primary model of prophet.

King

Once again, it is important to set aside the current understanding of monarchy and return to the earliest form of monarchical institution. The primary responsibility of the earliest kings was to protect the people of the country from attack or invasion. Thus, the king was the leader of the army, and the collector of taxes to support the royal household.

Whatever does kingship have to do with baptism or with pastoral ministry? At the time of its origin, the king was the pastoral minister of the people. He was to protect them and oversee the food and water supply.

As Jesus teaches in the Gospel, "The greatest among you will be your servant" (Matt 23:11). So, all who are baptized into Christ are to become servants to the whole people of God. Thus, one is reminded that the most important connection of liturgy and pastoral ministry is in the foundation of baptism. Furthermore, as the Eucharist is "source and summit" of the Christian life, it is source and summit of pastoral ministry.

MORE SPECIFIC AREAS OF PASTORAL MINISTRY

I might begin this section by quoting the familiar text from Paul in 1 Corinthians 12:4: "There are varieties of gifts, but the same

Spirit." Thus, there are different areas of pastoral ministry, with different gifts needed for each.

At the Candler School of Theology, the faculty articulates five areas of ministry in their guidelines for ecclesial practices. These include administration, liturgy, pastoral care, mission and outreach, and religious education. These seem to provide an excellent list on which to comment on liturgy and pastoral ministry.

Leadership and Administration

In my own congregation of St. Joseph, one of our four "Generous Promises" is: "We promise to be mutually responsible and accountable for leadership in our congregation." As such, we recognize the potential for leadership among every member, according to their gifts and experience.

This sentiment is expressed in the Constitution of the Church in the Modern World of Vatican II:

> This sense of responsibility comes as one is conscious of their dignity and then rises to their destiny in the service of God and others....[This responsibility] can be strengthened by undertaking the manifold demands of human fellowship, and by service to the community at large. (*Gaudium et Spes* 31)

Leadership is sometimes exercised as administration. In Don Senior's recent book *The Gift of Administration*, he makes the following observation:

> While it was easy to see the connection between my faith as a Christian and the vocation of studying and teaching the Scriptures, it took me some time to appreciate the fact that administration, too, was an authentic, Gospel-rooted ministry. While it makes sense to learn the art of administration from the wisdom of corporate leaders and social studies of effective management, what we might call "secular" sources, it is also important to know that from a Christian perspective, the

practices and virtues demanded by the work of administration have a solid biblical and theological foundation and as such can be an expression of one's Christian call to discipleship and service....Administration is also named by Paul as a "gift of God" given to the community to build it into the Body of Christ and one grounded in the very nature of the Christian mission to the World.[4]

Liturgy

The very title of this essay is "Liturgy and Pastoral Ministry." This topic can be addressed in two ways: the ministries that are necessary for "full, active, conscious" participation in the liturgy and the ministries to which the assembly is sent.

It is the whole community, the Body of Christ, that celebrates the liturgy. As the Body of Christ, the church, we each have a very important and necessary role in the celebration of the Eucharist. We become an assembly of worship, coming before God to offer our praise and thanksgiving.

The priest acts in the liturgy in the person of Christ: giving voice to the prayers of the church, presiding over the celebration of the mysteries of our faith, preaching God's Word, and feeding God's people with the Body and Blood of Christ. All these actions are pastoral in the exercise of care for God's people.

Other members of the Body of Christ, the church, are also called to service in roles of their own. These are not simply "jobs" or "tasks" that have to be done but real ministerial action. The planning of the Eucharist and preparation of the worship space in both art and environment and the immediate preparation for the celebration by sacristan and team are indeed pastoral ministry. The decoration of the church according to the liturgical seasons provides visual clues to the assembly, thus ministering to their senses. The sacristan and their team "set the table" for the Eucharist to take place, and the servers minister at that table. Ushers and greeters are indeed ministers of hospitality, welcoming those who have come to worship into the assembly. The music director, cantors, instruments, and choir all invite the assembly to raise their voices in song as appropriate to the season and readings of the day.

The lectors are called to be ministers of the Word, proclaiming in such a way that all can hear, and by the lector's very proclamation, all are drawn in to discern the meaning. ministers of holy communion offer the Body and Blood of Christ to the faithful, thus pastorally nourishing their souls.

Thus, the Liturgy of the Eucharist relies on the *pastoral ministry* of all who take part in providing a prayerful worship experience. The rite at the conclusion of the Mass sends everyone out on mission, as pastoral ministers by the very way they live their lives.

There are two versions of the dismissal rite, added in the recently revised Roman Missal; both stress this missionary function: "Go and announce the Gospel of the Lord," and "Go in peace, glorifying the Lord by your lives." Tony Gittins says, "Disciples are those who are called to be sent, who are co-missioned along with Jesus. He was sent to bring into the world the total and unconditional self-giving love of God."[5]

We are all called, each one of us, to be ministers of pastoral care: extending the love and care of God to one another.

Pastoral Care

> Ministry within the walls of the church is significant and must be shared, but it is only preparatory to our ministry in the world of work, of organizing, of bringing justice and the fulfillment of human dignity to all; for when we go forth from the Eucharist hand in hand, we are all, in partnership, going through the "servants' entrance" to the world.[6]

By the grace of baptism and sending from the Eucharist, all the baptized are called to pastoral ministry. For our purposes, the primary service of such ministry comes directly from this familiar Gospel text:

> For I was hungry and you gave me food, I was thirsty and you gave me something to drink, I was a stranger and you welcomed me, I was naked and you gave me clothing, I was sick and you took care of me, I was in prison and you

visited me....Truly I tell you, just as you did it to one of the least of these who are members of my family, you did it to me. (Matt 25:35–40)

It is important to note that these good works may look to some as simply social work. However, they become pastoral ministry when they are done with the awareness of being sent to serve God by serving the neighbor—the neighbor as one of God's beloved.

Special mention should be made here regarding pastoral care of and ministry to the sick.

Care of the sick and dying is a communal responsibility, an essential dimension of every Christian community. Many local churches have instituted a ministry of care that gives some structure to the work. Prior to the Second Vatican Council, this ministry would have been the work of the ordained. Today, however, all the baptized may be called to exercise this important ministry.

In 1983, the *Pastoral Care of the Sick* was published; it was revised and published in a second edition in 2016. Liturgy is the work of the assembled community of baptized persons. Persons who are sick or dying can so easily feel—and be—marginalized within their community. Those who minister to the sick represent the community and are encouraged to invite and engage the community to be present to the sick or dying person.[7]

Mission and Outreach

Most people in North America think of missionary activity as a service to a foreign country where there is a shortage of clergy and religious people. But the Decree on Missionary Activity of Vatican II, *Ad Gentes Divinitus*, says,

The mission of the Church is carried out by means of that activity through which, in obedience to Christ's command and moved by the grace and love of the Holy Spirit, the Church makes itself fully present to all peoples in order to lead them to the faith, freedom and peace of Christ by the example of its life and teaching, by the sacraments and other means

of grace. Its aim is to open up for all a free and sure path to
full participation in the mystery of Christ. (*Ad Gentes* 5)

Thus, the Council fathers understand the missionary activity of the
church to be any outreach to which the baptized are sent. Perhaps all
the areas being addressed in this essay exploring liturgy and pastoral
ministry come under the overarching umbrella of the church's mission.

I am blessed to work with colleagues at Catholic Theological
Union who are members of the Divine Word Missionaries. I will be
quoting from two of them, but, first, I would like to share the mission
of their congregation:

> We bring the Word of God to the most underserved and
> remote areas of the world, working first where the Gos-
> pel has yet to be preached and where local Churches are
> struggling to survive. We share Christ through service,
> teaching and caring for the sick and the poor. We do this
> through ministries that build and staff schools, hospitals,
> orphanages and hospices. We educate for AIDS preven-
> tion through centers that care for children and adults living
> with AIDS. We teach self-sufficient ways of life through
> land management, agricultural and ranching programs.
> And most importantly, by sharing the Word of God and
> celebrating the sacraments, we comfort those in need and
> bring peace to those in pain.[8]

This mission statement is explicit in serving both the physical and the
spiritual needs of those to whom the missionaries are sent. And it is
clear that the spiritual needs are nourished through celebrating the
sacraments.

Stephen Bevans, SVD, is a colleague at Catholic Theological
Union and is a specialist in missiology. He suggests that the mission
actually precedes the church. The church does not so much have a
mission as the mission has a church. The church is not about itself; it
is about the reign of God that it preaches, serves, and witnesses to,
and this makes all the difference.[9]

Roger Schroeder, SVD, is another colleague who, like his confrere Stephen Bevans, is a specialist in missiology. Roger has recently revised and expanded his book *What Is the Mission of the Church? A Guide for Catholics.* He includes a chapter titled "A Simple but Complex Reality." This is a phrase used by Pope John Paul II, speaking of the complexities of individual situations and contexts.

As part of this chapter, Roger writes specifically about liturgy, prayer, and contemplation. He introduces the section in this way:

> We normally may not consider liturgy, prayer and contemplation as acts of mission. However, centering our lives more and more on our God, who is missionary by nature, draws us into God's boundary-crossing mission.[10]

Roger also includes a very insightful message about the "out and in" of mission experience:

> Mission is not just from "inside" [the church] to "outside," but also the reverse. Bringing the voices and concerns of the neighborhood and world into liturgy in various ways prevents the community from focusing too much on itself and opens its members to being attentive, nourished, and challenged by God's movement in the wider world.[11]

If we begin to think of the church as missionary by its very nature, meaning that it is mission that gives identity and purpose to the church, any structure in the church will be understood not as an end in itself but as existing to contribute its part to serve the mission. The ministry of liturgy in the church exists not merely in order to contribute to or build up the church. The liturgy certainly does this, but its ultimate purpose is to form the church so that the church can get on with its work in the world.

Religious Education/Faith Formation

Years ago, the famous PBS personality Bill Moyers did a one-hour special, interviewing the then-archbishop of Milwaukee,

Rembert Weakland. Their topic was prayer as they walked through a park and came to sit on a bench. Moyers posed this question to Weakland: "Archbishop, how does one learn to pray?" He waited expectantly, supposing that Weakland would give something of a recipe for learning how to pray. The archbishop smiled a gentle smile and replied, "To learn to pray, one sits with one who prays."

Liturgists often use the Latin phrase *Lex orandi, lex credendi, lex vivendi.* It is loosely translated, "As we pray, so we believe, so we live." Though the primary intent of liturgy is to worship God, it always has an impact on the lives of participants that is educational.

> Awareness that liturgy "instructs" is as old as the people of Israel. Israel had summary statements that reflected, in story form, its identity in faith. Commentators note, however, that the formal context of those creedal stories and the occasions on which the people would hear them repeatedly was the liturgical life of Israel.[12]

As liturgy educates, so too the Christian community must educate itself for its liturgical work. Again, Vatican II emphasized the importance of such catechesis: "That all the faithful be led to the full, conscious and active participation in liturgical celebration which is demanded by the very nature of the liturgy, the Church must provide the needed program of instruction" (*Sacrosanctum Concilium* 14).

Since the Council, the centrality of liturgical/sacramental catechesis in Catholic religious education is evident. Many parishes involve parents in the sacramental catechesis of their children, especially in preparing for the sacraments of initiation and reconciliation. This faith formation of adults is important in renewing the liturgical life of the Catholic community.

In addition, the celebration of the Rite of Christian Initiation of Adults is a process of initiation of new members to the church that involves the parish community. Far from simply learning the doctrines of the Catholic faith, the RCIA welcomes new members into the community of faith, making them part of the parish community along with catechetical sessions of faith formation and education.

CONCLUSION

To reflect on and write about liturgy and pastoral ministry is a bit like untangling two strands that are intimately interwoven and connected. Beginning with baptism, the liturgical life sends Christians out to pastoral ministry, and pastoral ministry leads disciples back to liturgy.

I return to Godfrey Diekmann's article "Christian, Remember Your Baptism!" The baptized are sent forth to be the Light of Christ in the world and, thus, to share their particular gifts in pastoral ministry to God's people.

Our friend and colleague Jerry Austin, who cherishes the day of his own baptism, has spent his life of pastoral ministry teaching and celebrating liturgy.

Further Reading

Bernier, Paul. *Ministry in the Church: A Historical and Pastoral Approach.* Mystic, CT: Twenty-Third Publications, 1996.

Huebsch, Bill, with Paul Thurmes. *Vatican II in Plain English: The Constitutions.* Notre Dame: Ave Maria Press, 1996.

Oden, Thomas C. *Pastoral Theology: Essentials of Ministry.* San Francisco: HarperSanFrancisco, 1983.

O'Meara, Thomas Franklin. *Theology of Ministry.* New York: Paulist Press, 1983.

Osborne, Kenan B. *Ministry: Lay Ministry in the Roman Catholic Church, Its History and Theology.* Mahwah, NJ: Paulist Press, 1993.

Ostdiek, Gilbert. *Mystagogy of the Eucharist: A Resource for Faith Formation.* Collegeville, MN: Liturgical Press, 2015.

Philibert, Paul J. *The Priesthood of the Faithful: Key to a Living Church.* Collegeville, MN: Liturgical Press, 2005.

Senior, Donald. *The Gift of Administration: New Testament Foundations for the Vocation of Administrative Service.* Collegeville, MN: Liturgical Press, 2016.

Whitehead, Evelyn Eaton, and James D. Whitehead. *Community of Faith, Crafting Christian Communities Today.* Mystic, CT: Twenty-Third Publications, 1992.

Willimon, William H. *Worship as Pastoral Care*. Nashville: Abingdon Press, 1979.

Notes

1. *The Rite of Baptism for Children* (Collegeville, MN: Liturgical Press, 2002), 98.

2. Oscar Romero, *The Violence of Love* (Maryknoll, NY: Orbis Books, 1988), 24.

3. Bruce V. Malchow, *Social Justice in the Hebrew Bible* (Collegeville, MN: Liturgical Press, 1996).

4. Donald Senior, *The Gift of Administration: New Testament Foundations for the Vocation of Administrative Service* (Collegeville, MN: Liturgical Press, 2016), xi.

5. Anthony J. Gittins, *Called to Be Sent: Co-Missioned as Disciples Today* (Liguori, MO: Liguori Publications, 2008).

6. Msgr. John J. Egan in foreword to James D. Whitehead and Evelyn Eaton Whitehead, *The Promise of Partnership: A Model for Collaborative Ministry* (San Francisco: HarperOne, 1993).

7. Michael Ahlstron, Peter Gilmour, Robert Tuzik, eds., *A Companion to Pastoral Care of the Sick* (Chicago: Liturgy Training Publications, 1990).

8. Divine Word Missionaries website: http://www.svdmissions.org.

9. Stephen Bevans, "The Mission Has a Church: An Invitation to the Dance," *Australian E-Journal of Theology* 14, no. 1 (2009), http://aejt.com.au/__data/assets/pdf_file/0004/197644/Bevans_Mission _Has_Church.pdf.

10. Roger P. Schroeder, *What Is the Mission of the Church? A Guide for Catholics* (Maryknoll, NY: Orbis Books, 2018), 112.

11. Schroeder, *What Is the Mission of the Church?*, 113.

12. Gerhard Von Rad and M. G. Stalker, *Old Testament Theology: the Theology of Israel's Prophets*, vol. 2 (Louisville: Westminster John Knox Press, 2001), 418.

16

THE LITURGY-JUSTICE RELATIONSHIP

A Habit of Heart

—〰—

Anne Y. Koester

"How will our world be better off this day because we gathered to celebrate the Eucharist?" The Lutheran bishop's question was succinct and incisive. I have walked with this question, with respect not only to the Eucharist but also to liturgy in the broadest sense, ever since ELCA Bishop Stephen Bouman posed it at a 2003 colloquium on the liturgy-justice relationship.[1] The question captures the essence of the topic at hand; that is, the inseparability of the church's worship and justice.

Justice is a charged word. People have an instinctive sense of what justice is and carry understandings shaped by the society and culture in which they live. When *justice* is put in the same sentence as *liturgy*, reactions range from bewilderment to skepticism to disinterest. For some Catholics, to suggest that the church's worship is intertwined with justice seems incongruous. For others, while intrigued, the relationship might not be immediately apparent. Still for others, highlighting the inseparability of justice and liturgy might seem like some modern strategy to make liturgy more appealing to those who question its relevance not only to their daily lives but to a world fraught with injustices. And those who question whether the church itself is an authentic model of justice would likely dismiss the idea that the church's worship expresses justice.

The fact that the church's public prayer is rooted in justice has not been consistently apparent, which is regrettable. It has been obscured at times but recovered more recently. While obstacles to an understanding and living out of this relationship remain, I suggest that the symbiotic nature of liturgy and justice has worked its way into the Catholic imagination and way of being in the world, even if unarticulated and incomplete. It remains a process of discovery and wrestling individually and as a community with the forces that threaten the establishment of justice. Moreover, as will be discussed, the need for catechesis and reflection and for liturgy well-celebrated remains critical if justice is to become a habit of heart for the Body of Christ, that is, the baptized.

To begin this exploration of the liturgy-justice nexus, it is necessary to attempt to describe what *justice* means and to highlight key aspects of *liturgy*. Doing this work will enable us to recognize more readily that what might seem at first to be two separate dimensions of the Christian life are, in fact, tightly woven.

WHAT IS THE JUSTICE THAT LITURGY CELEBRATES?

Describing the contours of justice is no easy undertaking. It is a complex and slippery concept, with no single definition and layers of subjective interpretations. What justice is evolves continuously as it meets generations, cultures, and societies. We might speak of it in categories that are concerned with basic social relations and order, such as commutative, distributive, and legal justice. Social justice, aimed at ensuring that the structures of society further the common good, also rings familiar, especially in the context of modern Catholic social teaching. Each of these approaches has value and is necessary, yet each is imperfect. A more complete expression of justice and the justice that the liturgy proclaims is the *justice of God*. Divine justice transcends all human conceptions and expectations of justice, yet we know *something* of the justice of God because we know *something* of God.

Plainly stated, the justice of God is God's very self. It is another name for God. It follows, then, that God's justice is revealed in all the ways in which God is revealed. The justice of God is manifested, for instance, in God's creative action. From the beginning, God made things to be in right relationship. The Creation narrative of Genesis (1:1—2:2) provides a hymn-like description of the right relationships God intended. Out of a formless wasteland, the earth came to be; out of watery chaos, the sea. Two great lights to separate day and night were placed in proper relationship. God intended unceasing abundance and a world teeming with life. Human beings were created in God's likeness and entrusted with the responsibility of caring for all that had been created—all that God saw as good, all that God blessed.

Divine justice is a dominant theme of God's continuous outreach to humanity. Out of justice, God never tires of inviting human beings into right relationship with God, one another, and material creation. Even in the face of humanity's selfish and independent ways, even when people fail to respond to this invitation, God remains faithful. As is clear in Scripture, God responds to humanity's lack of faithfulness with justice.[2] The stories of the Old Testament tell of God's desire for communion with humanity and the establishment of a covenant relationship. God promises to be the God of Abraham and his descendants, who would be made into nations and given land as their permanent possession (Gen 17:6–8). For their part, this unique people was to live faithfully out of their relationship with the one true God. But the story of Israel became complex as the people repeatedly rebelled and turned away from God. Their infidelity strained right relationships with God, one another, and those outside of their community. Yet God never abandoned what God blessed. Out of justice, God was unremitting with calling the people back into relationship. When Israel worshiped other gods, when they failed to act justly toward others, the prophets warned the people of the consequences they would suffer if they neglected their covenant obligations.[3] At the same time, the prophets reassured Israel of God's undying love. While always respecting Israel's freedom to respond, God remained steadfast in fulfilling the promises made, calling them to conversion of life and a return to right relationships. God remained faithful to being their God. The justice of God, freely given, would not be withdrawn. Indeed, the Prophet Isaiah spoke of justice that "will renew the world through the coming Messiah" (Isa 9:6; 32:1).[4] God would fulfill God's promises of bringing justice and liberation to all. The covenant relationship would be restored.

Significantly, God's concern for those on the margins of society—the widow, the orphan, the poor, the stranger in the land—is also revealed in the story of Israel: "For the Lord your God...executes justice for the orphan and the widow, loves the resident alien, giving them food and clothing" (Deut 10:17–18).[5] Israel was to mirror the justice of God in its own actions toward the marginalized and oppressed.[6]

In the New Testament, the justice of God is definitively revealed in Jesus Christ: "Through Christ, God chose to re-establish the covenant relationship, thus restoring the broken relationship between the human community and God."[7] In the Gospel texts, Jesus's mission is presented as one of justice.[8] Given the conditions in Israel at the time, Jesus experienced firsthand a world where the elite and powerful oppressed the defenseless, the poor, and the marginalized. Considering Israel's history and hopes, Jesus saw the alleviation of Israel's bondage as essential to their salvation and, consequently, his mission.[9]

The way in which Jesus went about his mission of justice turned human expectations upside down. Consider Jesus's choice of disciples. He chose the powerless and socially insignificant. John Haughey says it well:

> It seems that he chose to minister to those in need with those who were uncredentialed, and in some cases even disreputable, in the eyes of society. The broadest of overviews of his life reveals a predilection toward the least favored, the "outs" of society.[10]

Jesus's mission of justice is further evidenced by the way in which he went about building right relationships. Jesus invited the people he encountered into relationship with himself and with one another. He was completely available to them because he had emptied himself of the human tendency to be self-centered. Jesus reached out to all persons regardless of social status, degree of faith, or any other characteristic. Jesus touched those thought to be untouchable, forgave sinners judged and rejected by the community, healed the sick and the brokenhearted, and shared life with an assortment of people, even society's most despised. His parables about the kingdom of God challenged his listeners to broaden their horizons and see anew.

The kingdom Jesus preached would be one in which he and those who followed him would serve others, not dominate or rule them. Jesus exhorted his followers to go beyond "abstract norms in [their] conduct to *a way of relating* because of the experience of God's own goodness." God's goodness was to be the norm for Jesus's followers as it was for him.[11] Moreover, Jesus's form of authority and power was far different from human assumptions. His form of authority and power was his person.[12]

Jesus not only spoke about the just reign of God; he embodied it. Mark Searle writes,

> In [Jesus's] life and activity he modeled the radically different justice which is that of the kingdom of God. By living and dying in total accord with his Father's will and by doing all he did in fulfillment of the Father's intentions for the world, Jesus lived the justice of God.[13]

Searle argues that because the justice of God has been realized on this earth in human form, the reign of justice is "no escapist utopia but a real possibility and the object of a well-founded hope" for the world.[14] He adds,

> And the fact that the same Spirit that animated [Jesus] has been poured out upon the rest of humanity meant that the realization of such justice may henceforth always be looked for and worked for. In every generation some people are called by name consciously to serve this kingdom and its justice as revealed in Jesus. They are called Christians, and they have the unenviable responsibility of representing the hope of a higher justice and working for its realization.[15]

St. Paul understands Jesus as the embodied justice of God and, as Haughey observes, uses the image of a new creation to describe the new order of justice God was to establish in Christ.[16] "One comes into the new creation by believing in Christ Jesus. And by believing one comes within range of and has access to the justice of God."[17] He adds that, for Paul, justice "comes from God, is received by believers, manifests God's presence in the world and leads to God. It flows into the world of persons and things, not through law but through [Christ]."[18] The kind of justice experienced in Christ transforms believers into ministers of reconciliation and "ambassadors for Christ, as if God were appealing through [them]" (See 2 Cor 5:17–21).[19] As part of the new creation, as sharers in the life of a just God, justice can be done through Christians individually and through the Body of Christ.[20] Indeed, this new, restored creation is fully realized when Christians actively participate in fostering right relationships, which can be accomplished only with Christ and through the power of the Holy Spirit. In sum, "[in] Paul, as in the whole New Testament, the gift of union with Christ becomes the radical basis of the Christian's social responsibility."[21] For Christians, this gift of union with Christ is realized and celebrated in baptism and sustained in the sharing of Eucharist.

The embodiment of justice in Jesus Christ is also at the heart of what it means to be human. The claim that Jesus is the justice of God insists on recognizing the inherent dignity of the human person. Humanity is what people and God have in common. The human experience is meaningful because it mediates something of the sacred. The justice of God is very clear, then, when the human person is approached as holy ground and when relationships with God, one another, and with material creation flourish. Words and actions that discount, violate, or isolate the human person or that are intended to destroy right relationships among people obscure God's justice.

We learn further about the justice of God in the believing community's patterns of worship and symbolic expressions, to which we now turn.

LITURGY 24/7

Like justice, liturgy is richly complex. Mindful of this, I want to highlight here four aspects of liturgy that are especially key to appreciating the depths of the liturgy-justice relationship. First, there are two dimensions of liturgy, which, while not identical, are inseparable. Asked what liturgy is, most people would likely think of the church's formal worship, with its seasons and feasts, sacred stories and images, and sacramental rituals. And they would be right; this is one dimension of liturgy. However, this dimension would not exist without the other, that is, the liturgy of the world, or the liturgy of life.[22] These two dimensions "interact with each other as two intrinsic dimensions of the one reality, correcting and enriching each other."[23] The baptized go from the church's liturgy to the liturgy of life and back to the liturgy. We never leave liturgy. It's 24/7.

According to Karl Rahner, the "primary and original liturgy" is "the human community's ongoing communion and cooperation with God in history."[24] Peter Phan, commenting on Rahner's approach, makes the case that "[it] is this liturgy of life that we must first think of when we speak of worship."[25] Quoting Rahner, Phan adds, "The liturgy of the church is the symbolic presentation of the liturgy of the world."[26] The "liturgy of life comes to be real, present and effective in the liturgy of the church," and, importantly, the source and summit of both dimensions is Jesus Christ, the justice of God.[27] In the Catholic imagination, baptism brings about both a right and a responsibility to participate—fully, consciously, and actively—in the liturgy of the church and in the "primary liturgy" of life. At this intersection lies justice, with the radical responsibility to rehearse the just reign of God through participation in the church's liturgy and to express it concretely in words and actions in the liturgy of life—*and*, having participated in the liturgy of life, to return to the church's liturgy as people who understand a little more about their role in furthering the just reign of God here and now. Indeed, the church's liturgy itself is shaped by and experienced anew because of the baptized assembly's work to make clearer the justice of God in the liturgy of life.

Second, closely related to these two dimensions of liturgy is the principle of sacramentality. Sacramentality is not some abstract theological construct; rather, it is a prism through which the Body of Christ looks. It is a worldview that recognizes that the things of this world and the human community itself are potential bearers of the Sacred. In other words, God's constant and active presence is experienced, at least partially, in the here and now. Sacramentality shapes the Catholic imagination and is foundational to the church's liturgy. Participation in the church's rituals stretches and shapes the sacramental imagination of the Body of Christ, sharpening its vision to recognize the innate goodness and sacredness of the world and all who live in it. A sacramental worldview has no place for injustices. For someone with a sacramental imagination, words and actions that harm or destroy right relationships belie the sacramentality of the people and things of this world and are thus intolerable.

Third, just as relationships are essential to justice, so too with liturgy. As Kathleen Hughes writes,

> While justice cares for the establishment of relationships, *liturgy* is their celebration. We gather to give praise and thanksgiving, to recall the mighty acts of God in human history, to make the memorial of Jesus' victorious death, to pray for the needs of our world, and to celebrate the kingdom of justice and love which is already and which is yet to be.[28]

Further, when the baptized gather for worship, they become conscious of their "union with Christ and of [their] dignity as sharers in the divine nature."[29] Their identity as the Body of Christ is concretely expressed. Virgil Michel, pioneer of the twentieth-century modern liturgical movement in the United States, pointed to the Body of Christ, visibly expressed in the liturgy of the church and of life, as the model, ideally anyway, "that we should try to follow in our human relations; for God constructed it on the basis of what is best in and for our natures."[30] Of course, it also needs to be admitted that the baptized assembly, while a holy people, is an incomplete manifestation of the Body of Christ and an imperfect model of human relations. Liturgy is a gathering not of the perfect but, as Hughes describes,

> [of] persons who need to let go, to give ourselves over, to surrender to the God of mystery, and to receive grace and strength to live no longer for ourselves. And in the very process of confessing the one true God and Jesus Christ

whom God has sent, the confessing community's self-awareness is purified and deepened, its commitment to justice reaffirmed.[31]

Liturgy is where the baptized can learn their name, "where actions must be repeated over and over until they are thoroughly assimilated and perfected—until, that is, the actors have totally identified with the part assigned to them."[32] Their assigned part is to be "other Christs"[33] who take seriously their mutual responsibility to one another within the Body of Christ and to the entire human community and the created world.

The last point to make about the nature of liturgy is that liturgy is not *our* idea. Neither is justice. Both are God's project. Both are God's gift. God summons; in freedom, Christians respond by assembling and celebrating all God has done, is doing, and will continue to do in Jesus Christ and through the power of the Holy Spirit. In freedom, Christians respond by participating in the work of justice in the world. All of this is at God's initiative; therefore, the Body of Christ must resist the temptation to superimpose on the church's liturgy its own notions about justice or unnecessarily add themes that are attempts to promote personal agendas. Rather, the liturgical assembly is called to join in the prayer and work of Christ and to be attentive and receptive to the justice *of God*. And when they are sent from the liturgy of the church to the liturgy of life, it is the justice of God they are to imitate.

WHAT HAS ALWAYS BEEN...YET NOT ALWAYS APPARENT

The liturgy-justice relationship is not a modern invention. There is evidence to support that Christians of the early church era (circa first through fifth centuries) appreciated that their worship and their actions in the world were inseparable. For instance, Justin Martyr, a second-century Christian apologist in Rome, spoke of the purpose of Sunday collection as helping those in need and of the Eucharist as something taken to those who were absent, presumably the sick.[34]

We see in the *Apostolic Tradition,* believed to be a third-century order in the church in Rome, that the determination of readiness for initiation into the Christian community included questions about whether the catechumens visited the sick and performed good works.[35] John Chrysostom, who became archbishop of Constantinople in 397, declared that one could not honor Christ "here [in the church] with silken garments, while neglecting him outside as he perishes from the cold and lack of clothing."[36]

Arguably, in the Catholic Church, the charge to rehearse God's just reign in the church's liturgy and promote the same in the liturgy of the world became less apparent in subsequent centuries. Among the reasons: the baptized lost their role in the church's liturgy. The clergy, rather than the assembly, assumed the role of primary liturgical actor. The original sense of liturgy—from the Greek *leiturgia,* meaning "public work," that is, the work of the people—was displaced by complex ceremonies that were the work of the clergy. How, then, could an alienated assembly imagine their passive attendance at liturgy as having anything to do with their daily affairs? Additionally, a spirit of uncompromising individualism in Western society spilled over into church life. As such, the baptized were unaware of themselves as a community, much less the church, the Body of Christ visible in the world. The Body of Christ metaphor, which St. Paul used to name and describe the baptized community—the church—got lost. The baptized were further distanced by an overemphasis on Jesus's divinity, which arguably overshadowed the faithful's sense of an intimate relationship with him and did not promote an understanding that through sharing in the very life of Christ, they became a visible sign of Christ's saving presence in this world.

The reawakening of the church to the liturgy-justice relationship came primarily in the twentieth century thanks to the vision of Virgil Michel, OSB, and other pioneers of the modern liturgical movement in the United States.[37] Michel saw the liturgy as a school for justice. Key to his thinking was the retrieval of the Body of Christ metaphor. It is through baptism that one is incorporated into the Body of Christ, "intimately united with Christ and through Christ [with one another]."[38] As members of the Body of Christ, Michel said, the baptized "are no longer to [themselves] alone but above all to Christ and his cause."[39] Virgil Michel believed that the life lived by Christians is "the same life possessed by Christ and all the other members of Christ";[40] thus, Christians are co-responsible for one another. Moreover, the baptized must be continuously tutored in the Christian ways of being and acting in the world. Michel saw the liturgy as the "pulse-beat of the Church,"[41] making it an indispensable source of learning and nourishment for the Body of Christ. For Virgil Michel, "full, conscious, and active participation" in the liturgy was a must. Membership in the Body of Christ comes with the call to foster right relationships, which are visibly expressed in the liturgy.[42]

Given the tremendous passion of people like Virgil Michel about the vital role of liturgy in the work of justice, one would think that this vision would have been clearly articulated in the Second Vatican Council's Constitution on the Sacred Liturgy (1963). Regrettably, it is not directly stated, but it is *implicit* in paragraph 14, which reads, "The faithful should be led to take that fully conscious, and active participation in liturgical celebrations *which is demanded by the very nature of the liturgy*. Such participation…is their right and duty by reason of their baptism" (emphasis added).[43] What is the participation that the liturgy demands? It demands a participation that extends beyond the walls of the church to the liturgy of life. It demands that the baptized live in right relationship with God, family, neighbors, coworkers, strangers, the local and global community—and thereby promote the just reign of God. The liturgy demands a participation that leads the assembly to assume an active role in bringing about a more just society and church.

LITURGY-JUSTICE: IT'S ONE PIECE

In the decades since the Second Vatican Council, many voices in the church have contributed to lifting up the liturgy-justice relationship and examining its various dimensions.[44] Still, questions remain. Has it been absorbed into the Catholic bones? Do people "get it"? Do they live out of this intrinsic relationship 24/7? There really is no way to measure accurately whether Catholics appreciate this relationship. It is all very subtle. People do not necessarily go about their daily lives consciously thinking that their desire to work for justice in the world is formed, at least to some degree, by their participation in liturgy. Rather, I suggest that the true measure of whether the baptized comprehend the inseparability of the liturgy-justice relationship is found in their very lives. Is it clear that the attitudes they carry, the choices they make, the actions they choose flow out of an imagination shaped by their participation in liturgy?

My own experience of listening to people during workshops and retreats on the liturgy-justice relationship gives me hope. The stories they tell! I think of the man who realized that the hospitality he experiences in his parish's liturgical celebrations keeps his heart open to others in need, such as the time he invited a jobless and distraught stranger to share his home until he could get back on his feet. I think of the woman who advocates for a refugee family from a war-torn country because she could not ignore what she understands as her baptismal responsibility to help people who are suffering. Life for both the family and the woman has been transformed as a result. I think of the people in my own parish who work closely with our sister parish in Haiti and who are model participants in the parish's liturgical life. I do not think it would cross their minds to engage in one without engaging in the other. I think of the many people who have reflected on the habits of heart that are habits of justice and that they believe have been shaped by their participation in liturgy. They speak of being formed into people who are more forgiving, welcoming, compassionate, and willing to expend themselves for others, whether family, neighbor, friend, or stranger. They become more aware of others' needs and feel compelled to respond. They discover, as Mark Searle wrote, "that the liturgy will not allow us to lose sight of who we are and what we are called to do. It will not allow us to forget... the eight hundred million people on this earth living at or below subsistence level," nor will the liturgy "allow us to shrug off the problems of violence and war, of systemic victimization, as something that has nothing to do with us."[45] These are only a small handful of stories.

It is when people tell their stories and reflect with one another about their lives that the inseparability of liturgy-justice becomes evident. As they unpack their experiences of life and liturgy, the insights flow and the level of enthusiasm and hope soars. This leads to a key point: given the opportunity for reflection, for sharing life, people really do "get it." The church needs to find more spaces for people to reflect on their experience of the church's liturgy and the liturgy of life. Mark Searle emphasizes the need for reflecting on liturgy to discover the reality of the just reign of God:

> What we need to do is simply reflect together on what it is we do when we celebrate liturgy and about what it means. We need to hear what we are saying when we pray, reflect on what we do when we celebrate. The more we understand the order of the world presented and rehearsed in the liturgy, the more we fall in love with the reality of the Kingdom which the liturgy presents and rehearses, the more we shall recognize the disparity between what is and what ought to be.[46]

Hopefully, the ripple effect of consistent reflection is increased and results in better participation in the liturgy of the church and of life. After all, participation is presupposed. One needs to "show up," that is, be *present* to the liturgy of the church and of life.

Related to providing occasions for reflection is the critical need for catechesis and faith formation that supports a culture of living the liturgy-justice relationship, so it is absorbed into the imagination early and strengthened over a lifetime. Liturgy-justice is not a one-session "topic"; rather, it is gradually learned, lived out, and reflected upon, with this cycle continuously repeating itself. How do church leaders—clergy, catechists, liturgists, social action leaders, among others—talk with the members of the Body of Christ about their baptismal responsibility? About their identity as eucharistic people—the Body of Christ shared with a world in need, the Blood of Christ poured out for others? For the liturgy-justice relationship to be clear and to thrive, the church needs to embrace their sacramental identity and responsibilities. They need to discover who they really are and are called to be.

Specifically, the baptized might be invited to consider what they learn about the justice of God and their responsibility to embody the same from the church's liturgical celebrations. We might ask, for instance:

- Are right relationships expressed in the assembly's gathering? Is the community's hospitality clear, that is, is it a community with a "big heart"? Do all feel that they belong, or are some isolated, judged, excluded? Who's there? Who's not there? Does the community make room for everyone? Is it evident that baptism is, in fact, the radical equalizer?

- Is the worship space an expression of justice? Does it provide an equivalent experience[47] for all, regardless of physical, intellectual, or mental ability? Do the images, design, art, and decor reflect the various ethnicities and cultures of the community or does one dominate?

- Is the baptized assembly's right and duty to fully, consciously, and actively participate truly supported? This is a matter of justice. An injustice is done if the assembly is relegated to an audience that watches a few "perform" the liturgy. At the same time, vibrant liturgical celebrations depend on everyone, not just a few. Being actively present encourages all to do the same. The justice of God becomes more readily apparent when celebrated with the assembly's active engagement.

- Is there an abundant use of the symbolic elements of the church's liturgy? Does their use engage the senses and impress upon the heart and mind the depth of meanings in their use? Or are we stingy? For example, a generous amount of water powerfully communicates that baptism is the most important day of the Christian's life, just as an abundance of wine invites the baptized to carry out their responsibility to share in the cup of suffering and pour themselves out for a world in need. The lavish use of oil more effectively conveys the gift of the Holy Spirit and the community's care. It is important to consider all the liturgy's symbols from this perspective of generosity. Anything less potentially decreases the assembly's engagement in and formation through the liturgical celebration, which itself would be an injustice.

- Is the just Word proclaimed with clarity and understanding? Do preachers break open the just Word in a way that inspires and challenges the assembly?

- Is there a regular opportunity to pray the Liturgy of the Hours and to be immersed more deeply in the scriptural texts that communicate the justice of God?

- Are the processions done in a way that all who are gathered learn their shared identity as the Communion of Saints, journeying as one people in Christ?

- Is the attitude of the Body of Christ one of reverence? Is the assembly rehearsed in this disposition of the heart, so they come to recognize the sacredness of every human person as one created and loved and chosen by God?

- Is there a spirit of mercy, forgiveness, and reconciliation, rather than an air of judgment and division?

- Is there space for silence? The assembly's experience of being with one another in silence can often be more powerful in fashioning hearts of justice than a multiplication of words.

- Do the intercessory prayers bid the assembly to turn outward and lift up in prayer the needs of the world, our nation, local communities and families, the church, and all of God's people?

- What is the language of the prayers, the preaching, the songs? Does the language communicate the justice of God? Does it in any way exclude, stereotype, or pass judgment?

- Does the music reflect the diversity of the assembly? Do the lyrics speak of justice, so that the assembly becomes and does what they sing?

- Does the sharing of Eucharist shape the assembly's willingness to share life with others? Does their experience of equal sharing in the Body and Blood of Christ transform the baptized into a eucharistic people who have the courage to seek the eradication of injustices and the elimination of that which engenders hatred, violence, and division within the human community? Does it instill a desire to live in unity with those they meet in daily life?

- Is the assembly dismissed from the liturgy of the church with a clear mandate to be "other Christs" in the liturgy of life?

- Does the community gather with Christians of other communions and people of other religions to pray, to lament, to celebrate, to give thanks, to envision, and to work together to promote a more just and compassionate world? Justice is about right relationships, which necessitates that the work of justice be ecumenical and interreligious in scope.

This list of considerations is by no means exhaustive. The church's liturgy is a dynamic force and inexhaustible in meaning. It is critical for the baptized to reflect on such questions to reinforce what they absorb from their rehearsal of justice in liturgy and to enable them to envision its impact on their way of being in the liturgy of life. Further, such questions are essential to creating an awareness among the baptized that will help them listen more deeply when participating in the church's liturgy, as well as the liturgy of life. It needs to be a listening that immerses them in the justice of God, forms them to have the mind of Christ, and exhorts them to be persons and communities through whom the justice of God is made visible.

To take seriously the intrinsic nature of the liturgy-justice relationship stretches us, and being stretched is often not comfortable. Perhaps because of this, some prefer to try to keep liturgy at a distance by not participating or "doing their own thing" when it comes to worship, and as a result, they fail to see any connection between the church's liturgy and furthering that which is right, just, and true in the world. Yet, the liturgy-justice relationship will not go by the wayside, even when people are inattentive or resist what liturgy demands. At the same time, I am convinced that once the baptized become more acutely aware of the church's liturgy as formative for the work of justice in the liturgy of life, they will never experience either the same way again. They will have discovered and embodied a significant dimension of the Catholic imagination.

All of this said, I return to the opening question—"How will our world be better off this day because we gathered for liturgy?"

Further Reading

Donnelly, Doris K., ed. *Sacraments and Justice*. Collegeville, MN: Liturgical Press, 2014.

Empereur, James L., and Christopher G. Kiesling. *The Liturgy that Does Justice*. Collegeville, MN: Liturgical Press, 1990. Reprinted by Wipf and Stock Publishers, 2006.

Himes, Kenneth R. "Eucharist and Justice: Assessing the Legacy of Virgil Michel." *Worship* 62, no. 3 (1988): 201–24.

Hughes, Kathleen, and Mark R. Francis, eds. *Living No Longer for Ourselves: Liturgy and Justice in the Nineties*. Collegeville, MN: Liturgical Press, 1991.

Koester, Anne Y., ed. *Liturgy and Justice: To Worship God in Spirit and in Truth*. Collegeville, MN: Liturgical Press, 2002.

Searle, Mark, ed. *Liturgy and Social Justice*. Collegeville, MN: Liturgical Press, 1980.

Scott, Margaret. *The Eucharist and Social Justice*. Mahwah, NJ: Paulist Press, 2009.

Wilbricht, Stephen S. *Rehearsing God's Just Kingdom: The Eucharistic Vision of Mark Searle*. Collegeville, MN: Liturgical Press, 2013.

Zimmerman, Joyce Ann, ed. *Liturgical Ministry* 7 (Fall 1998): 153–95. This issue includes: Camilla Burns, "Biblical Righteousness and Justice," 153–61; Kevin W. Irwin, "Liturgy, Justice and Spirituality," 162–74; Michael E. Moynahan, "The Concluding Rite: The Call to Do Justice," 175–81; David A. Stosur, "Bread of Life, Justice of God: Eucharistic Structures and the Transformation to Christian Justice," 182–89; and J. Frank Henderson, "Justice and the Jubilee Year," 190–95.

Notes

1. The colloquium was hosted by the former Georgetown Center for Liturgy, Washington, DC.

2. We are limited here to only a brief look at what is learned of God's justice from the scriptural texts. For a fuller treatment, see Camilla Burns, "Biblical Righteousness and Justice," *Liturgical Ministry* 7 (Fall 1998): 153–61; John R. Donahue, "Biblical Perspectives on Justice," in *The Faith that Does Justice: Examining the Christian Sources for Social Change*, ed. John C. Haughey (New York: Paulist Press, 1977), 68–112; Gregory J. Polan, "Justice," in *The Collegeville Pastoral Dictionary of Biblical Theology*, ed. Caroll Stuhlmueller et al. (Collegeville, MN: Liturgical Press, 1996), 510–22.

3. It is important to acknowledge the stories and images in the Old Testament where sinners are punished. They suffer when they stray from living in right relationship with God. This does not mean, however, that God is vindictive. As John Donahue cautions, "Though Yahweh punishes sinners there is no text in the Old Testament where [Yahweh's] justice is equated with vengeance on the sinner. Yahweh's justice is saving justice where punishment of the sinner is an integral part of restoration" ("Biblical Perspectives on Justice," 72).

4. As cited in Polan, "Justice," 511.

5. As cited in Polan, "Justice," 511.

6. Polan, "Justice," 511.

7. Burns, "Biblical Righteousness and Justice," 158.

8. See John C. Haughey, "Jesus as the Justice of God," in Haughey, *The Faith that Does Justice*, 264–90.

9. Haughey, "Jesus as the Justice of God," 270.

10. Haughey, "Jesus as the Justice of God," 271.

11. Haughey, "Jesus as the Justice of God," 278; emphasis mine.

12. Haughey, "Jesus as the Justice of God," 274.

13. "Serving the Lord with Justice," in *Liturgy and Social Justice*, ed. Mark Searle (Collegeville, MN: Liturgical Press, 1980), 17. Searle's article is reprinted in Anne Y. Koester and Barbara Searle, eds., *Vision: The Scholarly Contributions of Mark Searle to Liturgical Renewal* (Collegeville, MN: Liturgical Press, 2004), 4–22.

14. Searle, "Serving the Lord with Justice," 17.

15. Haughey, "Jesus as the Justice of God."

16. Haughey, "Jesus as the Justice of God," 284.

17. Haughey, "Jesus as the Justice of God," 284.

18. Haughey, "Jesus as the Justice of God," 284.

19. See also Eph 5:8–14, in which Paul speaks of those who follow Christ as "children of light," which is given to them by Christ and which produces "all that is good and right and true." He implores the Church at Ephesus to "take no part in the unfruitful works of darkness" but to expose them, for "everything exposed by the light becomes visible."

20. Haughey, "Jesus as the Justice of God," 285.

21. Haughey, "Jesus as the Justice of God," 286.

22. I use "liturgy of the world" and "liturgy of life" interchangeably here. "Liturgy of the world" is the primary characterization found in the scholarly literature to date; however, I agree with Peter C. Phan's preference for using "liturgy of life" because it "underlines its dynamic and personal character." "The Liturgy of Life as the 'Summit and Source' of the Eucharistic Liturgy: Church Worship as Symbolization of the Liturgy of Life?" in *Incongruities: Who We Are and How We Pray*, ed. Timothy Fitzgerald and David A. Lysik (Chicago: Liturgy Training Publications, 2000), 20.

23. Phan, "The Liturgy of Life," 24. Phan adds, "In its liturgical celebrations the church does not perform a worship *in addition to* the liturgy of life or unconnected with it; rather it makes explicit and intensifies through words and rituals the liturgy of life which takes place unceasingly through God's self-gift and humanity's acceptance of this divine self-gift" (ibid.).

24. Michael Skelley, *The Liturgy of the World: Karl Rahner's Theology of Worship* (Collegeville, MN: Liturgical Press, 1991), 93.

25. Phan, "The Liturgy of Life," 22.

26. Phan, "The Liturgy of Life," 22, quoting, Karl Rahner, *On Theology of Worship*, Theological Investigations 19 (New York: Crossroad, 1983), 146.

27. Phan, "The Liturgy of Life," 23, 25.

28. Kathleen Hughes, "Liturgy and Justice: An Intrinsic Relationship," in *Living No Longer for Ourselves: Liturgy and Justice in the Nineties*, ed. Kathleen Hughes and Mark R. Francis (Collegeville, MN: Liturgical Press, 1991), 41; emphasis original.

29. Virgil Michel, *The Liturgy of the Church* (New York: Macmillan, 1937), 60–61.

30. Virgil Michel, *Christian in the World* (Collegeville, MN: Liturgical Press, 1939), 76–77.

31. Hughes, "Liturgy and Justice," 41–42.

32. Searle, "Serving the Lord with Justice," 32.

33. Virgil Michel, "Liturgy and the Catholic Life," unpublished ms., 78 and 136.

34. Justin Martyr, *First Apology* 67 in Lawrence J. Johnson, *Worship in the Early Church: An Anthology of Historical Sources*, vol. 1 (Collegeville, MN: Liturgical Press, 2009), 68.

35. *Apostolic Tradition* 20, in Johnson, *Worship in the Early Church*, 1:205.

36. John Chrysostom, *Homilies on the Gospel of Matthew* 50.4, in Lawrence J. Johnson, *Worship in the Early Church: An Anthology of Historical Sources*, vol. 2 (Collegeville, MN: Liturgical Press, 2009), 178.

37. Other coworkers in the vineyard included, among others, William Heulsmann, Bernard Laukemper, Cecilia Himebaugh, Hans Ansgar Reinhold, and Reynold Hillenbrand, all of whom contributed to promoting the intrinsic relationship between liturgy and society. For further reading, see, e.g., Keith F. Pecklers, *The Unread Vision: The Liturgical Movement in the United States of America; 1926–1955* (Collegeville, MN: Liturgical Press, 1998); Gilbert Ostdiek, "Liturgy and Justice: The Legacy that Awaits Us," in *Liturgy and Justice: To Worship God in Spirit and Truth*, ed. Anne Y. Koester (Collegeville, MN: Liturgical Press, 2002), 1–18; Theodore Ross, "The Personal Synthesis of Liturgy and Justice: Five Portraits," in Hughes and Francis, *Living No Longer for Ourselves*, 17–35; and Margaret M. Kelleher, "Liturgy and Social Transformation: Exploring the Relationship," *U.S. Catholic Historian* 16, no. 4, Sources of Social Reform, Part Two (Fall 1998): 58–70.

38. Michel, *The Christian in the World*, 8.

39. Virgil Michel, "The Liturgy, the Basis of Social Regeneration," *Orate Fratres* 9 (1935): 543.

40. Michel, *The Christian in the World*, 8–9.

41. Virgil Michel, "The Meaning of the Church's Liturgy," *America* 34 (April 3, 1926): 586.

42. Michel, *The Liturgy of the Church*, 50–53.

43. For further reading on the meaning of participation in the liturgy, see Mark Searle, *Called to Participate: Theological, Ritual, and Social Perspectives*, ed. Barbara Searle and Anne Y. Koester (Collegeville, MN: Liturgical Press, 2006).

44. See, e.g., the authors recommended for "Further Reading" at the end of this chapter.

45. Mark Searle, "Grant Us Peace...Do We Hear What We Are Saying?" Talk by Mark Searle (date unknown); published in Stephen S. Wilbricht, *Rehearsing God's Just Kingdom: The Eucharistic Vision of Mark Searle* (Collegeville, MN: Liturgical Press, 2013), 225.

46. Searle, "Grant Us Peace," 225.

47. See Robert D. Habiger, "Equivalent Experience: Keys to Truly Accessible Worship Spaces," *Faith and Form* 48, no. 1 (2015): 26–28.

17

LIVING THE ECUMENICAL JOURNEY

—ᴍ—

John Borelli

The reform and renewal of the liturgy and efforts toward restoration of unity among Christians preceded the Second Vatican Council (1962–65) by decades. Through the actions of the Council, Catholics became formally and massively involved in reform, renewal, and ecumenism. Liturgical reform and ecumenical reconciliation spread among the churches, serving as two helping hands in the renewal of church life. This has been generally a successful story for the past five decades due in some measure to widespread acceptance of an ecclesiology of communion. Now, after many accomplishments and a growing consensus among the churches regarding the nature and mission of the church and the Eucharist and, to some extent, regarding the ministry of the church, Christians are exploring more visible ways to express how they see and accept one another as spiritual companions on "a journey of communion, the path of ecumenism awakened by the Holy Spirit," to use an expression of Pope Francis, and no longer as rivals and dissidents.[1]

EXPERIENCING ONE-MINDEDNESS

Those engaged in ecumenical dialogue often report greater one-mindedness and spiritual compatibility with their conversation partners in ecumenism than with members of their own church communities. Gerard Austin and Don Saliers recorded such feelings at the U.S. United Methodist–Roman Catholic Dialogue in 1982:

> It is both disturbing and promising to become aware that in respect to biblical, theological and liturgical matters we may share more in common with our dialogue partners than we do with many persons within our own communions....We are reminded that matters of unity...more specifically of Eucharistic faith and practice...are never simply theological or simply liturgical.[2]

The passage concludes "matters of unity are also political and historical." Pastoral application of ecumenical progress at times seems hostage to feuds and polarization within churches for political and historical reasons.

Sustained contact, conversation on matters of consequence touching our deepest commitments of faith, and the spiritual companionship in ecumenical dialogue affect us deeply, transforming how we view one another and our relations with one another in the Christian community. Bishop Munib Younan, then-president of the Lutheran World Federation, and Pope Francis met in Sweden and jointly inaugurated a year of common commemoration of the five hundredth anniversary of Luther's Reformation on October 31, 2016. They expressed agreement on three consequential observations. First, fifty years of sustained and fruitful ecumenical dialogue between Catholics and Lutherans have helped to overcome many differences and have deepened mutual understanding and trust. Second, having drawn closer to one another through dialogue and shared witness, we are no longer strangers. And third, what unites us is greater than what divides us. Consequently, they urged "all Lutheran and Catholic parishes and communities to be bold and creative, joyful and hopeful in their commitment to continue the great journey ahead of us."[3]

Friends in the circumstances of everyday life, though belonging to different churches, can always make room to grow in deeper mutual appreciation as spiritual companions. Church leaders and representatives must keep their behavior adjusted to corporate policies. They were once hindered by narrow understandings of church boundaries and membership as well as overwhelmingly negative views of one another's churches through most of the five centuries since Luther's

Reformation. Celebrations of Reformation Day, October 31, or Reformation Sunday, the last Sunday in October, became occasions to celebrate why Protestants were not Catholics. Particularly important were the centenaries of October 31, 1517, the day ascribed to Luther's action leading to the Reformation in German lands. Reviewing this history, Lutheran and Catholic representatives agreed that "political and church-political agendas frequently shaped these earlier centenary commemorations."[4]

In reaction to the negativity of Protestants celebrating their separation, Catholic teachings on the church reflected a more clerical perspective in that the Catholic view of the role of the priest as mediator grew in importance as the Catholic priest was seen as superior to Protestant ministers. The church for Catholics became more and more identified with the hierarchy and clergy than with the people.

In "The Church as Worshiping Community," an essay for a textbook on ecclesiology, *The Gift of the Church*, Gerard Austin reviewed briefly the important work of Yves Congar on identifying reasons for the development of that clerically focused understanding of the church. Austin then observed with hope and promise, "This clerical approach to understanding the Church would be reversed during the latter part of the nineteenth century and the twentieth century, culminating in the Second Vatican Council, by a retrieval of baptismal consciousness based on the earlier ecclesiology of communion."[5]

From the beginning, Pope St. John XXIII wanted the Second Vatican Council to be welcoming, merciful, and directed toward the unity that already exists among all people. Here are his words from his opening address to the Council: "This very unity which Christ implored for his Church seems to shine with a triple ray of heavenly and salvific light: the unity of Catholics among themselves which must always be kept most firm and as a splendid example; the unity of pious prayers and most ardent desire by which Christians separated from this Apostolic See desire to be linked with us; the unity, finally of esteem and respect for the Catholic Church shown by those who still profess the different non-Christian forms of religion."[6] This would be the first documentary indication that a theology of communion would characterize the work of Vatican II.

For Gerard Austin and many of us who have worked in theology and related fields for the past several decades, the Second Vatican Council is the point of departure for understanding why Catholics believe and practice what they do today. The theology of communion is the foundation for envisioning the church, reforming the liturgy, and reaching out to other Christians and peoples of all faiths, indeed to all humanity. Communion defines the role of bishops and of the laity and is the basis for daily renewal of a commitment to social justice and much more. Understanding the church as communion remarkably unifies the various acts and the sixteen final documents of Vatican II. This is how Gerard Austin summed up the importance of this theological insight for him personally:

> This baptismal ecclesiology of communion taught to me as a liturgy student in Paris was something that changed my whole life (and continues to do so). It permeated my entire faith and deeply affected the way I taught and preached.[7]

CHRISTIAN UNITY AND THE IMPORTANCE OF LITURGICAL REFORM

Pope St. John XXIII wanted Vatican II to be an outreach to other Christians from the start. The published notice of his original announcement of the Council offered three general reasons: "a means of spiritual renewal, reconciliation of the Church to the modern world, and service to the unity of Christians."[8] This was sufficient motivation for Cardinal Augustin Bea, SJ, to begin working behind the scenes to suggest that there be a commission on ecumenism by the end of 1959. Pope John accepted this idea and created the Secretariat for Promoting Christian Unity among the preparatory commissions. Then, less than a year before the Council convened, he allowed it to prepare drafts for the agenda; next, he authorized it as a commission of the Council. Pope Paul VI, his successor, made it a permanent body in the Roman curia.[9]

The theme of Christian unity was visible everywhere at the Council. First, there were the delegated observers and guests from other Christian churches and communities with a prominent place in the Council hall. There are also references to the seeking of Christian unity throughout the sixteen final documents. The first of the sixteen documents, the Constitution on the Sacred Liturgy (*Sacrosanctum Concilium*), opens this way: "This sacred Council has several aims in view: it desires to impart an ever increasing vigor to the Christian life of the faithful; to adapt more suitably to the needs of our own times those institutions which are subject to change; to foster whatever can promote union among all who believe in Christ; to strengthen whatever can help to call the whole of mankind into the household of the Church." Writing in 1988, Gerard Austin would observe, "In my opinion, the greatest gain of the Constitution on the Sacred Liturgy of Vatican II was the relationship that it set up between liturgy and ecclesiology."[10]

The third document promulgated by the Council, the all-important vision statement on the nature and mission of the church, *Lumen Gentium*, the Dogmatic Constitution on the Church, would refer to other Christians under its subheading "The People of God":

> The Church recognizes that in many ways she is linked with those who, being baptized, are honored with the name of Christian, though they do not profess the faith in its entirety or do not preserve unity of communion with the successor of Peter. For there are many who honor Sacred Scripture, taking it as a norm of belief and a pattern of life, and who show a sincere zeal....They are consecrated by baptism, in which they are united with Christ. They also recognize and accept other sacraments within their own Churches or ecclesiastical communities. (no. 15)[11]

A theology of communion allowed those working on the reform and renewal of the liturgy to underscore the fully conscious and active participation of all the faithful in the liturgical life of the church (*Sacrosanctum Concilium* 14) and those restoring an ecclesiology of communion to recover the priesthood of the faithful. The faithful, through their baptism, "exercise that priesthood in receiving the sacraments, in prayer and thanksgiving, in the witness of a holy life, and by self-denial and active charity" (*Lumen Gentium* 10).

The Decree on Ecumenism (*Unitatis Redintegratio*), promulgated on the same day as *Lumen Gentium*, addressed the current separation among Christians through the lens of a theology of communion: "For those who believe in Christ and have been properly baptized are brought into certain, though imperfect, communion with the Catholic Church" (no. 3). The decree encouraged prayer in common: "In certain special circumstances, such as in prayer services 'for unity' and during ecumenical gatherings, it is allowable, indeed desirable that Catholics should join in prayer with their separated brothers and sisters" (no. 8).

Now over fifty years later, the language sounds reserved, overly cautious, almost condescending. This was a truly major change at the time—encouraging prayer in common, something that the Holy See had discouraged in the past.[12] It was a major turnaround for the Council to commend prayer in common as the first among its recommendations of cooperative practices in ecumenism. The Council did draw a distinction between prayers in common (*communes preces*) and worship in common (*communicatio in sacris*).

A cautionary spirit prevailed when the Decree on Ecumenism advised that worship in common should not occur indiscriminately, without care and attention, because common worship proclaims a unity achieved and held fast but also serves as a means of grace toward that unity. These became the two leading principles for evaluating the significance of worship in common. Later, the Secretariat would provide more detailed norms when it supplied a directory for ecumenism, a project recommended on the floor of the Council and so approved.[13] The Secretariat issued the first versions in two parts, in 1967 and 1970, and supplemental advisories followed.[14] The recommendations were codified in the 1983 *Code of Canon Law* and the 1990 *Code of Canons of the Eastern Churches*. In 1993, the renamed Pontifical Council for Promoting Christian Unity released a revised *Directory for the Application of Principles and Norms on Ecumenism*, drawing from wisdom gained in the first twenty-five years of postconciliar ecumenism. It offered several suggestions based on the distinction between "non-sacramental liturgical worship" and "sharing in sacramental life" as two variations of worship in common.[15]

The recommendations of the Decree on Ecumenism in 1964 were released into a brave new world of ecumenical activity for Catholics. Most Catholic clergy, theologians, and the faithful in general were new to ecumenism. While Catholics had Christian friends and associates belonging to other churches and communities, now they were cognizant of a new dimension in these relationships and the prompting of their church to cooperate in the overall effort to restore Christian unity. Catholics were encouraged to join with other Christians in sharing their thoughts and feelings about the faith and in celebrating together morning and evening prayer, special vigils, the distribution of ashes, services of reconciliation, funerals, and weddings, and to accommodate, under conditions and with specific norms, sacramental services for baptism, anointing, marriage, and the Eucharist with other Christians present as guests.

By 1995, Pope St. John Paul II issued an encyclical on ecumenism, That All May Be One (*Ut Unum Sint*), declaring that "it is a source of joy to see that the many ecumenical meetings almost always include and indeed culminate in prayer" (no. 24).[16] By not unduly drawing immediate attention to sacramental sharing (*communicatio in sacris*), he expanded considerably on the many times when Christians can share in spiritual practices (*communicatio in spiritualibus*): the annual Week of Prayer for Christian Unity, many other occasions through the year, on pilgrimages, and especially when church leaders might recite the creed together (no. 24).[17]

In that encyclical, the pope drew attention to the 1982 convergence text of the Faith and Order Commission of the World Council of Churches, *Baptism, Eucharist and Ministry*.[18] It truly was an extraordinary achievement with official Catholic participation, demonstrating "the remarkable progress already made" and representing "a sure foundation for further study" (*Ut Unum Sint* 17). More specifically, the pope complimented its section on baptism for the way it articulated "the fundamental role of baptism in building up the church" (no. 42) and how the section on the Eucharist would inspire and had already inspired other churches "to renew their worship." In 1995, the pope read these shifts as "signs of convergence which regard various aspects of sacramental life" (no. 45). Thus, in a passage seldom cited, Pope St. John Paul II expressed great joy in the progress toward full communion:

> In this context, it is a source of joy to note that Catholic ministers are able, in certain particular cases, to administer the sacraments of eucharist, penance and anointing of the sick to Christians who are not in full communion with the Catholic Church but who greatly desire to receive these sacraments, freely request them and manifest the faith which the Catholic church professes with regard to these sacraments. Conversely, in specific cases and in particular circumstances, Catholics too can request these same sacraments from ministers of churches in which these sacraments are valid. (no. 46)

In support of his position, he cited the Decree on Ecumenism, the 1983 *Code of Canon Law*, and the revised 1993 *Directory on Ecumenism* for providing the norms.

Eight years later, in 2003, Pope St. John Paul II released his fourteenth and final encyclical, *Ecclesia de Eucharistia*, which conveyed a more juridical approach to the results of ecumenical progress than the pastoral approach that characterized *Ut Unum Sint*. In *Ecclesia de Eucharistia*, the pope cited that paragraph expressing his appreciation and joy that sacraments can be shared under certain "norms, which make it possible to provide for the salvation of souls with proper discernment." In this later instance, he adds a canonical judgment: "These conditions, from which no dispensation can be given, must be carefully respected, even though they deal with specific cases" (no. 46).

One should rightly ask why there is such severity in "proper discernment" of pastoral norms. Here is the first reason he gave in the later text: "Because the denial of one or more truths of the faith regarding these sacraments and, among these, the truth regarding the need of the ministerial priesthood for their validity, renders the person asking improperly disposed to legitimately receiving them." For his second reason, he appeals to a lack of reciprocity: "Catholics may not receive communion in those communities which lack a valid sacrament of Orders." The pope cites the Decree on Ecumenism (no. 22) for this second point (*Ecclesia de Eucharistia* 46).[19]

As Catholics were nearing the forty-year mark of steady ecumenical progress and widening agreement on the nature of the Eucharist and other topics once deemed "church-dividing," the Holy See intensified its efforts to promote rules rather than pastoral guidelines for ecumenical relations. The conditions listed in the *Directory on Ecumenism* for Catholic ministers to share the sacraments of reconciliation, anointing, and Eucharist with baptized persons were never intended to carry the same weight. Believing in the real presence and being properly disposed were considered more important than the circumstances, although situations of life and death would take priority. The original intention of Vatican II in approving a directory for ecumenism was to present such pastoral norms for implementing what is achieved toward the restoration of Christian unity. Also, while both canonical judgment and pastoral advice, for example, for Catholics attending the eucharistic celebration at an Anglican or Protestant church in 1965 would be very nearly the same, by 2003 Catholics might ask, along with their Anglican and Protestant relatives and friends, are we not in a different place theologically and spiritually in celebrating the unity we now know even more clearly that we already share? Unity is not complete, but ecumenically inclined Christians are closer in belief and practice than before.

When a Catholic participates in the Eucharist of another church, is she or he denying the truths that the Catholic Church teaches? I would suggest that their minds are far from denying what the Catholic Church teaches about the Eucharist and holy orders and are closer to that of guests welcomed into the eucharistic celebration of another community. They would understand they are participating as much as possible, with the permission of their hosts, in the Eucharist of that community as it "commemorate[s] the Lord's death and resurrection in the Holy Supper, [whereby they] profess that it signifies life in communion with Christ and await His coming in glory," using words taken from the Decree on Ecumenism 22.

In 1964, the decree identified "the Lord's Supper" and "worship, and ministry in the Church" as subjects for future dialogue because "we believe they [the separated churches and ecclesial communities of the West] have not preserved the proper reality of the Eucharistic mystery in its fullness, especially because of the absence [defect][20] of the sacrament of Orders" (no. 22). Furthermore, the decree cautioned against "any frivolousness or imprudent zeal" (no. 24). Very few Catholics at the time would have been comfortable in another church receiving communion, though in many places Catholic ministers began to share the sacraments of Eucharist, anointing of the sick, and reconciliation with other Christians.

The first edition of the ecumenical directory in 1967 advised that a Catholic who attends a Eucharist in one of these churches may not receive communion "except from a minister who has been validly ordained." The intention was to leave these topics for dialogue and clarification and not to allow prematurely drawn conclusions. The 1993 revised *Directory on Ecumenism* expanded on this due to the results of ecumenical discussion recommending that a Catholic may receive communion "only from a minister in whose Church these sacraments are valid or from one who is known to be validly ordained according to the Catholic teaching on ordination."

Ecumenical dialogue by then had revealed what was already suspected. Most Protestant churches retained baptism and Eucharist as sacraments because they were chief among the sacraments as practiced in the West at the time of the Reformation but had differing understandings of ministry. Gerard Austin concurred in an article published in 2000:

> All the sacraments of the Church are not on the same level, they are not all of equal value. The distinction made by the medieval theologians between the major and minor sacraments is helpful. The two premiere sacraments of the Church are baptism and Eucharist.[21]

After the signing of the Joint Declaration on the Doctrine of Justification by representatives of the Holy See and the Lutheran World Federation, acknowledging that this milestone in ecumenical achievements was a consensus allowing differing points of view, Lutherans and Catholics, particularly in Germany, wanted to move forward with joint celebrations of the Eucharist and with intercommunion, regular and reciprocal eucharistic sharing. The generous pastoral policy of the Catholic Church, as the 1983 *Code of Canon Law* and the 1993 *Directory on Ecumenism* attest, allows the sharing of the Eucharist with Lutherans, but concelebration is another matter entirely because that is a sign of full and complete unity. Cardinal Walter Kasper told a representative of *Lutheran World International* in a 2003 interview that the Joint Declaration was a milestone but not a sufficient reason yet to have joint Eucharist. He said that "individual pastoral solutions can be found, but unlike for Lutherans, a general invitation does not seem possible yet for the Roman Catholic Church."[22]

Opportunities to receive together and regularly are certainly a fundamental desire for Catholics and Lutherans living as close friends and spiritual companions and for those sharing the sacrament of marriage. Major theological breakthroughs in ecumenical relations do not necessarily bring major pastoral advances for the faithful. Individuals are left to decide for themselves, and church policies vary. In our ordinary lives, the glacial rate of progress among the churches is difficult to accept. This is where the ecumenical movement hits home, in our daily lives, in how we live our marriages and our spiritual friendships among a diversity of Christian traditions.

In November 2015, Pope Francis visited Christuskirche in Rome, the Lutheran parish church. He took a question from Anke de Bernardinis, the wife of a Roman Catholic, who expressed sadness over the lack of pastoral progress and asked what must happen for her to receive with her husband regularly. Pope Francis reflected aloud in response on the one baptism that we share and how this couple's journey together is an exploration of keeping baptism alive. He acknowledged that a Lutheran pastor friend had emphasized what the dialogues have already discerned, namely, how Lutherans and Catholics agree that Christ is truly present in the Eucharist. He concluded with the wise observation that "life is greater than explanations and interpretations." Then, after acknowledging one Lord, one baptism, one faith, he urged, "Speak with the Lord and go forward. I do not dare say more."[23]

If life is greater than explanations and interpretations, especially for a Lutheran-Catholic couple already sharing the sacraments of baptism and matrimony, should we not, in light of all the enormous progress in ecumenical relations, especially with Lutherans on the doctrine of justification on which Catholic and Lutheran differences fell into division, and with all the churches in the ecumenical movement on the essentials of baptism and Eucharist, find more pastoral space for sacramental sharing on a regular basis?

In 2015, a handpicked joint commission of Lutheran and Catholic theologians, well-experienced ecumenically, reviewed thirty-two ecumenical agreements between their churches on the topics of church, Eucharist, and ministry, in light of the Joint Declaration on the Doctrine of Justification. Their report, recommended by Cardinal Kurt Koch, Cardinal Kasper's successor as president of the Pontifical Council for Promoting Christian Unity, is titled "Declaration on the Way: Church, Ministry and Eucharist." It received unanimous approval of the church-wide assembly of the Evangelical Lutheran Church in America and of the U.S. Catholic Bishops' Committee on Ecumenical and Interreligious Affairs.[24] The authors of "Declaration on the Way" recommended that "the expansion of opportunities for Catholics and Lutherans to receive Holy Communion would be a significant sign of the path toward unity already traveled and a pledge to continue together on the journey toward full communion." This was but one of several practices recommended "that would express and advance this growing communion between them" because the actual reception of these many agreements invites the Lutheran World Federation and the Catholic Church to implement them.[25]

As I write this chapter, the German Episcopal Conference is preparing pastoral guidelines for determining situations in which a non-Catholic spouse married to a Catholic could receive the Eucharist. Pope Francis has invited the president of that conference, Cardinal Reinhard Marx, to Rome to discuss these suggestions, which have not yet been finalized, to determine if and under what circumstances couples of different denominations who regularly go to church together can receive the Eucharist together. Cardinal Marx gives as context "the high proportion of mixed marriages and families in Germany, where we recognize a challenging and urgent pastoral task."[26] Regarding such pastoral suggestions, the Pontifical Council for Promoting Christian Unity has consistently advised that bishops, taking into account pastoral norms established by episcopal conferences, institute guidelines for judging situations of pressing need and consult with the competent authorities of the interested churches and ecclesial communities involved.[27] Finally, after fifty years of such promptings, an episcopal conference is acting pastorally.

THE NEXT STEP

Though the work of fifty years of ecumenical dialogue, mostly in the form of agreed-upon statements, can fill shelves, most of it has not been received in any formal way. This is widely known. Unfortunately, in words from a recent address by experienced ecumenist Archbishop Donald Bolen, "their capacity to enliven and transform our churches is largely unrealized." Archbishop Bolen, by contrast, has pointed out why the Joint Declaration on the Doctrine of Justification was so significant: "It has been through an authoritative reception process in the signing churches, and as a result, has begun to have a transformative effective on our churches."[28]

On several occasions, especially during the common commemoration of the Reformation, Pope Francis has acknowledged the importance of the agreement on justification. Most recently, to representatives of the Lutheran World Federation, he concluded in light of this agreement, "The future challenges us: we can no longer refuse to seek and foster greater communion in charity and faith."[29]

Pope Francis has also revived the concept of accompaniment. For example, in his theme-setting apostolic exhortation *Evangelii Gaudium*, he described ecumenical relations this way:

> We must never forget that we are pilgrims journeying alongside one another. This means that we must have sincere trust in our fellow pilgrims, putting aside all suspicion or mistrust, and turn our gaze to what we are all seeking: the radiant peace of God's face. (no. 244)[30]

He further advised, "If we concentrate on the convictions we share, and if we keep in mind the principle of the hierarchy of truths, we will be able to progress decidedly towards common expressions of proclamation, service and witness" (no. 246).[31] When speaking in October 2016 to an ecumenical delegation, he was a little more specific. Speaking to the Secretaries of Christian World Communions, he acknowledged the necessity of theological agreement, but while we wait for it, there is so much more to do:

> However, in the meantime, ecumenism is created on the path. In walking with Jesus, it is not with my Jesus versus your Jesus, but our Jesus. The path is simple: it is made with prayer and with the help of others. Pray together: the ecumenism of prayer, for one another and for the unity of all. And then, the ecumenism of work for many needy people, for many men and women who suffer injustice, war... these terrible things. All together, we must help. Charity towards the other. This is ecumenism. Already, this is unity. Unity while walking with Jesus.[32]

In the Dogmatic Constitution on the Church (*Lumen Gentium*), Vatican II reminded the faithful that all are called to holiness: "Everyone whether belonging to the hierarchy, or being cared for by it, is called to holiness" (no. 39). Pope Francis reiterates this in his recently released apostolic exhortation *Gaudete et Exsultate*: "We are all called to be holy by living our lives with love and by bearing witness in everything we do, wherever we find ourselves....Are you married? Be holy by loving and caring for your husband or wife, as Christ does for the Church" (no. 14). He draws special attention the holiness of ordinary life: "Very often it is a holiness found in our next-door neighbors, those who, living in our midst, reflect God's presence" (no. 9).

In his discussion of prayer, Pope Francis recalls especially the powerful witness of ecumenical prayer. In particular, he recalled "the moving ecumenical commemoration held in the Colosseum during the Great Jubilee of the Year 2000" (May 7), when Pope St. John Paul II brought ecumenical leaders together to remember the martyrs for the faith in the twentieth century (no. 9). These Christians witnessed holiness and the presence of God in some of the worst of times of the previous century. Citing the pope's sermon from that day in May 2000, Pope Francis referred to "a heritage which speaks more powerfully than all the causes of division."[33] Thus, Pope Francis could write in his recent exhortation that "holiness is the most attractive face of the Church" and that among other Christians "the Holy Spirit raises up signs of his presence which help Christ's followers" (no. 9).

On several occasions, Pope Francis has referred to an "ecumenism of blood," a martyrdom for being Christian, no matter their particular churches. He did this with the Secretaries of Christian World Communions on October 12, 2016:

> When terrorists or global powers persecute Christian minorities or Christians, when they do this they do not ask: "Are you Lutheran? Are you Orthodox? Are you Catholic? Are you a Reformed Christian? Are you Pentecostal?" No. "You are Christian." They recognize this alone: the Christian. The enemy does not err; he knows well how to recognize where Jesus is. It is this ecumenism of blood....And so, ecumenism of prayer, ecumenism of walking; and the enemy teaches us the ecumenism of blood.[34]

The challenges of the present era and in the ordinary lives of Christians are great. With progress made by theologians in the areas of eucharistic theology and ecclesiology, we might find ways to encourage the spiritual companionship of all Christians as they face these great challenges.

For Pope Francis there is a creative tension between the work of theologians, which is necessary so that progress can be made, and the active ecumenical engagement of Christians living their lives in witness to their faith. He acknowledged to the Secretaries of World Communions, "Often, we think that the ecumenical endeavor is only for theologians;...this is very important....However, in the meantime, ecumenism is created on the path."[35] When Pope Francis preached at the conclusion of the Week of Prayer for Christian Unity on January 25, 2015, with several ecumenical guests present, he noted this tension:

Christian unity—we are convinced—will not be the fruit of subtle theoretical discussions in which each party tries to convince the other of the soundness of their opinions. When the Son of Man comes, he will find us still discussing! We need to realize that, to plumb the depths of the mystery of God, we need one another, we need to encounter one another and to challenge one another under the guidance of the Holy Spirit, who harmonizes diversities, overcomes conflicts, reconciles differences.[36]

The tension was also present in his advice at the Lutheran Church in Rome to the Lutheran woman married to a Catholic.

Especially after a successful and powerfully religious and enthusiastic common commemoration of the fifth centenary of the Lutheran Reformation, we are positioned for a new future of spiritual companionship. The new president of the Lutheran World Federation, Archbishop Panti Filibus Musa (archbishop of the Lutheran Church of Christ in Nigeria) said on his visit with Pope Francis, "Now, as we have jointly marked the 500th anniversary of the Reformation, I would like to add: We have begun our irreversible journey from conflict to communion and we do not wish to let it cease ever again."[37] He is saying that we are not at the beginning but at the point of no return. We need one another, and we need to recognize this more deeply through more frequent sacramental sharing.

Perhaps from this point on, Reformation Day and Reformation Sunday will become a Common Commemoration Day. Perhaps with the content of "Declaration on the Way" now moving to the international Lutheran–Roman Catholic Joint Commission, we will have greater public clarification of how Catholics, Lutherans, and all interested Christians can agree on the fundamental issues regarding church, Eucharist, and ministry but can allow a differentiating consensus on the major doctrines in the hierarchy of truths to enrich our understanding. Perhaps Christians will join more often in prayer and in other spiritual practices; will assist one another and serve together ever more in acts of service to the poor and needy and for the needs of their communities; and will find common expression for their friendship, companionship, and love. Friendships across the church boundaries will increasingly characterize Christian life in the future. Fortunately, we have considerable theological, biblical, and liturgical progress behind us as we live and work into the next fifty years since Vatican II and the next five decades of ecumenical relations.

In preparation for the fifth centenary, the Lutheran–Roman Catholic Joint Commission prepared a resource for common commemoration, *From Conflict to Communion*. It concludes listing five ecumenical imperatives to keep in mind. These remain relevant, now that 2017 has passed, and apply not only to Catholics and Lutherans but to all committed to restoring Christian unity.

> We should always begin from the perspective of unity and not from the point of view of division in order to strengthen what is held in common even though the differences are more easily seen and experienced.

> We must let ourselves continuously be transformed by the encounter with the other and by the mutual witness of faith.

> We should again commit ourselves to seek visible unity, to elaborate together what this means in concrete steps, and to strive repeatedly toward this goal.

> We should jointly rediscover the power of the gospel of Jesus Christ for our time.

> We should witness together to the mercy of God in proclamation and service to the world.

Notes

1. "Address of His Holiness Pope Francis to a Delegation of the Lutheran World Federation" (December 7, 2017), accessed November 18, 2018, http://w2.vatican.va/content/francesco/en/speeches/2017/december/documents/papa-francesco_20171207_federazione-luterana.html.

2. "Methodist-Catholic Statement: The Eucharist and the Churches," *Origins* 11, no. 41 (March 25, 1982): 653.

3. Their joint statement was issued on October 31, 2016. It can be found on the Vatican website here: https://w2.vatican.va/content/francesco/en/events/event.dir.html/content/vaticanevents/en/2016/10/31/dichiarazione-congiunta.html (accessed April 2, 2018). It was also published in *Origins* 46, no. 24 (November 10, 2016): 372–74.

4. *From Conflict to Communion* (Leipzig/Paderborn: Evangelische Verlagsanstalt/Bonifatius, 2013), 6. It is also available on several websites, e.g., http://www.vatican.va/roman_curia/pontifical_councils/chrstuni/lutheran-fed-docs/rc_pc_chrstuni_doc_2013_dal-conflitto-alla-comunione_en.html (accessed April 6, 2018).

5. Gerard Austin, "The Church as Worshiping Community," in *The Gift of the Church: A Textbook on Ecclesiology in Honor of Patrick Granfield, O.S.B.*, ed. Peter C. Phan (Collegeville, MN: Liturgical Press, 2000), 182.

6. *Gaudet Mater Ecclesia*, Pope John's Opening Speech to the Council (no. 19), https://jakomonchak.files.wordpress.com/2012/10/john-xxiii-opening-speech.pdf (accessed April 14, 2018). See also, Xavier Rynne, *Letters from Vatican City: Vatican Council II (First Session); Background and Debates* (New York: Farrar, Straus & Giroux, 1963), 270.

7. Gerard Austin, "Berakah Award Response: 'Liturgy/Church: Two Sides of One Coin.'" Response provided by the author for his reception of the Berakah award from the North American Academy of Liturgy.

8. "Bollettino," *L'Osservatore Romano* (January 26/27, 1959). See also: "Sollemnis Allocutio," *Acta Apostolicae Sedis* 51 (1959): 68–69; and commented on by Thomas F. Stransky, "The Foundation of the Secretariat for Promoting Christian Unity," in *Vatican II Revisited by Those Who Were There*, ed. Alberic Stacpoole (Minneapolis: Winston Press, 1986), 62.

9. For a history of the Secretariat for Promoting Christian Unity from its inception to the end of the Council, see Stransky, "The Foundation of the Secretariat," 62–87.

10. Gerard Austin, "Is an Ecumenical Understanding of Eucharist Possible Today?" *The Jurist* 48 (1988): 683.

11. The passage has a reference note to an apostolic letter of Pope Leo XIII, *Praeclara gratulationis*, June 20, 1894.

12. In an 1895 letter to the Apostolic Delegate in the United States, Archbishop Francesco Satolli, that had a long-lasting effect on U.S. bishops, Pope Leo XIII advised American Catholics no longer to hold "assemblies to which both Catholics and those who dissent from the Catholic Church come promiscuously to discuss together religion and morals."

Letter to Archbishop Satolli, September 18, 1895, *Leonis XIII Acta* 14, 323–24; see Francis J. Connell, "Pope Leo XIII's Message to America," *American Ecclesiastical Review* 109, no. 4 (October 1943): 244–56.

13. Archbishop Joseph J. Martin presented the first draft of the decree, *De Ecumenismo*, on November 18, 1963, for the Secretariat for Promoting Christian Unity. In his remarks, he indicated that the decree would state general principles but that the Secretariat was preparing a directory of norms for implementing the decree in response to the request of many bishops and that the Secretariat would continue its work on a directory unless if any action was taken to the contrary. When the debate on the draft was concluded on December 2, 1963, Cardinal Augustin Bea reiterated how a directory would be prepared by the Secretariat and what it would include. See *Acta Synodalia Sacrosancti Concilii Vaticani II*, II/5, 476–77 and II/6, 364–67.

14. Between 1968 and 1972, the Secretariat issued four separate notes and instructions with regard to sacramental sharing. See *Doing the Truth in Charity: Statements of Pope Paul VI, Popes John Paul I, John Paul II, and the Secretariat for Promoting Christian Unity 1964–1980*, ed. Thomas F. Stransky, and John B. Sheerin (New York: Paulist Press, 1982), 115–30.

15. Pontifical Council for Promoting Christian Unity, *Directory for the Application of Principles and Norms of Ecumenism* (Vatican City, March 25, 1993), nos. 116–36. Hereafter referred to as *Directory on Ecumenism*.

16. See http://w2.vatican.va/content/john-paul-ii/en/encyclicals/documents/hf_jp-ii_enc_25051995_ut-unum-sint.html (accessed April 14, 2018).

17. The first instance known to the author of a published distinction between *communicatio in sacris* and *communicatio in spiritualibus* in the first edition of the *Directory concerning Ecumenical Matters: Part One (Ad Totam Ecclesiam)* (1967), 25–63. See *Vatican Council II: The Conciliar and Post Conciliar Documents*, vol. 1, ed. Austin Flannery (New York/Dublin: Costello Publishing Company/Dominican Publications, 1975; rev. ed., 1996), 492–501.

18. *Baptism, Eucharist and Ministry*, Faith and Order Paper no. 111 (Geneva: World Council of Churches, 1982). The Faith and Order Commission invited "all churches to prepare an official response to the text at the highest level of authority." Christians worldwide prepared reports at varying levels of authority. These official reports appeared in six volumes

under the title *Churches Respond to BEM*, Faith and Order Paper nos. 129, 132, 135, 137, 143, 144, ed. Max Thurian (Geneva: World Council of Churches, 1986–88). The impact of BEM was enormously important, demonstrating substantial agreement on baptism among participating churches, causing the widespread restoration of a weekly Eucharist according to the principles of liturgical reform in many Protestant churches, and thus enabling some churches to enter into agreements of full communion.

19. See http://www.vatican.va/holy_father/special_features/encyclicals/documents/hf_jp-ii_enc_20030417_ecclesia_eucharistia_en.html (accessed April 14, 2018). Please note that *Ut Unum Sint* and *Ecclesia de Eucharistia* present these conflicting impressions on sacramental sharing in paragraphs 46 in each document.

20. Much appeared in print in 2000 and thereafter because the declaration *Dominus Iesus*, issued by the Congregation for the Doctrine of the Faith in that year. "Ecclesial communities" was an expression developed at Vatican II to identify those communities, which preserved much of what is needed to be church but lacked, primarily, the sacrament of orders along with other elements. The word in the Decree on Ecumenism for the condition of orders in these ecclesial communities is *defectus*, which can be translated as absence or defect. Ecumenists during the fallout after *Dominus Iesus* argued, based on the position of the Secretariat for Promoting Christian Unity at the time of Vatican II, that *defectus* meant that there were holy orders in these communities, but they were lacking one or more essential aspects. See, e.g., John F. Hotchkin, "Canon Law and Ecumenism: Giving Shape to the Future," *Origins* 30, no. 19 (October 19, 2000): 293–95; later published in *CLSA Proceeding* 62 (2000): 3–16; Thomas P. Rausch, "Has the Congregation for the Doctrine of the Faith Exceeded Its Authority," *Theological Studies* 62 (2001): 802–10; and Jared Wicks, "The Significance of the 'Ecclesial Communities' of the Reformation," *Ecumenical Trends* (December 2001): 10–13.

21. Austin, "The Church as Worshiping Community," 178.

22. See http://www.lutheranworld.org/lwf/index.php/cardinal-kasper-the-division-of-churches-increasingly-turning-into-a-scandal-before-the-world.html (accessed March 4, 2011). See also Cardinal Walter Kasper, *Harvesting the Fruits: Basic Aspects of Christian Faith in Ecumenical Dialogue* (New York: Continuum, 2009), 204–6.

23. See http://w2.vatican.va/content/francesco/en/speeches/2015/november/documents/papa-francesco_20151115_chiesa-evangelica

-luterana.html (accessed April 14, 2018). One should point out that Pope Francis began his reply noting with humor that he was expected to answer the question with Cardinal Kasper, the acknowledged expert in ecumenical matters, sitting in the front row.

24. The U.S. Catholic Bishops' Committee on Doctrine, as of this writing, has not approved of the text, already submitted to both the Pontifical Council for Promoting Christian Unity and the Lutheran World Federation. Competent theologians prepared the declaration; however, the theologians consulted by the doctrine committee were not in agreement. Nevertheless, on October 31, 2017, at ceremonies in the Vatican recognizing the conclusion of the year of common commemoration of the Reformation, the Pontifical Council for Promoting Christian Unity and the Lutheran World Federation announced that the next task of their formal dialogue commission would be "to discern in a prayerful manner our understanding on church, Eucharist and ministry, seeking a substantial consensus so as to overcome remaining differences between us." See https://cnstopstories.com/2017/10/31/vatican-lutheran-federation -announce-study-on-church-eucharist-ministry/ (accessed April 5, 2018).

25. *Declaration on the Way*, Bishops' Committee for Ecumenical and Interreligious Affairs, USCCB, and the Lutheran World Federation (Minneapolis: Augsburg Fortress, 2016), 114. Also available on several websites, e.g., http://download.elca.org/ELCA%20Resource %20Repository/Declaration_on_the_Way.pdf (accessed April 5, 2018).

26. "Marx to Meet Pope over Communion for Non-Catholics," *The Tablet*, accessed April 19, 2018, http://www.thetablet.co.uk/news/ 8918/marx-to-meet-pope-over-communion-for-non-catholics.

27. *Directory on Ecumenism* 129–31; see also previous notes 14, 15, and 17.

28. Archbishop Donald Bolen, "Towards Reconciliation: Recent and Future Steps as we Mark the 500th Anniversary of the Reformation," *Ecumenical Trends* 47, no. 2 (February 2018): 5.

29. Address of His Holiness Pope Francis to a Delegation of the Lutheran World Federation (December 7, 2017), accessed April 16, 2018, http://w2.vatican.va/content/francesco/en/speeches/2017/ december/documents/papa-francesco_20171207_federazione-luterana .html.

30. See http://w2.vatican.va/content/francesco/en/apost_exhortations/documents/papa-francesco_esortazione-ap_20131124_evangelii-gaudium.html (accessed April 14, 2018).

31. The concept of a hierarchy of truths was mentioned in the Decree on Ecumenism 11 to make the point that not all Christian doctrines are of equal value and that on the most fundamental of Christian teachings, Christians are in agreement: "When comparing doctrines with one another, they [Catholic theologians] should remember that in Catholic doctrine there exists a 'hierarchy' of truths, since they vary in their relation to the fundamental Christian faith. Thus the way will be opened by which through fraternal rivalry all will be stirred to a deeper understanding and a clearer presentation of the unfathomable riches of Christ." This passage concludes with a reference to Ephesians 3:8, referring to the boundless riches of Christ.

32. "Address of His Holiness Pope Francis to Participants in the Conference of Secretaries of Christian World Communions" (October 12, 2016), accessed April 15, 2018, https://w2.vatican.va/content/francesco/en/speeches/2016/october/documents/papa-francesco_20161012_christian-world-communions.html.

33. See "Homily of His Holiness John Paul II," May 7, 2000, accessed April 15, 2018, https://w2.vatican.va/content/john-paul-ii/en/homilies/2000/documents/hf_jp-ii_hom_20000507_test-fede.html.

34. See https://w2.vatican.va/content/francesco/en/speeches/2016/october/documents/papa-francesco_20161012_christian-world-communions.html (accessed April 15, 2018).

35. See https://w2.vatican.va/content/francesco/en/speeches/2016/october/documents/papa-francesco_20161012_christian-world-communions.html.

36. See https://w2.vatican.va/content/francesco/en/homilies/2015/documents/papa-francesco_20150125_vespri-conversione-san-paolo.html.

37. See https://www.lutheranworld.org/sites/default/files/171207greetings_to_hh_pope_francis_en.pdf (accessed April 16, 2018).

18

GERARD AUSTIN
Liturgical Theologian

—m—

Mark Wedig

Gerard Austin, Dominican friar, teacher, and Catholic priest, has devoted over fifty years to spreading the good news of liturgical scholarship and practice to the church across the globe. Austin, who is a founding member of the North American Academy of Liturgy, its fifth president, and recipient of that academy's 2017 Berakah Award, remains a seminal living figure for keeping the memory of the great epic of liturgical reform both in Roman Catholicism and across the Christian churches in the United States in the latter part of the twentieth century.

Gerard "Jerry" Austin's life can be viewed in terms of three major interrelated undertakings that are connected to his experience of liturgical reform, which will be addressed in this short biography. Austin's Dominican vocation, his years at The Catholic University of America, and his vast and comprehensive dedication to pastoral liturgy in the United States, Canada, Australia, New Zealand, South Africa, and many other places around the world can be seen as three related ventures of his life.

Gerard Austin's vocation as a Dominican friar began with his first religious profession in 1953. During his initial formation, Austin completed the bachelor's degree in philosophy at Providence College and then the licentiate in sacred theology (STLr) at the Dominican House of Studies in Washington, DC. His early postordination ministry between 1960 and 1964 for the Dominican Province of St. Joseph (Eastern United States) involved teaching theology at Aquinas College in Grand Rapids, Michigan. Nevertheless, Austin's Dominican vocation became focused in a new way when his brothers

343

sent him off to study liturgy in Paris in the wake of the Second Vatican Council and just after the promulgation of *Sacrosanctum Concilium*.

It was during this time at the Institut Superior de Liturgie, under the mentorship of the Dominican Pierre-Marie Gy, that the world of liturgical studies was opened up to him. It was in Paris at the Institut Catholique between 1964 and 1968 and then again for a postdoctorate in 1972 that the scholarship and direct influence of Yves Congar, Marie-Dominique Chenu, Irénée-Henri Dalmais, Pierre Jounel, Gy himself, and many others who were working on the reforms of the liturgy on the *Consilium* came to influence Austin tremendously. Those who have lived and worked with Jerry Austin relish the stories of his interactions both in the classroom and in the Dominican houses with Congar, Chenu, and other friar-giants of that age in the life of the church in France and during the initial post–Vatican II period. Austin often speaks of the tremendous influence of Congar on his thinking, especially concerning the centrality of baptism in the life of all Christians, and Gy's kind mentorship concerning his dissertation and postdoctoral research.

Over his many years as a Dominican friar, Jerry Austin has served the North American liturgical commission concerning the revisions and translations of the Dominican *Ordo* in the post–Vatican II period. In addition, Austin served twice as regent of studies for the Dominican Province of St. Martin de Porres, guiding and presiding over the intellectual life and study of the friar-preachers in the southern part of the United States. During his time as regent, Austin became a member of the worldwide Dominican study commission for the Order's intellectual life. The Dominicans awarded Austin an honorary doctorate in 2013 from the Aquinas Institute of Theology in St. Louis, Missouri. And for his great contribution to the intellectual life of the Dominicans, the master of sacred theology (STM) was conferred on Austin by the Master of the Dominican Order, a degree awarded by the Order of Preachers for the last eight hundred years on those of its members who have made an outstanding contribution to the theological sciences.

Gerard Austin brought the scholarship of his Paris experience and his enthusiasm for the church's liturgy resultant of those studies to The Catholic University of America when he began teaching there in 1968. A few years later, in 1970, Austin, Fred McManus, and Kevin Seasoltz founded the program in liturgy at CUA. With his colleagues in the liturgical program and during his tenure at CUA between 1968 and 1999 Austin helped to build an eminent liturgy faculty. Many who graduated from the liturgy program during those years reflect back on the great liturgical colleagueship of Austin, Seasoltz, McManus, David Power, Mary Collins, Kevin Irwin, Catherine Dooley, Mary Margaret Kelleher, Stephen Happel, and others. This period in CUA's history witnessed the convergence of an exciting "think tank" in liturgical studies, leading to innovative and groundbreaking research and writing in the field.

It was his fervor for the reform of the liturgy and the church itself that would take hold in Austin's classroom at The Catholic University of America. That in turn led to his scholarship on the sacraments of initiation and the liturgical year, eventually leading to numerous publications on the subject and his book on the sacrament of confirmation.[1] Moreover, for those who studied liturgy in the program at CUA, it would be Austin's "rite of passage" course in the medieval liturgical sources and his research in those sources in *Scriptorum* and other journals that would influence so many of his students. His incredible personal collection of sacramentaries, pontificals, ordines, lectionaries, and many other sources that he had collected in Paris were put on reserve for graduate students' research in the medieval liturgical texts of the church.

Finally and probably most significant in Gerard Austin's work as a teacher and scholar for the past fifty years has been his influence on and interest in pastoral liturgy. Austin's gregarious personality, genuine enthusiasm for the liturgy, and gift of networking across ecclesial contexts led to tremendous interaction with both clergy and laity in pursuit of liturgical education. His countless pastoral workshops and conferences have reached and influenced Catholic dioceses, Protestant seminaries, pastoral institutes, and religious congregations across the United States and Canada but also across Australia, New Zealand, South Africa, Pakistan, and so many other locations that Austin cannot fit them in his curriculum vitae. His impact on dioceses and pastoral leadership, preaching and teaching have constituted the bedrock of his Dominican vocation. Austin is apt to point out that his experience of lecturing and interacting with men and women throughout the world, especially "Down Under" and in other hemispheres, has strongly transformed and reoriented his thinking.

In 1999, Austin retired from The Catholic University of America after thirty-one years of teaching and embarked on a new adventure in spreading the good news about the church's liturgy. Between 1999 and 2012, Austin brought his pastoral and scholarly insight to the classroom of Barry University's pastoral theology master's degree program in the Diocese of Venice, Florida, at the Edmund Rice School for Pastoral Ministry. Relocating to Arcadia, Florida, and living at the faculty residence and library of the Rice School created a new synergy in Austin's outreach to laywomen and laymen in service to the church. Austin joined this program with Br. Paul Hennessy, Sr. Sallie Latkovich, Sr. Pam Owens, and eventually Dr. Andrea Molinari to contribute to a unique and innovative curriculum and pedagogy set out to transform the local church.

Austin is emphatic in saying that his years at the Rice School and teaching in its pastoral theology program were some of the happiest years of his academic career. Adult learners who offered themselves to the service of the Church of Southwest Florida in ministry, often after completing or complementing other successful careers, made Austin's teaching such a satisfying endeavor. While teaching in Florida, he was invited by the University of Notre Dame Center for Pastoral Liturgy to receive its 2002 Michael Mathis Award. That award remains eminently important to Jerry because it celebrates the outreach and communication of liturgy study to the pastoral setting: the true locus for that reflection.

Jerry Austin can be heard saying often that he has had such a rich, full, and interesting life made possible by his interactions with people and places over the course of his now eighty-five years. With a mind and wit as sharp as ever, he enjoys being a wisdom figure among his friends and colleagues. At the writing of this short biography of Gerard "Jerry" Austin, he resides at St. Dominic Priory in Miami, Florida, where he is honored as Dominican Scholar in Residence in the Department of Theology and Philosophy of Barry University.

Notes

1. Gerard Austin, *The Rite of Confirmation: Anointing with the Spirit* (New York: Pueblo, 1985).

CONTRIBUTORS

—⁓—

HELEN FRANCES BERGIN, OP, is a New Zealand Dominican sister who completed both her licentiate in sacred theology (1983–85) and her doctorate in sacred theology (1992–94) at The Catholic University of America in Washington, DC. Since then she has taught theology at the National Catholic Seminary in Dunedin, Otago, and most recently within an ecumenical consortium of theological colleges within the University of Auckland. Her main research and teaching interests have been God/Trinity/Holy Spirit, Christian anthropology, feminist theology, and introduction to theology. Helen retired from formal teaching at the end of 2016.

JOHN BORELLI, PhD, earned his doctorate at Fordham University and is special assistant for Catholic Identity and Dialogue to President John J. DeGioia at Georgetown University.

MICHAEL DOWNEY has served as professor of theology and spirituality at universities and seminaries in North America and abroad. Schooled in the spirituality of Jean Vanier and l'Arche, his abiding concern for the wounded and marginalized has brought him to serve those most in need through lectures, conferences, and retreats throughout the world. Author or editor of over twenty books, notably *Altogether Gift: A Trinitarian Spirituality* and *The New Dictionary of Catholic Spirituality*, his essays and articles on spirituality number in the dozens. His most recent book is *The Depth of God's Reach: A Spirituality of Christ's Descent* (Orbis, 2018).

TOM ELICH is a parish priest in the Archdiocese of Brisbane (Australia) and earned a doctorate of theology from the Institute Catholique de Paris and a doctorate in history of religions from the Université de Paris-IV (Sorbonne) in the area of medieval liturgy and sacramental theology. Since 1989 he has been director of liturgy in Brisbane and contributing editor of the quarterly journal *Liturgy News*. During the 1990s, he was executive secretary of the National Liturgical Commission of the Australian Catholic Bishops Conference and a member of the Advisory Committee of the International Commission on English in the Liturgy (ICEL) in Washington, DC. Since 2002, he has taught in liturgical studies programs, most recently at the Australian Catholic University where he is an honorary fellow. He is a member of the Australian bishops' National Liturgical Architecture and Art Board and a member of the international Societas Liturgica.

KEVIN IRWIN, STD, MDiv, is a priest of the Archdiocese of New York. He has been on the faculty at The Catholic University of America for over thirty years, currently serving as Ordinary Research Professor. His primary interest is in liturgy and sacraments.

ANNE Y. KOESTER works at Georgetown University, where she is an adjunct instructor with the Department of Theology at Georgetown University. She also oversees the RCIA process at Holy Trinity Catholic Church, Washington, DC.

SALLIE LATKOVICH is a Sister of St. Joseph, who completed her doctor of ministry degree in 1995 from the Graduate Theological Foundation. She taught in Trinity College's Education for Pastoral Service Program in Naples, Florida, and at the Blessed Edmund Rice School for Pastoral Ministry in the Diocese of Venice, Florida. In 2009, she moved to Chicago, where she was a member of the Bible Department at Catholic Theological Union and directed the Biblical Study and Travel Program as well as the Summer Institute. She was elected to leadership in her CSJ Congregation in April 2018, and now accepts speaking engagements, workshops, and retreats as her time allows.

ANNE MCGOWAN is assistant professor of liturgy at Catholic Theological Union in Chicago. A graduate of the University of Notre Dame, she is the author of *Eucharistic Epicleses, Ancient and Modern* (2014) and co-author of *The Pilgrimage of Egeria: A New Translation of the* Itinerarium Egeriae *with Introduction and Commentary* (2018).

PAUL MCPARTLAN, STL, DPhil, is a priest of the Archdiocese of Westminster (United Kingdom) and is the Carl J. Peter Professor of Systematic Theology and Ecumenism at The Catholic University of America.

GERARD MOORE earned his doctorate at The Catholic University of America, Washington, DC, and lectures in worship and practical theology at Charles Stuart University, Australia, where he is a member of its Public and Contextual Theology Research Centre and is Associate Head of School. He has been involved with the International Commission for English in the Liturgy (ICEL) and a range of ecclesial Australian worship bodies. He has published widely in liturgy, nationally and internationally, and his most recent publications are *Earth Unites with Heaven: An Introduction to the Liturgical Year* (Melbourne: Morning Star, 2014), and *The Disciples at the Lord's Table: Prayers over Bread and Cup across 150 Years of Christian Church (Disciples of Christ) Worship* (Eugene, OR: Wipf and Stock, 2015).

JOHN W. O'MALLEY, University Professor in the Theology Department of Georgetown University, is a specialist in the religious culture of modern Europe. His best-known book, *The First Jesuits* (Harvard University Press, 1993), is now available in twelve languages. His most recent monograph is *Vatican I: The Council and the Making of the Ultramontane Church* (Harvard University Press, 2018). *Trent: What Happened at the Council* was awarded best-book prize from both the American Catholic Historical Association and the American Society for Church History. In 2016, the Graduate School of Arts and Sciences of Harvard University conferred upon him its Centennial Medal, "the school's highest honor."

PATRICIA A. PARACHINI, SNJM, DMin, earned her doctorate from The Catholic University of America. A pastoral theologian and a spiritual director, she currently provides supervision and spiritual direction for lay and religious men and women and is a lecturer at CUA. She writes reflections for the daily prayer resource *Give Us This Day*; has written two books on lay preaching, a number of articles on topics related to liturgy, preaching, and spirituality; and has given preached retreats and presentations in national and international settings.

PETER C. PHAN, who has earned three doctorates, is the inaugural holder of the Ignacio Ellacuría Chair of Catholic Social Thought at Georgetown University, USA. His research deals with the theology of icon in Orthodox theology, patristic theology, eschatology, the history of Christian missions in Asia, and liberation, inculturation, and interreligious dialogue. He is the author and editor of over thirty books and has published over three hundred essays. His writings have been translated into Arabic, French, German, Italian, Polish, Portuguese, Romanian, Serbian, Spanish, Chinese, Indonesian, Japanese, and Vietnamese, and have received many awards from learned societies. He is the first non-Anglo to be elected president of the Catholic Theological Society of America and president of the American Theological Society. In 2010, he received the John Courtney Murray Award, the highest honor bestowed by the Catholic Theological Society of America for outstanding achievement in theology.

BARBARA REID, OP, PhD, is vice president and academic dean and professor of New Testament Studies at the Catholic Theological Union, Chicago, Illinois.

DON E. SALIERS, PhD, is a musician, theologian, and scholar of liturgy. He plays both the organ and piano and is a Methodist minister and poet. Saliers was the William R. Cannon Distinguished Professor of Theology and Worship at the Candler School of Theology at Emory University. He is the author of fifteen books. Although retired, he remains theologian-in-residence and professor emeritus at Candler. He has also taught at Notre Dame, St. John's, Vancouver School of Theology, and Boston College, and has served as president of the North American Academy of Liturgy and the Society for the Study of Christian Spirituality.

CATHERINE VINCIE, RSHM, PhD, is a member of the Religious of the Sacred Heart of Mary, Eastern American, for which she serves as a provincial councilor. She received her PhD in liturgical studies from The Catholic University of America in 1990 and has been on the faculty of the Aquinas Institute of Theology (1995–2015). She is author of *The Role of the Assembly in Christian Initiation*, *Celebrating Divine Mystery*, and *Worship and the New Cosmology* as well as numerous articles on Eucharist, initiation, liturgy and justice, and the liturgical year, among other topics. She is a member of the North American Academy of Liturgy, serving as president in 2012, and the Catholic Academy of Liturgy; she was a guest member of the ICEL Advisory Board from 1998 to 2000.

MARK E. WEDIG, OP, PhD, associate dean for graduate studies, College of Arts and Sciences, professor of theology in the Department of Theology and Philosophy, is a Dominican Friar of the Province of St. Martin de Porres (Southern Province, USA). Rev. Wedig's academic background is as follows: the bachelor of arts in history/medieval studies from Southern Methodist University; the master of divinity from the Dominican School of Philosophy and Theology, Berkeley, California; the master of arts in theology from the Graduate Theological Union, Berkeley, California; and the doctorate from The Catholic University of America. Mark's scholarly interests lie at the intersection between culture studies, liturgy, and the hermeneutics of the visual arts. He has been a member of the North American Academy of Liturgy since 1992 and the Catholic Academy of Liturgy since its inception.